CPE

Constitutional Law
Textbook

17th edition

Michael T Molan
BA, LLM (Lond), Barrister
Head of Law, South Bank University

HLT Publications

HLT PUBLICATIONS
200 Greyhound Road, London W14 9RY

First published 1979
17th edition 1995

© The HLT Group Ltd 1995

ISBN 0 7510 0546 0

British Library Cataloguing-in-Publication.
A CIP Catalogue record for this book is
available from the British Library.

Acknowledgement
The publishers and author would like to
thank the Incorporated Council of Law
Reporting for England and Wales for kind
permission to reproduce extracts from the
Weekly Law Reports.

Printed and bound in Great Britain

Contents

Preface

HLT Textbooks are written specifically for students. Whatever their course they will find our books clear and concise, providing comprehensive and up-to-date coverage. Written by specialists in their field, our textbooks are reviewed and updated on an annual basis.

In addition to the usual updating that we undertake each year for this book, we have added a new chapter called 'Recent Cases'. This chapter includes the most significant cases that have occurred in the last year. In order to assist the student extracts from the judgments and commentary, where appropriate, have been included. In many instances these cases highlight new interpretations of particular facets of existing law.

Knowledge of recent cases is extremely important for those studying for their examinations. It demonstrates not only an active interest in the law as it develops, but also the dynamic nature of the law which is constantly adapting to changing social and economic trends.

This *Constitutional Law Textbook* is designed for use by any undergraduates who have Constitutional Law within their syllabus. It will be equally useful for all CPE students who must study Constitutional Law as one of their 'core' subjects.

In addition, those studying for certain professional examinations, such as the Institute of Legal Executives, will find this Textbook gives them sufficient information for their appropriate examinations in Constitutional Law.

For its 17th edition this text has been significantly restructured so as to focus on the key constitutional principles, the institutions of government, and civil liberties. The chapters dealing with public order and police powers have been amended to take on board developments consequent upon the enactment of the Criminal Justice and Public Order Act 1994, although it should be noted that the key provisions of this Act will not be in force until May 1995. Students preparing for examinations in constitutional *and* administrative law are advised to refer to the companion *Administrative Law Textbook* for coverage of key areas, such as the application for judicial review, abuse of discretion, and remedies in public law.

The law is stated as of 31 December 1994.

Table of Cases

Table of Statutes

1

The Nature of Constitutional Law

1.1 Definition of a constitution

The constitution of a state may be defined as the body of rules relating to the structure, functions and powers of the organs of state, their relationship to one another, and to the private citizen.

The word constitution is also used to refer to a document containing the most important rules of a state's constitutional law. This document has usually been enacted by the legislature or adopted by some other constituent body, for example a Constituent Assembly. This is perhaps the more popularly understood meaning of the word constitution and this is one of the reasons that led de Tocqueville, the French political philosopher, to say that the English had no constitution, because the United Kingdom has no single special document in which the most important rules of the constitution are collected.

1.2 The organs of state

The legal criteria of statehood

Article 1 of the Montevideo Convention on Rights and Duties of States 1933 provides: 'The state as a person of international law should possess the following qualifications:

1. a permanent population;
2. a defined territory;

3. government; and
4. capacity to enter into relations with other states.'

Government

Government is one of the requirements of statehood and refers to the functions involved in the organisation and running of the state's affairs. There are three basic functions of government:

1. *Legislative functions.* These are comprised of the enactment of new law and the repeal or amendment of old law.
2. *Executive functions.* These include the making of policy and the general and particular carrying out of government according to law.
3. *Judicial functions.* These involve the determination of disputes between subjects, and between subjects and the state in accordance with the law.

The three organs of government

The three functions of government are executed by the three organs of government as follows:

1. *The Legislature.* This is the law-making body and consists in the United Kingdom of the 'Queen in Parliament', ie the House of Commons, the House of Lords and the Sovereign.
2. *The Executive.* This is the body responsible for the execution or enforcement or carrying into effect of the laws laid down by the Legislature. It also has responsibility for policy formulation. It consists of the Government, ie the Prime Minister and other ministers.
3. *The Judiciary.* This is the body responsible for settling legal disputes and interpreting and applying the law. It consists of the judges sitting in the courts of law.

1.3 The classification of constitutions

Constitutions can be classified in a number of different ways. The following are some of the most important classifications:

Written or unwritten

The traditional approach to the study of constitutions was to classify them as either 'written' or 'unwritten' depending on whether there was a single document containing the most fundamental constitutional rules (written constitution), or not (unwritten constitution). This classification may be misleading, because an unwritten constitution may have many important constitutional rules in statutory form and, on the other hand, a written constitution may, in its operation, be modified and qualified by important unwritten rules. The term 'enacted constitution' is sometimes used instead of written constitution. The United Kingdom is one of the few countries with an unwritten constitution. When United Kingdom colonies are granted independence it has been the invariable practice to provide for the adoption of a written constitution.

Rigid or flexible

This classification was first proposed by Lord James Bryce in a series of Oxford lectures at the end of the nineteenth century. A 'flexible constitution' Lord Bryce defined as one where all the laws of the constitution can be amended by the ordinary law-making process. By contrast, in a 'rigid constitution', the laws of the constitution can only be amended by some special procedure. Thus, according to Lord Bryce, the United States has a rigid constitution, since constitutional amendments cannot be made by an ordinary Act of Congress (the normal law-making process), but require a special procedure involving a two-thirds majority in each House of Federal Congress followed by ratification by at least three-quarters of the legislatures of the individual states of the Union. By contrast the United Kingdom constitution, any law of which can be changed by simple Act of Parliament, is flexible.

The terminology 'rigid' or 'flexible' was also adopted as one of six classifications of constitutions by Sir Kenneth Wheare in his book *Modern Constitutions*, 1951. However, Wheare used the terminology in a different sense, namely, to distinguish constitutions according to whether 'they are, in practice, through the force of a variety of circumstances, easily and often altered, or not'. On Wheare's classifications the United States constitution is 'rigid', because there have only been 26 amendments since its adoption in 1787. But the Swiss constitution, whose amendment requires a special procedure, usually a referendum of the people, is 'flexible' because, in fact, it has often been amended.

Unitary or federal

Under a federal constitution, government powers are divided between, on the one hand, the central (or federal) organs of state power and, on the other, the organs of the individual states or provinces which make up the federation. The United States of America, Canada, Australia, Malaysia and Nigeria are all examples of federal states. The essential point is that any alteration of the distribution of powers between the federal organs and the state organs can only be achieved by amendment of the constitution and not by simple act of the federal (central) Parliament. The individual states cannot have their powers reduced in that way. Any amendment to the constitution which involves a redistribution of powers between the federal and state organs will require some special procedure which, generally, allows the individual states some voice in the decision. Federal states have usually been formed by a group of states, each previously independent of one another or separately governed, coming together and transferring certain governmental powers to a set of central organs while retaining other powers themselves. Nigeria may be cited as an exception to this since the present 19 states of Nigeria were never separately governed.

Under a unitary constitution all state power is vested by the constitution in central organs. The United Kingdom has a unitary constitution since all state power is vested in central organs at Westminster and Whitehall. This is so despite the fact that the United Kingdom is regarded as having four component parts, England, Scotland, Wales and Northern Ireland. These four parts were, at one time, governed separately. However, today the Parliament at Westminster has power to make law for all four, and none has its own legislature. The United Kingdom does have a system of local authorities with power to make by-laws and administer certain services in their particular locality. However, this fact does not detract from the nature of the United Kingdom as a unitary state, since at any time Parliament at Westminster could, by simple Act of Parliament, reduce the powers of or even abolish these local authorities. Remember that the essential feature of a federal constitution is that the distribution of powers between the central organs and the individual state organs cannot be altered by simple act of the central Parliament.

Other classifications

Wheare's six classifications of constitutions were: written or unwritten, flexible or rigid, unitary or federal, and three classifications not yet mentioned:

1. *Supreme or subordinate.* That is, can the legislature acting on its own amend the constitution? If so, the constitution is subordinate. If not, it is supreme.
2. *Separated powers or fused powers.* This relates to the extent to which the functions and the personnel of the three organs of state overlap.
3. *Monarchical or republican.* This distinction is not as significant as it once was, since today many monarchies are, like the United Kingdom, constitutional monarchies where the monarch is practically without constitutional power, that power being vested instead in an elected Prime Minister or Cabinet.

The late S A de Smith in *Constitutional and Administrative Law* was influenced by Wheare's classifications. However, he abandoned the 'supreme or subordinate' distinction, and that based on 'fused or separated' powers, which he replaced by a distinction according to whether the state had a presidential or parliamentary executive. S A de Smith added two further classifications, the first being 'single-party and other constitutions'. The second classification he introduced was 'diarchical and other constitutions'. A diarchical constitution he describes as being one where 'there is a division of governmental competence between two or more authorities in the state otherwise than on a regional basis'. He cites France, where the constitution gives both the legislature and the president separate law-making powers each within defined fields, and the Cyprus constitution of 1960, which gave certain law-making powers to separate Greek and Turkish communal chambers, the division being purely ethnic and not regional.

Leslie Wolf-Phillips introduced a classificatory scheme based on 13 elements according to which constitutions can be categorised. Some of these categories are the familiar ones of 'rigid or flexible', 'monarchical or republican', 'unitary or federal', but others include 'indigenous or adventitious' (meaning home-produced or, alternatively, imposed from without for example by an imperial power); 'competitive or consolidatory' (according to whether the constitution allows 'competition' for power between various elements in the state or, alternatively, consolidates the power of one group, for example one party or one ethnic group); and 'programmable or confirmatory' (according to whether the constitution includes statements of aims yet to be fulfilled or whether it is, on the other hand, largely a confirmation of the existing state of affairs). Wolf-Phillips also points out that most, if not all, states have 'manifest' constitutions and 'latent' constitutions. The former refers to the formal constitutional text and the latter refers to those areas of vital political activity, for example the position and operations of political parties, which are unspecified in the constitutional texts. This viewpoint, whilst an interesting one from which to analyse other Commonwealth constitutions, may be less helpful in analysis of the United Kingdom constitution because there is no formal constitutional text or written constitution.

1.4 The British constitution classified

Unwritten character

The United Kingdom does not have a written constitution. There is no one document or group of documents which contain the constitution.

Unitary constitution

The United Kingdom is a unitary and not a federal state. Parliament, sitting at Westminster, is the only body competent to legislate for the United Kingdom.

Flexibility

The British constitution is flexible in the sense that all law in the United Kingdom, including laws relating to the constitution, may be enacted, repealed or amended by the Queen in Parliament using the same procedure. There is no 'superior' law. Changes in constitutional law can be effected by ordinary legislation.

Parliamentary sovereignty

Parliament may make or unmake any law. There is no limit to its competence to legislate. No Parliament may bind its successors or be bound by its predecessors.

Constitutional monarchy

The Queen is the Head of State. Succession to the throne is hereditary. Although the monarch retains many of the legal powers of government, by convention these powers are now exercised in her name by her ministers.

Bicameralism

The United Kingdom legislature is composed of two Houses. The House of Lords is the upper House of Parliament, and the House of Commons is the lower House of Parliament.

Democratic government

The membership of the House of Commons is elected at least every five years. The Government is drawn from the political party which has the majority of seats in the House of Commons and ministers of the Government are answerable to Parliament for the activities of their departments. Subject to the Prevention of Terrorism legislation few restrictions exist on the freedom of political activity.

Impartial Civil Service

The Civil Service is by convention non-partisan. Its membership does not change with a change of government.

1.5 Is a constitution a higher form of law?

In most states the constitution is a higher form of law in the sense that other laws must conform to it. In other words, the constitution imposes limits on what may be done by ordinary legislation. This is because, in the vast majority of states, the constitution is rigid in Lord Bryce's sense, or 'supreme' if we wish to use Wheare's terminology. The United Kingdom is one of the few exceptions, having a constitution which can be altered by ordinary legislation, and is, therefore, not a 'higher' form of law in any sense. The lack of a constitution with any greater legal sanctity than the ordinary law of the land is another reason for de Tocqueville's allegation that the English have no constitution. This principle that there are in the United Kingdom no laws, apart from arguably some European Community laws, which cannot be altered by ordinary Act of Parliament, is known as the principle of parliamentary sovereignty. See *Harris* v *Minister of the Interior* (1952) (2) SA 428(a).

1.6 The structure of the United Kingdom

The term 'United Kingdom' refers to the union of England, Wales, Scotland, and Northern Ireland. Although the countries making up this union may enjoy distinct legal systems, and hence laws peculiar to themselves, they are not sovereign states as that term is used in constitutional law. The countries comprising the union are governed by Parliament at Westminster, and it is this body which, subject to the effect of European Union law, enjoys sovereign power. It is in this sense, as considered above, that the United Kingdom constitution is described as being unitary in character.

The term 'Great Britain' should, strictly speaking, only be used when referring to the union of England, Scotland and Wales. 'British Isles' is a term of geographical, not constitutional significance, as it refers not only to the mainland, but also the Irish Republic and dependencies of the Crown such as the Isle of Man, Jersey and Guernsey.

The formation of the union

Although the two centuries following the Norman conquest saw periodic assertions of independence by Welsh princes and others holding power over parts of the principality, the status of Wales as an English colony became increasingly apparent and was evidenced by the enactment of measures such as the Statute of Wales 1284. The political union was effectively complete by 1536 with the passing of the Act of Union, and in due course Welsh representation at Westminster, and the integration of the Welsh and English legal systems followed.

In contrast to Wales, Scotland has a longer history of constitutional independence. Prior to the enactment of the Union with Scotland Act 1706, Scotland maintained its own monarchy, Parliament and, as the history of military engagements between English and Scottish forces attests, defended its geographical integrity with varying degrees of success. The legislation of 1706, and the complimentary Union with England Act passed by the Scottish legislature in 1707, effectively secured a political and constitutional union of what by then had become England and Wales and Scotland.

Attempts by the Westminster Parliament to establish authority over Ireland, as evidenced by measures such as the Union with Ireland Act 1800, culminated, in the early part of the twentieth century, in events such as the 1916 Easter rising, a rebellion by Irish nationalists, and the emergence of revolutionary parties such as Sinn Fein. In due course the British government faced up to the reality of the continued armed Irish resistance to rule from Westminster and, by means of the Irish Free State (Agreement) Act 1922, Irish Free State (Constitution) Act 1922, and the Irish Free State (Consequential Provisions) Act 1922, created a situation whereby the new Irish Free State could become a dominion within the British Commonwealth, with the six counties, making up what is now referred to as Northern Ireland, having the right to opt out of the arrangement. By 1948 Ireland had left the British Commonwealth and achieved the status of an independent sovereign state. With the enactment of the Ireland Act 1949, the British government formally recognised this independence, but also enshrined in statute the 'loyalist veto' whereby the reunification of Ireland would only be permitted if a majority of the population of Northern Ireland agreed. Predictably the predominantly protestant six counties of the north did exercise the right not to become part of a predominantly catholic Irish state and, under the terms of the Government of Ireland Act 1920, came to be governed by a Northern Ireland parliament sitting at Stormont. This body had the power to enact legislation for the province in most areas other than defence, foreign affairs and nationality, but financial control was effectively exercised from Westminster. Tension between the republican (catholic) and loyalist (protestant) communities in the north remained high, and following the outbreak of widespread civil disturbances in 1972, the Northern Ireland Parliament was disbanded and direct rule from Westminster imposed. After two decades of unsuccessful attempts at power-sharing between Westminster and Belfast, civil disobedience, public disorder, and terrorist atrocities committed by those on both sides of the sectarian divide, the prospects of a political settlement in Northern Ireland currently look promising. The Anglo-Irish Agreement of 1985 was followed by the joint Anglo-Irish Downing Street Declaration of 1993 and the 1994 cease-fire declared by the paramilitary forces on both sides. In early 1995 the Dublin and Westminster governments agreed a joint framework document for the province. Whilst reaffirming that a united Ireland cannot be achieved without the consent of a majority of those in Northern Ireland (and noting that this recognition would require amendment of the Irish constitution), the joint framework document acknowledges the legitimacy of the aspirations of the republican minority in Northern Ireland.

To promote cross-border cooperation, the document proposes the creation of a north-south body, comprising heads of relevant executive departments, to:

> '... discharge or oversee delegated executive, harmonising or consultative functions, as appropriate, over a range of matters that the two governments designate ... to discharge the functions ... designated for treatment on an all-Ireland basis ... to oversee the work of subsidiary bodies.'

Plans for a new Northern Ireland Assembly, empowered to take over much of the day-to-day running of the province, were also unveiled at the same time as the framework document. The proposed assembly would comprise 90 members, elected on a fixed-term basis, by means of proportional representation. The north-south body would be answerable to the Assembly, but the Assembly would not have competence in the areas of defence, law and order or foreign affairs, and would not have any revenue-raising powers. It remains to be seen whether the demands of the republicans can be met without the governance of the six counties effectively being ceded to Dublin.

Regionalism

Save the special arrangements that have existed in Northern Ireland from time to time during the twentieth century, the British constitution has not featured any system of what might be termed 'regional government'. Powers and functions have been allocated between central government at Westminster and local government based on (largely) county boundaries. The special needs of both Scotland and Wales have been recognised at an executive level by the creation of government departments to take particular responsibility for aspects of regional policy. Thus, in 1884 the Scottish Office was created, and in 1892 the post of Minister for Scotland was accorded Cabinet rank. By 1926 the significance of the post was reflected in its being elevated to the rank of Secretary of State for Scotland. The post of Secretary of State for Wales was created in 1964, the holder being a member of the Cabinet. A Welsh Office, based in Cardiff, was created to provide an administrative base for its functions. The extent to which the creation of government departments based on regional lines has worked to the benefit of those regions remains open to question. The Welsh and Scottish Secretaries of State are, of course, bound by collective responsibility, and thus may have to be party to decisions that run counter to the interests of their regions as a whole. Given the secrecy attaching to Cabinet proceedings it is impossible to know the extent to which such ministers actually fight for their regions' interests. Perhaps effectiveness can only be measured in terms of economic prosperity.

The Welsh and Scottish Secretaries of State are answerable to the Westminster Parliament, but there is limited scope for scrutiny of their functions. Parliamentary questions for these ministers come around approximately once every three weeks. Since 1979 there have been select committees for Welsh and Scottish affairs, and there are standing committees which look at legislation exclusively concerned with Scotland.

Devolution

Some would argue that at the heart of the debate on devolution is the issue of legitimacy. Can a government based at Westminster claim to represent the whole country, or is it iniquitous that, for example, a Conservative government should exercise power over a region such as Scotland where it might command less than 20 per cent of the popular vote? The significance of devolution as a political issue seems to ebb and flow, depending upon a whole host of other factors. Disillusionment with central government, its apparent failure to take on board the needs of the regions, and grievances, both perceived and real, over the allocation of resources will generally provide fertile soil for the seeds of nationalism and calls for regional independence. This sense of alienation of regions such as Scotland and Wales was aggravated during the 1980s, with its prolonged period with a large Conservative majority in the House of Commons, by the perception in some quarters that what happened in Scotland and Wales did not matter as there were few Conservative voters there anyway. Another factor relevant to the growth in nationalism and support for devolution may be the decline in the power and influence of large (metropolitan) local authorities which have been gradually denuded of their functions and status. Municipal power bases for the opposition in Wales and Scotland have effectively been emasculated by successive reforms of local government in the period from 1979–1995. The resurgence of nationalism following the break-up of the former Soviet Union may also be a relevant underlying trend.

Opponents of devolution argue that it is unnecessary, would simply increase bureaucracy, would result in inconsistent standards in the delivery of public services, would place an unnecessary burden on the taxpayer, and could ultimately undermine the continued existence of the United kingdom as a political entity and world power.

In order to better understand these moral, political and economic arguments for and against devolution, some thought needs to be given to exactly what devolution would involve. Would a regional government take functions and powers from central government or local government? Which would it be closer to? Would local government still be answerable to the centre, or to the newly created regional assembly? How would national standards in social services be maintained? Is there any real case for regional government in England?

Many of these issues were addressed by the Kilbrandon Commission which defined devolution (para. 543) as '... the delegation of central government powers without the relinquishment of sovereignty'. This definition is necessarily imprecise, as the devolution of power can take a variety of forms, depending on the type of power being devolved and the degree of devolution involved. Broadly speaking it is possible to identify three variants:

1. *Legislative devolution* – the power to legislate for, and execute policy in relation to, certain defined matters delegated to a regional assembly. Central government retains an overriding power to legislate in respect of any matter (ie can repeal any measure introduced by the regional assembly).
2. *Executive devolution* – legislation is passed by Parliament at Westminster, with regional assemblies determining local policy and the manner in which it is to be put into effect.
3. *Administrative devolution* – does not involve the creation of a regional assembly. Central government arranges for the discharge of its policies on a regional basis.

Attempts at reform

In 1969 a Labour government under Harold Wilson sought to address the issue of regional government by establishing a Royal Commission on the Constitution. Its terms of reference, although broad, related particularly to the question of the desirability or otherwise of devolving power to the regions. The Commission, ultimately chaired by Lord Kilbrandon, eventually reported in 1973, although there was considerable dissent amongst its members as to the course to be adopted in order to promote regionalism. In its report the Commission claimed a lack of any significant 'grass-roots' support for wholesale independence in Wales or Scotland, and emphasised the need for the United Kingdom to remain a coherent political and economic entity.

A majority of its members favoured elected assemblies for Scotland and Wales with delegated legislative powers in relation to matters exclusive to those regions (ie largely co-terminus with the matters falling within the province of the respective Secretaries of State for Scotland and Wales). Dissenting voices amongst the Commission's members argued that the regions of England had an equally strong claim to the right to be well governed and could not agree to any scheme for devolution that overlooked the interests of the English regions.

By the time the Commission's report was published in 1973, a Conservative government was in power and, perhaps unsurprisingly, the somewhat incoherent range of findings in the report led to its usefulness being doubted.

Although there had been a notable increase in the nationalist vote in parliamentary elections and by-elections in the late 1960s and early 1970s, it was not until the mid-to-late 1970s that a Labour government, heavily dependent upon the support of minority parties, took determined steps to put into effect policies designed to devolve power to regional assemblies for Wales and Scotland. Two measures were enacted, the Wales Act 1978 and the Scotland Act 1978, providing for legislative devolution in the case of the proposed Scottish Assembly and executive devolution in the case of the Welsh Assembly. The implementation of these proposals was made dependent upon the outcome of referendums to be held in Scotland and Wales. As a result of backbench opposition to these Acts when they were before Parliament, a clause was inserted to the effect that both Acts would be repealed unless 40 per cent of those entitled to vote in the referendums voted in favour of the proposed assemblies. In the event, only 11.9 per cent of registered voters in Wales supported the proposals and in Scotland the figure was 32.9 per cent. Thus the scheme came to nothing, and the Scottish National Party was to some extent responsible for the Labour government's fall from power when it subsequently withdrew its support in the House of Commons in 1979.

The constitutional dimension

One of the persistent problems arising in the devolution debate is the so-called 'West Lothian Question', so named after the MP for that area, Tam Dalyell, who persistently raised the issue in the House of Commons. If real power is to be devolved to regional assemblies, for instance the power to levy taxes, what would be the role of Welsh and Scottish MPs at Westminster? If their powers and rights were to continue unabated, a situation would be created whereby English MPs would not be able to vote upon matters directly affecting Wales or Scotland, but Welsh and Scottish MPs would be able to vote on matters directly affecting England and Northern Ireland. The irony in such an arrangement is, of course, that it turns the moral justification for devolution, the unfairness of an unrepresentative English majority legislating for regional minorities, on its head. The Welsh and Scottish MPs would be wholly unaccountable in terms of their voting on matters relating to England alone.

The problem is particularly acute for any Labour government, given the current distribution of parliamentary seats, as the Scottish and Welsh constituencies return primarily Labour candidates. The logical response to the 'West Lothian Question' would be for Welsh and Scottish MPs to cease to have the right to vote at Westminster on matters exclusive to other regions. A Labour government could find itself in the uniquely uncomfortable position of having an overall majority in the House of Commons, but only when the Scottish and Welsh MPs were included in the total. It is perhaps worth noting in this regard that to date the Labour Party has only won a majority of *English* seats on two occasions, 1945 and 1966. It could, therefore, be in a minority, and thus effectively unable to govern, as regards internal English affairs. Such a situation, especially if a Labour Cabinet comprised a significant number of MPs with Scottish constituencies, would in all likelihood be politically untenable.

The reality, it is submitted, is that it is not possible to tamper with one aspect of Parliament's powers, for example by devolving power to Scottish and Welsh assemblies, without also looking at what reforms this would necessitate as regards the 'rump' of the Parliament that would remain to govern England.

The political dimension

In party-political terms, the Conservative Party has consistently adopted a centrist line, being opposed to the devolution of power to elected regional assemblies. Even in the case of Northern Ireland it has emphasised that it is the Conservative *and Unionist* Party and has set its face against policies that would involve any weakening of the Union. The difficulty for the Conservative Party is that Scottish voters, faced with a stark choice between Westminster conservatism and Scottish nationalism, may opt for the latter for the want of any intermediate choice. Furthermore, the continued efforts to reach an accommodation with republicans in Northern Ireland, when considered alongside the Conservative government's refusal to contemplate devolution on the mainland, do make the latter stance appear somewhat hypocritical.

The recent history of local government possibly contains a warning to any

Conservative government contemplating devolution. It can be argued that voters are willing to express their unhappiness with the party in power, by voting for the opposition in local government elections, because legislation passed by successive Conservative-dominated Parliaments has ensured that local authorities have very little power. They can no longer engage in the pursuit of outlandish political philosophies at the ratepayers' expense. The local elector knows that a vote for the Labour or Liberal Parties cannot have dire financial consequences for him because of the centrally imposed controls on spending. Similarly, with elected regional assemblies. They are likely to become sounding boards for the opposition to whichever party is in power, so long as they do not possess untrammelled power to levy taxes. The paradox, of course, is that if true devolution is to be achieved the regional assemblies would have to be given such powers.

The Labour Party has also, historically, embraced centralism as a means of effectively pursuing socialist policies. Much Labour support is, however, based in the more remote regions, and the Labour Party has shown greater readiness than the Conservative Party to recognise the moral argument for regional empowerment. A political difficulty for the Labour Party, however, is in espousing the nationalist cause, whilst retaining a political identity distinct from the nationalist parties. It is a difficult balancing act for any mainstream *national* political party to propose an effective and real devolution of power, without also advocating that the extent of its own writ as a party of government should not also be curtailed. In its 1987 election manifesto the Labour Party committed itself to legislating to establish an elected Scottish Assembly with '... a wide range of powers over health, education and housing and over significant aspects of industrial and economic policy'. No mention was made of power to raise funds by way of taxation. Wales was promised a strengthened Welsh Development Agency and a separate Arts Council. The commitment to a Scottish Assembly was reaffirmed in the 1992 manifesto, with an additional undertaking to introduce an elected Welsh Assembly '... with powers and functions which reflect the existing administrative structure'. Current Labour Party policy promotes the cause of an elected Scottish Assembly.

The cause of regionalism has perhaps been most consistently espoused by the so-called 'centre parties', currently the Liberal Democrats. In its election manifesto of 1987, the (then) SDP/Liberal Alliance undertook to establish elected Welsh and Scottish assemblies, in addition to regional assemblies throughout England. By 1992, these pledges had evolved into the Liberal Democrat commitment to introduce 'home rule' for both Scotland and Wales, by means of elected Parliaments.

2

The Sources of Constitutional Law

2.1 The sources of constitutional law

2.2 Non-legal rules of the constitution

2.1 The sources of constitutional law

Introduction

In the United Kingdom, the sources of our constitutional law are the same as the sources of our general law. There is no complete written constitutional document. In addition to these legal rules of the constitution there are also many non-legal rules which are nonetheless considered to be binding.

The legal rules of the constitution

In the United Kingdom there are three main sources of legal rules of the constitution.

Legislation

Legislation is the most important source of constitutional law. The doctrine of parliamentary sovereignty provides that legislation has precedence over all other law, including judicial precedent and earlier legislation. Major statutes of constitutional significance include: Magna Carta 1215; Petition of Rights 1628; Bill of Rights 1689; Act of Settlement 1700; Act of Union with Scotland 1707; Parliament Acts 1911 and 1949; Statute of Westminster 1931; Crown Proceedings Act 1947; and the European Communities Act 1972.

Judicial precedent

Under the doctrine of precedent (or stare decisis), decisions of the superior courts are binding on all courts below, thus enabling a body of 'case law' to be built up. Important rules of constitutional law may be found in many judicial decisions. For example, the case of *Entick* v *Carrington* (1765) determined that general warrants are illegal. In *Burmah Oil* v *Lord Advocate* [1965] AC 75, it was held that at common law the Crown may in certain circumstances be under a duty to compensate the subject for property seized in exercise of the royal prerogative. Judicial decisions may also interpret legislation of constitutional significance. For example, in the case of *Fox* v *Stirk* [1970] 2 QB 463, the relevant section of the Representation of the People Act was interpreted in such a way as to permit students to register as electors in either their home town or their university town.

European Community law
Since the accession of the United Kingdom to membership of the European Communities on 1 January 1973, European Community law has been applied by the United Kingdom courts and forms a source of our constitutional law. Community law is found in the Community treaties; regulations; directives and decisions of Community organs; and in rulings and decisions of the European Court of Justice. Where Community law is in conflict with national law of Member States, Community law prevails. For a more detailed consideration of Community law, see Chapter 5.

2.2 Non-legal rules of the constitution

There are two sources of non-legal rules of the United Kingdom constitution:

1. Constitutional conventions.
2. Custom.

Conventions of the constitution

A great many rules of the constitution are not contained in Acts of Parliament or judicial decisions but are to be found in those rules of conduct called conventions. They have been defined as:

> '... rules of constitutional behaviour which are considered to be binding by and upon those who operate the constitution but which are not enforced by the law courts ... nor by the presiding officers in the Houses of Parliament.'

Examples of conventions of the constitution
Conventions relating to the Executive. The Sovereign must not exercise on her own initiative her legal right to refuse to assent to Bills which have passed through both Houses of Parliament.

The Sovereign must act in accordance with the advice of her ministers.

The Government shall be headed by a Prime Minister and the Prime Minister shall choose a Cabinet of ministers to lead the Government.

The Sovereign shall appoint as Prime Minister the leader of the party with the majority of seats in the House of Commons.

The Prime Minister and the Chancellor of the Exchequer must be members of the House of Commons.

Ministers are collectively and individually responsible to Parliament. The Government must resign or advise a dissolution of Parliament if it loses the confidence of the House of Commons.

Ministers must be members of the House of Commons or the House of Lords.

Conventions relating to the Legislature. The majority in the House of Commons shall not expel the minority to gain political advantage.

The House of Lords ought ultimately to defer to the will of the House of Commons.

The representation of political parties in Parliamentary Committees ought to be proportionate to their strength in the House.

Money Bills shall only be introduced in the House of Commons and only by a Government minister.

Parliament must be summoned to meet at least once a year.

Conventions relating to the Judiciary. Judges should not be active in party politics.

Members of the House of Lords who have not been appointed Lords of Appeal in ordinary must not participate in the judicial functions of the House.

Conventions relating to the Commonwealth. The Governor-General of a Commonwealth country within Her Majesty's Dominions must be appointed by the Queen on the advice of the Government of the country concerned.

The Governor-General of a Commonwealth country within Her Majesty's Dominions must act on the advice of the Government of that country and not on the advice of the United Kingdom Government.

Governments of Commonwealth countries should inform each other about foreign policy and treaty negotiations.

Why conventions of the constitution are obeyed
According to Dicey:

> '... the sanction which constrains the boldest political adventurer to obey the fundamental principles of the constitution and the conventions in which these principles are expressed, is the fact that the breach of these principles and of these conventions will almost immediately bring the offender into conflict with the courts and the law of the land.
>
> For example, by convention Parliament must meet at least once each year. If that convention were disobeyed the Government would soon find itself running out of money or having to raise illegal taxes, as the power to levy taxes is granted by Parliament for only a year at a time.'

However, there are many conventions the breach of which would not result in any illegality. For example, the conventions that lay peers do not take part in the judicial functions of the House, or that the majority in the Commons should not expel the Opposition, or that Parliament should not legislate for a Dominion against its will, if breached, would not entail the breach of any legal rule. Therefore obedience to conventions cannot be explained by reference to legal sanctions alone. As Professor Jennings has suggested, conventions are obeyed 'because of the political difficulties which follow if they are not'. In a democracy this means the pressure exerted through public opinion and the Opposition for Government conforming to the principles on which the system is based.

The distinction between law and convention

According to Dicey the main distinction between law and convention is simply that laws are enforced by the courts, while conventions are not:

> '... the rules which make up constitutional laws, as the term is used in England, include two sets of principles or maxims of a totally distinct character.
>
> The one set of rules are in the strictest sense "laws" since they are rules which (whether written or unwritten, whether enacted by statute or derived from the mass of custom, tradition, or judge-made maxims known as the common law) are enforced by the courts; these rules constitute "constitutional law" in the proper sense of that term and may for the sake of distinction be called collectively "the law of the constitution".
>
> The other set of rules consists of conventions, understandings, habits or practice which, though they may regulate the conduct of the several members of the sovereign power, of the Ministry, and of other officials, are not in reality laws at all, since they are not enforced by the courts.'

However, Dicey's approach may be too simplistic. Not all rules of law are justiciable. Professor Jennings sees the real distinction between law and convention as resting upon the fact that when a rule is a rule of law, it is generally speaking the function of the courts to declare that it is broken. The legal rule is either formally expressed or formally illustrated by a decision of a court, whereas conventions arise out of practice. Formal enunciation through the proper constitutional authorities gives a rule of law a greater sanctity than a convention. The Opposition feels that it has a more effective remedy if it can point out that the Government has acted illegally, than it would have if it could say only that it has acted unconstitutionally.

Why not enact conventions as law?

Conventions have several advantages over legal rules in the context of constitutional law. They provide a means of bringing about constitutional change without the need for formal change in the law. For example, many conventions concern the powers of the Sovereign. They allow the legal powers of the Queen to remain intact while allowing the democratically-elected Government to exercise those powers, and they allow flexibility. Law is rigid and may be difficult to change. Conventions allow the constitution to evolve and keep up to date with changing circumstances without the need for formal enactment or repeal of law.

Law must be followed in every case. Conventions allow discretion and can be waived if the particular circumstances make this desirable. Most conventions concern matters of a political nature. Their non-legal nature thus helps to keep the judiciary and the courts out of politics and political controversy. As long as conventions are obeyed there is no need for legal codification. If a particular convention is disregarded then it can be formally enacted and given legal status.

The courts and conventions

Conventions, being non-legal rules, cannot be enforced through the courts. But the courts have, in appropriate cases, been prepared to recognise the existence of conventional rules when deciding points of law. For example, in *Liversidge* v *Anderson* [1942] AC 206, the court gave as one reason for refusing to exercise judicial review of a minister's discretionary power, the fact that through the convention of ministerial responsibility, the minister was responsible to Parliament for the exercise of the power. Thus an alternative 'remedy' was available. Similarly, in *Attorney-General* v *Jonathan Cape Ltd* [1976] QB 752, which concerned the Crossman diaries, the Lord Chief Justice decided that an injunction could, in suitable cases, be granted to protect Cabinet secrecy, and hence collective responsibility.

Perhaps the most significant example of the courts adjudicating on the existence or otherwise of a convention arose in *Re Amendment of the Constitution of Canada* (1982) 125 DLR (3d) 1. The Canadian Government had submitted to the United Kingdom proposals for a draft constitution which would effectively give Canada complete control over its own constitution. Provinces opposed to the changes sought, by way of a declaration, the view of the Supreme Court of Canada in relation to the following question:

> 'Is it a constitutional convention that the House of Commons and Senate of Canada will not request Her Majesty the Queen to lay before the Parliament of the United Kingdom of Great Britain and Northern Ireland a measure to amend the Constitution of Canada affecting federal-provincial relationships or the powers, rights or privileges granted or secured by the Constitution of Canada to the provinces, their legislatures or governments without first obtaining the agreement of the provinces?'

By a majority of six to three the court confirmed the existence of such a convention. In coming to this conclusion the majority of the court had been guided by the views of Sir Ivor Jennings, as stated in *The Law and the Constitution* (5th ed p136):

> 'We have to ask ourselves three questions: first, what are the precedents; secondly, did the actors in the precedents believe that they were bound by a rule; and thirdly, is there a reason for the rule? A single precedent with a good reason may be enough to establish the rule. A whole string of precedents without such a reason will be of no avail, unless it is perfectly certain that the persons concerned regarded them[selves] as bound by it.'

The court's declaration was clearly not binding on the Canadian Government as a matter of law, but it is significant that a revised proposal was drawn up to which all provinces agreed, with the exception of Quebec. The result was the enactment of the Canada Act 1982 which repatriated the Canadian constitution: see further *Manuel* v *Attorney-General* [1983] Ch 77.

Custom

A further source of constitutional rules is custom, ie 'rules of conduct based upon social or commercial custom which are recognised by judicial decision as having binding force'. Two important customary sources are:

1. the Royal Prerogative; and
2. the law and custom of Parliament.

The Royal Prerogative

The Royal Prerogative comprises those privileges and immunities recognised at common law as belonging to the Crown. The existence and extent of the prerogative is determined by the courts and no new prerogatives can be created.

The law and custom of Parliament

These comprise the rules relating to the functions, procedure, privileges and immunities of each House of Parliament. Some are to be found in resolutions of each House, while others remain unwritten, being based solely on informal understandings or practice. Generally the ordinary courts have no jurisdiction over the law of Parliament.

Other non-legal sources of constitutional law

The writing of eminent constitutional lawyers forms a subsidiary source of constitutional law. When determining questions of constitutional law the courts may seek the guidance of writers of repute such as Dicey, Maitland, Anson, Jennings, Wade, de Smith, Wolf-Phillips and Erskine May, all of whom are of great persuasive authority.

3

The Separation of Powers – The Rule of Law – The Independence of the Judiciary

3.1 The rule of law

3.2 The separation of powers

3.3 The independence of the Judiciary

3.1 The rule of law

Introduction

In the United Kingdom the general concept of the rule of law has become identified with Professor A V Dicey's usage of that phrase in his work *The Law of the Constitution* first published in 1885. The phrase has been in use since at least as early as the time of Aristotle in the fourth century BC, and it has certainly meant different things to different thinkers and theorists. Aristotle's concept of the rule is encapsulated in his phrase:

'The rule of the law is to be preferred to that of any individual.'

The essence of this is that even rulers should be subject to some sort of higher law and should govern in accordance with that higher law. By higher law in this context is meant some form of natural law governing the universe. From this flows the idea that man-made law, if it is to be properly regarded as law, must conform to the standards of that natural law. Thus, law must conform to certain minimum standards of justice as a reflection of that absolute justice which obtains in the natural world. At different times throughout the centuries there have been different views as to how man may ascertain what this natural law or absolute justice consists in.

Dicey certainly took over this thinking, the general idea that law, of its very nature, embodies certain principles. For Dicey the rule of law existed most strongly in those societies where the content of the legal rules on certain matters was to a certain specified effect.

Dicey's rule of law

In *The Law of the Constitution*, Dicey stated that the rule of law was one of the main features of the constitution of the United Kingdom and that, in this context, the phrase embraced 'at least three distinct though kindred concepts'.

Dicey's first concept

'That no man is punishable or can be lawfully made to suffer in body or goods except for a distinct breach of law established in the ordinary legal manner before the ordinary courts of the land. In this sense the rule of law is contrasted with every system of government based on the exercise by persons in authority of wide, arbitrary, or discretionary powers of constraint.'

Professor Jennings in his book *The Law and the Constitution* writes of Dicey's first concept:

'... it involves the notion that all governmental powers, save those of the representative legislature, shall be distributed and determined by reasonably precise laws. Accordingly a King or other person acting on behalf of the State cannot exercise a power unless he can point to some specific rule of law which authorises his act ...'

Jennings makes it clear that Dicey is saying something about the content of the law in a society where the rule of law obtains – the law does not give those in authority wide, discretionary powers to interfere with the personal freedom or property of subjects. This view of Jennings is justified, as is shown by Dicey's own reference to the first concept:

'It means ... the absolute supremacy or predominance of regular law as opposed to the influence of arbitrary power, and excludes the existence of arbitrariness, of prerogative, or even of wide discretionary authority on the part of the Government.'

Thus, according to Dicey, those in authority in the United Kingdom where, he claimed, the rule of law was most emphatically present, in contrast to continental countries such as Switzerland and France, could only interfere with the personal freedom or property of a subject if the subject had breached a specific law of the land and the breach had been established 'in the ordinary legal manner before the ordinary courts of the land'.

Dicey's second concept

'We mean in the second place, when we speak of the "rule of law" as a characteristic of our country, not only that with us no man is above the law, but (which is a different thing) that here every man, whatever be his rank or condition, is subject to the ordinary law of the realm and amenable to the jurisdiction of the ordinary tribunals.'

He comments further:

'With us every official, from the Prime Minister down to a constable or a collector of taxes, is under the same responsibility for every act done without legal justification as any other citizen.'

Here Dicey was concerned to distinguish English law from the law of, for example, France, where there was, in contrast to England, a separate set of administrative courts for adjudicating in legal disputes between a subject and a Government official. Such disputes would in England at that time be dealt with in the ordinary civil courts. In France they would be dealt with in the administrative courts, separate from the ordinary civil courts which dealt with disputes between subject and subject. The law applied in the administrative courts contained certain rules and principles different from those of the civil law applied in the ordinary civil courts. Dicey's contention was that in England every man, whether subject or Government official, must justify his acts by reference to the same body of law, being the ordinary law applied in the ordinary courts of the land.

Dicey wrote of this second concept:

> ' "The rule of law" in this sense excludes the idea of any exemption of officials or others from the duty of obedience to the law which governs other citizens or from the jurisdiction of the ordinary tribunals ... The notion which lies at the bottom of the administrative law known to foreign countries is, that affairs or disputes in which the government or its servants are concerned are beyond the sphere of the civil courts and must be dealt with by special and more or less official bodies ...'

By 'more or less official bodies' he meant tribunals or courts which were essentially a part of the Executive machinery as opposed to part of the regular and independent court structure.

Dicey's third concept

> '... the general principles of the constitution (as for example the right to personal liberty, or the right to public meeting) are with us as the result of judicial decisions determining the rights of private persons in particular cases brought before the courts; whereas under many foreign constitutions the security (such as it is) given to the rights of individuals results, or appears to result, from the general principles of the constitution ...'

The point being made by Dicey here is that in English law the rights of the individual are determined by and are dependent upon the ordinary law of the land as developed by the ordinary courts adjudicating in particular cases. In England they do not arise from and are not dependent upon any special 'Bill of Rights' or other declaration in a written constitution. Dicey regarded the protection given to the rights of the individual in the United Kingdom as superior to that given in countries with a special declaration of rights or bill of rights, since he claimed the emphasis in English law was on giving a remedy when a right was infringed and not resting content with a mere statement or declaration of rights – a mere piece of paper.

To what extent is Dicey's formulation of the rule of law relevant today?

Dicey's first concept

Many present-day statutes give the police the power to arrest where they have reasonable grounds for suspecting certain facts. The police have powers of arrest whereby they may detain a person for at least a short time upon reasonable suspicion alone. It is quite clear that all Governments need certain legal powers to detain persons for trial even though it may later be established in court that the detainee had committed no crime. In this situation, the detainee is 'made to suffer in body' although he has committed no 'distinct breach of the law'. This legal power existed in Dicey's time as in our own and the police must justify the detention by reference to some fairly specific provision of common law or statute. A person who suspects that he is unlawfully detained may apply to the Divisional Court of the Queen's Bench Division of the High Court for a writ of habeas corpus ordering his release. The writ will be issued if the court is not satisfied that the detention is justified by law. Since the Petition of Rights 1628 it has not been sufficient answer in habeas corpus proceedings to state that the imprisonment is 'by special order of the King' – this answer had satisfied the court in the *Case of the Five Knights* (1627).

Social and political developments in the twentieth century have led to developments in law which give certain wide discretionary powers to the Government to interfere with a man's property ('make him suffer in ... goods') in the absence of any 'distinct breach of the law'. The extensive powers of compulsory purchase of land available to the Government today is, perhaps, the most outstanding illustration of such powers.

Dicey's second concept

The monarch in her personal capacity is not subject to the jurisdiction of the ordinary courts of the land. Although the Crown Proceedings Act 1947 has reduced the legal immunities and privileges of the Crown in its public capacity, there are still many aspects in which the Crown is in a privileged position in litigation.

Government officials have a vast array of legal rights and powers which the ordinary members of the public do not. For example, to take money as income tax, to exercise a power of compulsory purchase, to deport a person. In addition, the subject who wishes to contest whether the official has exercised these powers in accordance with law, is often required by law to take the matter, not to the ordinary courts of the land, but to a special tribunal. Such a tribunal may be closely connected with the Government department involved in the dispute or, to put it in Dicey's words, may be a 'more or less official' body. In some cases there is an appeal on a point of law to the ordinary courts, but not in the case of every tribunal.

The range of matters falling within the jurisdiction of bodies referred to generically as tribunals, is vast. It encompasses the determination of tax due, eligibility for social security payments, regulation of civil aviation, awards of compensation to victims of crime, immigration, decisions to release prisoners on parole, rent assessment, and regulation of broadcasting. Whilst it is true that proceedings of tribunals may not be subject to the legal restraints operating in respect of courts of law, such as contempt, privilege and the rules of evidence, but they are subject to the rules of administrative law as developed at common law. In addition, many of the most important tribunals are listed in Schedule 1 to the

Tribunals and Inquiries Act 1992, thus ensuring that they are required to give reasons for their decisions if so requested, and that a right of appeal to the High Court on a point of law is available.

Judicial immunity. The public interest in the proper administration of justice has led to the rule that no civil legal action may be brought in respect of anything said or done by a judge in the exercise of his judicial functions (*Anderson* v *Gorrie* [1985] 1 QB 668); in respect of a jury verdict (*Bushell's Case* (1670) 6 St Tr 999); or in respect of words spoken by the parties, counsel or witnesses in the course of judicial proceedings (*Munster* v *Lamb* (1883) 11 QBD 588). Note also that the Crown cannot be sued in tort in respect of the actions of its servants discharging judicial functions.

In contrast to certain groups of people who have certain legal immunities, other groups are subject to more legal restraints than the general public. Clear examples are members of the army, air force and navy who are subject to legal codes of discipline over and above those contained in the general law of the land. The Army Act 1955 creates a large number of offences, such as desertion, absence without leave, and disobedience to duty.

Dicey's third concept

It is still true today that such legal protection as is given to the rights of the individual in the United Kingdom depends on the ordinary law of the land as contained in statutes and judicial decisions, and not upon any special declaration or Bill of Rights. The question of whether the United Kingdom should adopt an entrenched bill of rights is one which is much discussed. Some of the participants in this discussion believe, contrary to Dicey's view, that individual rights would be better protected in the United Kingdom if such an entrenched bill of rights existed.

Jennings on Dicey's rule of law

In his book, *The Law and the Constitution*, Sir Ivor Jennings carried out a sustained critique of Dicey's views, including his treatment of the rule of law. Jennings points out that the phrase could be used simply to denote a society where a state of law and order existed. For this usage, even an absolutist regime would qualify. Clearly, however, Dicey does not use the phrase to mean this and no more. Dicey is only prepared to give the label 'the rule of law' to societies where the legal rules on individual liberty and individual property rights conform to the standards he has set and which he considers desirable. To put it another way, Dicey makes a value judgment about what the content of law should be and then takes the next step of saying that that is what law is. The rule of law operates most strongly in those societies where the legal rules conform most perfectly to the standards he has set. It is Jennings who points out that Dicey's political views influence his judgment in setting those standards. Jennings states that those elements or features in the law of a society which Dicey relies on as constituting the rule of law are all consequences which follow naturally from the existence of a democracy with free elections and a recognition that criticism of the Government is a positive merit. Jennings, by implication, denies that the prevalence of law is greater in a community which has these elements or features, than in a community where these features are absent. He is prepared to recognise that law may also rule in a society where the principles Dicey favours for the protection of individual liberty are quite absent. For Jennings states that the principles enunciated by Dicey 'depend essentially upon the existence of a democratic society' and, by implication, Jennings is not prepared to deny that law prevails in a community where the political system is not one of the Western liberal-democratic type favoured by Dicey. Jennings does not deny the desirability, in political terms, of the features Dicey stresses, but he does deny the specifically 'legal' character of a community where they are present. He says of Dicey's three concepts:

'These are intangibles which nevertheless produce an impression on the mind of any observant person who crosses the boundary from a dictatorial state into a free country. They cannot easily be forced into a formal concept dignified by such a name as the rule of law ...'

Putting the matter more bluntly, he says of Dicey's use of the phrase 'the rule of law':

'If it is merely a phrase for distinguishing democratic ... government from dictatorship, it is wise to say so.'

Sir Ivor Jennings thus attempts to lay bare what he presumably believes to be the fallacy of supposing that societies adhering to political systems of the typical Western liberal-democratic type, with their stress on the rights of the individual, have any specially 'legal' character which is missing in countries with political systems of the socialist, collectivist type. Two points may be made about this. Firstly, political theorists and jurists in socialist countries of the Maoist type are well aware of the political connotations of the phrase the rule of law. They write and speak of the desirability of their own societies conforming to 'socialist legality' rather than to 'the rule of law'. Secondly, there is a tendency even – or, perhaps, especially – in jurists in many parts of the world to assume that law in the area of civil liberties has some logical and necessary connection with certain principles which those concerned hold dear. One might say more specifically, although also more tentatively, that there has been a tendency at times to stress respect for the individual as, in some sense, an essential of law. This can be seen in the content of discussions surrounding the Declaration of Delhi 1959.

The Declaration of Delhi 1959

The International Commission of Jurists, which is affiliated to UNESCO, convened a number of conferences for the purpose of agreeing upon an adaptation of Dicey's rule of law which could be made world-wide. The most important result of these conferences was probably the Declaration of Delhi 1959, which resulted from a congress held by the International Commission of Jurists in New Delhi and attended by jurists from over 50 countries.

In answer to a questionnaire distributed to those attending, 'respect for the supreme value of human personality' was stated to be the basis of all law. Clearly this is a statement in general terms about what the content of law should or must be. Taking this as a starting point, the Declaration stated that the rule of law involved:

1. The right to representative and responsible government – that is, the right to be governed by a representative body answerable to the people.
2. That the citizen who is wronged by the Government should have a remedy.
3. Certain minimum standards or principles for the law – those contained in the Universal Declaration of Human Rights 1948 and the European Convention on Human Rights 1953 – including freedom of religion, freedom of assembly and association, the absence of retroactive penal laws.
4. The right to a fair trial, which involves:
   a) certainty of the criminal law;
   b) the presumption of innocence;
   c) reasonable rules relating to arrest, accusation and detention pending trial;
   d) the right to legal advice;
   e) public trial;
   f) the right of appeal;
   g) the absence of cruel and unusual punishments.
5. The independence of the Judiciary including proper grounds and procedure for the removal of judges.

The influence of Dicey's first and second concepts can be seen in the declaration. His third concept was abandoned since most other countries in the world have a bill of rights of some description.

The rule of law today

S A de Smith wrote in his book *Constitutional and Administrative Law* regarding Dicey's rule of law:

> 'His ideas, rooted in Whiggish libertarianism, were very influential for two generations; today they no longer warrant detailed analysis.'

It cannot, however, be denied that some general concept of the rule of law is frequently used today as a yard-stick against which law on individual freedom is measured. It is not unusual to hear civil rights groups protest that certain legal provisions in the United Kingdom or other Commonwealth countries are 'contrary to the rule of law'. Often the speaker or writer might be strained to say exactly what he understands the rule of law to involve. The criticism is usually levelled at legal provisions which give to the Executive branch of Government power to deprive individuals of their personal liberty for a considerable time on the basis of some vague suspicion of wrongdoing, and without the courts having an opportunity to adjudicate on whether there is substantial ground for suspicion.

'Liberty', formerly The National Council for Civil Liberties, claims in its publication *The Prevention of Terrorism Act: The Case for Repeal* that the Act has 'severely undermined the principles of natural justice and the rule of law', because it allows the Home Secretary to authorise detention for up to seven days without access to a court. The Act, in effect, it is claimed, authorises detention for questioning since the detainee only needs to be suspected of some involvement in terrorism and not of any specific act of terrorism. In addition the Home Secretary may, by an exclusion order, exclude an individual from one part of the country to another, for instance, from Great Britain to Northern Ireland, without the right to a court hearing, and indeed without the suspect having the right to know or challenge the evidence against him.

Although there are many respects in which English law deviates from the strict norms set up by Dicey's rule of law, references to those norms will be made when certain groups feel that deviation has gone beyond what is acceptable in increasing Executive discretionary power at the expense of individual freedom, and the right of the courts to decide when the legal preconditions for loss of liberty are satisfied.

3.2 The separation of powers

Introduction

As with the rule of law, the doctrine of separation of powers can be tracked back to Aristotle. It was developed by John Locke in the seventeenth century in his *Second Treatise of Civil Government*, 1690. He wrote:

> 'The Three Organs of State must not get into one hand ... It may be too great a temptation to human frailty, apt to grasp at power, for the same persons who have the power of making laws, to have also in their hands the power to execute them, whereby they may exempt themselves from obedience to the laws they make, and suit the law, both in its making and execution, to their own private advantage.'

The doctrine was developed further by the French jurist Montesquieu (1689–1755) who based his exposition on the British constitution of the early eighteenth century. The doctrine is briefly as follows:

1. There are three functions of Government: legislative, executive and judicial.
2. Each of these three functions should be vested in one organ of Government: the legislative, the executive and the judiciary, with no overlap. Each should then act as a check and balance on the others.
3. To concentrate more than one function in any one organ of Government is a threat to individual liberty.

According to Wade and Bradley in *Constitutional and Administrative Law* the concept of separation may, in the phrase 'separation of powers' mean at least three different things:

1. That the same persons should not form part of more than one of the three organs of Government, for example, that ministers should not sit in Parliament.
2. That one organ of Government should not control or interfere with the work of another, for example the Judiciary should be independent of the Executive, and ministers should not be responsible to Parliament.
3. That one organ of Government should not exercise the functions of another, for example, ministers should not have legislative powers.

The extent to which separation of powers may be said to exist in the United Kingdom is the subject of some controversy. According to de Smith:

> 'No writer of repute would claim that it is a central feature of the modern British system of government.'

However, in *R* v *Hinds* (1976) Lord Diplock, in delivering the judgment of the Privy Council, referred to:

> '... the basic concept of separation of legislative, executive and judicial power as it had been developed in the unwritten constitution of the United Kingdom.'

How far is separation of powers a feature of the British constitution?

Relationship between Legislature and Executive
Do the same persons form part of the Legislature and the Executive? The Sovereign is head of the Executive and also an integral part of the Legislature. Her powers are, however, theoretical rather than real. More importantly, by convention ministers must be members of one or other House of Parliament. The vast majority of persons who hold positions within the Executive are disqualified from membership of the House of Commons. These include civil servants, members of the armed forces and police forces, and other holders of offices of profit under the Crown (House of Commons Disqualification Act 1975).

Does the Legislature control the Executive or the Executive control the Legislature? Ultimately Parliament controls the Executive in that Parliament can oust a Government by withdrawing support. However, because of the distortion produced by the United Kingdom electoral system together with party discipline, a Government with an overall majority in the House of Commons has a large measure of control over Parliament. Government backbenchers will be unwilling to go too far in challenging the Government for fear of causing a General Election. The Government also has available several devices for curtailing parliamentary debate, and the House of Lords can now only delay the passage of legislation. It can be argued that the Legislature has been deprived of its legislative function in all but form because of the Government majority in the House of Commons, together with strict party discipline and devices for curtailing debate. In substance it is the Government making the law.

Some parliamentary control of the Executive exists in the form of question time, select committees, adjournment debates and Opposition days.

Do the Legislature and the Executive exercise each other's functions? There is a vast number of statutory instruments issued by ministers every year. The authority for this derives from statute, but little control is retained by Parliament over the legislation that is finally produced. Thus the Executive exercises a considerable legislative function.

Relationship between the Executive and the Judiciary
Do the same persons form part of the Executive and the Judiciary? The Lord High Chancellor is a member of the Executive as head of the Lord Chancellor's department and a member of the Cabinet. He is also the head of the Judiciary, entitled to preside over the House of Lords when it sits as a court. A member of the House of Lords, he is also a member of the Legislature.

Does the Executive control the Judiciary or the Judiciary control the Executive? The Judiciary are appointed by the Executive. Magistrates and circuit judges are appointed by the Lord Chancellor. High Court judges are appointed by the Queen on the advice of the Lord Chancellor. Lords Justice of Appeal and Lords of Appeal in Ordinary are appointed by the Queen on the advice of the Prime Minister after consulting the Lord Chancellor.

Magistrates are dismissible by the Lord Chancellor without cause shown. Circuit judges are dismissible by the Lord Chancellor for incapacity or misbehaviour.

Superior judges, under the Act of Settlement 1700, hold office during their good behaviour, rather than at Her Majesty's pleasure, but can be removed upon an address from both Houses of Parliament. The Supreme Court Act 1981 re-enacted the provision of 1700 in slightly different words, stating that judges of the High Court and Court of Appeal hold office during their good behaviour, 'subject to' a power of removal by the Queen on an address by both Houses of Parliament. A similar provision applies to Lords of Appeal in Ordinary: Appellate Jurisdiction Act 1876 s6. This power of removal upon an address from Parliament has only been exercised once since 1700. In 1830 Jonah Barrington, an Irish judge, was removed, having misappropriated money belonging to litigants and having ceased to perform his judicial duties many years previously.

Financial independence of the Judiciary is guaranteed under the Act of Settlement 1700 which provided that salaries of judges shall be 'ascertained and established'. This provision has been taken to mean that the salary of judges shall be charged on the consolidated fund, meaning that their payment is permanently authorised.

Immunity of the Judiciary from Executive criticism is supported by the convention that the Government should not criticise judicial decisions.

Judicial control of the Executive exists in that it is the duty of the courts, if proper application is made to them by a citizen or a body with locus standi, to check the Executive authorities from exceeding their powers, and, in some instances, to order the performance of duties owed by public officials. For example: *R* v *Metropolitan Police Commissioner, ex parte Blackburn* [1968] 2 QB 118; *Secretary of State for Education and Science* v *Tameside Metropolitan Borough Council* [1977] AC 1014; *Congreve* v *Home Office* [1976] QB 629; *Laker Airways* v *Department of Trade* [1977] QB 643.

Do the Executive and the Judiciary exercise each other's functions? There are a great many administrative tribunals, so called because of their comparatively close connection with the administrative (Executive) authorities. These tribunals are set up by statute, some, such as rent tribunals and industrial tribunals, to resolve disputes between two private individuals; others, such as social security tribunals and Special Commissioners of Income Tax, to resolve disputes between a citizen and a Government department. Many of these tribunals work largely independently of any Government department. The Special Commissioners of Income Tax, for example, is a panel of five full-time officials of the Inland Revenue department responsible for dealing with disputes between the citizen and the Inland Revenue about income tax assessments, and generally regarded as doing so with great impartiality.

Apart from the existence of these administrative tribunals, whose connections with a Government department may be strong or weak, there are many disputes which a citizen may have with an Executive authority, which will not be referred to a tribunal, but are instead decided by a minister. These include disputes over refusal to grant planning permission by a local authority, or over the making of compulsory purchase orders. They fall for decision by the minister at the head of the relevant Government department. This is a very clear example of the Executive exercising a judicial function. The question can, of course, arise as to whether a particular function is more properly classified as 'administrative' or 'judicial'. The line between the two can be difficult to draw. For example, in an application for a licence or a dispute over the making of a clearance order, the deciding body has to apply the legal provisions of the relevant statute to the facts before it. But the legal provisions may allow for the exercise of considerable discretion on the part of the deciding body. Is the function then administrative or judicial?

Relationship between the Judiciary and the Legislature
Do the same persons form part of the Judiciary and the Legislature? Under the House of Commons Disqualification Act 1975 all full-time judicial appointments disqualify the holder from membership of the House of Commons. But, the House of Lords is both the second chamber of the Legislature and the highest Court of Appeal in the United Kingdom. Also the Lord High Chancellor presides over the

House when it is sitting in its legislative capacity, and is entitled to preside over the Appellate Committee when hearing appeals.

Does the Legislature control the Judiciary or the Judiciary control the Legislature? Parliament can control the courts, in a sense, by legislation. But judges' salaries are charged on the consolidated fund, meaning that their payment is permanently authorised, and this authority does not need to be renewed, and hence reviewed, each year by Parliament. Thus Parliament is denied an annual opportunity to discuss and possibly criticise the activities of judges.

There is also a long-standing rule of the House of Commons that, except upon a substantive motion on the question of whether to request dismissal, Members of Parliament should not make comments or reflections upon the activities of particular judges, or judges generally. This convention is recorded in Erskine May. Members of Parliament may, with the exception of those holding office in the Government, criticise a judgment rather than a judge. It is for the Speaker to ensure that MPs observe this nice distinction, which may be no easy task. In recent years, several of Lord Denning's judgments have caused an angry response among some MPs. On the occasion of his judgment in *Duport Steels Ltd* v *Sirs* (1980) – a Court of Appeal decision which was reversed on appeal to the House of Lords, where adverse comment was made on the highly political flavour of parts of Lord Denning's judgment – the Speaker quoted a ruling given by the late Selwyn Lloyd when Speaker:

> 'It can be argued that the judge made a mistake and was wrong and the reason for this contention can be given within certain limits. What is wrong is to impute any motives to judges acting in their responsible office.'

Regarding judicial control of the Legislature, the doctrine of parliamentary sovereignty applicable in the United Kingdom must be contrasted with those written constitutions which vest in a state's Supreme Court the power to declare legislation unconstitutional and invalid. No such power exists in the United Kingdom, in relation to primary legislation. As far as delegated legislation is concerned, the courts can invalidate statutory instruments or Orders in Council by invoking the ultra vires doctrine; see the comments of Sir John Donaldson MR in *R* v *HM Treasury, ex parte Smedley* [1985] 1 QB 657 at 666.

Do the Legislature and the Judiciary exercise each other's functions? It may certainly be argued that the judges in the United Kingdom to some extent make law – the legislative function. The creative or legislative function of the judiciary is perhaps greater in a common law system than in a civil law system based on a code. The 'declaratory theory' of precedent – the theory that judges do not make law but only declare the common law or common custom of the realm – persisted into the 19th century, but it is now generally recognised that the judges in the United Kingdom do exercise some law-making function, with the silent acquiescence of

Parliament. A particularly striking example of this creative function was the House of Lords' decision in *Shaw* v *DPP* [1962] AC 220.

Shaw proposed to publish a 'ladies' directory' giving details of prostitutes. Prostitution is not, and was not at that time, a criminal offence in the United Kingdom. Shaw was convicted of conspiracy to corrupt public morals, and his conviction was upheld by the House of Lords, although this was not a statutory offence and there had never previously been a conviction for this offence. Indeed, when Shaw had consulted his lawyers and Scotland Yard to enquire whether, in the event of publication, he would be committing any criminal offence, the reply was that he would not. Lord Simmonds stated, giving his judgment in the House of Lords:

> 'In the sphere of criminal law I entertain no doubt that there remains in the courts of law a residual power to enforce the supreme and fundamental purpose of the law, to conserve not only the safety and order but also the moral welfare of the state, and that it is their duty to guard it against attacks which may be the more insidious because they are novel and unprepared for.'

In 1972 in *Knuller* v *DPP* [1973] AC 435, the House of Lords upheld another conviction of conspiracy to corrupt public morals. As a point of interest, it is indicative of one aspect of the Judiciary's power to create new law that Lord Reid, who had dissented in *Shaw*'s case, taking the view that there could not be a conviction for such an offence, concurred in the decision in *Knuller*, feeling obliged to do so in view of the majority decision in *Shaw*'s case.

Conclusion

Although in 1976 in *R* v *Hinds* Lord Diplock, delivering the judgment of the court, referred to 'the basic concept of separation of legislature, executive and judicial power as it had been developed in the unwritten constitution of the United Kingdom', there is certainly some evidence of lack of separation or, at least, important modifications of the doctrine in any pure form. In the United Kingdom probably the most striking modification of the concept of separation is that all ministers, heading the Executive, are drawn from and are responsible to Parliament. This has been the convention since the latter part of the eighteenth century. In addition, the picture in the twentieth century has been one of increased Executive activity in the legislative and adjudicative fields, which many regard as a cause for alarm.

Clearly, however, judges have very great discretion as to the extent to which they want to be 'pro-active'. Respect for the doctrine of the separation of powers can be relied upon as a justification for not intervening, as was the case in *Malone* v *Metropolitan Police Commissioner* [1979] Ch 344. Sir Robert Megarry V-C refused to grant a declaration that 'telephone tapping' was illegal per se under English law, since the matter was not governed by legislation, and in the absence of authority he was not prepared, sitting at first instance, to create any legal principles at common law.

Separation of powers in the constitution of the United States

In the United States constitution of 1787, separation of powers was clearly expressed. Each of the three primary constitutional functions was vested in a distinct organ.

1. Legislative power was vested in Congress, consisting of a House of Representatives and a Senate.
2. Executive power was vested in the President.
3. Judicial power was vested in the Supreme Court and such other federal courts as might be established by Congress.

The President holds office for a fixed term of four years. If he resigns his deputy succeeds. He is not dependent on support in Congress to continue in office, and cannot use the threat of dissolution to make Congress, particularly those members who are of his party, co-operate. The President is separately elected from Congress, therefore he may be of a different party from that which has a majority in either or both Houses of Congress.

The constitution states both the President's powers and the power of Congress.

Heads of the chief departments of state are known as the Cabinet, but they are individually responsible to the President and not to Congress. That is, the President is directly answerable to the electorate because he is directly elected. In the United Kingdom, where ministers are not directly elected as such, they are answerable to Parliament which is directly elected and therefore answerable to the electorate.

The part played by the President and Cabinet with regard to legislation
Neither the President nor members of his cabinet can sit or vote in Congress. They have no direct power to initiate Bills, but the President can merely recommend legislation in his message to Congress. The President can veto legislation but can be overridden by a two-thirds vote in both Houses. Treaties are negotiated by the President, but must be approved by a two-thirds majority of the Senate.

The President has the power to nominate certain key officers, including judges of the Supreme Court, but the Senate must confirm these appointments and may refuse to do so. Once appointed, the judges of the Supreme Court are independent of both Congress and the President. They may be removed by impeachment by the Senate, but only for treason, bribery or similar offences.

The Supreme Court has ruled that the separation of powers expressed in the constitution excludes any extensive delegation of legislative power by Congress to executive agencies: *Schechter Poultry Corporation* v *US* (1935). There is also the historic decision of Chief Justice Marshall in *Marbury* v *Madison* (1803), by which the Supreme Court assumed the power of declaring both Acts of Congress and Acts of the President to be unconstitutional.

In fact, the separation of powers in the United States constitution does not involve the isolation of each organ from the other two, but rather an elaborate system of checks and balances. The system rests upon an open recognition that particular functions belong primarily to a given organ, while at the same time superimposing a power of limited interference by another organ in order to ensure that the first does not exercise its acknowledged functions in an arbitrary and despotic manner.

3.3 The independence of the Judiciary

As Professor Wade has written of the United Kingdom:

> 'The separation of powers means little more than an independent Judiciary.'

It this context judicial independence involves the following, security of tenure, immunity from civil and criminal liability, as regards the discharge of judicial functions, and restrictions upon parliamentary criticism of decisions.

Security of tenure

Magistrates may be dismissed by the Lord Chancellor without cause shown.

Judges of inferior courts may be dismissed by the Lord Chancellor for incapacity or misbehaviour. Judges of superior courts – High Court, Court of Appeal and House of Lords – hold office during good behaviour subject to a power of removal by the Queen on an address to the Queen by both Houses of Parliament: Act of Settlement 1700 re-enacted in the Appellate Jurisdiction Act 1981 and the Supreme Court Act 1981.

Freedom from criticism

By convention the judicial conduct of judges may not be the subject of criticism in parliamentary debate, except upon a motion for an address for their removal. Breach of this convention may amount to a contempt of Parliament. Criticism of a judge may also amount to contempt of court.

Judicial immunity

Judges are immune from suit in the law of defamation for anything said in court, as are parties, lawyers and witnesses. This applies to all the judges no matter what their rank in the judicial hierarchy. However, the liability of judges in tort for actions in the course of judicial proceedings depends upon the rank of the judge concerned. In the superior courts a judge is not liable even for an act in excess of his jurisdiction, provided he was acting bona fide, as illustrated in *Sirros* v *Moore* [1974] 3 All ER 776.

The plaintiff was a citizen of Turkey brought before a magistrate for breach of the Aliens Order 1953. The magistrate fined him £50, recommended that he be deported, but directed that he should not be detained pending the Home Secretary's decision on deportation. The plaintiff appealed to the Crown Court against the recommendation for deportation. At the hearing the judge accepted the prosecution's submission that the court had no jurisdiction to hear an appeal against a recommendation for deportation, and announced the court's decision that the appeal be dismissed. Thereupon the plaintiff made his way out of the court, but when the judge realised that he was leaving court he called out 'stop him' and sent police officers after him. They found him in the street and brought him back to the cells. He was detained in custody. On the following day the plaintiff applied to the Divisional Court for habeas corpus. He was successful. He later issued a writ claiming damages for assault and false imprisonment against, inter alia, the circuit judge in the Crown Court who had given the decision on appeal. The matter went to the Court of Appeal. The Court of Appeal held that the Crown Court had jurisdiction to hear the appeal. The Crown Court had merely, however, dismissed the appeal and thus at the time the plaintiff's detention was ordered there was in force no order under which the plaintiff could be detained.

The instruction from the judge that he be detained was therefore unlawful. The plaintiff had, however, no cause of action against the judge in respect of this unlawful detention. The majority of the court (Lord Denning MR and Ormerod LJ) stated that every judge of the superior and inferior courts, including a Justice of the Peace, was entitled to protection from liability and damages in respect of what he had done provided that he was:

1. acting judicially; and
2. under the honest belief that his act was within his jurisdiction.

This was to be so even though in consequence of a mistake of law or fact, what the judge had done might be outside his jurisdiction. This then was the principle laid down by the majority: that a judge should have immunity provided that at the time he was acting judicially and also honestly believed that what he did was within his jurisdiction.

Buckley LJ, while holding that the judge was protected since what he had done was within his jurisdiction, although he had adopted an erroneous course of procedure, was of the view that the act in question, if the judge is to be protected, must not only have been done in his judicial capacity but also be an act upon which he has jurisdiction to adjudicate. But this was the minority view, and the case can be seen as moving in the direction of increasing judicial immunity rather than restricting it.

The dicta of the majority in *Sirros* v *Moore*, to the effect that all judges should enjoy the same immunity, were disapproved by the House of Lords in *Re McC* [1984] 3 All ER 908 where damages were awarded against magistrates who had failed to notify an accused of his right to legal representation before imposing a custodial sentence. The Lords considered that the historic distinction between judges of the superior and inferior courts should be preserved. They affirmed that judges of the inferior courts remain liable for acts in excess of their jurisdiction.

Immunity applies to both civil and criminal liability and is based upon public policy requiring the judiciary to be free to pursue the administration of justice.

Independence distinguished from neutrality

In his book *The Politics of the Judiciary* Professor J A G Griffith seeks to explode what he refers to as 'the myth of judicial neutrality'. This is the theory that a court order is a product of the law and only marginally of the judicial mind.

In practice, as Griffith points out, judges are faced with cases involving questions of the powers of government or the right of individuals – essentially political questions in the eyes of most people – and the guidance given to the judges by statute and common law is inadequate and imprecise. They must, however, give a decision; they cannot remain silent. Griffith carries out his own analysis of the sort of decisions judges are likely to give and comes to some conclusion as to the sort of factors that are likely to influence those decisions.

Early in his book Griffith reviews surveys on the social and educational background of the Judiciary. Looking at surveys covering the last century or so, Griffith observes that 70 per cent of the judiciary are products of Oxford or Cambridge University and about 75 per cent to 80 per cent have attended public school. These figures, he observes, have changed very little over the last 30 years or more and show in broad terms that four out of five professional judges are products of public school and Oxbridge.

He also observes early in his book that in political cases:

> 'We find a remarkable consistency of approach ... concentrated in a fairly narrow part of the spectrum of political opinion. It spreads from that part of the centre which is shared by right wing Labour, Liberal and 'Progressive' Conservative opinion to that part of the right which is associated with traditional Toryism – but not beyond it into the reaches of the far right.'

Judges in the United Kingdom, according to Griffith, are not beholden politically to the Government of the day. They seek to give decisions which accurately apply the law, and where the law leaves some latitude as to what the decision in a particular case should be, judges seek to give decisions which serve the public interest as they perceive it. However, as Griffith observes, 'what is or is not in the public interest is a political question which admits of a great variety of answers'. The judicial concept of the public interest, at least seen in the cases discussed in his book, is according to Griffith three-fold. It concerns:

1. The interests of the State and the preservation of law and order broadly interpreted.
2. The protection of property rights.
3. The promotion of certain political views normally associated with the Conservative Party.

The first point Griffith illustrates by reference to such decisions as *Liversidge* v *Anderson* [1942] AC 206 and *R* v *Secretary of State for Home Affairs, ex parte Hosenball* [1977] 1 WLR 766. In both cases the interests of the State were seen to outweigh the interests of the individual.

On the law and order matter, Griffith claims that in perhaps the most important area of all, that of police powers, the judges have left largely unfulfilled their self-styled role as protectors of the individual. He claims of the (sometimes illegal) practices of the police in relation to questioning, search and seizure: 'these: practices have been generally supported by the judiciary'.

As far as the protection of property rights is concerned, Griffith claims that, apart from a brief period during and after the Second World War, the courts have continuously intervened to limit and curtail the powers of Government to interfere with property rights, and have been far more assiduous in this than in the protection of civil rights and liberties. He refers, for example, to squatters cases and cases involving governmental power of compulsory purchase.

Concerning the promotion of certain political views normally associated with the Conservative Party, Griffith comments that the attitude of the court to trade union members who incur the displeasure of the union officials is one of considerable sympathy. He comments to the same degree on those who claim that their companies have unjustly dismissed them. He concludes that the suspicion arises that the courts in protecting the individual trade unionist are motivated more by their dislike of organised trade unions than by their wish to advance the personal rights of individuals.

It is trade union cases which Griffith selects to illustrate most strongly his point that judicial decisions are affected by the judge's view of what will best serve the public interest. He selects the case in 1972 when five dockers, who had been imprisoned for disobedience to an order of the National Industrial Relations Court, were released from prison following the House of Lords judgment in *Heaton's Case*. Griffith claims that the decision in *Heaton's Case* did nothing to change any law which was relevant to the dockers' imprisonment for contempt of the National Industrial Relations Court. He sees the decision of the National Industrial Relations Court to release the dockers, following the decision in *Heaton's Case*, as using a flimsy justification for their release, which the court regarded as essential if a general strike was to be avoided.

Whereas the courts had previously regarded the upholding of the rule of law as being in the public interest, they now saw the avoidance of this general strike as being most forcibly in the public interest. Griffith sees the House of Lords as being involved in this matter as well, and it is true that judgment in *Heaton's Case* was given one week after the hearing. In other words the giving of the judgment was expedited.

By way of conclusion Griffith states of the Judiciary:

'I mean to absolve them of a conscious and deliberate intention to pursue their own interests or the interests of their class. I believe that ... within the considerable area of decision making open to them they look to what they regard as the interest of the whole society.'

Griffith takes the view that in our society political power and the power of Government are exercised by a relatively small number of people, and that the senior judges are undeniably among those few. They are bound therefore to protect the social order which allows them a position of power from threats to its stability or to the existing distribution of political and economic power.

He says finally of the politics of the Judiciary:

'It is not the politics of the extreme right ... but is it demonstrable that on every major social issue which has come before the courts during the last thirty years – concerning industrial relations, political protests, race relations, government secrecy, police powers, moral behaviour – the judges have supported the conventional, established and settled interests. This conservatism does not necessarily follow the day-to-day political policies currently associated with the party of the same name. But it is a political philosophy nonetheless.'

4

The Sovereignty of Parliament

4.1 Introduction

4.2 The continuing nature of parliamentary sovereignty

4.3 Sovereignty and the courts

4.4 Limitation upon the exercise of parliamentary sovereignty

4.1 Introduction

The phrase 'sovereignty of Parliament' is generally used to mean the absence of any legal restraint on the legislative powers of the United Kingdom Parliament. This absence of legal restraint has three aspects:

1. Parliament is legally competent to legislate upon any subject matter.
2. No Parliament can bind its successors or be bound by its predecessors.
3. Once Parliament has legislated no court or other person can pass judgment upon the validity of the legislation.

Whilst this is broadly correct as a statement of principle it must be considered in the light of membership of the European Community, considered in Chapter 6. The examples given below will serve to illustrate the basic principle of parliamentary sovereignty and the primacy of that concept within the British constitution.

The Act of Settlement 1700 and His Majesty's Declaration of Abdication Act 1936

Although in 1700 Parliament laid down in the Act of Settlement the law governing accession to the English throne, Parliament was legally competent to alter the right of succession by the later Act of 1936 which provided that Edward VIII, his issue, if any, and the descendants of that issue should not thereafter have any right to the succession.

Burmah Oil Co v Lord Advocate *[1965] AC 75, and the War Damage Act 1965*

In the case of *Burmah Oil Co* v *Lord Advocate* the House of Lords held that where private property was taken or destroyed (except by battle damage) under the Royal Prerogative, the owner was entitled at common law to compensation from the Crown.

Parliament, however, reversed the effect of this decision in the particular case by enacting the War Damage Act 1965, which retrospectively provided that no person should be entitled at common law to receive compensation in respect of damage to or destruction of property caused by lawful acts of the Crown during, or in contemplation of the outbreak of, a war in which the Sovereign is or was engaged. This Act effectively removed Burmah Oil's common law right to compensation. Such retrospective legislation is rare but quite within Parliament's competence; see further the War Crimes Act 1991.

Mortensen *v* Peters *1906 14 SLT 227*

The appellant was a Dane and the master of a Norwegian ship. He was convicted by a Scottish court of otter trawling in the Moray Firth, contrary to a by-law issued by the Fishery Board for Scotland under the Herring Fishery (Scotland) Act 1889. He argued that international law recognised the right of a state to control fishing only within its territorial waters, and that the by-law was in contravention of a rule of international law limiting territorial waters to bays and estuaries of no greater breadth than 10 miles.

His appeal against conviction was dismissed unanimously by a full bench of 12 judges. The Lord Justice-General, Lord Dunedin, said:

> 'In this court we have nothing to do with the question of whether the Legislature has or has not done what foreign powers may consider a usurpation in a question with them. Neither are we a tribunal sitting to decide whether an Act of the Legislature is ultra vires as a contravention of generally acknowledged principles of international law. For us an Act of Parliament duly passed by Lords and Commons and assented to by the King is supreme, and we are bound to give effect to its terms.'

It can be seen from this case that, traditionally, for a United Kingdom court, United Kingdom municipal law is paramount even where there is a conflict between a rule of United Kingdom law and a rule of public international law. See further on this point *Cheney* v *Conn* [1968] 1 All ER 779. Thus, the United Kingdom may sign and ratify an international treaty, but the provisions of the treaty do not affect United Kingdom municipal law unless a statute is passed providing for the incorporation of the provisions as a part of United Kingdom law. There is now, however, one major qualification to this, and that is in relation to United Kingdom membership of the European Communities. The relationship between United Kingdom law and Community law cannot be analysed in terms of the relationship between United Kingdom law and public international law. The special problems raised as regards the doctrine of parliamentary sovereignty by United Kingdom membership of the European Communities are considered in Chapter 6.

4.2 The continuing nature of parliamentary sovereignty

Perhaps the most important aspect of the doctrine of parliamentary sovereignty is the inability of Parliament to limit its own legislative powers for the future. This is often expressed by saying that Parliament cannot bind its successors. Professor E C S Wade has encapsulated this aspect of the doctrine of parliamentary sovereignty in his observation that:

'There is one, and only one, limit to Parliament's legal power: it cannot detract from its own continuing sovereignty.'

Where Parliament intends to repeal earlier legislation it normally does so by means of an express clause to that effect in a later Act. Where later legislation is simply inconsistent with earlier legislation the courts invoke the doctrine of implied repeal whereby the earlier Act is impliedly repealed to the extent that it is inconsistent with the later Act.

Two cases illustrate this point. In *Vauxhall Estates Ltd* v *Liverpool Corporation* [1932] 1 KB 733 the Corporation of Liverpool proposed a scheme for the improvement of a certain area of the city. The Minister of Health confirmed the scheme in an order which incorporated the provisions of the Acquisition of Land (Assessment of Compensation) Act 1919 and the Housing Act 1925. These two Acts each provided a different scheme of compensation for compulsorily acquired land. The 1919 Act provided in s7(1):

'The provisions of the ... order by which the land is authorised to be acquired, or of any Act incorporated therewith, shall in relation to the matters dealt with in this Act, have effect subject to this Act, and so far as inconsistent with this Act those provisions shall ... not have effect.'

The question arose as to whether the compensation due to the appellants should be calculated in accordance with the 1919 Act or in accordance with the 1925 Act. The appellants argued that, because of s7(1) of the 1919 Act, it must be calculated in accordance with that Act. It was held that the compensation should be assessed in accordance with the later Act. Parliament had exercised its power of overriding the provisions of s7(1) of the 1919 Act by enacting in the later Act of 1925 a set of provisions totally inconsistent with those of the 1919 Act. As Avory J stated:

'We are asked to say that by a provision of the Act of 1919 the hands of Parliament were tied in such a way that it could not by any subsequent Act enact anything which was inconsistent with the provisions of the Act of 1919. It must be admitted that such a suggestion as that is inconsistent with the principle of the constitution of this country. Speaking for myself, I should certainly hold until the contrary were decided, that no Act of Parliament can effectively provide that no future Act shall interfere with its provisions.'

Similarly, in *Ellen Street Estates Ltd* v *Minister of Health* [1934] 1 KB 590 the material facts of which were identical to those in *Vauxhall Estates* v *Liverpool Corporation*, counsel for Ellen Street Estates Ltd argued that although the provisions of the 1919 Act could be repealed by express words in a later Act, they could not, because of s7(1), be repealed by implication by provisions in a later Act which were inconsistent with those in the 1919 Act.

It was held that the provisions of an earlier Act could always be repealed by implication by provisions in a later Act which were inconsistent with those in the earlier Act. Parliament could not, by a statement in an earlier Act, effectively provide that the provisions of that Act cannot be repealed by implication by inconsistent provisions in a later Act.

Scrutton LJ stated:

'Parliament can alter an Act previously passed, and it can do so by repealing in terms the previous Act ... and it can do so in another way – namely, by enacting a provision which is clearly inconsistent with the previous Act.'

Maugham LJ stated:

'The Legislature cannot, according to our constitutions, bind itself as to the form of subsequent legislation, and it is impossible for Parliament to enact that in a subsequent statute dealing with the same subject-matter there can be no implied repeal.'

This aspect of parliamentary sovereignty, the doctrine of implied repeal, may be the aspect that has been most significantly affected by United Kingdom membership of the European Communities.

4.3 Sovereignty and the courts

Prior to the great constitutional re-settlement of the seventeenth century, the courts claimed the right to challenge Acts of Parliament. In the *Case of Dr Bonham* (1610) Coke CJ stated:

'And it appears in our books, that in many cases, the common law will control Acts of Parliament, and sometimes adjudge them to be utterly void: for when an Act of Parliament is against common rights or reason, or repugnant, or impossible to be performed, the common law will control it and adjudge such Act to be void.'

Today the courts acknowledge that they must apply the law as laid down by Parliament. But it is only Acts of Parliament which are recognised by the courts as having the attributes of legal sovereignty. The courts will not allow a mere resolution of the House of Commons, for example, to alter the existing law of the land. The legal sovereignty of Parliament can only be exercised through Acts of Parliament.

What is an Act of Parliament?

Since there is no basic statutory definition of an Act of Parliament, what constitutes an Act of Parliament is primarily a matter of common law. At common law, a Bill becomes an Act of Parliament when it has been approved by the House of Lords and the House of Commons and has received the Royal Assent. Standing orders of each House of Parliament, together with other conventions and practices which have not been reduced to writing, govern the procedure on the passage of a Bill through each House. The enforcement of these procedural rules is entirely a matter for the House concerned, and the courts refuse even to consider the question as to whether there have been any procedural defects in the passage of a Bill through Parliament.

In *Edinburgh and Dalkeith Railway* v *Wauchope* (1842) 8 Cl & F 710, the respondent claimed that under the private Act of Parliament incorporating the railway company he was entitled to payment for every carriage loaded with passengers which passed over his land. The appellants argued that this provision had been repealed by a later private Act. (Note: a private Act of Parliament is one which only affects the legal rights and liabilities of certain persons or bodies and not those of the whole community.) The respondent countered with the argument that this later Act was invalid since it adversely affected his rights and according to the Standing Orders of the House of Commons, should not have been introduced without his having been given notice, and he had not been given such notice. The respondent had abandoned this argument by the time the case reached the House of Lords but, as it had found some support in the lower court, the House of Lords considered the argument and rejected it. Lord Campbell, for example, stated:

> 'All that a Court of Justice can do is look to the parliamentary roll; if from that it should appear that a Bill has passed both Houses and received the Royal Assent, no Court of Justice can inquire into the mode in which it was introduced into Parliament, nor into what was done previous to its introduction, or what passed in Parliament during its progress in its various stages through both Houses. I trust therefore, that no such inquiry will again be entered upon in any court ... but that due effect will be given to every Act of Parliament, private as well as public, upon what appears to be the proper construction of its existing provisions.'

Note that Lord Campbell stated that all the courts can do in order to ascertain the existence of an Act of Parliament is to look at the 'parliamentary roll' to see whether it appears from that, that the Bill passed both Houses and received the Royal Assent. Since 1848 there has been no parliamentary roll. Since 1849 the practice has been for the Queen's printer to make two copies of each Act of Parliament which are duly authenticated by the proper officers of each House; one is then kept in the Public Record Office, and the other in the House of Lords. Inspection of these 'Queen's printer's copies' would today be equivalent to inspection of the parliamentary roll before 1849.

The courts have similarly refused to investigate the validity of legislations where allegations have been made of procedural impropriety prior to enactment.

In *Lee* v *Bude and Torrington Junction Railway Co* (1871) LR 6 CP 577, one of the arguments of the defendant was that the plaintiff company was a legal nonentity because Parliament was induced to pass the Act forming the company by fraudulent recitals on the part of the plaintiffs. Again the court refused to question any of the matters which had led to the passing of the Act.

Willes J, with whom the other two members of the court agreed, stated:

> 'I would observe, as to these Acts of Parliament, that they are the law of the land ... We sit here as servants of the Queen and the Legislature. Are we to act as Regents over what is done by Parliament with the consent of the Queen, Lords and Commons? I deny that any such authority exists. If an Act of Parliament has been obtained improperly, it is for the legislature to correct it by repealing it: but, so long as it exists as law, the courts are bound to obey it.'

The principle recognised in these nineteenth century cases was more recently reaffirmed by the House of Lords in *Pickin* v *British Railways Board* [1974] AC 765.

By s259 of a private Act of Parliament of 1836 setting up a railway line it was provided that, if the line should be abandoned, the lands acquired for the track should vest in the owners of the adjoining lands. Subsequently the line became vested in the British Railways Board who promoted a private Bill, which was unopposed, and became the British Railways Act 1968. The effect of s18 of this Act was to cancel the effect of s259 of the 1836 Act and to vest in the Board instead any land over which abandoned tracks of lines passed. The plaintiff owned land adjoining an abandoned track. He brought an action against the Board claiming that by virtue of s259 of the 1836 Act he was the owner of the land under the track to mid-track. The Board claimed that, by virtue of s18 of the 1968 Act, the land under the track had vested in the Board. The plaintiff argued that the Board had obtained the passage of the 1968 Bill as unopposed, by misleading Parliament by a false recital in the preamble to the Bill that the requisite documents had been deposited with the local authority as required by standing orders. In fact, the plaintiff claimed, all the requisite documents had not been deposited and he, as owner of the land affected, had not been given notice of the intention to promote the Bill, which he would have opposed. Thus, he argued, the 1968 Act was ineffective to modify his legal rights.

It was held that the function of a court was to apply the enactment of Parliament. Thus it was not lawful, in the course of litigation, to call into question the validity of a statute by attempting to establish that Parliament, in passing it, was misled by fraud or otherwise.

Note that nothing in these cases denies the principle that a Bill must receive the approval of both Houses – unless it is a measure passed under the provisions of the Parliament Acts 1911–49 which dispense with the need for the consent of the House of Lords in certain circumstances – and the Royal Assent before it becomes an Act of Parliament. However, if it appeared from the Queen's printer's copy of an Act that such approval and assent had been given, the approach of the courts in the above cases shows that a court will not be prepared to consider extraneous evidence that such approval and assent had not in fact been given. See further *Murray* v *Rogers* 1992 SLT 221.

4.4 Limitation upon the exercise of parliamentary sovereignty

Only Parliament can limit its own sovereignty and such limitations must have been enacted in the form of a statute. No Parliament can bind its successors, therefore whatever limitations are imposed upon the sovereignty of Parliament by one statute may be repealed by a subsequent Act. However, in theory there are means by which limitations can be placed upon the sovereignty of Parliament. Such limitations fall into two main categories – as to the scope and subject-matter of parliamentary legislation, and as to the manner and form which legislation must take.

Limitations as to scope and subject-matter

Examples of such limitations are to be found in the Statute of Westminster 1931 and the various colonial Independence Acts. For example, s4 of the Statute of Westminster 1931, provides that:

'[N]o Act of the Parliament of the United Kingdom shall extend to a Dominion as part of the law of that Dominion unless expressly requested and consented to by the Dominion.'

Therefore any Act of the United Kingdom Parliament purporting to apply to a Dominion, but passed without the consent and request of that Dominion, might be ignored by the Dominion's courts. Of course, the United Kingdom Parliament might first repeal s4 of the Statute of Westminster, but as Lord Sankey observed in *British Coal Corporation* v *R* [1935] AC 500 'that is theory and has no relation to realities'.

Limitations as to manner and form

An example of such a limitation is to be found in the Colonial Laws Validity Act 1865: *Attorney-General for New South Wales* v *Trethowan* [1932] AC 526. Under the Colonial Laws Validity Act 1865, the Legislature of New South Wales had full power to make laws regarding its own constitution, powers and procedures, provided such laws were passed 'in such manner and form' as might be required from time to time by any Act of Parliament or other law for the time being in force. An Act passed in 1929 provided that the Upper House of the Legislature should not be abolished until a Bill passed by both Houses had been approved by a referendum. Amendments to the 1929 Act also required a referendum. Subsequently a Bill was passed by both Houses seeking to abolish both the Upper House and the referendum requirement. An injunction was granted by the New South Wales Court to restrain the Government of New South Wales from presenting the Bill for Royal Assent until a referendum had been held. On appeal, the Judicial Committee of the Privy Council held that the requirement of a referendum was binding on the Legislature until it had been abolished by a law passed in the 'manner and form' required by the law for the time being, that is, with the approval of a referendum.

However, the 'manner and form' provision in Trethowan was entrenched in that it was imposed on the New South Wales Legislature by a higher authority: the United Kingdom Parliament. Such entrenched provisions are only really possible where such higher authority exists, either in the form of a written constitution or a colonial power. As neither situation applies in the United Kingdom, parliamentary legislation cannot be 'entrenched' in this way. For further examples of the 'manner and form' limitation upon parliamentary sovereignty: see *Bribery Commissioner* v *Ranasinghe* [1965] AC 172; *Harris* v *Minister of the Interior* (1952) (2) SA 428(a); *Manuel* v *Attorney-General* [1983] Ch 77.

Other practical limitations on the exercise of parliamentary sovereignty

The doctrine of the mandate

According to this general and rather vague doctrine, which seems to be a product of the nineteenth century, the Government is expected to carry out the policy indicated in its manifesto at the General Election. Thus it should present to Parliament for enactment the Bills necessary to implement its manifesto proposals, as the fact that they were elected to power signifies they have popular support. The doctrine is subject to two important modifications. First, a government is expected and required to deal with situations which arise during its lifetime and some of these will not have been foreseeable at the time of the General Election. An unforeseen emergency may, for example, arise. Secondly, a government is not expected to 'mark time' because it has carried out all its manifesto commitments. Sir Ivor Jennings has referred to the doctrine of the mandate as 'a stick used by the Opposition to beat the Government'.

Public opinion

A government is constrained, in fact, by public opinion as to the Bills it presents to Parliament for enactment, for any government will have to face a General Election within a few years. Thus a government will be constrained from promoting legislation which favours one group too much against the interests of the general public. Reports of parliamentary debates in the press and on radio and television, and the publication of Bills after the first reading, mean that the public are, to some extent, informed about proceedings in Parliament. Public opinion is communicated to the Government in various ways, particularly through the activities of organised interest groups.

The European Community and parliamentary sovereignty. For a discussion of the effects of membership of the European Communities on the sovereignty of the United Kingdom Parliament see Chapter 6: Parliamentary Sovereignty and European Union Membership.

5

The European Union

5.1 Introduction

5.2 The institutions of the European Union

5.3 European Union law

5.4 The powers of the Court of Justice

5.1 Introduction

The origins of the European Union can be traced back to 9 May 1950, when the French Foreign Minister, Robert Schuman, (working closely with Jean Monnet) outlined the aims and methods of the so-called Schuman plan. The aim of the plan was to integrate the coal and steel industries of those Western European countries who wished to participate in the scheme, creating a European Coal and Steel Community (ECSC). It was formally established in 1951 when six countries – Belgium, France, the Federal Republic of Germany, Italy, Luxembourg and the Netherlands – signed the Treaty of Paris. Common institutions were established to govern the operation and development of the coal and steel industries in the member states. The establishment of the European Coal and Steel Community was seen by many as the first step towards greater unity in Europe. First, certain industries such as coal and steel would be integrated; then the economies as a whole of the member countries would be integrated. Ultimately, this would give way to broader unity and possibly the formation of a United States of Europe. In 1957, the process of integration was taken a step further with the signing of the Treaty of Rome (hereinafter referred to as the EC Treaty) establishing what is now referred to as the European Community (EC), to integrate the member countries' economies as a whole. This period also saw the formation of the European Atomic Energy Community (Euratom), to encourage co-operation in the peaceful use and development of nuclear energy.

The objectives of the European Union

The European Union has as its aim the welding of Europe into a single prosperous area by abolishing restrictions affecting the movement of people, of goods and of capital; in effect an internal market without internal frontiers in which the free movement of goods, persons, services and capital can be achieved.

Article 2 of the EC Treaty provides:

'The Community shall have as its task, by establishing a common market and progressively approximating the economic policies of member states, to promote throughout the Community a harmonious development of economic activities, a continuous and balanced expansion, an increase in stability, an accelerated raising of the standard of living and closer relations between the States belonging to it.'

Article 3 of the Treaty details the means by which these aims are to be achieved. First, the elimination of customs duties and quantitative restrictions on the import and export of goods between member states. With the abolition of all customs duties between member states there will be a single European market of approximately 270 million customers available to producers in Europe, and European manufacturers will be able to produce goods more cheaply on the scale that is practised for example in the United States. Second, the establishment of a common customs tariff (CCT) on goods entering any member state of the European Union from a third country and the establishment of a common commercial policy. Third, the free movement of workers of members states within the community. Fourth, the establishment of a common agricultural policy (CAP), designed to keep the price of foodstuffs at a sufficiently high level to ensure an adequate return for farmers without the need for subsidies. Foodstuffs entering member states from outside the European Union have levies placed upon them to make them as expensive as those offered for sale by producers in the European Union. Prices are not allowed to fall to their natural level because producers can insist on designated national authorities intervening to buy foodstuffs at a certain price – the 'intervention price' fixed each year by the Council – hence the butter, beef and grain 'mountains' and the wine, milk and olive oil 'lakes'. Fifth, the regulation of restrictive trade practices, ie those which tend to limit competition, for example, an agreement between producers that they will not supply below or above a certain price. State aid to industries which tends to distort competition between member states is also, in general, prohibited. Sixth, the approximation of laws of member states to the extent required for the proper functioning of the Common Market.

In 1973 the original six member countries were joined by Denmark, Ireland and the United Kingdom. In January 1981 Greece joined the Community and Spain and Portugal also became members on 1 January 1986. With effect from 1 January 1995 membership will increase to 15, with the addition of Austria, Finland and Sweden. The original Treaty of Rome has since been amended by the Acts of Accession relating to new member states, and the Single European Act, which came into force on 1 July 1987. The Single European Act introduced a new Article 8a, which committed member states to the adoption of measures which aimed at the establishment of an internal market by 31 December 1991. The Act also introduced some institutional changes, for example by widening the scope for majority voting in the Council of Ministers and by introducing a new procedure for co-operation between the Council and the European Parliament.

Maastricht

Following a meeting of heads of government of members states in Maastricht in December 1991, the Treaty on European Union – the 'Maastricht Treaty' – was signed by all member states, with certain exceptions being made by the United Kingdom, on 7 February 1992. The treaty accelerates the move towards a federal, unified, Europe, providing that every national of the member states is a citizen of the Union. It lays down a timetable for monetary union, with the aim of producing a single currency by 1999, although the United Kingdom was granted a possible 'opt out' clause. The appendices to the treaty stipulate the requirements for member states wishing to join the single currency. As with previous Community treaties, and in accordance with constitutional requirements, the Maastricht Treaty had to be incorporated into United Kingdom law by means of domestic legislation, hence the enactment of the European Communities (Amendment) Act 1993. Section 1(1) of the 1993 Act gives effect to the Maastricht Treaty, with the exception of the Protocol on Social Policy (in particular its limitation upon working hours), by providing that references in the European Communities Act 1972 to 'Community Treaties' now include the Treaty on European Union. Section 1(2) provides that, for the purposes of s6 of the European Parliamentary Elections Act 1978 (which provides that no treaty which provides for any increase in the powers of the European Parliament shall be ratified by the United Kingdom unless it has been approved by an Act of Parliament), the Maastricht Treaty (meaning 'the Treaty … signed at Maastricht …') has received such parliamentary approval. The purpose of this provision is that, once enacted, the United Kingdom Government would become entitled to exercise its prerogative power in order to ratify the Maastricht Treaty without contravening s6 of the European Parliamentary Elections Act 1978, as the treaty referred to in s1(2) is the Maastricht Treaty in its entirety, and not just those parts of the treaty referred to in s1(1). Section 2 of the 1993 Act provides that no notification shall be given to the Council of the European Communities that the United Kingdom intends to move to the third stage of economic and monetary union unless a number of preconditions have been satisfied. These include (inter alia) the requirements that a draft of that notification should have been approved by Act of Parliament, and that the Government has reported to Parliament on its proposals for the co-ordination of economic policies. Section 7 provides that the European Communities (Amendment) Act 1993 could only come into force once each House of Parliament has come to a resolution on a motion tabled by a minister of the Crown considering the question of adopting the Protocol on Social Policy.

The resolution required by s7 was considered by the House of Commons on 22 July 1993. Before the vote could take place, however, the House had to consider an Opposition amendment which called for the adoption of the Protocol on Social

Policy before ratification of the Maastricht Treaty. The vote on the Opposition motion produced an apparent dead heat, the Speaker exercising her casting vote in the Government's favour. In the subsequent vote on the substantive motion, put forward by the Government for the purposes of satisfying the requirements of s7 of the 1993 Act, a number of rebel Conservative MPs voted with the Opposition and the motion was defeated by 324 votes to 316. The following day the Prime Minister tabled a motion stating that 'This House has confidence in the policy of Her Majesty's Government on the adoption of the Protocol on Social Policy'. The motion was carried. The Act received royal assent on 20 July 1993, and came into force on 23 July 1993. The Maastricht Treaty was ratified on 2 August 1993.

A question may be raised as to whether or not the motion passed on 23 July, which was in effect a confidence motion, was the type of motion envisaged by Parliament when enacting s7 of the 1993 Act. The judiciary may be precluded from commenting on the propriety or otherwise of parliamentary proceedings, but it would be open to the courts to consider the wording of s7 with a view to evaluating what type of resolution it required.

The subsequent ratification of the Maastricht Treaty was the subject of an application for judicial review in *R* v *Secretary of State for Foreign Affairs, ex parte Rees-Mogg* [1994] 2 WLR 115. The applicant sought a declaration that any such ratification would be unlawful, citing three objections: (1) A ratification of the protocol on social policy would be in breach of the European Parliamentary Elections Act 1978 because the 1993 Act, which evidenced Parliament's approval of the Maastricht Treaty, expressly excluded approval of the Protocol on Social Policy – hence the protocol would not have been approved by Parliament prior to ratification as required by the 1978 Act; (2) Following from (1), the ratification of the Protocol on Social Policy (that protocol being specifically excluded from the operation of the European Communities Act 1972, by the 1993 Act) would be an unlawful exercise of prerogative power as it would involve an alteration to Community law without parliamentary approval; (3) The establishment of a common foreign policy (under Title V of the Maastricht Treaty) would involve a loss of prerogative power, which could only be achieved by way of statutory enactment. Dismissing the application the court held that, notwithstanding the provisions of s1(1) of the 1993 Act, the reference to 'Treaty' in s1(2) was a reference to the Maastricht Treaty in its entirety. By using the phrase 'the Treaty ... signed at Maastricht ...' in s1(2), it was clearly the intention of Parliament that the United Kingdom Government should have been able to subsequently ratify the Maastricht Treaty without contravening s6 of the European Parliamentary Elections Act 1978. On the basis that Parliament, when it intends to limit the scope of prerogative power, does so by express words, an intention to limit the prerogative power of Her Majesty's ministers to amend the EC Treaty could not be discerned from a reading of s2(1) of the European Communities Act 1972. In any event, the protocol did not fall within the definition of 'the Treaties' in s1(2) of the 1972 Act, being specifically excluded by s1(1) of the European Communities (Amendment) Act 1993, thus the court felt that any argument based on s2(1) of the 1972 Act was without foundation. Any agreement on allowing other member states to move towards the implementation of the Protocol on Social Policy, signified by ratification, created only international obligations for the United Kingdom Government and did not affect domestic law. There was no evidence that it had been the intention of Parliament, by way of the 1972 Act, to curtail the treaty making powers of the Crown under the prerogative. On the facts, the ratification of Title V of the Maastricht Treaty did not involve a diminution of prerogative power as it would be open to the United Kingdom to renege on its obligations under the treaty, and reassert the prerogative power to formulate and execute foreign policy in the areas affected.

Terminology

Following the signing of the Treaty on European Union (TEU), what was formerly referred to as the European Economic Community (EEC) becomes simply the European Community (EC), with the Treaty of Rome, as amended, being referred to as the EC Treaty. The EC is itself now part of the European Union (EU), a term that can be used in two senses. First, in describing the physical territory of the member states as a whole. Secondly, to describe member states acting other than under the EC Treaty, ie in relation to common foreign and security policy, or co-operation in justice and home affairs. In the technical sense the expression 'community law' should now only be used in respect of law arising under the EC Treaty.

5.2 The institutions of the European Union

Responsibility for achieving the aims of the three Communities lies with four institutions:

1. The Council of Ministers (or the Council of the European Union as the Commission would like it to be known following the signing of the TEU).
2. The Commission.
3. The European Parliament.
4. The Court of Justice of the European Communities.

The Council of Ministers

The Council is the Communities' principal decision-making body. Its function is to make policy decisions and to issue regulations and directives, and other 'acts', on the basis of proposals from the Commission.

The Government of each nation in the European Union has a seat on the Council. The foreign minister is usually a country's main representative, but a Government is free to send any of its ministers to Council meetings. Its membership thus varies with the subject scheduled for discussion. Unlike the Commission, the

Council's members represent their national interests first and foremost. Three times a year Government heads meet in the European Council or 'summit' to discuss broad areas of policy. The presidency of the Council rotates between the member Governments at six-monthly intervals.

The Council can determine issues by a simple majority vote, by qualified majority voting, or by means of a unanimous decision, depending on the procedure required by the EC Treaty as amended by the Single European Act. The provisions regulating the voting procedures of the Council attempt to fulfil two aims: firstly, to ensure that the Council cannot easily take a high-handed approach to Commission proposals, and secondly, to ensure that important proposals aimed at promoting greater integration of member states should not be held back by the veto of one Member State. Hence the Council may be able to accept Commission proposals by a qualified majority, but unanimity is required if it seeks to amend a Commission proposal.

For some particularly important decisions, such as acceptance of a new member state, or changes in the number of Commissioners, unanimity is required.

As Article 148 explains, under the system of qualified majority voting the votes of members are weighted according to population. In effect a country will be allocated roughly one vote for every six million of population, although there are anomalies in respect of the smaller nations so as to ensure that their views are not totally marginalised. France, Germany, Italy and the United Kingdom have ten votes each; Spain eight votes; Belgium, Greece, the Netherlands and Portugal five votes each; Denmark and Ireland three votes each; and Luxembourg two votes. A total of 54 votes is needed for a proposal to be passed. The entry into the European Union of Austria, Finland and Sweden will increase the number of votes to 90. If the 'blocking minority', currently 23 votes, is to be increased proportionately, it will rise to 26. The United Kingdom is concerned that the enlargement of the European Union may make it possible for a coalition of smaller nations to outvote the larger countries on issues where qualified majority voting is permitted. However, under what is known as the Luxembourg Accord (the Luxembourg Agreement of 1966) the Council will not normally impose a decision on a member in a matter that the member considers to be of vital national interest. The significance of the Single European Act is that it extends qualified majority voting to areas where previously unanimity would have been required. It is extended in the context of the policies listed as New Policy Objectives. The criterion is that, while the general principle of a new policy requires unanimous approval, the implementation of that principle through regulations or directives will be carried out by qualified majority voting. Under the amendment to Article 100 (Article 100A), the Council can act by way of a qualified majority vote to give effect to measures proposed by the Commission 'which have as their object the establishment and functioning of the internal market'. It should be noted that at present, unanimity would still be required for the adoption of acts relating to free movement of persons, rights of employed persons, and fiscal provisions. In most decisions of the Council of Ministers, however, unanimity is aimed at and generally achieved.

The Council is assisted in its work by COREPER, the Committee of Permanent Representatives of Member States, which not only undertakes the preparatory work for Council meetings but also co-ordinates meetings of senior civil servants from Member States.

The Commission

The European Union treaties assign the Commission a wide range of duties. It is the guardian of the treaties setting up the European Community and is responsible for seeing that they are implemented. The Commission therefore is the initiator of Community policy and exponent of the Community interest in the Council; and the Executive arm of the Communities and responsible for the administration of the Community.

The Commission, an independent body with Executive powers and responsibility, has 17 members (20 from January 1995) chosen for their all-round capability by agreement between the governments of the member states. Commissioners are obliged to act in the Communities' interests and not in the interests of the country from which they come. Throughout their four-year term of office members must remain independent of the Governments and of the Council. The Council cannot remove any member from office; only Parliament can compel the Commission to resign as a body by passing a motion of censure.

Each Commissioner heads a department with special responsibilities for one area of Community policy, such as economic affairs, agriculture, the environment and transport. Regular discussions are held between a Commissioner's department and interested parties. As a result of these discussions the Commissioner formulates draft proposals which he believes will help to improve the quality of life of Community citizens. The draft proposals are discussed by all the Commissioners who then decide on the nature of the final proposal. Decisions are taken on a collegiate basis. The Treaty on European Union seeks to expand the scope of the Commission's competence as regards policy initiatives.

The European Parliament

The European Parliament (EP) is not to be equated with the Westminster model. It cannot legislate in its own right, it does not possess any form of parliamentary sovereignty, and it exercises limited but growing supervisory powers. In particular the Parliament:

1. Advises the Council of Ministers on Commission proposals.
2. With the Council of Ministers, determines the budget for the Community.
3. Exerts some political control over the Council and Commission.

4. By debate can attract publicity to issues which then have to be considered by the Commission or the Council.

The European Parliament currently has 518 members who represent the citizens of the European Union. Members are directly elected and serve for a period of five years. The citizens of France, Germany, Italy and the United Kingdom are each represented by 81 members; Spain by 60 members; the Netherlands by 25 members; Belgium, Greece and Portugal each by 24 members; Denmark by 16, Ireland by 15 and Luxembourg by six members. The composition of Parliament makes it a fully integrated Community institution. The members do not sit in Parliament in national groups but in political party groups. The six main political party groups at present are the Communists, Socialists, European People's Party, European Progressive Democrats, European Democrats and the Liberal and Democratic Group. From January 1995 membership will increase to 626, with the United Kingdom having 87 MEPs.

The European Parliament meets on average once a month, for sessions which last up to a week. It has 18 standing committees which discuss proposals made by the Commission. The committees present reports on these proposals for debate by the full Parliament. Decisions made by Parliament are influential on the Council of Ministers, but are not binding. However, direct elections have given Parliament greater political authority and new prestige both inside and outside the European Union. The Parliament has the right to question. members of the Commission and Council and is therefore able to monitor the work of these institutions. It has the power to dismiss the Commission by a two-thirds majority vote, and to reject the Council's proposals for the Community budget.

The role of the Parliament has been strengthened by the provisions of the Single European Act, which requires the Council to 'co-operate' with the Parliament before adopting Commission proposals aimed at implementing the internal market. Under Article 149 of the Treaty, such co-operation requires the Council to obtain the opinion of the Parliament on a Commission proposal, develop its own common position which is then communicated to the Parliament, and await the approval of the common position by Parliament. If no response is received within three months, the Council can proceed with the adoption of the proposal. If the Parliament rejects or seeks to amend the proposals – a decision which must be carried by an absolute majority of the Parliament's members – the Commission may present an amended proposal to the Council, which may then be accepted by a qualified majority. Unanimity is required if the Council seeks to amend proposals re-examined by the Commission.

The effect of these changes is that, instead of simply giving a consultative opinion on Community legislation, the European Parliament now has the opportunity of pronouncing on the final decision of the Council. This procedure has effect only in those cases where the Council acts by qualified majority voting.

The Court of Justice of the European Communities

The Court is the European Union's supreme judicial authority; there is no appeal against its rulings. Each of the treaties establishing the European Communities uses the same broad terms to define the specific responsibilities of the Court of Justice, which is to 'ensure that in the interpretation and application of this treaty the law is observed'. The Court therefore interprets and applies the whole corpus of European Union law from the basic treaties to the various implementing regulations, directives and decisions issued by the Council and the Commission.

Although its jurisdiction is principally concerned with European Union law, the Court is not cut off from national law, since it draws its inspiration from the legal traditions that are common to the member states. This ensures respect both for the general principles of law and for fundamental human rights insofar as they have been incorporated into the European Union legal order.

There are three significant processes by which a matter may be raised before the European Court. Firstly, an action by a member state against another member state alleging a failure to comply with the requirements of European Union law. Secondly, the courts of member states can refer questions of law concerning the interpretation of the treaties to the European Court, under Article 177 of the EC Treaty. Thirdly, the European Court may quash any measure introduced by either the Council or Commission which is incompatible with the objectives of the Community treaties. Such intervention may be initiated by a Community institution, a member state, or even an individual: see further section 5.4 (below).

The judges

The judges are appointed by common accord of the governments of the member states. The treaties require them to be chosen 'from persons whose independence is beyond doubt and who possess the qualifications required for appointment to the highest judicial offices in their respective countries or who are jurisconsults of recognised competence'. There is no specific nationality requirement, but at the present time the Court has one judge from each member state. The judges select one of their number to be President for a renewable term of three years.

Members hold office for a renewable term of six years. Every three years there is a partial replacement of the Court's membership; five or six judges and two or three advocates-general are replaced alternately. This ensures continuity of the Court's decisions, especially as most of the judges have had their term of office renewed at least once and sometimes twice. The independence of the judges is guaranteed by their statutes and is based on three fundamental rules of procedure – their deliberations are secret; judgments are reached by majority vote; judgments are signed by all the judges who have taken part in the proceedings. Dissenting opinions are never published.

The advocates-general

The advocates-general are appointed on the same terms and have to satisfy the same criteria with respect to independence and training as the judges. Nationality is immaterial. In practice, until recently the advocates-general were all nationals of the larger community countries, but lately a post of advocate-general has gone to a national of one of the smaller member states. According to the treaties the function of the advocates-general is 'acting with complete impartiality and independence, to make, in open court, reasoned submissions on cases brought before the Court, in order to assist the Court in the performance of the tasks assigned to it'. The advocates-general do not represent the Communities and cannot initiate proceedings themselves. Their duties should not be confused with those of a public prosecutor. At a separate hearing some weeks after the lawyers have addressed the Court the advocate-general comments on the various aspects of the case, weighs up the provisions of European Union law, compares the case in point with previous rulings, and proposes a legal solution to the dispute. The advocate-general does not participate in the Court's deliberations.

The Court of First Instance

Since 1988 the European Court has been assisted in its work by the Court of First Instance, comprising 12 judges, created under the Single European Act. Advocates-general may assist the court but there are none specifically assigned to it. The role of the court is to deal with cases that turn primarily on issues of fact, rather than law, brought by natural or legal persons, rather than member states. Initially its caseload was limited to disputes related to production quotas, competition law and staff cases, but since 1993 its jurisdiction has been extended to all matters, other than cases involving anti-dumping proceedings. Appeal on a point of law lies to the ECJ.

Economic and Social Committee

In addition to the three main institutions considered above, there is also a body known as the Economic and Social Committee which plays a consultative role in the decision making processes of the Council and Commission. The committee represents a wide spectrum of Community interests, such as those of workers, consumers and farmers.

The EC Ombudsman

Following the 1994 European Parliament elections an Ombudsman for the EC will be appointed by the European Parliament, pursuant to Article 138e of the EC Treaty, to investigate allegations of maladministration made by any EU citizen or resident against any EC institution other than the European Court of Justice. Complaints considered by the EC Ombudsman will not have to pass through an MEP filter (he will be able to act on his own initiative), and are not subject to any specific time limit. Given that serious violations of EC law can be pursued by individuals taking cases to the European Court of Justice, it seems likely that the EC Ombudsman will be concerned with less serious cases, perhaps where there may be no obvious judicial remedy, and political pressure to achieve a settlement or redress is more appropriate. The only sanction available to the EC Ombudsman in the event that he finds an institution guilty of maladministration is the making of an adverse report to the European Parliament.

The Council of Europe and the European Council

The Council of Europe exists quite independently of the European Union, being the creation of the Treaty of Westminster in 1949. It has a much larger membership than the European Union, comprising many states that, for political or economic reasons, find the concept of EU membership unacceptable or unattainable. The Council of Europe operates essentially as an intergovernmental organisation, that from time to time generates conventions on key aspects of international law. Its most notable achievement is the European Convention on Human Rights. A possible consequence of failing to comply with the Convention's requirements is expulsion from the Council of Europe. The European Council has existed since 1972 and is comprised of the heads of state or government and the President of the European Commission. Although it originally existed as an ad hoc organisation, its existence has now been formally recognised by the Single European Act. The European Council provides a forum for discussion of strategic issues related to EU policy, and for reviewing the operation of the EU. Meetings, normally held three times a year, are chaired by the head of the member state currently holding the presidency of EC.

5.3 European Union law

There are three main sources of European Union law: the Community treaties; the Acts of the Community institutions; and the decisions of the Court of Justice of the European Communities. Essential to the effective operation of the European Union is the principle that the primary law of the Union, the treaties, applies to the same extent in the legal system of each member state, and that it takes precedence over the domestic law of any member state, to the extent that there is any conflict between the two. Article 5 of the EC Treaty provides:

> 'Member states shall take all appropriate measures, whether general or particular, to ensure fulfilment of the obligations arising out of this Treaty or resulting from action taken by the institutions of the Community. They shall facilitate the achievement of the Community's tasks. They shall abstain from any measure which could jeopardise the attainment of the objectives of this Treaty.'

The 'appropriate measures' for the implementation of the Treaty depend upon the nature of the member state's legal system. Where it is monist, the Treaty will automatically become part of domestic law that can be relied upon in the courts of that member state (to the extent that it creates rights for individual litigants, as to which see below). Where the member state has a dualist system, as is the case with the United Kingdom, the Treaty has to be incorporated into domestic law in order to be effective; see the European Communities Act 1972, the impact of which is considered further in Chapter 6.

As regards the secondary legislation of the European Union, namely regulations, directives and decisions, Article 189 of the EC Treaty provides:

> 'A regulation shall have general application. It shall be binding in its entirety and directly applicable in all member states. A directive shall be binding, as to the result to be achieved, upon each member state to whom it is addressed, but shall leave to the national authorities the choice of form and methods.
>
> A decision shall be binding in its entirety upon those to whom it is addressed. Recommendations and opinions shall have no binding force.'

Decisions of the Court of Justice may be treated as a secondary source of European Union law. The Court is not bound to follow its previous decisions and they may therefore be treated as persuasive rather than binding authority.

Any doubt as to the primacy of Community law over national law was resolved by the European Court of Justice in *Costa* v *ENEL* [1964] ECR 585 where the Court stated:

> 'By creating a Community of unlimited duration, having its own institutions, its own personality, its own legal capacity of representation on the international plane and, more particularly, real powers stemming from a limitation of sovereignty or a transfer of powers from the States to the Community, the member states have limited their sovereign rights, albeit within limited fields, and have thus created a body of law which binds both their nationals and themselves. The integration into the laws of each member state of provisions which derive from the Community, and more generally the terms and spirit of the Treaty, make it impossible for the States, as a corollary, to afford precedence to a unilateral and subsequent measure over a legal system accepted by them on a basis of reciprocity ... The executive force of Community law cannot vary from one State to another in deference to subsequent domestic laws, without jeopardising the attainment of the objectives of the Treaty set out in Article 5(2) and giving rise to the discrimination prohibited by Article 7. The obligations undertaken under the Treaty establishing the Community would not be unconditional, but merely contingent, if they could be called in question by subsequent legislative acts of the signatories ...'

The primacy of European Union law prevails even where the domestic law is penal in nature, thus creating a defence of reliance on European Union law: see *Pubblico Ministero* v *Ratti* (Case 148/78) [1979] ECR 1629.

Direct applicability

It will be seen, therefore, that provisions contained in the treaties and regulations enacted by the Council are of 'direct applicability', by which is meant that they become part of the law of member states without further intervention by the member state; see further *Van Duyn* v *Home Office* (Case 41/74) [1974] ECR 1337, and *Re Export Tax on Art Treasures (No 2)* [1972] CMLR 699. Proceedings can be brought in the European Court by any member state against another member state failing to fulfil its obligations under the treaties. Directives, by contrast, are not directly applicable in that they require further enactment by a member state before they can take effect within the domestic law of that member state; see further *Marleasing SA* v *La Commercial Internacional De Alimentacion SA* considered below.

Direct effect

The extent to which the primacy of EU law is made effective depends largely upon the degree to which compliance is policed. Clearly, large-scale failure by a member state to comply with the requirements of EU law would be raised by the Commission, or other member states. It is through the empowerment of individual EU citizens, however, that the monitoring process is made most effective, and this has been achieved by the European Court's development of the concept of 'direct effect'. In basic terms, if a given provision of EU law is held to have the characteristic of direct effect it can be invoked by a individual against a member state in the courts of the relevant member state.

That Treaty provisions can have direct effect, where they are found to be sufficiently precise and unconditional in their effect, was established in *Van Gend en Loos* v *Nederlandse Administratie der Belastingen* [1963] ECR 1, where the Court held:

> 'The objective of the EEC Treaty, which is to establish a Common Market, the functioning of which is of direct concern to interested parties in the Community, implies that this Treaty is more than an agreement which merely creates mutual obligations between the contracting states. This view is confirmed by the preamble to the Treaty which refers not only to governments but to peoples. It is also confirmed more specifically by the establishment of institutions endowed with sovereign rights, the exercise of which affects member states and also their citizens. Furthermore, it must be noted that the nationals of the states brought together in the Community are called upon to cooperate in the functioning of this Community through the intermediary of the European Parliament and the Economic and Social Committee ... the task assigned to the Court of Justice under Article 177, the object of which is to secure uniform interpretation of the Treaty by national courts and tribunals, confirms that the states have acknowledged that Community law has an authority which can be invoked by their nationals before those courts and tribunals.
>
> The conclusion to be drawn from this is that the Community constitutes a new legal order of international law for the benefit of which the states have limited their sovereign rights, albeit within limited fields, and the subjects of which comprise not only member states but also their nationals. Independently of the legislation of member states, Community law therefore not only imposes obligations on individuals but is also intended to confer upon them rights which become part of their legal heritage. These rights arise not only where they are expressly granted by the Treaty, but also by reason of obligations which the Treaty imposes in a clearly defined way upon individuals as well as upon the member states and upon the institutions of the Community ...'

The same reasoning can be applied to regulations, provided the preconditions for direct effect are met; see *Politi* v *Ministry of Finance* [1971] ECR 1039.

The question of the extent to which, if at all, directives can have direct effect was considered by the European Court of Justice in *Van Duyn* v *Home Office* (Case 41/74) [1974] ECR 1337. The United Kingdom government allowed the Church of Scientology to operate in England, but sought to limit its activities by not granting work permits to foreign nationals seeking to take up employment with the church in England. Ms Van Duyn, a Dutch national offered employment by the church in England, was refused a work permit by the Home Office. She sought a declaration that the minister's prohibition was in contravention of Article 48 of the EC Treaty, and was not permitted under Council directive No 64/221. Amongst the questions referred under Article 177, the court asked whether the directive in issue was directly applicable so as to confer on individuals rights enforceable by them in the courts of a member state. The European Court of Justice, holding that the directive could have direct effect, observed:

> 'If ... by virtue of the provisions of Article 189 regulations are directly applicable and, consequently, may by their very nature have direct effects, it does not follow from this that other categories of acts mentioned in that article can never have similar effects. It would be incompatible with the binding effect attributed to a directive by Article 189 to exclude, in principle, the possibility that the obligation which it imposes may be invoked by those concerned. In particular, where the Community authorities have, by directive, imposed on member states the obligation to pursue a particular course of conduct, the useful effect of such an act would be weakened if individuals were prevented from relying on it before their national courts and if the latter were prevented from taking it into consideration as an element of Community law. Article 177, which empowers national courts to refer to the Court questions concerning the validity and interpretation of all acts of the Community institutions, without distinction, implies furthermore that these acts may be invoked by individuals in the national courts. It is necessary to examine, in every case, whether the nature, general scheme and wording of the provisions in question are capable of having direct effects on the relations between member states and individuals.'

Horizontal direct effect

The type of direct effect recognised in cases such as *Van Duyn* is sometimes described as 'vertical' in the sense that it permits an individual to invoke the provisions of EU law against a member state. Perhaps not surprisingly individual litigants have since raised the question of the extent to which Treaty provisions, regulations and directives can have 'horizontal' direct effect, in the sense that they can be invoked by one individual against another natural or private legal person in the courts of member states.

The horizontal direct effect of Treaty provisions has been recognised by the European Court of Justice in decisions such as *Walrave and Koch* v *Union Cycliste Internationale* [1974] ECR 1405, and *Defrenne* v *Sabena* [1976] ECR 455, where it has been seen as a necessary step towards ensuring that the objectives of the Union are not thwarted by private law bodies exercising their rights to legal autonomy. A distinction has been drawn, however, between Treaty provisions and regulations on the one hand, that are directly applicable and hence become part of domestic law without further enactment, and directives on the other, that require the state to which they are addressed to carry out the necessary procedures for implementation. Whilst it might be justifiable to permit proceedings against a private party for non-compliance with a Treaty provision or regulation, should that private party be at risk of litigation because of the member state's failure to implement a directive? In a number of cases, most notably *Marshall* v *Southampton & South West Hampshire Area Health Authority* [1986] QB 401, *Marleasing SA* v *La Commercial Internacional De Alimentacion SA* [1992] 1 CMLR 305 and *Faccini Dori* v *Recreb Srl* (Case C-91/92) 14 July 1994, the European Court of Justice has ruled that directives cannot have horizontal direct effect so as to impose liabilities and duties on individuals and private companies. As the court observed, recognising the limits of the scope of EU law in *Faccini Dori* v *Recreb Srl*:

'The effect of extending ... to the sphere of relations between individuals [the case law on horizontal direct effect to directives] would be to recognise a power in the Community to enact obligations for individuals with immediate effect, whereas it has competence to do so only where it is empowered to adopt regulations.'

The unwillingness of the European Court of Justice to recognise the horizontal direct effect of directives has, however, to been seen in the light of three other factors, the concept of the public body, the doctrine of indirect horizontal effect, and the availability of damages.

What is a public body for the purposes of direct effect?

As has been noted above, the term vertical direct effect has been used to describe the position where a directive can be invoked by an individual against a member state. The scope of vertical direct effect depends, therefore, on the extent to which defendant bodies are perceived to be emanations of the state, eg the armed forces, the police, regulatory bodies, colleges and universities etc. The extent to which an employer could be regarded as falling within the sphere of public law (and hence amenable to the doctrine) was considered in *Marshall* v *Southampton & South West Hampshire Area Health Authority* (above), and *Johnstone* v *Chief Constable of the Royal Ulster Constabulary* [1987] QB 129, where the European Court of Justice ruled respectively that employees of the National Health Service, and those of constitutionally independent authorities responsible for maintaining law and order, could invoke provisions contained in directives against their employers on the basis that they were agents of the national authority. In *Foster* v *British Gas* [1991] QB 405 the European Court of Justice suggested that:

'... a body, whatever its legal form, which has been made responsible pursuant to a measure adopted by the state, for providing a public service under the control of the state and which has for that purpose special powers beyond those which result from the normal rules applicable in relations between individuals is included in any event among the bodies against which the provisions of a directive capable of having direct effect may be relied upon.'

Following this ruling the House of Lords proceeded on the basis that British Gas was a state body for the purposes of vertical effect; see further *Doughty* v *Rolls Royce* [1992] CMLR 1045 (ownership by the Crown not the sole determining factor).

Indirect horizontal effect

The European Court of Justice has also recognised what might be described as an 'indirect' form of horizontal direct effect, where a directive is relied upon in litigation between two private parties of member states. In *Marleasing SA* v *La Commercial Internacional De Alimentacion SA* (above) the plaintiff company had sought the nullification, in the Spanish courts, of the creation of the defendant company, on the basis that it had been formed with the sole purpose of defrauding creditors. The plaintiffs' legal challenge was based on the provisions of Spanish law (sections 1261 and 1275 of the Civil Code) which rendered invalid contracts which were without legal purpose or caused unlawful consequences. The defendants called in aid Article 11 of the Council directive 68/151 claiming that it listed exhaustively the circumstances in which the nullity of a company could be declared, and that the ground relied upon by the plaintiffs was not listed therein. The directive had not, at the time this came before the Spanish courts, been incorporated into the domestic law of Spain. The question referred to the European Court of Justice was as to whether the Article in question was directly applicable so as to preclude a declaration of nullity of a public limited company on a ground other than those set out in the Article. The European Court of Justice ruled that, whilst directives were not of themselves capable of having direct effect between individuals, the national courts of member states were obliged to interpret domestic law so as to ensure conformity with EC directives, whether the domestic law originated before or after the incorporation of the directive. The effect of the decision was to prevent the Spanish court from declaring the defendant company to be a nullity on any ground other than one listed in the relevant directive; see further *Faccini Dori* v *Recreb Srl* (above). In the light of this ruling the views to the contrary expressed by the House of Lords prior to the *Marleasing* decision, in *Duke* v *GEC Reliance Ltd* [1988] AC 618, must be doubted.

Remedies for non-implementation of directives

The failure of a member state to implement an EC directive as required may also give rise to a right in damages on the part of an individual adversely affected by the failure. In *Francovich (and others)* v *Italian Republic* [1992] IRLR 84, a number of Italian workers who had been made redundant found that, following their employer's insolvency, there were insufficient funds to pay their salaries. The workers complained that the Italian Government had failed to implement legislation, required by an EC directive, to guarantee that such salary arrears should be paid by the state. The European Court of Justice held that, even in situations such as presented by the case under consideration where the directive in question could not be regarded as one having direct effect, member states were obliged to provide protection for clearly defined individual rights granted by EC law to defined groups, and a failure to provide such protection, if resulting in economic loss to individuals within those groups, rendered the member state in question liable in damages. The court based its reasoning on the ground that the full effectiveness of European Union law might be called into question, and the protection of the rights which they conferred would be weakened, if individuals could not obtain compensation where their rights were infringed by a breach of European Union law for which a member state was responsible. In other words, a member state should not be able to hide behind its own failure to implement a directive when defending such proceedings.

The true significance of this ruling has yet to be established. In principle it could have huge significance for litigants in areas such as employment protection and equal opportunities, although it is open to question as to what extent it will apply to the more general rights for employees arising under the social chapter of the Treaty on European Union. As regards the United Kingdom, it raises the prosect of a right to damages where a litigant applies for judicial review for non-implementation of a directive, even though O.53 clearly states that damages are only available if they could have been awarded had the litigation proceeded by way of action. Where a causal link cannot be established between the failure to implement a directive and financial loss on the part of the applicant, declaratory relief will be more appropriate, see *R* v *Secretary of State for Employment, ex parte Equal Opportunities Commission and Another* [1994] 2 WLR 409.

Note that in *Kirklees BC* v *Wickes Building Supplies* [1992] 3 WLR 170, Lord Goff observed that the decision in *Francovich* cast doubt on assertions in earlier House of Lords' cases, such as *Bourgoin SA* v *Ministry of Agriculture* [1986] QB 716, to the effect that a breach of Article 30 would not of itself give the injured party a right to damages against the state. His Lordship was of the view that if the House of Lords were to hold that s47 of the Shops Act was found to be invalid as being in conflict with Article 30, the United Kingdom could be obliged to pay damages to individuals suffering loss for the breach of Article 30 for which the state was responsible.

In *Francovich* the issue for the court was the availability of damages for non-implementation, but clearly the same question could arise in relation to a member state that has failed to alter its domestic law so as to ensure conformity with EU law. A number of key issues in this respect may well be resolved by the European Court of Justice when it delivers its ruling in *Brasserie du Pecheur* v *Federal Republic of Germany* (Case C-46/93). The plaintiff, a French brewery company, incurred considerable financial loss as a result of not being permitted to sell its beer in Germany. The German authorities justified this restriction by reliance on the

Reinheitsgebot (German beer purity law). In 1987 the *Reinheitsgebot* was adjudged by the European Court of Justice to be incompatible with EC Treaty Article 30, on the ground that it gave an unfair advantage to German beer producers in their own market. The German Federal Court has now referred the following questions to the European Court of Justice for a preliminary ruling:

1. Does EU law require a member state to provide compensation in the form of damages for failure to adapt a national law to the requirements of EU law?
2. Are there limits on the availability of damages, as there would be, for example, if Federal German law was found to be incompatible with the basic law of the Republic?
3. Is the payment of damages dependent on proof of fault by the state officials responsible for ensuring conformity of domestic law?
4. If damages are available, not subject to other limits laid down by the domestic law of a member state, does liability extend to pure economic loss?
5. If damages are available, not subject to other limits laid down by the domestic law of a member state, does liability extend to losses incurred prior to the ruling of the European Court of Justice to the effect that the *Reinheitsgebot* conflicted with EU law?

The two key policy issues for the European Court of Justice to consider would appear to be whether liability should arise for errors in compliance that do not amount to negligence, and the financial consequences for member states of any such failure. The ruling will also be of direct relevance to those Spanish trawler owners still seeking financial compensation as a result of the *Factortame* affair; see further Chapter 6.

5.4 The powers of the Court of Justice

There are a variety of ways in which recourse to the Court may be had. A distinction is made between direct actions, which involve disputes between parties, and requests for preliminary rulings, which take the form of questions put by national judges. Direct actions may be divided into four categories:

1. Proceedings against a member state for failure to fulfil an obligation.
2. Proceedings for annulment.
3. Proceedings for failure to act
4. Proceedings to establish liability.

Proceedings for failure to fulfil an obligation

In the first place it is up to the Commission, as guardian of the treaties and of the decisions taken by the institutions, to initiate proceedings for failure to fulfil an obligation. If it considers that any part of the administration of a member state has not honoured a Community obligation, it asks that state to make its comments and then issues a reasoned opinion. If the state does not act on the opinion within the time allowed, it may be taken to the Court. After notifying the Commission, a member state may also initiate this procedure. If the Court agrees that the case is well founded, it declares that an obligation has not been fulfilled: see for example *EC Commission* v *Italy* (Case 39/72) [1973] ECR 101.

All the authorities of the member state concerned are required to take the necessary measures to comply with the Court's judgment in their respective areas of competence. If a state does not comply with the initial ruling, new proceedings may be brought for a declaration by the Court that the obligations arising from its first decision have not been complied with. *EC Commission* v *Italy* [1989] 3 CMLR 25 makes it clear that the member state's duty in such cases is to make the necessary amendments to its domestic law. The Treaty on European Union provides that the Court can, in extreme cases, fine states for non-compliance with EC obligations.

Proceedings for annulment

Proceedings for annulment are directed against binding Community acts, be they general regulations and directives or decisions addressed to individuals, taken by the Council and the Commission. Because opinions and recommendations do not have binding force, proceedings may not be brought in respect of them. In the words of the Treaty, grounds for annulment include lack of power, infringement of an essential procedural requirement, infringement of the treaties or of any rules of law relating to their application, and misuse of powers.

The member states and the Community institutions can seek the annulment of any act by an institution, including those which, like regulations and directives, are of general application. Private citizens and companies, on the other hand, may initiate proceedings only against decisions which are specifically addressed to them or which, despite being in the form of regulations or decisions addressed to another person, concern them directly and individually. If the Court regards the action as well founded, it declares the act in question void and of no effect, and the act then ceases to have any legal force as from the date when it originally took effect. Nevertheless, in the case of a regulation, the Court may confirm the validity of certain provisions.

Proceedings for annulment are a way of reviewing the legality under the treaties of Community acts and of Commission decisions and regulations and of settling conflicts between the institutions over their respective powers under the treaties.

Failure to act

Proceedings for failure to act provide a means of penalising inactivity on the part of the Council or the Commission. Should the Council or the Commission infringe the Treaty by failing to act, the member states and the other institutions of the

Community may bring an action before the Court of Justice to have the infringement established. Such actions are admissible only if the institution in question has previously been called upon to act. If it has not acted within two months of being invited to do so, an action may be brought within a further two months.

The institutions have considerable scope for taking proceedings for failure to act, but such cases can also be brought under identical conditions by private individuals or firms, who can accuse a Community institution of having failed to take a binding decision (ie one other than a recommendation or opinion) concerning them. Admissibility is subject to the same conditions as those which apply to actions for annulment; the act not taken must have been of direct and personal concern to the plaintiff.

Actions to establish liability

The Community may incur civil liability for damage caused by its institutions or servants in the performance of their duties in accordance with the general principles common to the laws of the member states. The treaties confer on the Court of Justice the exclusive jurisdiction to order the Community to pay damages because of its actions or its legislative acts, on the principle of non-contractual liability. In exercising its unlimited jurisdiction, the court decides the basis on which liability is to be determined, whether the damage is due to Community action, the amount of damage caused and the sum to be paid in compensation. By contrast, the Community's contractual liability is subject to the general law of the member states and to the jurisdiction of their courts.

Requests for preliminary rulings

The Court is, by its very nature, the supreme guardian of Community law. But it is not the only Court that has the power to apply and interpret this body of law that is common to all the member states. Unlike most classical forms of international treaty, there is a mass of provisions set out in the treaties themselves and in the secondary legislation of the Council and the Commission, and agreements entered into by the Community, that are directly and immediately applicable in the legal systems of all the member states. These acts have a direct effect in that they can confer individual rights on nationals of member states. Private individuals may invoke them in their national courts both in relation to other individuals and in relation to the national authorities. The courts in each member state have thus become Community courts.

To avoid differing and even conflicting interpretations, the treaties introduced a system of preliminary rulings, which is the real keystone to the whole system. Preliminary rulings can also be requested in order to test the validity of acts adopted by the institutions; this, like the system of proceedings for annulment, is part of the mechanism for ensuring that what the Community does is always lawful.

Under the EC Treaty, where a national court from which appeals may be made finds there is a problem regarding the interpretation of the treaties or of measures taken by the institutions, or some question arises as to the validity of these measures, it may apply to the European Court for a preliminary ruling if it considers that it needs to do so in order to come to its judgment. When a problem or question of this type arises in a national court against whose decisions there is no judicial remedy under national law (eg the House of Lords), that court must refer the matter to the Court of Justice. This system has resulted in valuable collaboration between the Court of Justice and national courts in ensuring the uniform application and interpretation of Community law.

In *Srl CILFIT* v *Ministry of Health* [1982] ECR 3415, the Court defined the extent and limits of the obligation on courts of final instance to request preliminary rulings. The Court stated that national courts did not need to refer questions if:

1. the question raised was irrelevant, as, for instance, if it could have no possible influence on the outcome of the dispute;
2. the Community rule had already been interpreted by the Court, whatever the circumstances leading to this ruling and without the matters in dispute necessarily being absolutely identical; and
3. there was no reasonable doubt about how the question should be answered.

Opinions vary on the authority enjoyed by preliminary rulings and particularly on whether they have general effect or are binding only on the parties concerned. However, three points seem to have been accepted regarding references for interpretation:

1. the interpretation given by the Court is binding on the judge who requested it, who refers the matter back to the Court if he considers that there is still a question to be answered;
2. the interpretation serves as a basis for applying the relevant law in any subsequent case and other courts may invoke it without further reference to the Court of Justice; and
3. a judge may always ask the Court of Justice for a new interpretation.

Preliminary rulings may be applied for only by a national court or tribunal and not by the parties to the case.

6

Parliamentary Sovereignty and European Union Membership

6.1 European Union law in the United Kingdom

6.2 The European Communities Act 1972

6.3 European Union law and United Kingdom sovereignty

6.4 Conclusion

6.1 European Union law in the United Kingdom

The United Kingdom became a member of the European Communities with effect from 1 January 1973, by virtue of the Treaty of Accession 1972. For the Treaty of Accession and the Community treaties and law to have legal effect in the United Kingdom it was necessary for Parliament to pass legislation incorporating them into domestic law. This was achieved by the European Communities Act 1972, as amended.

6.2 The European Communities Act 1972

The main provisions of the Act are as follows:

Section 1   This defines the Community treaties to which the Act relates and includes the treaties entered into by the Communities prior to 22 January 1972. Any subsequent treaties entered into by the Communities may be incorporated into United Kingdom law by Order in Council.

Section 2(1)   This is probably the most important provision of the Act. It provides that:

> 'All such rights, powers, liabilities, obligations and restrictions from time to time created or arising by or under the Treaties, and all such remedies and procedures from time to time provided for by or under

68

the Treaties, as in accordance with the Treaties are without further enactment to be given legal effect or used in the United Kingdom shall be recognised and available in law, and be enforced, allowed and followed accordingly; and the expression "enforceable Community right" and similar expressions shall be read as referring to one to which this subsection applies.'

The effect of this subsection is that all the provisions of European Union law which are, in accordance with European Union law, intended to take direct effect in the United Kingdom, are given the force of law. This applies to the law of the European Union made both before and after the coming into force of the Act.

Section 2(2)   Provides that where Community law requires legislative implementation in the United Kingdom, for example, directives, this may be achieved by means of delegated legislation.

Section 2(3)   Grants permanent authority to the United Kingdom Government to make payments in respect of its Community obligations. Annual parliamentary approval for payment to the Community is therefore unnecessary.

Section 2(4)   This provides that:

'The provision that may be made under subsection (2) above includes, subject to Schedule 2 to this Act, any such provision (of any such extent) as might be made by Act of Parliament, and any enactment passed or to be passed, other than one contained in this Part of this Act, shall be construed and have effect subject to the foregoing provisions of this section; but, except as may be provided by an Act passed after this Act, Schedule 2 shall · have effect in connection with the powers conferred by this and the following sections of this Act to make Orders in Council and regulations.'

The 'foregoing provisions' include s2(1) which states that directly applicable Community law shall have effect in the United Kingdom. Therefore s2(4) seems to amount to a statement that United Kingdom Acts of Parliament 'shall be construed and have effect subject to' directly applicable Community law.

Section 3(1)   This provides that:

'... for the purposes of all legal proceedings, any question as to the meaning or effect of any of the Treaties or as to the validity, meaning or effect of any Community instrument, shall be treated as a question of law (and if not referred to the European Court) be for determination as such in accordance with the principles laid down by the European Court.'

6.3 European Union law and United Kingdom sovereignty

Despite Lord Denning's words in *Bulmer* v *Bollinger* [1974] Ch 401, to the effect that 'when we come to matters with a European element the [T]reaty is like an incoming tide. It flows into the estuaries and up the rivers. It cannot be held back', there are several possible interpretations of s2(4) European Communities Act 1972.

It could be seen as amounting to a statement that all United Kingdom legislation shall only take effect to the extent that it is consistent with Community law, however clearly it may appear from the United Kingdom legislation that it is intended to have effect notwithstanding any Community law to the contrary. It is clear both from the Treaty and from statements made by the European Court of Justice, that the Community view is that Community law should prevail over national law in all circumstances. The European Court of Justice, in *Costa* v *ENEL* [1964] CMLR 425, stated that accession to the European Communities 'has as a corollary the impossibility, for the member state, to give preference to a unilateral and subsequent measure against a legal order accepted by them on a basis of reciprocity'. In *Re Export Tax on Art Treasures (No 2)* [1972] CMLR 699, the European Court of Justice stated:

> 'The grant to the Community by the member states of the rights and powers envisaged by the provisions of the Treaty implies in fact a definitive limitation of their sovereign powers over which no appeal to provisions of international law of any kind whatever can prevail.'

This makes it clear that, as far as the European Court of Justice is concerned, any United Kingdom constitutional law doctrine of the legislative sovereignty of Parliament is irrelevant.

The approach of the European Court of Justice runs contrary to the traditional doctrine of the sovereignty of Parliament as enunciated in *Vauxhall Estates Ltd* v *Liverpool Corporation* (1932) and *Ellen Street Estates* v *Minister of Health* (1934). The strict traditionalist, who insists on the retention of the doctrine of implied repeal as set out in *Ellen Street Estates* v *Minister of Health* (1934), would refuse to give any effect to s2(4), insisting that later United Kingdom legislation always, by implication, repeals earlier legislative provision with which it is inconsistent.

A third approach to s2(4) is to treat it as amounting to a rule of interpretation that there shall be a presumption that the United Kingdom Parliament, in passing legislation, intends to legislate consistently with Community law. This approach differs from the first since it allows that if the United Kingdom Parliament were to make it clear in an Act that it intended to legislate contrary to Community law, or that it intended the legislation to take effect notwithstanding any provision of Community law to the contrary, then the United Kingdom legislation would prevail to the extent that it was in conflict with Community law. This is the approach that was favoured by the Court of Appeal in *Macarthys Ltd* v *Wendy Smith* [1979] 3 All ER 325.

A man had been employed as a stockroom keeper at £60 per week. Subsequently a woman was employed in this position at £50 per week. She took the matter to an industrial tribunal on the grounds that this was contrary to law. Three main questions arose: first, was this arrangement contrary to the Equal Pay Act 1970 as amended by the Sex Discrimination Act 1975? Secondly, if it was not, was it contrary to Article 119 of the Treaty of Rome which provides: 'Each Member State shall ... ensure and ... maintain the application of the principle that men and women should receive equal pay for equal work ... '? Thirdly, in the event of a conflict between the United Kingdom legislation and Article 119 of the Treaty, which should prevail in the English courts? The Employment Appeal Tribunal held that the 1970 Act provided Ms Smith with the right to equal pay where she had performed identical duties in succession to a male employee, a decision which was upheld by the Employment Appeal Tribunal. The employers appealed to the Court of Appeal. It was held (per Lawton and Cumming-Bruce LJJ) that the Equal Pay Act 1970, as amended by the Sex Discrimination Act 1975, only required equal pay for men and women employed in like work contemporaneously, and thus afforded no protection for the female plaintiff in the present case. There was uncertainty, however, as to whether or not Article 119 of the Treaty covered the situation where a woman was employed on certain work that had previously been performed by a man. Since the proper interpretation of Article 119 was uncertain, the matter was referred to the European Court of Justice under Article 117 for a preliminary ruling.

It is interesting to note the views that were expressed by Lord Denning MR regarding the primacy of Community law:

'It is unnecessary, however, for these courts to wait until all that procedure has been gone through. Under ss2(1) and (4) of the European Communities Act 1972 the principles laid down in the Treaty are "without further enactment" to be given legal effect in the United Kingdom; and have priority over "any enactment passed or to be passed" by our Parliament. So we are entitled and I think bound to look at Article 119 of the EEC Treaty because it is directly applicable here; and also any directive which is directly applicable here: see *Van Duyn* v *Home Office (No 2)*. We should, I think, look to see what those provisions require about equal pay for men and women. Then we should look at our own legislation on the point, giving it, of course, full faith and credit, assuming that it does fully comply with the obligation under the Treaty. In construing our statute, we are entitled to look to the Treaty as an aid to its construction, but not only as an aid but as an overriding force. If on close investigation it should appear that our legislation is deficient or is inconsistent with Community law by some oversight of our draftsmen then it is our bounden duty to give priority to Community law. Such is the result of ss2(1) and (4) of the European Communities Act 1972.

I pause here, however, to make one observation on a constitutional point. Thus far I have assumed that our Parliament, whenever it passes legislation, intends to fulfil its obligations under the Treaty. If the time should come when our Parliament deliberately passes an Act with the intention of repudiating the Treaty or any provision in it or intentionally of acting inconsistently with it and says so in express terms then I should have thought that it would be the duty of our courts to follow the statute of our Parliament. I do not however envisage any such situation.'

Thus Lord Denning put forward the view that if Parliament, in an Act, stated an express intention to legislate contrary to Community law or notwithstanding

Community law, then in that one situation the United Kingdom court would give preference to the United Kingdom legislation over the Community law. The other members of the court expressed the same view, Lawton LJ saying:

> '... I can see nothing in this case which infringes the sovereignty of Parliament ... Parliament by its own act in the exercise of its sovereign powers has enacted and followed in the United Kingdom (s1(1) European Communities Act 1972) and that any enactment passed or to be passed ... shall be construed and have effect subject to (s2 in accordance with s2(4) of the Act). Parliament's recognition of European Community law and the jurisdiction of the European Court of Justice by one enactment can be withdrawn by another. There is nothing in the Equal Pay Act 1970 as amended by the Sex Discrimination Act 1975, to indicate that Parliament intended to amend the European Communities Act 1972, or to limit its application ...'

On the reference under Article 177, the European Court ruled that Article 119 did not require contemporaneous employment (*Macarthys Ltd* v *Smith* [1980] ECR 1275), and the case was referred back to the Court of Appeal for the implementation of this interpretation: *Macarthys Ltd* v *Smith* [1981] QB 180. Although his comments were obiter Lord Denning took the opportunity afforded by the second hearing to state the following view:

> 'Article 119 now takes priority over our English statute ... Community law is now part of our law; and, whenever there is any inconsistency, Community law has priority. It is not supplanting English law. It is part of our law which overrides any other part which is inconsistent with it.'

This 'rule of construction' approach, whereby domestic law is always interpreted in a manner that ensures its compliance with Community law, amounts to a retention of the doctrine of express repeal of earlier law by later legislation, but involves the abandonment of the doctrine of implied repeal as far as Community law is concerned. In this approach it is neither consistent with the traditional United Kingdom doctrine of the sovereignty of Parliament, nor with the Community doctrine of the supremacy of Community law over national law. However, it is yet to be seen how the United Kingdom courts would act if faced by a United Kingdom Act of Parliament expressing an intention of Parliament to legislate contrary to Community law.

The matter was considered further by the House of Lords in *Garland* v *British Rail Engineering Ltd* [1983] 2 AC 751. The appellant was a female employee of the respondent company. Employees enjoyed (ex gratia) free travel on British Rail. Upon retirement male employees continued to enjoy this benefit for themselves and their families. In the case of retiring female employees, the benefit did not extend to their families. The appellant contended that this discrimination was not permitted by s6(4) of the Sex Discrimination Act 1964, and was in breach of Article 119 of the EEC Treaty. The complaint was dismissed by an industrial tribunal, allowed on appeal to the Employment Appeal Tribunal, and the respondent employers appealed successfully to the Court of Appeal. On appeal to the House of Lords, the issue was referred to the European Court of Justice, which held that the discrimination was in breach of Article 119, which was directly applicable where a domestic court found such discrimination to exist. On reference back to the House of Lords the decision of the Employment Appeal Tribunal was restored. Lord Diplock observed that:

'... it is a principle of construction of United Kingdom statutes, now too well established to call for citation of authority, that the words of a statute passed after the Treaty has been signed and dealing with the subject matter of the international obligation of the United Kingdom, are to be construed, if they are reasonably capable of bearing such a meaning, as intended to carry out the obligation, and not to be inconsistent with it. A fortiori is this the case where the Treaty obligation arises under one of the Community treaties to which section 2 of the European Communities Act 1972 applies ...'

To some extent Lord Diplock side-stepped the key question of when, if ever, domestic law would be allowed to prevail where it was in conflict with Community law. He expressed the view that:

'The instant appeal does not present an appropriate occasion to consider whether, having regard to the express direction as to the construction of enactments "to be passed" which is contained in s2(4), anything short of an express positive statement in an Act of Parliament passed after 1 January, 1973, that a particular provision is intended to be made in breach of an obligation assumed by the United Kingdom under a Community treaty, would justify an English court in construing that provision in a manner inconsistent with a Community treaty obligation of the United Kingdom, however wide a departure from the prima facie meaning of the language of the provision might be needed in order to achieve consistency.'

See further *Pickstone* v *Freemans plc* [1989] 1 AC 66.

Note that the *Macarthys* and *Garland* cases were concerned with the relationship between domestic legislation and directly enforceable Community legislation. Where the alleged conflict is between domestic law and Community law that is not directly enforceable, in the sense that it has no direct effect between individuals, the courts have been less willing to adopt the 'rule of construction' approach. In *Duke* v *GEC Reliance Ltd* [1988] 1 All ER 626, the House of Lords considered an action for wrongful dismissal brought by a woman who had been forced to retire at 60, while her male colleagues were not required to retire until they were 65. She claimed that the Equal Pay Act 1970, and the Sex Discrimination Act 1975, had to be construed so as to ensure compliance with EEC directive 76/207 (the equal treatment directive). It was held that the directive required the UK to prohibit unequal treatment by employers, but did not create a right for individuals to sue their employers for damages for non-compliance. In reaching this conclusion, Lord Templeman stated:

'Section 2(4) of the European Communities Act 1972 does not in my opinion enable or constrain a British court to distort the meaning of a British statute in order to enforce against an individual a Community directive which has no direct effect between individuals. Section 2(4) applies and only applies where Community provisions are directly applicable.'

It may be the case that in the light of the *Marleasing* case (considered in Chapter 5), the English courts will not be able to maintain this view.

A situation where there is a clear conflict between domestic law and Community law is, perhaps, unlikely to arise since it would amount to a blatant repudiation by the United Kingdom of its international obligations under the European Community treaties, but problems have arisen as regards the availability of interim relief while the issue of the validity of domestic law is being determined by the European Court of Justice; see the *Factortame* litigation.

6.4 Conclusion

The United Kingdom Parliament has forfeited its sovereignty by the European Communities Act 1972, which provides for the direct applicability of Community law in the United Kingdom, and the enforceability of Community rights before United Kingdom courts. However, this forfeiture of sovereignty is better described as a limited and partial surrender of sovereignty. The European Communities Act 1972 is not entrenched. Parliament can in theory repeal the Act at any time and thus regain its full supremacy as a sovereign legislature. With the passage of time, however, this regaining of sovereignty becomes more theoretical and less practical. The political realities of the situation will dictate that the greater the degree of integration in terms of economic, monetary, and commercial union, the more difficult it will be for any UK Government to extricate itself from the European Union. As successive generations grow up, not having known anything of life prior to membership, it may be unlikely that any prospective UK Government would receive a mandate for withdrawal.

The view expressed by Hoffmann J in *Stoke-on-Trent City Council* v *B & Q plc* [1991] 2 WLR 42 displays increasing realism on the part of the judiciary. His Lordship stated (at p45):

> 'The EEC Treaty is the supreme law of this country, taking precedence over Acts of Parliament. Our entry into the European Economic Community meant that (subject to our undoubted but probably theoretical right to withdraw from the Community altogether) Parliament surrendered its sovereign right to legislate contrary to the provisions of the Treaty on matters of social and economic policy which it regulated.'

7

The Electoral System – Membership of the House of Commons

7.1 The composition of the House of Commons

The membership of the House of Commons is elected on the basis of universal adult suffrage. Under s7 of the Parliament Act 1911, a General Election to determine the membership of the House of Commons must be held at least every five years.

The franchise

The law relating to the franchise is now contained in the Representation of the People Act 1983. In order to vote in a parliamentary election a person must be included in the electoral register for a parliamentary constituency. To qualify for inclusion in the register, a person must be:

1. eighteen years of age (or be due to attain his 18th birthday within 12 months of the publication of the register);
2. a British subject or a citizen of the Republic of Ireland;
3. not subject to any legal incapacity; and
4. resident in the constituency on the qualifying date for compiling the register. The Representation of the People Act 1985 makes provision for postal voting by those living overseas, and the 1990 Act enables a voter who changes address to vote by proxy for the rest of the period for which the register is in force without having to make a fresh application on each occasion.

The register of electors

The register is prepared once a year by the registration officer of each constituency. To be included in the register, a person must be resident at an address in the constituency on the qualifying date, 10 October. Except for Northern Ireland, no period of residence is necessary. A provisional register is issued on 28 November and exhibited to the public. Any objections to the inclusion or exclusion of any person in or from the register must be made by 16 December. Such objections are heard by the registration officer. Appeal lies from his determination to the County Court and thereafter, on a point of law, to the Court of Appeal. The determination of the registration officer and any decision of the County Court may also be reviewed by the Divisional Court of the Queen's Bench Division. The register comes into force on 16 February and remains operative for 12 months.

The meaning of residence for electoral purposes was considered by the Court of Appeal in *Fox v Stirk* [1970] 2 QB 463.

The question before the court was whether two students who took up residence in their university towns a few days before the qualifying date, and who might spend as little as 26 weeks a year in residence in those towns, spending the rest of their time at their parents' home in another part of the country, could be regarded as ordinarily resident in their university town for the purpose of the electoral register. The court held that there was a sufficient degree of permanence in the students' residence in their university towns for them to be placed on the electoral register. The court held further that a person could, for these purposes, be regarded as resident in more than one place at any one time. However, it is a criminal offence for a person to vote in more than one constituency, even though his name appears on the electoral register for each constituency.

Service voters – members of the armed forces, whether serving at home or abroad, Crown servants and British Council staff overseas, and their spouses – shall be registered as if they were living at the address at which, but for the service, they would normally be resident.

Disqualification

The following persons are not entitled to vote, even if their names appear on the electoral register:

1. Aliens, excluding citizens of the Republic of Ireland.
2. Minors (persons under 18 years of age).
3. Peers and peeresses in their own right (Irish peers may vote).
4. Convicted persons undergoing sentences in penal institutions.
5. Persons convicted of corrupt or illegal practices at elections. The former are disqualified from voting for five years, the latter for five years in the constituency in question.

6. Those who, for reasons such as mental illness, subnormality, drunkenness or other infirmity, lack the capacity at the moment of voting to understand what they are about to do. It is for the presiding officer at the polling station to decide whether or not a person lacks such capacity.

Parliamentary constituencies

The United Kingdom is currently divided into 651 parliamentary constituencies, each of which is represented by one member in the House of Commons.

The delimitation of constituency boundaries

Under the House of Commons (Redistribution of Seats) Acts 1949 and 1958, four permanent Boundary Commissions, for England, Wales, Scotland and Northern Ireland, were created to undertake a review of constituencies at intervals of not less than ten or more than 15 years, and report to the Secretary of State any redistribution of seats necessary to ensure, as far as possible, equal electorates. The Boundary Commissions Act 1992 amends the Parliamentary Constituencies Act 1986 with the effect that the next Boundary Commission report will have to be submitted by 31 December 1994. The aim is to ensure that the next general election, which must be held by April 1997, will be contested on the basis of revised constituencies.

The chairman of each Commission is the Speaker of the House of Commons and a High Court judge is appointed deputy chairman. Each Commission has two other members who must not be MPs. When a Commission has decided to recommend changes, notice must be given in the constituencies affected and representations must be invited. A local inquiry may also have to be held. The Commission must then submit its report to the Secretary of State, who must lay it before Parliament together with a draft Order in Council for giving effect, with or without modifications, to its recommendations. The draft order must then be approved by resolutions of each House before the final order is made by the Queen in Council.

The principle underlying the redistribution of seats

As a basic principle each constituency should have the same number of voters within it to ensure that all votes have equal value. However, a Boundary Commission is entitled to depart from the strict application of this principle if 'special geographical considerations including in particular the size, shape and accessibility of a constituency' so require. Parliamentary constituencies shall, as far as practicable, follow local government boundaries and local ties and any inconvenience caused by the proposed alteration must also be considered. The ideal size for each constituency is found by dividing the total electorate in each Commission area by the number of constituencies in that area. Because of population distribution as in, for example, the Highlands of Scotland or rural Wales, this formula may be departed from. A constituency in the Scottish Highlands would be so large as to be unworkable if constituencies were arranged on the equal average population basis.

In practice this means that an individual vote in Scotland or Wales is more powerful than an individual vote in other parts of the United Kingdom, as because of the smaller constituency population, fewer votes are required to elect a member. In other words the weight which your vote carries varies according to where you live. The essence of democracy is the principle of 'one man, one vote, one value', but in the United Kingdom it appears that, since not all votes have the same value, some electors are more equal than others.

Challenging the process

Those involved in the redistribution of parliamentary constituencies, such as the Boundary Commissions and the Home Secretary, are, in theory, subject to control by the courts if they act unlawfully in the discharge of their functions. Putting the theory into practice has not proved easy.

In *Harper* v *Secretary of State for the Home Department* [1955] 1 Ch 238 the court rejected the contention that it had any jurisdiction to comment on the validity of Commissioners' reports placed before Parliament by the Home Secretary in the form of a draft Order. Lord Evershed MR commented that, in his view, if the courts were competent to pass judgment on the reports there might be no end to the process of challenge.

There are clearly constitutional difficulties in delaying any legal challenge to the process until the report is before Parliament. Hence in the most significant case to come before the courts on this issue, *R* v *Boundary Commission for England, ex parte Foot* [1983] QB 600, the Labour Party leader, who believed that the Commission had acted unreasonably in compiling its report, sought an order to prevent the report being put before Parliament. On the facts the Court of Appeal felt there was insufficient evidence to show that in compiling its report the Commission had failed to take into account relevant considerations, or conversely had taken into account irrelevant considerations.

Given current demographic trends, it is the Labour Party that seems most likely to suffer as a result of constituency boundaries being withdrawn, the shift of population from urban centres to the shires being the primary cause. The 1992 General Election was fought on the basis of boundaries based, in many cases, on electoral registers dating back to 1976. It is predicted that the next General Election may be fought against a background of boundary changes ensuring an increase of approximately 20 Conservative MPs. In London alone, 13 of the present 84 seats may disappear. The Boundary Commission has until the end of 1994 to finalise its report.

7.2 The electoral system

At present Members of Parliament are elected under the 'relative majority' or 'first past the post' system. Each Parliamentary constituency returns a single member.

Each elector can vote for one candidate only, and the candidate who polls the most votes within a given constituency wins that seat. It is a 'winner takes all' system. If you vote for the candidate who comes second in the poll, your vote is quite simply disregarded. It is a very crude system. There is no relationship between the number of votes cast nationally for a particular party and the number of seats allocated to that party in the House of Commons. In practice the system produces exaggerated majorities for the two major parties and discriminates against the minority parties.

The results of the April 1992 General Election demonstrate this clearly.

Party	Actual seats	% Seats	% Popular vote
Conservative	336	51.7	43
Labour	271	41.6	35
Liberal Democrats	20	3	18
Others	24	3.7	4

Advantages of the simple majority voting system

1. The voting procedure is simple and the results may be quickly and easily calculated.
2. There is a link between the member and his constituency.
3. One party usually obtains an absolute majority of seats in the House of Commons thus leading to strong government. There is no coalition Government with minor parties holding the balance of power being able to exert influence out of all proportion to their popular support in the country.

The Liberal Democrats indicated that if they were asked to form a Government, or if they held the balance of power in a 'hung' Parliament, they would introduce reforms to allow for elections on the basis of proportional representation. This would clearly be to their political advantage. By allowing a more accurate reflection of the preferences expressed by voters, it would reduce the wastage of votes which is a feature of the relative majority system. The apparent injustices of the 1983, 1987 and 1992 General Elections would therefore be avoided.

Electoral reform

Public interest in the issue of electoral reform has been wavering since the 1930s but there are now signs that it is reviving. At the beginning of the 20th century one would have been entitled to expect an early introduction of some form of proportional representation into the United Kingdom. A Royal Commission on Electoral Systems was appointed in 1900 and reported in favour of changing to a system known as the alternative vote in 1910. In the Representation of the People Act 1918, Parliament began to pave the way towards a system of proportional representation by single transferable vote when it introduced that system for the university constituencies. The university vote was abolished in 1948.

In 1930 a Bill which sought to introduce the alternative vote passed the Commons but was lost, never to be revived, when the Labour Government fell in 1931. Thereafter the climate of opinion changed and in 1944 a Speaker's Conference rejected the idea of proportional representation.

Despite the fact that the Speaker's Conference of 1973 did not even consider the question of electoral reform, there is evidence that public opinion is in favour of a proportional voting system. Moreover, there is likely to be pressure from Europe for electoral reform. Article 138(3) of the Treaty of Rome provides that:

> 'The Assembly shall draw up proposals for elections by direct universal suffrage in accordance with a uniform procedure in all Member States.'

In a Europe where most other member states have a system of proportional representation it seems unlikely that the crude first past the post system will become that uniform procedure, despite the House of Commons' initial rejection of proportional representation in the voting procedure for elections to the European Parliament.

When faced with the choice, the House of Commons also rejected proposals that the single transferable vote system should be used for elections to the regional assemblies which were once proposed in Scotland and Wales. Having analysed the alternatives, the report of the Royal Commission on the Constitution made a positive recommendation in favour of using the single transferable vote system for elections to the proposed assemblies. The fact that the House of Commons rejected this proposal shows the depth of resistance to electoral reform which comes from the Commons itself. Members who feel that their seat in the Commons would be threatened by reform have a vested interest in perpetuating the first past the post system. Given its fourth successive election defeat, the Labour Party has, not surprisingly, increased its interest in electoral reform, inviting Professor Raymond Plant to head an inquiry on the issue. It remains to be seen to what extent its proponents are successful in making it part of the mainstream of that party's policy. The danger for any opposition party in embracing electoral reform is that it can be seen as an admission that it cannot win under the current system.

The alternative vote system

Under this system the voter is asked to list the candidates within the constituency in order of preference. If no candidate gains an absolute majority of first preference votes then the lowest candidate is eliminated and his second preference votes are distributed amongst the other candidates. The process may be repeated until a candidate emerges who has an absolute majority – more than half the votes. This system is used to elect the Australian Lower House. It is not a proportional system, but it does reduce the number of wasted votes and has the advantage of being easy to understand and administer.

The party list system

The ultimate and only precise means of achieving direct proportionality is to have only one constituency, composed of the whole country, with the parties presenting lists of candidates and electors voting, not for individual candidates, but for the whole party list. Seats are then allocated to the parties in proportion to the votes received by each party list. However, difficulties may be encountered in drawing up the list and in particular determining the order of candidates. It would also destroy the territorial constituency system with its strong link between one MP and one constituency.

The single transferable vote system

The single transferable vote system is an alternative to the party list system. It requires multi-member constituencies of between five and seven members. Voters list the individual candidates in order of preference. In counting the votes, the principle that applies is that the candidate only needs a certain number, or quota of votes, to be elected, and any votes that he receives beyond this figure are surplus and serve only to build up an unnecessary majority. So, once the candidate has received the quota necessary to secure his election, the 'surplus' votes are redistributed among the other candidates according to second preferences.

There are several variations based on the procedures used to determine the quota, count the votes, and redistribute the surplus votes, but the quota is generally established by the following formula:

$$\frac{\text{Number of votes cast} + 1}{\text{Number of seats} + 1}$$

Political parties in the United Kingdom

The origin of the Conservative and Liberal Parties

During the constitutional conflicts of the seventeenth century there emerged in Parliament two main groups:

1. The Royalist or Court group (Tories).
2. The Parliamentary or Country group (Whigs).

These names were retained throughout the eighteenth century but group organisation in Parliament in the eighteenth and early nineteenth centuries consisted of little more than informal meetings. The late eighteenth century saw the emergence of Whips to organise MPs for voting purposes, and bitter controversies over the 1832 Reform Bill led to a hardening of 'party lines'.

Following Sir Robert Peel's declaration in his 1834 election address that the Tory policy was to conserve all that was good in existing institutions, the Tory Party became generally known as the Conservative Party. The repeal of the Corn Laws in 1845 split the Conservative Party. One group, the Protectionists, led by Disraeli, opposed the repeal, and another, the Peelites, supported Peel's free trade policy. The Peelites gradually merged with the Whigs and Radicals during the 1850s and 1860s to form the new Liberal Party.

The origins of the Labour Party

At the beginning of the nineteenth century, in an attempt to get working class representation in Parliament, the Labour Representations Committee was formed by an alliance between various trade unions and socialist societies. In 1906 the name of the Labour Representation Committee was changed to the Labour Party. By 1922, when 142 Labour members were returned to Parliament, the Labour Party had replaced the Liberals as one of the two major parties.

The Liberal Democrats

In 1988, following the demise of the Social Democratic Party led by Dr David Owen, the bulk of its members agreed to merge with the Liberal Party to form a new centre party, the Liberal Democrats.

Other parties

The other parties of any importance are, on the whole, parties whose support is concentrated in some particular geographical area of the British Isles. Thus the Scottish Nationalist Party (SNP) and Plaid Cymru (Welsh Nationalist Party) command some support in Scotland and Wales respectively. Their high point of electoral support was, however, the early to mid 1970s. Since the proposals for devolution of power to Scotland and Wales were rejected by the electorate of those areas in 1979, their electoral fortunes have suffered a reverse.

In Northern Ireland the Official Unionist Party and the Ulster Unionist Party are both predominantly Protestant and in favour of Northern Ireland continuing as a part of the United Kingdom. The Social Democratic and Labour Party is Roman Catholic-based and favours, at the very least, reforms which would give the Roman Catholics in Northern Ireland a greater say in Government affairs.

The growth of mass party organisations outside Parliament

The Reform Act 1832 widened the franchise considerably. After 1832 the political clubs, particularly the Tory Carlton Club and the Whig Reform Club, became centres of party loyalties. Various local Registration Societies were also formed after 1832 to persuade new voters to support particular party candidates. The further extension of the franchise in 1867 led to the main developments in local party organisation outside Parliament. With a larger electorate, the need arose for machinery to distribute party propaganda, and the national organisations of the Liberal and Conservative Parties both date from this period.

7.3 The conduct of elections

The conduct of elections is regulated by the Representation of the People Act 1983 so as to eliminate, as far as possible, corrupt and illegal electoral practices and other unfair methods. Each candidate must appoint an election agent, which may be himself, and all campaign expenditure must be authorised by the candidate or his agent. A maximum limit is imposed on election expenditure and it is an illegal practice for the candidate or his agent knowingly to exceed this limit. Certain forms of expenditure are prohibited altogether.

The prohibition on election expenditure without the consent of the candidate extends equally to expenditure designed to prevent the election of other competing candidates. Hence in *DPP* v *Luft* [1977] AC 962, the House of Lords upheld the convictions of the respondents who, without the authority of any of the 'candidates' had distributed leaflets urging voters not to support National Front candidates.

By contrast, there are no legal limits on the amount of money a party may spend on its national campaign (ie the campaign that is not designed to support any particular candidate in any particular constituency). Calls have been made for regulation of such expenditure, or at least greater openness regarding the sources of finance and levels of spending, but there are at present no moves towards reform. The conventional view is that the Conservative Party has an inevitable advantage given its higher level of funding by private industry than that received by the Labour Party from the trade unions. The conduct of the 1992 General Election campaign perhaps cast doubt on the view that the most expensive campaign is always the most effective, despite the Conservative Party's narrow victory. Should the Labour Party lose the financial backing of the trade unions, its ability to conduct a sustained, sophisticated and effective campaign would clearly be called into doubt, perhaps raising the question of state funding of political groups.

Bribery, cheating and the use of fraudulent devices would also constitute election offences. In *R* v *Rowe, ex parte Mainwaring and Others* [1992] 1 WLR 1059, the appellants were successful candidates for the Liberal Democrats at local government elections. The respondents, unsuccessful Labour Party candidates, presented election petitions claiming that the appellants had engaged in corrupt electoral practices, namely the publication by them of a leaflet, designed to appear as if it was a Labour Party leaflet, containing factually accurate but politically contentious accounts of Labour Party policies that might not have been popular with the Labour Party voters in the areas in which it was distributed. The leaflet complied with the requirement that it should carry the details of the distributing party's agent, but this was in minuscule print. The Court of Appeal found that a leaflet issued by one political party designed so as to appear as if it had been issued by a rival party could be a fraudulent device, notwithstanding that the contents were factually correct. For an offence to be made out, however, it had to be shown that an elector had in fact been impeded or prevented in the free exercise of the franchise, and the evidence of this was lacking in the present case. The result induced Nolan LJ to express the view that s115(2)(b) of the Representation of the People Act 1983 should be replaced by a more effective provision that could deal with '... less blatant and less easily detected but no less effective methods of exerting influence ...'.

Election petitions

Since 1868 Parliament has entrusted the duty of hearing petitions against the validity of elections to an election court consisting of two judges of the Queen's Bench Division in England or of the Court of Session in Scotland. An election petition complaining of illegal or corrupt practices or other irregularities must be presented within 21 days of the official return of the result. The court, which usually sits in the constituency concerned, determines whether the candidate in question was duly elected and whether any illegal, corrupt or other irregular practices have been proved. If the petition alleges that the successful candidate was subject to a legal incapacity, and this is proved, the court may either declare the election void or award the seat to the runner-up. The decision of the court is notified to the Speaker of the House of Commons and is recorded in the journals of the House. Such petitions are now extremely rare, but perhaps the most celebrated example is provided by the challenge to Tony Benn's election as an MP following his inheritance of his father's viscountcy: see *Re Parliamentary Election for Bristol South-East* [1964] 2 QB 257.

7.4 Membership of the House of Commons

There is no qualification requirement for membership of the House of Commons, but certain categories of persons and office holders are disqualified from sitting and voting in the House.

Disqualification

The following are disqualified:

1. Aliens, but not including citizens of the Republic of Ireland.
2. Persons under 21 years of age.
3. Persons suffering from mental illness. Under the Mental Health Act 1983 the Speaker must be notified when a member is detained as a person suffering from mental illness. The Speaker must then obtain a medical report. If the detention is confirmed by this report and the member is still detained as a mental patient according to a second report six months later, his seat is vacated.
4. Peers and peeresses in their own right. Peers of Ireland, who are not qualified to sit in the House of Lords, are not disqualified.
5. Clergy who have been episcopally ordained into the Church of England and the Church of Ireland, Roman Catholic priests and Ministers of the Church of Scotland.

6. A person convicted of treason is disqualified from membership until receipt of a Royal Pardon or expiry of the sentence. Until recently, if a member was convicted of any crime other than treason, and was sentenced to imprisonment, the Speaker was to be informed of the nature of the offence and sentence; but the prisoner remained a member unless a motion was passed by the House of Commons to expel him. Now, under the Representation of the People Act 1981 a person who has been sentenced to one year's imprisonment or more is disqualified from membership of the House of Commons during his period of detention. A Member of Parliament who is sentenced to one year's imprisonment or more must vacate his seat.

7. Bankrupts are disqualified and remain disqualified until five years after discharge, unless discharged with a certificate that bankruptcy was a result of misfortune and not misconduct. A member who becomes bankrupt may continue to sit until the House takes notice of his bankruptcy and orders him to withdraw.

8. Persons convicted of corrupt and illegal practice at elections. Corrupt practices include impersonation, bribery, treating and undue influence. Illegal practices include false statements as to candidates; corruptly inducing a person's withdrawal from candidature; payments for exhibition of election notices, except to a commercial advertising agent; employment of paid canvassers; any other payments contrary to, or in excess of, those allowed by the Representation of the People Acts. According to s159(1) Representation of the People Act 1983, if a candidate who has been elected is reported by an election court to be personally guilty, or guilty by his agents, of any corrupt or illegal practice, his election is void. If he has been reported personally guilty he is incapable of being elected for the constituency concerned for ten years in the case of a corrupt practice and seven years in the case of an illegal practice. If guilty by his agents the incapacity is for seven years in the case of a corrupt practice and the duration of that Parliament in the case of an illegal practice. A candidate reported personally guilty of corrupt practice is also incapable of being elected to the House of Commons in any constituency for five years.

Disqualification of office-holders

There are four main reasons for disqualification of certain office-holders from membership of the House of Commons:

1. The risk of patronage.
2. The physical impossibility of certain office-holders being able to attend Parliament.
3. The conflict of constitutional duties.
4. The need for political impartiality in certain offices.

Disqualifying offices are now set out in the House of Commons Disqualification Act 1975, and, under s1 of the Act fall into six categories:

1. Judicial offices. No person may hold a full-time judicial appointment and at the same time be a practising politician. Lay magistrates are not affected.
2. Civil servants. Full- or part-time civil servants who wish to stand as parliamentary candidates must first resign the service.
3. Members of the regular armed forces. Retired officers and members of the Territorial Army and other reserve or auxiliary forces are not disqualified.
4. Full-time members of any police force.
5. Members of the Legislatures of non-Commonwealth countries.
6. Members of certain commissions, tribunals and other bodies listed in the first Schedule to the Act. This schedule may be amended by Order in Council.

Resignation from the House of Commons

In law, a member of the House of Commons is unable to resign his seat. The only way to be released from membership is to accept a disqualifying office. Traditionally the office of Steward or Bailiff of the Chiltern Hundreds or of the Manor of Northstead were used for this purpose. They are expressly preserved as a ground of disqualification by s4 of the 1975 Act.

Ministers of the Crown

Not more than 95 holders of specified ministerial offices may sit and vote at any one time in the House of Commons (House of Commons Disqualification Act 1975, s52(1).) Additional appointments must therefore be made from the House of Lords.

Effect of disqualifications

If a person who is disqualified from membership of the House of Commons is elected, his election is void. If a member becomes disqualified after election, his seat is vacated. If the disqualification has been removed, the House may direct that the disqualification be disregarded. This does not affect any proceedings on an election petition or the determination of an election court; the obligation of the House of Commons to make an order implementing the finding of an election court remains.

Under s7 of the 1975 Act anyone who claims that a person purporting to be a member of the House of Commons is disqualified by the Act may apply to the Privy Council for a declaration to that effect. The House itself may petition the Crown to have the matter referred to the Judicial Committee of the Privy Council for an advisory opinion.

8

The Functions of the House of Commons – Parliamentary Privilege

8.1 Introduction

8.2 The Speaker of the House of Commons

8.3 The legislative process

8.4 Opportunities for debate in the House of Commons

8.5 Parliamentary questions

8.6 Parliamentary committees

8.7 Parliamentary control of national finance

8.8 Introduction to parliamentary privilege

8.9 Privileges of the House of Commons

8.10 The courts and parliamentary privilege

8.11 MPs as representatives of outside interests

8.1 Introduction

The main functions of Parliament include the passing of legislation and the scrutiny of the Administration through debate, the committee system and the control of national finance.

A select committee report on sittings of the House (HC 20) noted that the Commons sits on more days and for longer hours than any comparable legislative body. Amongst the report's recommendations were proposals that the business of the House should be concluded by 10pm Monday to Wednesday; the number of Friday sittings should be reduced, with additional consideration of Private Members' Bills on Wednesdays; Thursday sittings to finish at 7pm.

8.2 The Speaker of the House of Commons

History of the Speakership

The Speakership dates back under its present title to 1377 when Sir Thomas Hungerford was appointed. Up to the seventeenth century the Speaker was often an agent of the King. By the Civil War the Speaker's duty to the House of Commons had been recognised, as illustrated by Speaker Lenthall's reply in the House to King Charles I who had come to arrest five members for treason:

> 'May it please Your Majesty, I have neither eyes to see nor tongue to speak in this place, but as the House is pleased to direct me, whose servant I am here, and I humbly beg Your Majesty's pardon that I cannot give any other answer than this to what Your Majesty is pleased to demand of me.'

Election of the Speaker

The Speaker is elected at the beginning of every new Parliament or when the previous Speaker dies or retires. He does not generally change with a change of Government. In the past when a new Speaker has been required, the practice has been for the longest serving member of the House to move the election of the member, selected from the Government party, whose name has been previously agreed between the party leaders in consultation with backbenchers. The House then votes for this member. Following the General Election of April 1992, and the retirement of Sir Bernard Weatherill as Speaker, the post was contested by a number of Members of Parliament, the House of Commons ultimately opting for its first ever female Speaker, the Labour MP Miss Betty Boothroyd.

Duties of the Speaker

The Speaker must be seen to be completely impartial and be above party politics and preserve the rights of minorities in the House, hence the requirement that on taking office he should sever his party connections. While the Speaker must continue as a Member of Parliament, he does not speak in debate or vote in the House, and is usually returned unopposed at General Elections. Although unable to represent his constituents' interests in the House, he is able to deal with their individual grievances privately with the government departments concerned.

The Speaker acts as chairman during debates and generally presides over the House, except when it is in committee. It is the Speaker who calls members to speak and decides how many supplementary questions shall be allowed at Question Time. He is responsible for the maintenance of order and the general conduct of debates. He can request members using unparliamentary language or behaviour to withdraw. In cases of grave general disorder he may suspend the sitting. If a member is wilfully disobedient to a ruling the Speaker can 'name' the member, thereby suspending him from the House. He guides the House on all questions of procedure and privilege. He will rule as to whether a certain matter is in accordance with the rules and precedents of the House. It is the Speaker who reprimands on behalf of the House offenders brought to the Bar.

The Speaker does not vote in division unless there is a tie, in which case, according to the ruling of Speaker Addington (1796):

'... the Speaker should always vote for further discussion where this is possible.'

See, for example, the use of the casting vote by Speaker Boothroyd during the debate on the resolution required by s7 of the European Communities (Amendment) Act 1993. The speaker will usually give his casting vote in favour of the introduction of a Bill, in favour of a Bill being given its Second Reading, or against a guillotine motion.

He also decides which of the amendments proposed at the Report Stage of legislation shall be debated. This is an important power. The Speaker's decision to allow debate on a long list of proposed amendments obviously affects the speed with which a Bill is passed, and may even result in the Bill not completing all of its stages in both Houses before the end of the session. This is particularly relevant in the case of Private Members' Bills for which there is in any case little time made available for debate.

The Speaker also determines whether a Bill is a money Bill within the meaning of the Parliament Act 1911. He decides as to whether an application for an emergency debate under Standing Order No 10 is proper to be put to the House. He is partially responsible for the selection of the topic for the daily adjournment debate on Thursdays. The Speaker also decides whether to put a closure motion proposed during the passage of legislation to the House. A closure motion occurs where an MP, usually a Government Whip, moves 'that the question be now put', that is, that the debate terminate and that a vote be taken immediately. If a closure motion is put and the House passes it, with at least 100 members voting in favour, then there can be no further debate and the question must immediately be put to the vote. The Speaker may refuse to put the closure motion on the grounds that it is an abuse of the rules of the House or an infringement of the rights of minorities. It is for the Speaker to decide whether the termination of debate at that point would involve too drastic a curtailment of the rights of MPs to debate proposed legislation. Because of the lack of parliamentary time and the rule that a Bill must go through all its stages in both Houses within one session of Parliament, the exercise of the Speaker's discretion on the question of a closure motion can be of great significance.

The Speaker is also chairman of the Boundary Commissions which review the distribution of seats, and represents the Commons in its relations with the Lords and the Sovereign.

8.3 The legislative process

Introduction

A proposed piece of legislation is called a Bill. It becomes an Act when it has been passed by Parliament and has received the Royal Assent. A distinction must be drawn between Public and Private Bills.

Public Bills seek to alter the general law and concern the whole community. They are introduced into Parliament under the Standing Orders of the two Houses relating to public business.

Private Bills affect only a section of the community and relate to matters of individual corporate or local interest. They are promoted by interested persons or bodies outside Parliament and are subject to separate Standing Orders relating to private business.

Hybrid Bills are Public Bills that are classified by the Speaker as having a particular effect on one section of the community. They are defined by Erskine May as 'a Public Bill which affects a particular private interest in a manner different from the private interests of other persons or bodies of the same category or class'.

Public Bill procedure

Most Public Bills are Government Bills introduced and promoted by the Government; but some may be Private Members' Bills introduced by backbench Members of Parliament. Bills may be introduced into either House, but politically controversial legislation, financial legislation, and electoral legislation begin in the House of Commons. In the case of a Government Bill, introduced in the House of Commons, the procedure for enactment is as follows:

First Reading

A 'dummy' copy of the Bill is placed on the table on the day of presentation; when the moment of presentation is reached, after questions, the Speaker calls the sponsoring minister, the Clerk reads the short title of the Bill and the minister, or a Whip acting on his behalf, names a (notional) day for the Bill's Second Reading. No debate takes place at the First Reading. The Bill is then printed and published and the Opposition, particularly, can study it with a view to criticism and amendment.

Second Reading

When the Bill is printed it can proceed after examination for compliance with the House's rules, to its first substantive stage, which is called the Second Reading. The date on which the debate is to take place will be announced by the Leader of the House. Wherever possible the Government aims to leave two weekends between the printing and Second Reading of a Bill. The Second Reading is the time at which the House considers the principle and merits of the Bill, and a vote is taken on whether to give the Bill a Second Reading. It is rare however for a Government Bill to be denied a Second Reading. Some non-controversial Bills are dealt with in a Second Reading Committee, and exclusively Scottish Bills in Scottish Grand Committee.

Committee stage

After Second Reading, a Bill is normally referred to a Standing Committee consisting of between 16 and 50 members nominated by a committee of selection and reflecting party strength in the House. Standing Committees are constituted to deal with Bills as and when necessary, and there have been up to ten sitting at one time. They are designated by letters – eg Standing Committee A, Standing Committee B – and two, the first and second Scottish Standing Committees, deal with Bills relating exclusively to Scotland.

The Committee stage involves detailed clause by clause consideration of the Bill. The committee may generally amend the Bill as it thinks fit, provided that the amendments made are relevant to the subject matter of the Bill. Amendments and new clauses may be moved by the minister, the Opposition spokesmen, or by any member of the committee. Instead of referring a Bill to a Standing Committee the Bill may be considered by a Committee of the Whole House. In general, this procedure will be used for Bills of constitutional importance, those requiring a very rapid passage, and certain financial measures, including at least part of each year's Finance Bill. Exceptionally, Bills may be referred to a Select Committee, in which case evidence may be taken and a report made.

Report stage

When a Bill has completed its Committee stage, it is reported as amended to the whole House. Further amendments, alteration of amendments made by the committee, and new clauses, may be made at this stage. All members may speak and vote at this stage, unlike in a Standing Committee.

Third Reading

The final Commons stage of the Bill is the Third Reading. The Bill is debated once more in general terms with only verbal amendments allowed. Except for Bills of major political or constitutional importance the Third Reading is usually brief and formal.

House of Lords stages and amendments

After its Third Reading, the Bill is sent to the House of Lords where it goes through stages similar to those in the Commons. The House of Lords has no Standing Committees and the Committee stage is usually taken by a Committee of the Whole House. If the Lords amend the Bill, their amendments are printed and considered by the Commons and agreed to, amended, or disagreed to. If they are disagreed to, the Commons send to the Lords a note of the reasons for the disagreement and the Lords consider the matter further. In the case of an impasse between the Houses, the Parliament Act 1949 provides for the will of the Commons to prevail. The Lords have no power to amend a Money Bill.

The Parliament Act 1911 annulled the power of the Lords over Money Bills, reducing it to a delaying power of one month only, after which a Money Bill sent up from the Commons may receive the Royal Assent even if it has not been approved by the House of Lords. The Lords' power over all other Public Bills (except a Bill to extend the maximum life of a Parliament beyond five years) was reduced to a delaying power, and this delaying power was reduced even further by the Parliament Act 1949. The position now is that a Bill which the Lords refuse to pass within one month may nevertheless receive the Royal Assent provided that it has been passed by the House of Commons in two successive sessions, and one year has elapsed between the date of the Bill's Second Reading in the first session and its Third Reading in the second session.

Royal Assent

The assent of the Sovereign is required after a Bill has passed through both Houses, for it to pass into law. Such assent has not been withheld since 1707, but every Bill is still required to go through the procedure appointed. After the Royal Assent has been given the Bill becomes an Act.

Commencement Orders

Some Acts are brought into force immediately, some at a date specified in the Act and others by Commencement Orders, which may activate all or part of the Act at a date determined by the Government by Order in Council or a minister by statutory instrument.

Private Members' Bills procedure

Although the bulk of the legislative programme is taken up by Government Bills there are a number of procedures under which private members may initiate Bills.

The ballot

Because the time set aside by the House for consideration of private members' legislation is limited, there is always great pressure on the time available for the discussion of Bills introduced by backbench members. Priority in the use of this time is established by a ballot drawn on the second Thursday the House sits in each session. The 20 members who are successful in this stand at the front of the queue to introduce private members' legislation. The ballot therefore establishes an order of priority enabling those successful in it to use the limited private members' time for debate of their Bills which, given the Government's control of the parliamentary timetable, might otherwise not make progress. The ten members placed highest in the ballot may claim some of the expenses incurred in drafting their Bills.

The Ten Minute Rule

Bills introduced under the Ten Minute Rule are not in general serious attempts at legislation. The procedure is mainly used as a means of drawing attention to a particular subject or testing parliamentary opinion on a subject. Members wishing to present a Ten Minute Rule Bill must give notice of a motion for leave to bring in a Bill at 10am every Tuesday and Wednesday, for a Tuesday or Wednesday three weeks ahead. The member may speak briefly in support of the Bill and an opponent may reply. The House may then decide on whether the Bill should be introduced. Upon occasion such Bills do become law through general consent, though there is rarely time for debate after the introduction.

Standing Order No 39

Standing Order No 39 allows every member the right to introduce a Bill after due notice. The Bills introduced under this procedure cannot be high on the list on Second Reading Fridays and there is little practical likelihood of their being debated, unless the Government makes time available on other days in the week. However, Bills which are totally non-controversial are sometimes introduced under this system, and these have occasionally passed into law.

Proceeding on Private Members' Bills

Standing Order No 6 relating to the precedence of Government business lays down that ten Fridays be set aside for Private Members' Bills and ten Fridays for private members' motions. Time for debate on Private Members' Bills is therefore severely restricted. Members may nominate a day for the Second Reading of their Bill, and it is obviously to the advantage of the member drawn first in the ballot to nominate the first Friday available, for the second member to nominate the second Friday, and so forth. But on only six Fridays is precedence given to Second Readings. Since debate on an important or contentious Bill can be expected to last for nearly the whole of the short Friday session, not all, even of the ballot Bills, will be debated. On the remaining four Fridays, precedence is given to the later stages of those Bills which received their Second Readings earlier in the session.

A member who is low down in the ballot may nevertheless succeed. If he puts his Bill down for the first Friday, for example, he may hope for two courses of action. Firstly, if the Bill named first is not particularly controversial, and few members wish to speak on it, he may hope to get a debate during part of the time available. Otherwise he may hope to have his Bill given a Second Reading without debate at 2.30pm, when the Clerk reads out the titles of Bills which are on the order paper, in their order of precedence. But if a member should shout 'object', the Bill is not given a Second Reading and the member in charge of the Bill must nominate another day, failing which the Bill is regarded as dropped. A Bill whose sponsoring member is placed very low in the ballot, or one introduced under the Ten Minute Rule or Standing Order 39, is bound to have to take its chance at 2.30pm. It follows that such a Bill is very unlikely to make any further progress unless its contents are such as to arouse absolutely no dissent. A Bill that gets read a second time on a Friday will usually then be committed to a Standing Committee, but it may go to Committee of the Whole House if the member so moves after Second Reading. There is a single Standing Committee for all Private Members' Bills (except Scottish Bills) which have been read a second time. The same queuing system applies here as at the other stages, and this is a substantial impediment to the passage of Bills, particularly long and complex ones.

Another impediment to a Bill getting a Second Reading or negotiating its Report Stage in time is the necessity to secure the closure. Many Private Members' Bills are 'talked out'; in other words, the debate on them has not been concluded when the available time is exhausted. This occurs more frequently than is the case with Government Bills, not only because less time is available, but also because the 'guillotine' (ie a time allocation order whereby debate on a particular matter can be brought to a close once the time limit is reached) is not used on Private Members' Bills. If opponents of the Bill, therefore, are still speaking just before 2.30pm, its sponsor or a colleague must seek to move 'that the question be now put', otherwise the debate would be interrupted and stand adjourned without the question having been put. The Chair will not permit the closure to be moved if insufficient debate has taken place. In addition a motion of closure requires the support of 100 votes if it is to be carried, and this is difficult to achieve on a Friday, when attendance at the House is low.

Private Members' Bills cover a variety of subjects, often controversial matters of social reform such as divorce, abortion and homosexuality, for which the Government has no time, or is disinclined to introduce itself because of adverse public opinion. A private member may not propose a Bill the main object of which is the creation of a charge on the public revenue.

All members of the House of Lords are free to introduce Bills into the House, and there is sufficient time for them to be debated. But it may be difficult to find time for such Bills to be considered in the House of Commons.

The success of Private Members' Bills

Session	Number of Private Members' Bills becoming law	Number unsuccessful
1974 (short session)	7	32
1974–75	10	76
1975–76	16	69
1976–77	11	78
1977–78	11	78
1978–79 (short session)	3	55
1979–80 (long session)	10	115
1980–81	14	64

1981–82	8	72
1982–83 (short session)	10	71
1983–84 (long session)	13	105
1984–85	21	76
1985–86	21	91
1986–87 (short session)	15	70
1987–88 (long session)	13	106
1988–89	9	132

The numbers include all Bills originating in the Commons or brought from the Lords, but exclude Lords Bills which did not reach the Commons. Unsuccessful motions to bring in Bills under the Ten Minute Rule are also excluded.

Private Bill procedure

A Private Bill is a Bill seeking to alter the law relating to a particular locality (Local Bill) or seeking to confer rights on or absolve from liability a particular person or body of persons (Personal Bill). The procedure for private legislation is regulated by Standing Orders of each House relating to private business. They are initiated by petition from persons or bodies (promoters) outside Parliament. The Standing Orders require that full notice shall be given to persons and bodies where legal rights may be affected by the proposed legislation, so that they may, if necessary, oppose it. In the House of Commons the Bill is introduced by being presented at the table by the clerk of the Private Bill office. It is then deemed to have been read for a first time. At the Second Reading debate, the House determines whether, assuming the facts stated in the preamble to the Bill to be true, the Bill is unobjectionable from the point of view of national policy. If read a second time, the Bill is committed to a committee of four members in the Commons (or five members in the Lords).

The Committee stage of a Private Bill has some of the features of a quasi-judicial proceeding. The promoters and the opponents of the Bill are often represented by counsel and may call evidence. The Committee first considers the preamble of the Bill. If the preamble is accepted the clauses are then considered and may be amended. If the preamble is rejected the Bill falls. After Committee stage the Bill is reported to the House. It then follows a procedure similar to that of a Public Bill.

Hybrid Bill procedure

The Standing Orders for private business apply to a hybrid Bill so that, if opposed after its Second Reading, it goes before a Select Committee where those whose legal rights are affected by the Bill may raise their objections and petition against it. After the petitioners have been heard by the Select Committee, the Bill then passes through its Committee stage and later stages as if it were an ordinary Bill.

8.4 Opportunities for debate in the House of Commons

Apart from the opportunities for debate during the legislative process, there are various other opportunities for debate in the House of Commons.

Adjournment Debates

At the end of every day's business, when the adjournment of the House is formally moved, half an hour is made available for a private member to raise a topic in debate and for a ministerial reply to be given. Members with topics they want debated enter a ballot. The ballot determines what the topic is going to be on Monday, Tuesday, Wednesday and Friday. For Thursday the Speaker selects one of the submitted topics. Usually, Adjournment Debates are on some matter of local interest, so the debates tend to be constituency orientated. Often, if a member is dissatisfied with an answer he has received in correspondence with a minister or in answer to a parliamentary question, he may raise the matter 'on the adjournment'. However Adjournment Debates usually take place in an almost empty House and at an inconvenient time for press coverage. Such debates are not followed by a vote of the House.

Standing Order No 10 – motion to adjourn

Standing Order No 10 allows members to suggest that a specific and important matter should have urgent consideration and that an emergency debate be held upon it. It is for the Speaker to decide whether the matter is sufficiently important and urgent to warrant giving it precedence; the Chair in general gives leave very seldom. If leave is granted, and if the motion is approved by the House or supported by 40 members, the motion will be debated either that evening or the following day.

Recent topics where leave has been given include the invasion of Grenada and policing operations connected with the coal mining dispute.

The final day before each of the four parliamentary recesses is also devoted to a series of private members' debates and ten Fridays per session are also set aside for private member motions. Other opportunities for debate occur in the debate on the address in reply to the Queen's Speech, the debate on the Budget, debates on motions of censure, the 19 Opposition Days, the three Estimate Days and on the Second Reading of Consolidated Fund Bills.

Devices for curtailing debate

Delay of Bills in the House of Commons is a threat to the Government's legislative programme. The more time which one Bill takes, the less time is available for other legislation, and a Government with a heavy legislative programme may find its plans frustrated by the Opposition or individual members seeking to prolong proceedings.

To overcome this threat, various methods of curtailing debate have been adopted by the House.

Standing Order 22

The Speaker or chairman may require a member to discontinue his speech if he persists in irrelevance or tedious repetition.

The closure

Under Standing Order 30 any member, either in the House or in Committee, may move 'that the question be now put'. If the chairman finds the application in order the closure motion must be put forthwith and voted upon without debate. Not fewer than 100 members must vote for the motion. If carried the debate ceases and the motion under discussion must be voted upon.

The kangaroo

This is the power of the Speaker at the Report stage (or the chairman at the Committee stage) to select from among the various proposed amendments those which are to be discussed.

The guillotine motion

The term 'guillotine motion' is a colloquial expression for an allocation of time motion. The purpose of such a motion is to provide that one or more stages of a Bill be disposed of either by a fixed date, or by a fixed number of sittings of the House, or a committee, or both. Each guillotine motion is specific, and devised by the Government for the particular Bill or Bills to which it applies. The guillotine motion may be debated for no more than three hours. If a Bill before a Standing Committee is the subject of an allocation of time order, a detailed timetable is recommended to the Standing Committee. Some or all of the details of the timetable may be prescribed in the allocation of time order itself, or left to the Business Committee to recommend.

The Business Committee, set up under Standing Order No 45, consists of the Chairman of Ways and Means (the Deputy Speaker) who acts as chairman, and no more than eight MPs nominated by the Speaker in respect of each Bill. The function of the committee is to divide the Bill into various parts and allot time to each part. The effect of the order is that at the end of each allotted period the part of the Bill in question is voted upon forthwith, although substantial parts of the Bill may not yet have been discussed at all.

The guillotine is not lightly used and is not applied without reason, for instance, in the face of delaying tactics amounting to obstruction. In other cases the guillotine could not be applied because the Government could not be sure of carrying the necessary motion.

On the whole, these devices are unpopular with parliamentarians because they can restrict valuable criticism and amendment of legislation. If used extensively –

and they are being used increasingly – it can be argued that they deny the legislative role of Parliament.

8.5 Parliamentary questions

Since the late seventeenth century it has been the practice to question ministers in Parliament. There are three categories of question:

1. Question for oral answer which is intended to be given an oral answer in the House during Question Time.
2. Private notice question which can be asked if the Speaker judges its subject matter to be urgent and important. These are taken orally in the House at the end of Question Time.
3. Question for written answer, which is not taken orally in the House but is printed in the Official Report (Hansard).

Parliamentary question procedure

The process for asking a question in the Chamber is fairly lengthy. The member must first give notice of his question by handing it to the clerks in the Table Office not more than ten sitting days and not less than two sitting days before it is to be asked. The question, either seeking information or pressing for action, must be addressed to a specific minister and must concern a matter for which he is responsible as a minister. A question addressed to the wrong minister may be transferred to the minister actually responsible. Ministers are questioned on a rota basis, each department being allocated particular days of the week. The Prime Minister answers questions every Tuesday and Thursday from 3.15 to 3.30pm. No member may ask more than eight questions in every ten sitting days, with a maximum of two questions on any one day. Only one question may be put to each minister on any day. Answers to questions are drafted in the appropriate department. They provide not only an answer for the particular question asked, but also prepare sufficient background material to enable the minister to deal with any supplementary questions that may be asked. Ministers may refuse to answer questions affecting State security, or which touch on matters which are sub judice.

Procedure at Question Time

Question Time takes place on Monday, Tuesday, Wednesday and Thursday, after prayers from 2.35 to 3.30pm. The Speaker calls the member whose question stands first on the Order Paper. The minister reads out his prepared answer. Supplementary questions may then be asked which must relate to the original question. These will be unscripted and contain an element of surprise. When the

Speaker considers that enough supplementaries have been asked he calls question number two on the Order Paper, and so on until the time allocated to questions has expired. Any oral questions which have not been answered by then will receive a written answer printed in the next issue of Hansard.

Private notice questions

Questions concerning sudden emergencies or developments which require immediate attention may be raised with the appropriate minister by means of the private notice question. To ask a question by private notice, a member must apply to the Speaker before 12 noon on the day on which an answer is required. Private notice is given to the minister concerned and his department is immediately informed. Besides being subject to the same rules as to form and content as ordinary questions, a private notice question must satisfy two additional criteria – it must be urgent, and it must be of public importance. If the Speaker allows a private notice question it will be answered immediately after Question Time.

Questions for written answer

There is no limit to the number of questions for written answer which may be tabled and these form the majority of questions answered in each session. Written questions are subject to the same rules of order as oral questions. Usually written questions are answered within seven days of being tabled. If an earlier answer is required a priority written answer may be requested provided a minimum of two sitting days notice is given.

The statistics for the 1985–86 session (which was of average duration) provide a good indication of the volume of parliamentary questions to ministers:

Number given an oral answer – 2,480

Number put down for an oral answer receiving a written answer – 14,852

Number put down for a written answer – 31,718

Private notice questions (excluding the weekly business question) – 43

The effectiveness of Question Time as a device for achieving parliamentary control of the Executive

Generally, the private member is no match for the minister with his Civil Service brief. When a parliamentary question is submitted it is passed immediately to the relevant Government department, and the officials in that department will give priority to preparing a brief for the minister enabling him to answer not only that question, but also any supplementary questions that the officials anticipate. The department knows by whom the question is asked, and in preparing the brief will bear in mind the interest and concerns of the questioner and other MPs who are similarly interested and likely to put supplementary questions.

The Opposition parties ask more questions than the Government party but because there are more Government backbenchers they may catch the Speaker's eye and ask more supplementary questions. Some questions are 'arranged' by the Government so that it can publicise or emphasise a particular matter, especially Government success.

No direct sanction is involved when a minister is asked a question. Nevertheless it may get a matter publicised. Prime Minister's Question Time is usually broadcast live.

Government policy is not often changed by a question but it can be pushed faster in a particular direction. Questions very often uncover some administrative flaw and secure a remedy because of the publicity given the matter.

Ministers rarely gain or lose in reputation at Question Time. Most of them can cope quite satisfactorily with it having risen through the House themselves. Often a minister will deal with a question simply by a party gibe, stonewalling or evasion.

The effectiveness of Question Time as a method of securing control of the Executive by Parliament is limited. This is due in part to the vast library and research facilities available to the minister through his department. In contrast the private member has comparatively small library facilities available. The private member may also be unsuccessful in securing the information he requires from the department, and indeed, the reticence of the department in giving information may mean that he is not even aware of difficult and pertinent questions which he could and should be asking.

8.6 Parliamentary committees

The committees of the House of Commons fall into two main categories:

1. Standing Committees.
2. Select Committees.

Standing Committees

These are responsible for the Committee stage in the passing of Bills. They consist of between 16 and 50 members nominated by a Committee of Selection, and reflect party strength in the House. Standing Committees are constituted to deal with Bills as and when necessary; there have been up to ten sitting at one time. They are designated by letters: eg Standing Committee A, Standing Committee B. In addition there are a Scottish Grand Committee, a Welsh Grand Committee and a Northern Ireland Committee. Occasionally a Bill may be considered by a Committee of the Whole House, when the entire House sits to take the Committee stage. In general this procedure is used for Bills of constitutional importance, those requiring a very rapid passage, and certain financial matters.

Select Committees

Select Committees of the House of Commons can be sub-divided into three main categories:

1. Ad hoc Select Committees.
2. Sessional Select Committees.
3. Departmental Select Committees.

Ad hoc Select Committees

Ad hoc Select Committees are set up for a specific purpose when the need arises. Their inquiries are specified and limited in their extent and they are dissolved when their inquiries are concluded. They are employed less frequently than in the past. Today the device of a Royal Commission, a department committee of inquiry, or a judicial inquiry is more common.

Sessional Select Committees

Sessional Select Committees are those set up at the beginning of the session and remaining throughout the session. They comprise those committees concerned with the domestic running of the House and members, and those concerned with the scrutiny of some aspects of Government activity. The latter have been largely superseded by the Departmental Select Committees. The following Select Committees and sub-committees currently exist:

1. European Legislation
2. Liaison
3. Members' Interests
4. Parliamentary Commissioner for Administration
5. Privileges
6. Procedure
7. Public Accounts (see below)
8. Sound Broadcasting
9. Statutory Instruments (Select Committees)
10. House of Commons (Services)
    a) Accommodation and Administration Sub-Committee.
    b) Catering Sub-Committee.
    c) Computer Sub-Committee.
    d) Library Sub-Committee.
    e) New Building Sub-Committee.
11. Consolidation Bills (Joint Committee)
12. Statutory Instruments (Joint Committee).

(Joint Committees are Select Committees whose membership is drawn from both Houses of Parliament and they are set up to consider matters of concern to both Houses.)

The Public Accounts Committee. The Public Accounts Committee was established in 1861 and has been reappointed annually since then. It has 15 members, all backbenchers selected so as to represent the composition of the House. The chairman is always a member of the Opposition, usually with ministerial experience in finance. The committee is generally regarded as one of the most successful Select Committees. It is concerned with accounts of money already spent, not with estimates of proposed expenditure. Its brief is to see that public money has been spent economically, and not wastefully. It has the power, under Standing Orders, to call for papers and civil servants and ministers for questioning. It reports to the Treasury and to the department concerned, as well as to Parliament. One day a session is reserved for debating the reports of the Public Accounts Committee. Parliamentary questions may also be asked as a result of the committee's reports. The knowledge of the existence of the Public Accounts Committee undoubtedly has an effect on checking wasteful expenditure by Government departments.

Departmental Select Committees

On 25 June 1979 the House of Commons considered several motions relating to the structure and scope of its own Select Committee system, based upon proposals for reform contained in the first report from the Select Committee on Procedure, Session 1977–78. After debate, the House approved a package of reforms amounting to the establishment of a system of new Departmental Committees to replace the rather ad hoc system which had been developing piecemeal since the 1960s. The reform left untouched many of the then existing committees (see above), but those which closely resembled the new departmentally based committees were abolished so as to avoid confusion, duplication of effort and unnecessary cost. Prior to the General Election of April 1992, the organisation of committees was set out as below:

Government Departments and the Committees

	Name of committee	Principal Government department(s) of members concerned	Maximum number	Quorum
1.	Agriculture	Ministry of Agriculture, Fisheries and Food	11	3
2.	Defence	Ministry of Defence	11	3
3.	Education, Science and Arts	Department of Education and Science Office of Arts and Libraries	11	3
4.	Employment	Department of Employment	11	3
5.	Energy	Department of Energy	11	3
6.	Environment	Department of the Environment	11	3

7.	Foreign affairs	Foreign and Commonwealth Office	11	3
8.	Home affairs	Home Office	11	3
9.	Scottish affairs	Scottish Office	13	5
10.	Social Services	Department of Health and Social Security	11	3
11.	Trade and Industry	Department of Trade and Industry	11	3
12.	Transport	Department of Transport	11	3
13.	Treasury and Civil Service	Treasury, including former Civil Service department functions, Board of Inland Revenue, Board of Customs and Excise	11	3
14.	Welsh affairs	Welsh Office	11	3

Sub-committees. The Foreign Affairs Committee, the Home Affairs Committee and the Treasury and Civil Service Committee each have the power to appoint one sub-committee. The sub-committees are styled the Overseas Development, Race Relations and Immigration, and Treasury and Civil Service Sub-Committees respectively.

Scope of enquiries. The committees are appointed to examine the expenditure, administration and policy of the principal Government departments and associated public bodies.

Mr Norman St John-Stevas, the then Leader of the House, explained this as follows:

'The objective of the new committee structure will be to strengthen the accountability of Ministers to the House for the discharge of their responsibilities. Each Committee will be able to examine the whole range of activity for which its Minister or Ministers have direct responsibility. The Government also accepts the Procedure Committee's view that the Committees must be able to look at the activities of some public bodies that exercise authority of their own and over which Ministers do not have the same direct authority as they have over their own Departments. The test in every case will be whether there is a significant degree of ministerial responsibility for the body concerned.' (H C Deb, Vol 969 c44, 25 June 1979.)

The committees were not to concern themselves with draft legislation or Bills. They are empowered to take evidence and issue reports, but they may not amend a Bill as though they were one of the rare Select Committees to which a Bill is occasionally committed in preference to the more usual Standing Committee. However, in the 1980–81 Sessional, Special Standing Committees were set up on an experimental basis to provide such an opportunity and have been reinstituted from time to time since then.

Membership and chairman. The maximum membership for each committee is laid down in Standing Orders. Members are nominated or discharged on a motion tabled by the Committee of Selection. This replaces the previous system where members were nominated on a motion tabled by the Government Whips after consultation with other parties and interested members. The field from which the membership is drawn is limited by convention. The Committee of Selection does not nominate members of the Government, parliamentary private secretaries or regular Opposition front bench spokesmen. Once nominated, members normally serve for the life of a Parliament. But a member of a Select Committee who is made a minister, parliamentary private secretary, or an Opposition front bench spokesman, is discharged. Chairmen of Committees are chosen from the membership of each committee and it is a tradition of the House that they sometimes come from Opposition parties.

Liaison Committee. The Liaison Committee is a Select Committee appointed to co-ordinate the work of committees, to consider general matters relating to the work of Select Committees, and to give such advice relating to their work as may be sought by the House of Commons Commission. The committee has the power to send for persons, papers and records and may report from time to time to the House.

Staff and specialist advisers. The House of Commons Commission is responsible for the provision of adequate support staff for committee work. Under Standing Order No 99, each committee has the power to appoint persons with technical knowledge either to supply information which is not readily available, or to elucidate matters of complexity within the committee's order of reference.

The numbers and distribution of these specialist advisers vary according to the needs of each committee and the particular inquiry undertaken, but it has become possible for a pool of expertise to be permanently available, unlike the old system where advisers were appointed only for specific inquiries. Most committees have appointed specialist advisers, and also full-time researchers known as Select Committee temporary assistants.

Powers. Under the terms of the motion approved on 25 June 1979 the Departmental Select Committees have the following powers:

1. To send for persons, papers and records, to sit notwithstanding any adjournments of the House, to adjourn from place to place and to report from time to time. The refusal of the two sons of the late Robert Maxwell to answer questions put by members of the select committee on social security was referred

to the House of Commons as a possible contempt. The Maxwell brothers, who initially refused to attend, claimed privilege against self-incrimination (14 January 1992).

2. To appoint persons with technical knowledge either to supply information which is not readily available or to elucidate matters of complexity within the committee's order of reference.

3. To report from time to time the minutes of evidence taken before sub-committees; and the sub-committees appointed under this Order shall have power to send for persons, papers and records, to sit notwithstanding any adjournment of the House, and to adjourn from place to place, and shall have a quorum of three.

These powers are essentially the same as those granted to the old Select Committees. In its report, the Procedure Committee had suggested stronger powers, particularly to order the attendance of ministers:

'(64) Select Committees should be empowered to order the attendance of Ministers to give evidence to them ... and to order the production of papers and records by Ministers, including Secretaries of State (65). In the event of a refusal by a Minister to produce papers and records required by a Select Committee the Committee should be empowered to claim procedure over public business for a debate on a Motion for an Address or for an Order for the Return of the Papers, unless time is provided by the Government by the sixth sitting day after the first appearance of the Motion ...'

The Government raised three main objections to these proposed powers:

1. It was not appropriate for a Select Committee to order about members of the House. Only the House as a whole had such a constitutional power.

2. It was not appropriate for the committee to have procedure for a debate unless it was shown that the matter was one of general concern to the House as a whole.

3. The whole question was one of judgment sometimes involving public interest and not amenable to hard and fast rules.

The Leader of the House declared:

'I give the House the pledge on the part of the Government that every Minister from the most senior Cabinet Minister to the most junior Under Secretary will do all in his or her power to co-operate with the new system of Committees and to make it a success. I believe that declaration of interest to be a better guarantee than formal provisions laid down in Standing Orders.'

Certain Select Committees were granted an increase in their powers following the second Report of the House of Commons Select Committee on Procedure (Cmnd 1532). The Home Affairs Select Committee has been given power to examine the work and spending of the Lord Chancellor's Department, the Attorney-General's Office, the Treasury Solicitor's Department, the Crown Prosecution Service and the Serious Fraud Office. The committee will be allowed to examine the judicial appointments system but not individual judicial appointments. It will not have power to consider court cases or the confidential advice given by the Law Officers to the Crown. The Education, Science and Arts Select Committee has been enlarged from 11 to 13 MPs, with power to appoint a sub-committee to examine science and technology issues.

In a report from the Commons Select Committee on MPs' Interests (HMSO, March 1991) it was advised that chairmen of Select Committees should give up all outside business interests which might conflict with their committee duties. Further, no committee member should have a client relationship with the Government department being scrutinised by his committee.

Reports. Departmental Committees have the power to report to the House. Standing Order No 81 provides:

> 'Every Select Committee having power to send for persons, papers, and records shall have leave to report to the House their opinion and observations upon any matter referred to them for their consideration, together with the minutes of the evidence taken before them, and also to make a special report of any matters which they may think fit to bring to the notice of the House.'

There is no specific provision for debating such reports. The suggestion of the Procedure Committee that eight 'Select Committee Mondays' be set aside in each session for such debates was not taken up by the Government, but the Leader of the House did declare the Government's intentions to give substantially increased priority to such debates.

Limitations of the present Select Committee system

There is still no effective sanction available against a minister who refuses to appear, or refuses to allow civil servants to appear, before a Select Committee to give evidence. Ministers have sometimes refused to appear or to answer certain questions.

In the past Select Committees, partly because of inadequate funding, have enlisted the assistance of too few 'support' staff, such as secretarial staff, researchers and technical experts, and their inquiries and reports have not been as penetrating as they could have been. MPs themselves also have limited time available for committee work.

There is still no guaranteed time set aside for debating Committee reports (other than those of the Public Accounts Committee).

Although the House of Commons Committee of Selection formally makes appointments to the committees, the party Whips have considerable influence over who is chosen. This enables the front bench of a party to exclude from a committee any MP who is likely to act in committee in a way contrary to the policy of the front bench. Thus the Government may attempt to exclude from a committee MPs of its own party who are likely to join with those from the Opposition to produce a report highly critical of the Government. Nevertheless, reports critical of the Government are produced, but this 'packing' of committees by the party Whips clearly reduces the potential effectiveness of Select Committees as a device for exercising control over the Government.

The advice and criticism of a non-partisan committee will never have great influence in British politics while there continues to be among MPs, particularly those on the front benches, such a strong belief in the notion and practice of party Government, with a single party having the right to formulate policy.

The Select Committees should not be dismissed as completely ineffectual in putting pressure on the Government. Some commentators have seen in their increased use the key to a more effective role for Parliament vis-à-vis Government, and see Select Committees as a device for reasserting parliamentary control over the Executive. The more cautious saw Select Committees as generators of advice and information which would have some influence because of their non-partisan nature. In this respect committees have been remarkably successful in producing 'non-partisan' reports rather than dividing down party lines and producing a majority report by the Government party and a minority report by the other parties.

8.7 Parliamentary control of national finance

Introduction

Parliamentary control of national finance has two aspects. The first is control over Government expenditure. The second is control over the raising of revenue by the Government to finance that expenditure. Two principles must be noted:

1. A charge, whether upon the public revenue (expenditure) or upon the people (taxation) does not become valid until authorised by legislation. The latter is provided for in the Bill of Rights 1689 and the former by long standing convention.
2. A charge may not be considered by the Commons unless it is proposed or recommended by the Crown. This financial initiative of the Crown is expressed in a Standing Order of the House of Commons which in part dates from 1713.

Parliamentary control of Government expenditure

As far as parliamentary control over expenditure is concerned supply is granted by Parliament annually in the Appropriation Act. This does not complete its passage through Parliament until July or August, and since the financial year ends on 31 March the Government requires parliamentary authorisation to spend between the two dates. In order to provide this authorisation, one or more Consolidated Fund Acts are passed in the meantime. These include the following items:

The Civil Vote(s) on Account – in effect the giving of permission to the Government to go on spending money from 1 April while Parliament is considering the estimates.

Defence Vote(s) on Account – as above, but authorising spending on defence as opposed to 'civil' matters.

The approval of Supplementary Estimates needed to cover any deficits in the financial year about to end.

Excess votes to cover deficits in the previous financial year, not the one just ending but the one before that.

The Appropriation Act, passed in July or August, grants the remainder of the money requested for the current year. It also appropriates all the sums involved to their specific purposes, hence its name.

Financial procedures of the House

There were four main changes implemented in the 1982–83 Session resulting from the first report of the Select Committee on Procedure (Supply).

1. There are now three annual 'estimate days' devoted to consideration of the main and supplementary estimates. For the first time the House of Commons is able to debate and vote on the details of public expenditure. The Select Committee had recommended eight days for the purpose, but the Government was able to persuade the House that three would be adequate, subject to reviews once the scheme was in operation.
2. The Second Reading debates on Consolidated Fund Bills are replaced by adjournment debates, set aside for private members. The Second Reading of the Consolidated Fund Bill was a pure formality, so now the remaining time is given over to private members.
3. 'Supply days', previously taking 29 parliamentary days, are replaced by 20 'Opposition days'. Seventeen of these days are at the disposal of the Leader of the Opposition, and matters selected by him take precedence over Government business. The three remaining days are allotted to the leader of the second largest Opposition party, which is defined as the party of those not represented in the Government which has the second largest number of members elected to the House as members of that party.
4. To ensure that the Opposition does not lose ten days in that change, various regular items of business, traditionally taken as Supply time, are transferred to Government time.

These changes are a step towards recognising, as the Select Committee put it, that 'the House's financial procedures are antiquated and defective and need a thorough overhaul'. See further the effect of the National Audit Act 1983, considered below.

The role of Select Committees in checking expenditure

The Expenditure Committee (disbanded in 1979), like the Estimates Committee before it, used to examine the estimates of proposed Government spending. On two days in the parliamentary year, time was guaranteed in the Commons for debating the reports of this committee and its sub-committees. However, since the setting up of the new Specialist Select Committee system in 1979, Government estimates have been laid before the appropriate committee according to department. But there is no time guaranteed for the House to debate the reports of these committees, and certainly not before it has to vote the authorisation of the expenditure proposed. The degree of control exercised by these committees over Government expenditure must therefore be regarded as quite limited.

National Audit Act 1983

This Act is intended to strengthen parliamentary control and supervision of expenditure of public money by making new provision for the appointment and status of the Comptroller and Auditor General, establishing a Public Accounts Commission and a National Audit Office, and making new provision for promoting economy, efficiency and effectiveness in the use of public money by Government departments and other authorities and bodies.

Section 1 of the Act provides for the appointment of the Comptroller and Auditor General to be by the Prime Minister acting with the agreement of the chairman of the Committee of Public Accounts. The Comptroller and Auditor General shall by virtue of his office be an officer of the House of Commons. He shall have complete discretion in the discharge of his functions and as to the manner in which any examinations are carried out. But in determining whether to carry out any such examinations, he shall take into account any proposals made by the Committee of Public Accounts.

Section 2 creates the Public Accounts Commission consisting of the chairman of the Committee of Public Accounts, the Leader of the House of Commons, and seven other members of the House of Commons appointed by the House, none of whom shall be a minister of the Crown.

Section 3 sets up a National Audit Office consisting of the Comptroller and Auditor General and his staff.

Section 6 provides that the Comptroller and Auditor General may carry out examinations into the economy, efficiency and effectiveness with which any department, authority or other body to which the section applies has used its resources in discharging its functions. He may not question the merits of the policy objectives of any department, authority or body in respect of which an examination is carried out.

Section 7 provides that if the Comptroller and Auditor General has reasonable cause to believe that any authority or body to which the section applies has in any of its financial years received more than half its income from public funds, he may carry out an examination into the economy, efficiency and effectiveness with which it has in that year used its resources in discharging its functions. Again, he may not question the merits of policy objectives. Section 7 applies to any authority or body appointed, or whose members are required to be appointed, by or on behalf of the Crown, except a body specified in Schedule 4 to the Act. Schedule 4 lists certain bodies that would have fallen within the section and has the effect of excluding the nationalised industries.

Section 8 provides that the Comptroller and Auditor General shall have a right of access to all such documents as he may reasonably require for carrying out any examinations under s6 or s7, and shall be entitled to require from any person holding or accountable for any such document such information and explanation as are reasonably necessary for that purpose.

Section 9 provides that the Comptroller and Auditor General may report to the House of Commons the results of any examination carried out by him under s6 or s7.

Control over taxation

In April the Government indicates how it will raise money in the Budget which sets out proposed rates of income tax and customs and excise duties. These Government proposals are given immediate effect by resolutions of the House of Commons; the Provisional Collection of Taxes Acts 1913–68 permits the collection of taxes up to 5 August on the strength of what is proposed in the Budget resolutions. The resolutions are then incorporated into a Finance Bill which from April to July goes through the normal procedure for legislation. Obviously the Committee stage of this Bill is a detailed consideration of finance and a job for experts. Since 1968 the Committee stage has been divided between the whole House and a standing committee of 50 which is staffed by MPs with financial skills. The end result is the annual Finance Act which must be passed by 5 August.

8.8 Introduction to parliamentary privilege

Parliamentary privilege is part of the law and custom of Parliament. It allows Parliament to conduct its affairs without improper interference by the Sovereign, the courts or other bodies or persons outside Parliament. Privilege, unless created by statute, forms part of the common law. It is defined in Erskine May as:

> ' ... the sum of the peculiar rights enjoyed by each House collectively as a constitutional part of the High Court of Parliament and by members of each House individually, without which they could not discharge their functions, and which exceed those possessed by other bodies or individuals.'

8.9 Privileges of the House of Commons

At the opening of each Parliament, the Speaker formally claims from the Crown for the Commons 'their ancient and undoubted rights and privileges'. These are:

1. Freedom of speech in debate.
2. Freedom from arrest.
3. Freedom of access to Her Majesty whenever occasion shall require; and that the most favourable construction should be placed upon all their proceedings.

The other privileges of the House of Commons, not expressly claimed by the Speaker, include:

1. The right of the House to regulate its own composition.
2. The right to take exclusive cognisance of matters arising within the precincts of the House.
3. The right to punish both members and non-members for breach of privilege and contempt.
4. The right of impeachment.

Freedom of speech

The right is guaranteed by Article 9 of the Bill of Rights 1689 which provides:

> '... the freedom of speech and debates or proceedings in Parliament ought not to be impeached or questioned in any court or place out of Parliament.'

The effect of Article 9 is that no member may be made the subject of an action in the courts on the basis of statements made in the course of parliamentary proceedings. The rationale for the privilege is that members should not be inhibited in representing their constituents, challenging the executive, or discharging their legislative functions by the threat of possible legal action. If a member is sued for defamation in respect of something said during the course of parliamentary proceedings, the writ should be struck out as disclosing no cause of action. Were the matter to come to trial the court would presumably hold that the defendant's comments were protected by absolute privilege. The privilege avails a member of Parliament whether he is defending proceedings for defamation or initiating them. In *Prebble* v *Television New Zealand Ltd* [1994] 3 WLR 970 the defendant television company broadcast a programme in which allegations were made of impropriety on the part of the Labour government. The plaintiff, the minister for state-owned enterprises, alleged that the programme had defamed him by implying, inter alia, that he had misled the House of Representatives concerning the government's policy on the sale of state-owned industries. The defence contended that either the programme had not conveyed any defamatory meaning, or to the extent that it had its contents were true. At first instance those elements of the defence statements that sought to rely on statements made in proceedings in Parliament in order to refute the plaintiff's claim were struck out, on the basis that reliance on them infringed Article 9 of the Bill of Rights 1689. The decision was upheld by the Court of Appeal, but in addition a majority of the court held that the plaintiff's action should be stayed unless and until privilege in respect of the statements relied upon was waived by the House of Representatives. The Privileges Committee of the House of Representatives had concluded that it did not have the power to waive the privilege. The plaintiff appealed to the Privy Council against the stay of his action, and the defendants sought to appeal against the upholding of the first-instance decision to strike out parts of the defence submission. The Privy Council, allowing the plaintiff's appeal, and dismissing the defendants', held that the fact that the person making the impugned statement in Parliament was also the initiator of the legal proceedings did not justify any departure from the principle enshrined in Article 9 of the Bill of Rights 1689. The privilege in question belonged to Parliament, not to individual members. Whether or not a member had misled Parliament was a matter to be dealt with by Parliament and fell outside the jurisdiction of the courts. If the defendants had intended to adduce evidence of proceedings in Parliament simply to prove what had been said or decided, there would have been no objection. In the instant case, however, the defendants sought to adduce the evidence in order to prove that the House had been misled. The Privy Council accepted that there might be cases where justice demanded a stay of proceedings, where for example the majority of the evidence relied upon by the defendant was protected by privilege and it would be impossible for him to defend a libel action unless that privilege was waived. Failure to grant a stay in such cases could result in a significant restriction on the freedom of the press to comment on political affairs. The present case did not fall within that category, however. The majority of the statements relied upon by the defence were not protected by privilege and it was not unjust in the circumstances to allow the action to proceed.

Even where an action in defamation is brought against a member of Parliament in respect of statements made other than in parliamentary proceedings, the action cannot normally be supported by reference to other non-defamatory statements made in the course of parliamentary proceedings. In *Church of Scientology* v *Johnson-Smith* [1972] 1 QB 522, where the defendant MP, who was being sued for a libel in respect of comments alleged to have been made during a television interview, raised the defence of fair comment, it was held that the plaintiffs, who needed to prove malice on the defendant's part, could not use speeches made by the defendant in the House of Commons as evidence to substantiate their allegation of malice.

The House of Lords has stressed that the ruling in *Pepper (Inspector of Taxes)* v *Hart* [1993] 1 All ER 42, to the effect that extracts from Hansard can be cited to assist a court in interpreting legislation, should not be seen as undermining the parliamentary privilege enshrined in Article 9. Lord Browne-Wilkinson expressed the view of the majority in observing that there could be sound reasons for departing from the long standing rule that no account should be taken of extracts from Hansard in construing Acts of Parliament, where the legislation in question was ambiguous or obscure, or where adherence to the literal rule produced an absurd result and there was evidence in Hansard that would reveal the mischief aimed at by the legislation, or the very question before the court had been considered in Parliament. It was envisaged that, provided only comments made by a minister or other person promoting a Bill were taken into account under this exception, the courts would be giving effect to Parliament's intentions, rather than undermining the independence of MPs.

Proceedings in Parliament

What are 'proceedings in Parliament'? Remarks made in debate, discussions in committee, parliamentary questions and answers, and votes are clearly within the definition. Other words spoken within the precincts of Parliament unconnected with parliamentary proceedings are not protected.

In *Rivlin* v *Bilainkin* [1953] 1 QB 485 the posting of libellous material in the House of Commons post box to members was held to be insufficient in itself to render the communications the subject of parliamentary privilege.

In between these two situations lies a grey area. In particular, problems have frequently arisen regarding the status of communications between constituents and their MPs and between members and ministers. The leading modern case is that of *G R Strauss* (1957–8).

Strauss, a Labour MP, wrote to the Paymaster-General complaining about the way in which the London Electricity Board disposed of their scrap cable. The Paymaster-General denied responsibility on the ground that the matter concerned day-to-day administration rather than policy, and he passed the letter to the board. The board took exception to Strauss' allegations and threatened to sue him for libel unless he withdrew and apologised. Strauss raised the threat as a question of privilege and the matter was referred to the Committee of Privileges. The committee reported that in writing his letter Strauss was engaged in a proceeding in Parliament for the purposes of Article 9 and that the board, in threatening to sue, were in breach of parliamentary privilege. However when the report of the committee was debated in the House, on a free vote it rejected the findings of the committee. The House resolved that Strauss' letter was not a proceeding in Parliament.

The decision in *Strauss* is not binding on the House in future cases, and the Select Committee on Parliamentary Privilege recommended in 1967 that the decision of the House in *Strauss* should be reversed by legislation. Communications between members and ministers, while not perhaps covered by parliamentary privilege, may however be protected by qualified privilege in the law of defamation.

In *Beach* v *Freeson* [1972] QB 14 qualified privilege was held to attach to the sending of a letter from a member to the Lord Chancellor containing the complaints made by a constituent about the plaintiff's firm of solicitors. The Lord Chancellor's responsibility for the courts and the fact that solicitors are officers of the court were sufficient to bring the case within the general common law rule under which, where both sender and recipient have a special interest, a duty respectively to send and receive the communications, the publication is protected by qualified privilege.

Letters from members of the public to MPs enjoy only qualified privilege.

In *R* v *Rule* [1937] 2 KB 375 qualified privilege was held by the Court of Criminal Appeal to attach to the sending of two letters from a constituent to his MP containing complaints about the conduct of a detective sergeant and a justice of the peace. Lord Hewart CJ said:

> 'A Member of Parliament to whom a written communication is addressed by one of his constituents asking for his assistance in bringing to the notice of the appropriate minister a complaint of improper conduct on the part of some public official acting in that constituency in relation to his offices, has sufficient interest in the subject-matter of the complaint to render the occasion of such publication a privileged occasion.'

In *Rost* v *Edwards* [1990] 2 WLR 1280, the plaintiff, an MP, sued the defendants for libel. He had been the subject of an article in *The Guardian* newspaper which allegedly implied that he had used his membership of the House of Commons Select Committee on Energy to acquire information, which he in turn sold to companies overseas. As a result, so the plaintiff claimed, he had been de-selected from membership of the Standing Committee of the Electricity Privatisation Bill and had not been appointed as Chair of the Energy Select Committee. To support these claims the plaintiff sought to adduce evidence of the appointment procedures of the House of Commons committees. In relation to his failure to register his business interests, the plaintiff further sought to adduce evidence as to the criteria for registration in the Register of Members' Interests and his reasons for non-registration. The question arose during the trial as to whether or not the evidence the plaintiff sought to adduce was inadmissible on the ground that it was protected by parliamentary privilege as it related to proceedings in Parliament. Popplewell J held that the evidence relating to appointments to committees could not be adduced, but that relating to the Register of Members' Interests could.

In the course of his decision Popplewell J expressed some sympathy with the plaintiff's contention that no breach of privilege arose in this case because he sought only to ascertain what had happened in the House of Commons, as opposed to wanting to question the propriety of the proceedings, but felt that the weight of authority prevented him from accepting the submission. In the circumstances the only option open to the plaintiff seeking to adduce such evidence was to petition the House for permission to do so.

In relation to the Register of Members' Interests he observed:

> '... There are clearly cases where Parliament is to be the sole judge of its affairs. Equally there are clear cases where the courts are to have exclusive jurisdiction. In a case which may be described as a grey area a court, while giving full attention to the necessity for comity between the courts and Parliament, should not be astute to find a reason for ousting the jurisdiction of the court and for limiting or even defeating a proper claim by a party to litigation before it. If Parliament wishes to cover a particular area with privilege it has the ability to do so by passing an Act of Parliament giving itself the right to exclusive jurisdiction. Ousting the jurisdiction of the court has always been regarded as requiring the clearest possible words. Nothing in the authorities, as I have indicated, in any way covers the instant situation. It is true that courts have over the years enlarged the

definition of "proceedings" from the formal speeches in the House to other matters, as appears from the various authorities to which I have been referred ... but ... there are plenty of areas which are not covered by "proceedings in Parliament". It is clearly not possible to arrive at an exhaustive definition ... A line has to be drawn somewhere. As Lord Pearce once said: "I do not know, I only feel."

In the result, I conclude that claims for privilege in respect of the Register of Members' Interests does not fall within the definition of "proceedings in Parliament" ...'

The Parliamentary Commissioner Act 1967 s10(5) accords absolute privilege to communications between MPs and the Parliamentary Commissioner for Administration.

Reports of parliamentary proceedings

The House has persistently claimed the right to prevent or limit reporting of its deliberations, but it resolved in 1971 to entertain complaints of breach of privilege or contempt in relation to such reports only where the sitting of the House or committee in question was in private. At common law the fair and accurate reporting of parliamentary debates is protected by qualified privilege (see *Wason* v *Walter* (1869) LR 4 QB 73). This privilege was confirmed by the Court of Appeal in *Cook* v *Alexander* [1974] QB 279, a case which also established qualified privilege for the 'parliamentary sketch' – or summary of debate – so long as it is fair and accurate. This privilege holds notwithstanding notice on the part of a participant in the debate.

Parliamentary papers

The Parliamentary Papers Act 1840 s1 provides that any civil or criminal proceedings arising out of the publication of any papers or reports made by the authority of either House must be stayed on the production of a certificate to that effect from an officer of the House. By s3 of the Act, qualified privilege attaches to fair and accurate extracts from, or abstracts of, papers published under the authority of Parliament.

Freedom from arrest

Immunity from arrest is now of little importance and in 1967 the Committee on Parliamentary Privilege appointed to review the law of parliamentary privilege recommended its abolition. The immunity only applies to civil arrest and extends not only while Parliament sits, but also for 40 days before and after.

In *Stourton* v *Stourton* [1963] P 302, which concerned the Baron and Baroness Mowbray, the Baroness issued a summons for leave to issue a writ of attachment because the Baron was in breach of an order made under s17 of the Married Women's Property Act 1882. Parliament was sitting. Scarman J held that the Baron was protected from arrest by parliamentary privilege because the writ of attachment was to compel performance of acts required by civil process and not for a criminal contempt of court.

The immunity does not protect members from arrest on criminal charges, nor from detention under regulations made under the Defence of the Realm Acts in time of war. In 1940, for example, the Commons Committee of Privileges was of opinion that there had been no breach of privilege when Captain Ramsay, a member, had been detained under regulations made under the Emergency Powers (Defence) Act 1939.

It is a contempt of the House for any person to seek to serve a writ or other legal process upon a member within the precincts of the House.

The right of the House to regulate its own composition

The House used to have the right to determine disputed elections. This is now regulated by statute, the matter being committed to an election court consisting of two judges of the Queen's Bench Division. Subject to provisions applying where the judges disagree, the determination certified by the court 'shall be final to all intents and purposes'. The House of Commons, on being informed by the Speaker of a certificate of the court, shall order it to be entered in their journals and shall give the necessary direction for confirming or altering the return, or for issuing a writ for a new election, or for carrying the determination into execution as the circumstances may require.

The House still retains the exclusive right to determine by resolution when a writ for the holding of a by-election shall be issued. The House also maintains the right to determine whether a member is qualified to sit in the House, and can declare a member's seat vacant on grounds of legal disqualification or for any other reason it thinks fit. Legal disqualification may be determined by an election court or the Judicial Committee of the Privy Council.

The right of the House to expel a member whom it considers unfit to sit has been used sparingly. One example is that of Gary Allighan MP who in 1947 was expelled from the House for contempt. He had falsely alleged that MPs had given details of parliamentary party meetings held within the Palace of Westminster to journalists in return for money or while under the influence of drink. He was himself guilty of this behaviour and his contempt was compounded by his lying to the Committee of Privileges. The House voted to expel him.

The right to take exclusive cognisance of matters arising within the precincts of the House

Proceedings in Parliament cannot be called in question in any court. The House maintains the right to control its own proceedings and regulate its internal affairs without interference from the courts. The leading case is *Bradlaugh* v *Gossett* (1884).

Charles Bradlaugh was elected as Member of Parliament for Northants. He was an atheist and refused to take the oath. Eventually the House allowed him to make an affirmation of allegiance under the Parliamentary Oaths Act 1866, in lieu of taking an oath. A common informer then sued Bradlaugh for penalties on the ground that he did not come within the classes of persons permitted by the statute to affirm instead of taking an oath, and therefore he was not qualified to sit and vote in the House. The court held that Bradlaugh was not entitled to affirm and his seat was declared vacant. He was re-elected and rather than be excluded again he sought to take the oath. The House would not allow him to do so, and in July 1883 they passed a resolution: 'That the Serjeant-at-Arms do exclude Mr Bradlaugh from the House until he shall engage not further to disturb the proceedings of the House.' In August 1881 Bradlaugh tried to enter the House and was forcibly ejected by the Serjeant-at-Arms (Gossett). Bradlaugh claimed an injunction to restrain the Serjeant-at-Arms from excluding him, and a declaration that the resolution was void. The court held that it had no jurisdiction to interfere. As Lord Coleridge CJ observed:

'What is said or done within the walls of Parliament cannot be inquired into in a court of law. On this point all the judges in the two great cases which exhaust the learning on the subject – *Burdett* v *Abbott* 14 East 1, 148 and *Stockdale* v *Hansard* 9 Ad & E 1 – are agreed, and are emphatic. The jurisdiction of the Houses over their own members, their right to impose discipline within their walls, is absolute and exclusive. To use the words of Lord Ellenborough, "They would sink into utter contempt and inefficiency without it" ...'

Stephen J said:

'I think that the House of Commons is not subject to the control of Her Majesty's Courts in its administration of that part of the statute-law which has relation to its own internal proceedings, and that the use of such actual force as may be necessary to carry into effect such a resolution as the one before us is justifiable.

Many authorities might be cited for this principle ... Blackstone says 1 Com 163: "The whole of the law and custom of Parliament has its origin from this one maxim, "that whatever matter arises concerning either House of Parliament ought to be examined, discussed, and adjudged in that House to which it relates, and not elsewhere." '

The court also expressed extreme reluctance in any case to declare a resolution of the House void. The injunction was refused because reasonable force could be used to exclude any person from premises where he would be a trespasser.

If a statute is to bind the House it must do so clearly.

In *R* v *Graham-Campbell, ex parte Herbert* [1935] 1 KB 594, A P Herbert, an Independent MP, applied for summonses against the members of the House of Commons Kitchen Committee for selling drinks in the members' bar without a justices' licence. The Chief Metropolitan Magistrate refused to issue the summonses and the Divisional Court of the King's Bench Division held that he had been right to decline jurisdiction because of parliamentary privilege.

The House does not generally assert jurisdiction over matters arising within its precincts if they have no direct connection with its proceedings. The penal powers of the House are inadequate to deal with ordinary crimes and these are usually left to the criminal courts.

The right to punish for breach of privilege and contempt

The House has the power to maintain its privileges and to punish those who break them or commit contempt of the House. All breaches of privilege are contempts of the House but not all contempts involve the infringement of the privileges of the House. Contempt of the House is a very wide concept. Erskine May describes it as:

> '... any act or omission which obstructs or impedes either House of Parliament in the performance of its functions, or which obstructs or impedes any member or officer of such House in the discharge of his duty, or which has a tendency, directly or indirectly, to produce such results, may be treated as a contempt even though there is no precedent of the offence.'

While the House cannot create new privileges, except by statute, there is no complete list of behaviour which constitutes contempt, though the following are examples: attempting to disrupt the proceedings of the House; attempting to bribe members; casting imputations reflecting upon the dignity of the House; refusing to give evidence, or giving false evidence, or tampering with witnesses before a committee of the House; the service of writs on members within the precincts of the House; obstructing an Officer of the House while in the execution of his duty.

Complaints of breach of privilege may be raised by a member or in the House by the Speaker. If the Speaker rules that a prima facie case has been made out, a motion is proposed, by the Leader of the House or the member who raised the matter, that the matter be referred to the Committee of Privileges. The motion may then be debated and voted upon. The committee, comprising the 15 most senior members of the parties in the House, is the master of its own proceedings. It can compel the attendance of witnesses and the production of documents, failure to comply being a contempt. There is no requirement of legal representation, indeed the 'defendant' may not be given any hearing at all. At the conclusion of its investigation the committee reports its findings to the House and may recommend the action that the House should take. The House need not accept the committee's findings or recommendations, but it almost always does. This procedure has been criticised. The Select Committee on Parliamentary Privilege in 1967 recommended that persons directly concerned in the committee's investigations should have the right to attend its hearings, make submissions, call, examine and cross-examine witnesses, and, with leave of the committee, be legally represented and apply for legal aid. These recommendations were not adopted.

If the House finds that a breach of privilege or a contempt of the House has been established it may adopt one of several courses of action. It may order the offender to be reprimanded or admonished by the Speaker at the Bar of the House. A member may be suspended or expelled from the House. Although the House no longer has the power to impose a fine, it may commit a person to prison. The commitment cannot last beyond the end of the session and the prisoner must be released upon the prorogation or dissolution of Parliament. Officials of the House may be dismissed and persons such as lobby correspondents, who are granted special facilities in the Palace of Westminster, may have those facilities withdrawn.

It is interesting to speculate upon the possible repercussions of the decision of the European Commission on Human Rights in *Application No 13057/87* v *Malta*, in which it was held that the jurisdiction of the Maltese House of Representatives, to punish those alleged to have been in breach of its privileges, contravened Article 6 para 1 of the European Convention on Human Rights, because such proceedings involved the House as victim, prosecutor and judge. In theory the same objections could be raised to the jurisdiction of the House of Commons to deal with breaches of its privileges and contempt. It should be remembered, however, that the convention currently forms no part of English law, and thus decisions of the Commission would not be legally binding.

8.10 The courts and parliamentary privilege

The House of Commons claims to be the absolute and sole judge of its own privileges and maintains that its judgment cannot be called into question by any other court. The courts do not agree. They maintain the right to determine the nature and extent of parliamentary privilege when adjudicating upon the rights of individuals outside the House. This disagreement has given rise to constitutional conflict.

Stockdale v *Hansard* (1839) 9 Ad & E 1. Stockdale published an illustrated treatise on the reproduction system. A copy was found in possession of a prisoner in Newgate and was described by the inspectors of prisons in a report to the Government as 'disgusting and obscene'. The report was printed by order of the House of Commons and was sold by Hansard, the parliamentary printers. The plaintiff brought an action for libel against Hansard. The defendants, acting under the direction of the House of Commons, pleaded that the publication was covered by parliamentary privilege. The Court of Queen's Bench rejected this plea and awarded damages to Stockdale. Regarding the power of the House of Commons to create new privileges by resolution, Lord Denman CJ commented:

> 'The supremacy of Parliament, the foundation on which the claim is made to rest, appears to me completely to overturn it, because the House of Commons is not Parliament, but only a co-ordinate and component part of the Parliament. That sovereign power can make and unmake the laws; but the concurrence of the three legislative estates is necessary; the resolution of any one of them cannot alter the law, or place anyone beyond its control. The proposition is therefore wholly untenable, and abhorrent to the first principles of the constitution of England.'

Stockdale then brought another action against Hansard. On the instructions of the House the defendants entered no plea, and the plaintiff was again awarded damages.

Case of the Sheriffs of Middlesex (1840) 11 Ad & E 273. The Sheriffs of Middlesex, in pursuance of a writ from the Court of Queen's Bench in the case of

Stockdale v *Hansard*, levied execution upon property of Hansard. The House of Commons thereupon committed the Sheriffs for contempt, and breach of privilege. A writ of habeas corpus was applied for on the ground that the Sheriffs were unlawfully detained. Upon motion to discharge the Sheriffs from custody, the Court of Queen's Bench held that the court had no jurisdiction to interfere.

In 1840 the House of Commons secured the passing of the Parliamentary Papers Act, conferring absolute privilege on matters contained in parliamentary papers.

There is therefore in effect a dualism:

> '... there may be at any given moment two doctrines of privilege, the one held by the courts, the other by either House, the one to be found in the Law Reports, the other in Hansard.'

However, in allowing the House to enforce its own view of privilege and commit the Sheriffs of Middlesex, the courts have perhaps recognised their subordination to Parliament.

8.11 MPs as representatives of outside interests

Interference with the exercise of a member's freedom of speech in debate and proceedings in Parliament, by threats, is considered by the House to be a contempt of Parliament and breach of privilege. If a member agrees to represent an outside interest group in Parliament, is a threat by that group to remove support from the member a breach of privilege?

In the case of *W J Brown* (1947), Brown, an Independent MP, agreed to become the salaried 'parliamentary general secretary' of the Civil Service Clerical Association. Disagreement arose between Brown and the association over his political attitudes and the latter proposed the termination of the agreement. Brown claimed the proposal was a breach of parliamentary privilege as it was calculated to influence him in his conduct as an MP. The Committee of Privileges reported that on the particular facts no breach of privilege had been committed. Commenting generally on such agreements, the committee was of opinion that it would be improper for a member to enter into any arrangement fettering his complete independence by undertaking to press some particular point of view on behalf of an outside interest, whether for reward or not. It would be improper to attempt to punish a member financially because of his actions as a member. The committee refused to condemn contractual relationships, recognising that many members received financial assistance from outside bodies. The payments in themselves did not involve a breach of privilege and the committee concluded that if the contract itself were not a breach, then neither was a legitimate decision to terminate it. Allegations that a number of MPs agreed to ask questions in the House of Commons in return for cash payments during 1993–94 are currently the subject of investigation by the Committee of Privileges.

9

The House of Lords

9.1 The composition of the House of Lords

9.2 The functions and work of the House of Lords

9.3 House of Lords reform

9.1 The composition of the House of Lords

From the earliest times the House of Lords has been composed of Lords Spiritual and Temporal. The Lords Spiritual originally comprised the bishops and certain abbots and priors whose membership lasted as long as they held their office. Membership of the Lords Temporal became almost entirely hereditary by the fifteenth century. The Lords Temporal were known as peers, indicating that they were then equal in standing. Today they are divided in rank, there being five degrees – dukes, marquesses, earls, viscounts and barons.

The members of the House of Lords are not elected and sit either by virtue of the hereditary principle or by Crown appointment. At present the following are entitled to membership:

The Lords Spiritual

There are the Archbishops of Canterbury and York, the Bishops of London, Durham and Winchester, and the next 21 diocesan bishops of the Church of England according to the seniority of their appointment. When such a bishop dies or resigns, his seat in the House is taken by the next senior diocesan bishop. They hold their seats in the Lords until they resign from their episcopal office.

The Lords Temporal

These comprise:

1. Hereditary peers and peeresses in their own right of England (created before the union with Scotland in 1707); Great Britain (from 1707 to 1801 when the union of Great Britain and Ireland took effect); and the United Kingdom (1801 to date). Hereditary peerages may be created by the Queen on the advice of the

Prime Minister, recent examples being William Whitelaw, created Viscount Whitelaw in 1983, and the late Harold Macmillan, created Earl Stockton in 1984.

In *Re Parliamentary Election for Bristol South-East* [1964] 2 QB 257, Gorman J observed:

'The hereditary principle is still firmly embodied in the Constitution. Though by legislation starting with the Parliament Act 1911, the powers of the House of Lords have been curtailed, it still remains the law that the composition of the House of Lords is largely based on the hereditary principle, namely, that persons of a certain class, that is to say, persons who by creation by letters patent or by succession have become peers of the realm, have the right and duty to sit in the House of Lords. A peerage (and for this purpose we confine our consideration to United Kingdom peers) constitutes a complex of rights, privileges and duties. As stated above in *Viscountess Rhondda's case* [1922] 2 AC 339, Lord Wrenbury used these words: "A peerage is an inalienable incorporeal hereditament created by the act of the Sovereign which, if and when he creates it, carries with it certain attributes which attach to it not by reason of any grant of those attributes by the Crown, but as essentially existing at common law by reason of the ennoblement created by the grant of the peerage." '

2. Hereditary peers of Scotland created before the Act of Union 1707. From 1707 until the Peerage Act 1963 there were 16 representative peers for Scotland elected by the Scottish peers for the duration of a Parliament. Since 1963 all holders of peerages of Scotland have had the right to be admitted to the House of Lords. Peers of Ireland no longer have any right to sit in the Lords but may be elected to the Commons.

3. Life peers created under the Life Peerages Act 1958. The Sovereign may grant by Letters Patent baronies for life, without limit of number, to persons of either sex. The object is to strengthen and broaden the composition of the House by securing the experience of distinguished men and women without conferring the right of succession upon their issue.

4. The Lords of Appeal in Ordinary. Not more than 11 Lords of Appeal in Ordinary may be appointed by the Crown to perform the judicial duties of the House. They are entitled to sit and vote for life, notwithstanding retirement from their judicial office, and may participate in general debate.

Membership of the House of Lords

As of 28 February 1994 membership of the House of Lords numbered 1,202, comprising:

1. 428 life peers (including Law Lords and bishops), 61 of whom are women;
2. 774 hereditary peers, of whom 17 are women (inheriting under ancient Scottish titles).

The 'working peers' (those attending on a regular basis) number between 350 and 400, the majority of whom are life peers.

Writs of summons are issued for each new Parliament. They are sent to those who have had peerages conferred on them, but others have to satisfy the Lord High Chancellor of their right to sit before a writ of summons can be issued for the first time. Bankrupts and aliens are disqualified from receiving a writ of summons. On first attending the House in each new Parliament, Lords present their writ of summons at the table of the House and take an oath or affirmation of allegiance to the Queen. Leave is granted for the duration of a Parliament to those Lords who are unable or unwilling to attend the House. While on leave of absence Lords are expected not to attend the sittings of the House. Leave may be rescinded on giving one month's notice.

Party allegiance in the House of Lords

All the mainstream political parties are represented in the House, although a large number of members remain unattached to any political party. In February 1994 the major groupings in the House of Lords were as follows:

	CON	LAB	LIB-DEM	Cross-benchers	OTHS
Life peers	147	103	31	114	15
Hereditary peers	328	12	24	161	73
Totals	475	115	55	275	88

(NB figures do not tally with those for overall membership as they were not compiled at the same time.)

While the House traditionally has an in-built Conservative majority, in recent years the Conservative Government has not always been able to command a majority. For example the first Thatcher administration (1979–83) sustained 45 defeats in the House of Lords. During the 1983–87 Parliament the Government sustained 62 defeats in the House of Lords. Between 1987 and May 1990 the Government sustained 40 defeats in the House of Lords.

Salaries and expenses

Members of the House of Lords do not receive a salary. Salaries are paid to Government ministers in the Lords, the Leader of the Opposition, Opposition Chief Whip, the Chairman of Committees, the Principal Deputy Chairman of Committees and the Lords of Appeal in Ordinary. Members of the House are entitled to expenses incurred for the purpose of attending the sittings of the House or its committees, such as accommodation, subsistence, travel, general office expenses or secretarial or research assistance.

9.2 The functions and work of the House of Lords

The 1968 Government White Paper *House of Lords Reform* referred to seven functions of the House of Lords.

Its appellate role as the supreme court of appeal

The House of Lords acts as the final court of appeal for the whole of the United Kingdom in civil cases and for England, Wales and Northern Ireland in criminal cases. The House may also hear certain other appeals, including those from the Courts-Martial Appeal Court. The judicial work of the House is separate from its other functions. The only peers who participate are the Lord High Chancellor, the Lords of Appeal in Ordinary, who are expressly appointed for the purpose, and Lords who hold or have held high judicial office.

The provision of a forum for free debate on matters of public interest

In the House of Lords Wednesday is traditionally set aside for special debates on a wide range of subjects. Debates may be initiated by the Government, Opposition, backbench or independent members. Once a month, from the beginning of the session until the Spring Bank Holiday recess, there are two short debates, limited to two and a half hours each. The right to initiate such debates is confirmed to backbenchers and crossbenchers, and the subjects for debate are chosen by ballot.

The revision of Public Bills brought from the House of Commons

About one half of the time of the House of Lords is devoted to the consideration of Public Bills. Most of this time is spent on revising Bills which have already passed the Commons, where most of Government legislation is introduced. There are four main reasons why most legislation is introduced in the House of Commons:

1. In most cases the relevant departmental minister is a member of the House of Commons.
2. The House of Commons, as the elected chamber, is the political forum in the legislature.
3. Many Bills have a significant financial content even if they are not strictly Money Bills.
4. The provisions of the Parliament Acts are only available to enforce the will of the Commons in respect of Bills introduced in that House.

While the procedure of the two Houses for considering Public Bills is very similar, there are some significant differences. It is an established convention that the Lords do not ordinarily divide upon the Second Reading of a Government Bill, which usually goes to committee. While in the Commons Public Bills usually go to a

Standing Committee, in the Lords they are almost always considered by a Committee of the Whole House. The Lords, unlike the Commons, allow amendments to be tabled at Third Reading.

The Lords have nothing corresponding to the Commons guillotine and there is no effective machinery for curtailing debate. Nor is there provision for the selection of amendments for debate and all amendments tabled may be debated.

The legislative powers of the House of Lords are limited by the Parliament Acts 1911 and 1949 under which certain Public Bills may be presented for the Royal Assent without the consent of the Lords. The Parliament Acts do not apply to:

1. Bills introduced in the House of Lords.
2. Bills to extend the life of a Parliament beyond five years.
3. Provisional Order Bills.
4. Private Bills.
5. Delegated legislation.

The conditions to be fulfilled before a Bill can be presented for the Royal Assent under the provisions of the Parliament Acts vary according to whether or not it is certified by the Speaker as a Money Bill, that is, one containing only provisions dealing with national taxation, the expenditure of public money, or loans or their management. The certificate of the Speaker is conclusive. Under the provisions of the Parliament Act 1911, if a Money Bill passed by the Commons and sent to the Lords at least one month before the end of a session, is not passed by the Lords without amendment within one month, it may be presented for Royal Assent without the Lords' consent. This does not debar the Lords from amending Money Bills provided they are passed within the month, but the Commons are not bound to consider the amendments.

An amended Bill is returned to the Commons for consideration of the Lords' amendments. Usually most Lords' amendments are accepted, but if the Commons reject them, the Lords do not usually insist on them. Should they do so, and should no compromise solution be found, or should the Lords reject a Commons Bill altogether, then – unless it is a Money Bill – it cannot become law during that session. Parliamentary sessions last about a year and normally begin in October or November. Bills which are not enacted in the course of a session are lost at the end of the session.

A Commons Bill lost because it is not accepted by the Lords can be passed in the following session without the Lords' consent. Under the Parliament Acts, if the Lords reject a Public Bill other than a Money Bill which has been sent from the Commons in two successive sessions, then it may be presented for the Royal Assent without the consent of the Lords. The Bill, which with certain exceptions must be identical to the Bill that was lost, must be sent up to the Lords at least one calendar month before the end of a session. Provided there is a gap of at least a year between the Commons Second Reading of the original Bill in the first session and the

Commons Third Reading of the identical Bill in the second session, then the Bill may receive the Royal Assent and become an Act.

The effect of the Parliament Acts is that the Lords have power to delay a Public Bill brought from the House of Commons until the session after that in which it was first introduced, and until not less than 13 months have elapsed from the date of the Second Reading in the Commons in the first session.

The initiation of Public Bills

The more important and controversial Bills almost invariably begin in the House of Commons. However, Bills which are relatively uncontroversial in party political terms have recently been introduced in the House of Lords with a fair degree of regularity. These include the Wildlife and Countryside Bill (1980–81 session), the National Heritage Bill, Data Protection Bill and the Health and Social Services and Social Security Adjudications Bill (1982–83 session). By convention all Consolidation Bills (Bills which do not alter the law but replace a number of Acts dealing with a particular subject by a single Act), and most Bills to give effect to changes in the law proposed by the Law Commissions, are introduced in the Lords.

Unlike members of the House of Commons, members of the Lords are free to introduce Private Members' Bills, and there is usually sufficient time for them to be debated. However, if they are passed there is no guarantee that time will be found for them in the House of Commons. The fact that the Lords have no constituents makes it easier for them to discuss measures proposing controversial changes, and they played a significant part in reforming the law relating to homosexuality and abortion.

The consideration of subordinate legislation

Subordinate or delegated legislation is made by ministers under powers conferred upon them by statute. There are three main categories:

1. Affirmative instruments, which require the approval of both Houses of Parliament before they can come into or remain in force.
2. Negative instruments, which may be annulled by resolution of either House.
3. General instruments, which are not subject to any parliamentary proceedings.

The powers of the House of Lords over delegated legislation were not curtailed by the Parliament Acts and are the same as those enjoyed by the House of Commons. When a resolution of each House approving the instrument is required, the House of Lords always has an opportunity to debate it. In the case of a negative instrument, any member may move a motion to annul it, and while in the Commons time often cannot be found to debate such motions, in the Lords there is no such difficulty.

The scrutiny of the activities of the Executive

There are several means of questioning ministers in the House of Lords about Government policy in addition to those provided by general debates. Each day up to four oral or 'starred' questions may be asked of the Government and are taken as first business. No Lord may ask more than two questions on any day nor may he have more than three questions on the order paper at any time. Supplementary questions may be asked by any member, but there may not be a debate. 'Unstarred' questions are taken at the end of business. The member asking the question makes a speech, and a debate may take place before the minister's reply, which concludes the proceedings. Private Notice Questions may be asked on matters of urgency. It is for the Leader of the House or as a last resort for the House itself, to decide what constitutes a matter of urgency.

Questions for Written Answers may be placed on the Order Paper. They are normally answered within a fortnight, and the answers are printed in the Official Report (Hansard). In all cases questions are addressed to Her Majesty's Government and not to individual ministers.

The scrutiny of private legislation

Unlike Public Bills, which are introduced by members, Private Bills originate outside Parliament and are promoted by bodies and individuals seeking special powers not available under the general law. The powers of the House of Lords in relation to private legislation were not limited by the Parliament Acts and are the same as those of the House of Commons. The procedure for considering Private Bills is generally the same in both Houses. They are subject to consideration by counsel to the Chairman of Committees in the Lords and counsel to the Speaker in the Commons. For the most part their consideration takes place in Committee.

The privileges of the House of Lords

The privileges of the House of Lords are similar to those enjoyed by the House of Commons, as outlined in Chapter 8. They include freedom of speech – Article 9 of the Bill of Rights applies to the Lords as it does to the Commons; freedom from civil arrest. Individual peers may claim privilege from civil arrest at any time: see *Stourton* v *Stourton* (1963). The House of Lords has the right to regulate its own composition, via its Committee of Privileges, including the determination of the right of newly created peers to sit and vote. Claims to established peerages are also determined by the Committee. It also enjoys the right to punish for contempt. The Lords can commit a person for a definite term and may also impose fines.

9.3 House of Lords reform

At the beginning of this century the powers of the House of Lords in respect of legislation were equal to those of the House of Commons, with one exception. The Lords recognised Commons privilege in financial matters, which prevented them from initiating or amending Bills granting aids and supplies or imposing charges on the people. However, the House of Lords retained the right to reject financial legislation outright.

The Parliament Act 1911

In 1909 the Lords rejected the Budget which Lloyd George had presented to the Commons. The Liberal Government, re-elected in the ensuing election, introduced the Parliament Bill to restrict the powers of the House of Lords. This Bill was passed by the House of Lords in August 1911, under the threat that sufficient Liberal peers would be created to ensure its passage should the Bill have been rejected. The Parliament Act 1911 made three main changes:

1. A Bill certified by the Speaker as a Money Bill should receive the Royal Assent and become an Act of Parliament without the consent of the House of Lords if, having been sent up from the House of Commons at least one month before the end of the session, it had not been passed by the Lords without amendment within one month of its being sent up.
2. Any other Public Bill, except one for extending the life of a Parliament, could become an Act of Parliament without the consent of the House of Lords if it had been passed by the House of Commons in three successive sessions, two years having elapsed between its first Second Reading and its final passing in the House of Commons, and if it had been sent up to the House of Lords at least one month before the end of each of the three sessions.
3. The maximum duration of a Parliament was reduced from seven years to five.

Only four Acts have been passed under the Parliament Act procedure: the Welsh Church Act 1914 disestablishing the Church of Wales; the Government of Ireland Act 1914, providing for Irish home rule; the Parliament Act 1949; and the War Crimes Act 1991.

The most recent use of the Parliament Act procedure merits some attention. On its first journey through the House of Lords, the War Crimes Bill (which proposed changes in English law to enable the prosecution in English courts of Nazi war criminals living in the UK) was defeated at Second Reading by 207 votes to 74. Utilising the procedures of the 1911 and 1949 Acts the Government decided to re-introduce the Bill. On the second journey through the House of Lords the Bill was again defeated at Second Reading, this time by 131 votes to 109. The Bill was sent direct to the Queen for Royal Assent, which was granted in the summer of 1991.

This was the first time the procedure had been used since the enactment of the 1949 Act, which itself had been passed without the consent of the House of Lords under the 1911 Act procedure.

A number of constitutional questions arise from this. Was it legitimate for the House of Lords to reject the principles of the Bill at Second Reading when the House of Commons had indicated its view (on both occasions) by overwhelmingly voting in favour of those principles? Can the War Crimes Act 1991 be regarded as an Act or merely a special species of delegated legislation authorised by the 1911 Act? If it is an Act in the sense of primary law, does this indicate a change in the sovereign body? See further, articles on the similar question of the status of the Parliament Act 1949: (1976) 92 Law Quarterly Review 591; (1979) 95 LQR 36 and 386; and (1981) 97 LQR 265.

The Bryce Report

The Parliament Act 1911 was regarded as a temporary measure pending further reform of the composition of the Lords and the relationship between the two Houses of Parliament. In 1917 a conference consisting of 15 members of each House and chaired by Viscount Bryce, was appointed to consider both the composition and powers of a reformed Second Chamber. The conference reported in 1918. It stated that the primary functions of a Second Chamber included:

1. Examination and revision of Commons Bills.
2. Initiation and discussion of non-controversial Bills.
3. Interposition of so much delay (and no more) in the passing of a Bill into law as might be needed to enable the opinion of the nation to be adequately expressed upon it.
4. Discussion of general questions of policy.

The conference recommended, in its majority report, that the House of Lords should consist of 246 members indirectly elected by MPs representing regional units. A further 81 members would be chosen by a Joint Standing Committee of both Houses. The 81 were to be hereditary peers and bishops, and the number was to be gradually reduced to 30 hereditary peers and bishops and 51 others. The Law Lords were to sit ex-officio. With the exception of those sitting ex-officio, all members would hold seats for 12 years, one-third retiring every fourth year. The reformed Second Chamber was to have full powers over non-financial legislation. Any differences between the two Houses was to be resolved by a Free Conference Committee consisting of up to 30 members of each House. A Bill that had been passed by the House of Commons and agreed to by a majority of the Free Conference might, in certain circumstances, become law without the agreement of the Second Chamber. No action was ever taken to implement the Bryce Report.

The Parliament Act 1949

In 1947 the Parliament Bill was introduced by the Labour Government in the House of Commons to further regulate the powers of the House of Lords. Under pressure from the Conservatives and Liberals the Second Reading of the Bill in the House of Lords was adjourned to enable a conference of party leaders to take place. Agreement was reached on certain principles regarding the role and composition of a reformed House, such as the need for the Second Chamber to be complementary to, and not a rival to, the Lower House; that no one political party should have a permanent majority; that heredity should not by itself constitute a qualification for admission; and that women should be admitted. In April 1949 the conference broke down following disagreement over the period of the Lords' delaying powers. The House of Lords then rejected the Parliament Bill on Second Reading, and it was passed into law under the provisions of the 1911 Act. The Parliament Act 1949 amends the Parliament Act 1911 by reducing from three to two the number of sessions in which a Bill must be passed by the Commons, and reducing the period between the first Second Reading and final passing in the House of Commons from two years to one.

Leave of absence 1958

On the recommendation of the report of the Select Committee chaired by the Earl of Swinton, standing orders were amended to enable peers unable or unwilling to attend the House regularly to apply for leave of absence, thus preventing the 'backwoodsmen' from suddenly appearing to determine the result of a particular division. A peer granted leave of absence is not expected to attend sittings until his leave has expired or been terminated, except to take the Oath of Allegiance. At least one month's notice of intended termination is expected.

The Life Peerages Act 1958

This empowers the Crown to create life peers who are entitled to sit and vote in the House of Lords and whose peerages expire on their death. Life peerages may be conferred upon women.

The Peerage Act 1963

This Act enables hereditary peers, other than those of the first creation, to renounce their titles for life by disclaimer. The peerage remains dormant and devolves upon the heir in the normal manner on the renouncer's death. Under the Act, if a sitting member of the House of Commons succeeds to a title, he has one month after the death of his predecessor in which to disclaim, or, if the death occurs during an election campaign, one month from the declaration of the poll in favour of a successful peer. Existing peers had 12 months from the Royal Assent to the Act on 31 July 1963 in which to disclaim. Peers who succeed thereafter have 12 months from succession or their coming of age. A person who has disclaimed a peerage is entitled to vote in parliamentary elections and is eligible for election to the House of Commons. The 1963 Act also provides that peeresses in their own right should be admitted to the House of Lords and should be subject to the same disqualifications in respect of election to and membership of the House of Commons as hereditary peers. The system of Scottish representative peers was abolished, all Scottish peers being now admitted to the House.

The Parliament (No 2) Bill 1969

The Queen's Speech for the 1967–68 Session contained the following provision:

> 'Legislation will be introduced to reduce the powers of the House of Lords and to eliminate its present hereditary basis, thereby enabling it to develop within the framework of a modern Parliamentary system. My Government are prepared to enter into consultations appropriate to a constitutional change of such importance.'

Accordingly inter-party talks on Lords Reform took place at a conference between party leaders from 8 November 1967 to 20 June 1968, when talks were broken off by the Government following the rejection by the House of Lords of a Government Order continuing sanctions against the Government of Rhodesia. In November 1968 the Government published a White Paper, *House of Lords Reform*, which was later embodied in the Parliament (No 2) Bill 1968–69. Its main proposals were as follows:

1. The reformed House of Lords was to be a two-tier structure comprising voting peers and non-voting peers.
2. Succession to a hereditary peerage was no longer to carry the right to a seat in the House of Lords, but existing peers by succession would have the right to sit as non-voting members during their lifetime, or might be created life peers to enable them to continue in active participation as voting members.
3. Voting peers were expected to play a full part in the work of the House and be required to attend at least one-third of the sittings. They would be subject to an age of retirement. Non-voting peers would be able to play a full part in debates and in committees but would not be entitled to vote.
4. The voting House would initially consist of about 230 peers, distributed between the parties in such a way as to give the Government a small majority over the Opposition parties, but not a majority of the House as a whole when those without party allegiance were included.
5. The reformed House would be able to impose a delay of six months from the date of disagreement between the two Houses on the passage of non-financial public legislation. After this delay a Bill could be submitted for Royal Assent by resolution of the House of Commons.

6. The Lords would be able to require the House of Commons to reconsider subordinate legislation, but would not be able to reject it outright.

7. A review would be made of the functions and procedures of the two Houses once the main reform had come into effect.

The White Paper was debated in both Houses. In the Lords it was approved by 251 votes to 56, but in the Commons more criticism was raised. This was particularly because of the extension of patronage which a nominated and paid Upper Chamber would produce, and of the political power which the proposals would place in the hands of cross-bench voting members. With the imposition of a three-line whip by the Government, and on a free vote by the Conservative and Liberal parties, the motion to reject the White Paper was defeated by 270 votes to 159.

Despite the Commons opposition to the White Paper, the Government decided to honour its pledge in the Queen's Speech and implement the proposals. Accordingly the Parliament (No 2) Bill was introduced in 1968, to make the constitutional changes. As this was a constitutional Bill, its Committee stage was taken on the floor of the House of Commons, giving opponents the opportunity to prolong proceedings and table a large number of amendments. The Opposition did not co-operate to impose a guillotine, and after the House had spent 11 days in Committee and only the preamble and the first five clauses out of 20 had been considered, the Prime Minister announced the abandonment of the Bill on 17 April 1969.

The current debate

The conventional wisdom would appear to be that there is a good case to be made for effecting some reform of the House of Lords, but rather less agreement as to what form those changes should take and how radical they should be.

Those who argue for the outright abolition of the House of Lords, in other words those who advocate a unicameral legislature, contend that, in a unitary constitutional structure, a second chamber is redundant. Abolitionists reject the notion that the House of Lords can be justified on the basis that it acts as a necessary check on the Commons and can provide more effective scrutiny of legislative proposals. The rationale for abolition is that if there are defects with the representativeness and effectiveness of the Commons, it is the House of Commons itself that needs to be reformed so that it operates properly. They might add that the space and resources currently utilised by the House of Lords could be more effectively deployed by an expanded House of Commons. Criticisms to the effect that a unicameral legislature could aggregate unlimited power to itself are usually met with the response that the control exercise by the House of Lords under our current system is at best sporadic. Rather than being occasionally contained, obstructed or thwarted by the House of Lords, the House of Commons could be required to operate within the confines of a written constitution, if necessary with entrenched provisions, perhaps requiring a referendum for amendment.

Those who advocate the retention of a second chamber tend to focus their proposals for reform either on the method of appointment for members, or the rights of members. The House of Lords is unique amongst the legislative bodies of industrialised democratic nations in that the majority of its members are entitled to attend on the basis of the hereditary principle, rather than nomination or election.

Those who advocate a directly elected second chamber face a number of obvious difficulties. Why duplicate the House of Commons? If the proposal is that election should be on some basis other than that used at present for parliamentary elections, it is open to criticism that it will either produce a less representative assembly, leaving it open to questions as regards its legitimacy, or that it could produce a more representative assembly, perhaps by the adoption of proportional representation, and thus represent a threat to the House of Commons. The adoption of the model based on a powerful second chamber, such as can be found in federal constitutions such as that in Australia, Switzerland and the United States of America, would require some fundamental changes to the British constitution, particularly in terms of ministerial responsibility to the House of Commons.

In countries such as Iceland and Norway the second chamber is elected by the lower house, so the party-political composition of the second chamber will normally mirror that of the lower house. The attraction of this method is that there is still an indirect link with the democratic process, in that the membership is determined by those who have been elected, and it ensures that the second chamber is unlikely to be able to thwart the will of the democratically elected legislative body. A variation on this theme, encountered in countries such as France and Austria, is for the second chamber to be elected by an electoral college, or by regional assemblies, thus ensuring that the legislature represents a wider group of interests than might otherwise be the case. Difficult questions will remain, however, as to the extent to which the indirectly elected body can be permitted to obstruct the will of the directly elected body. A further possible variant is to assemble a second chamber on a functional basis, in the sense that the membership is made up of the holders of specific posts, for example local authority chief executives, designated trade union leaders, university vice-chancellors, heads of quangos such as the Equal Opportunities Commission, English Heritage, the Countryside Commission, etc. The presence in the House of Lords of the Lords Spiritual and the Law Lords to some extent provides a skeletal model of this approach. The advantage of such a model is that it brings a varied range of experience and wisdom to bear upon the legislative proposals of the House of Commons, but it also raises questions as to where the power of patronage would lie. One would also have to question the extent of the 'checking' powers to be given to such an assembly, and the extent to which individuals, holding influential and demanding posts in commerce, industry and the public sector, would be able to attend regularly to discharge their legislative duties.

The Labour Party is currently committed to reforming the House of Lords, by ending the voting rights of hereditary peers. While this would go some way to deflecting the criticisms of the Lords on the grounds of it being an unrepresentative and undemocratic body, the question nevertheless arises as to what extent the *life* peers can claim that they have any stronger claim to vote. Taken to its logical conclusion, all current peers should be deprived of the right to vote. A further constitutional question arises as to how such a change would be accomplished. Assuming opposition from the House of Lords, and setting aside the possible creation of hundreds of pro-reform life peers, could a Labour government push legislation through, utilising the Parliament Acts, to effect these changes without the consent of the Lords? Given that it would arguably be seen as a matter touching upon the privileges of the House of Lords, the courts might be sympathetic to an argument that ultimately it is a matter for the House of Lords itself to resolve; see further the *Bradlaugh* litigation considered in Chapter 8.

10

The Central Government – Responsible Government – Ministers' Powers – The Civil Service

10.1 The Prime Minister and the Cabinet

10.2 Ministerial responsibility

10.3 Government departments

10.4 The principal departments of State

10.5 The Civil Service

10.6 The relationship between ministers and civil servants

10.7 Rules affecting the political activities of civil servants

10.8 Tenure of appointment of civil servants

10.9 The Privy Council

10.1 The Prime Minister and the Cabinet

Introduction

One of the principal features of the modern British constitution is the concentration of the control of both legislative and executive functions in the Cabinet, a small body of men presided over by the Prime Minister. All important questions of policy and the general scope and nature of the legislation to be initiated by the party in power are decided by the Cabinet. Both the existence of the Cabinet and the pre-eminence of the Prime Minister are the result not of law, but of convention.

The Prime Minister

Formal position of the Prime Minister

The office of Prime Minister is a de facto institution recognised by statute but governed mainly by convention. It is invariably held together with the office of First Lord of the Treasury. In the eighteenth and nineteenth centuries, when Walpole, William Pitt the Younger, Disraeli and Gladstone were shaping the Prime Ministerial role into its present form, the holder of the office of First Lord of the Treasury had powers of patronage which enabled him to control departmental appointments so as to secure advantage for his party. The title Prime Minister only dates from 1905 and before 1937 the salary of the Prime Minister was derived from holding the office of First Lord of the Treasury.

The Ministerial and Other Salaries Act 1975 and the Parliamentary and Other Pensions Act 1972, now refer to the 'Prime Minister and First Lord of the Treasury' and it seems unlikely therefore that the two offices will become separated again. The last occasion on which they were separated was between 1895 and 1902, when Lord Salisbury was Prime Minister and Balfour was First Lord of the Treasury. Although the First Lord of the Treasury ceased to have responsibility for civil service affairs on the creation of the Civil Service Department in 1968, the Prime Minister now becomes Minister for the Civil Service as well as First Lord of the Treasury, and so retains ultimate responsibility for the Civil Service. With this responsibility go certain rights of patronage, as the appointment of senior civil servants is made on the Prime Minister's recommendation. On the abolition of the Civil Service Department in 1981 the Prime Minister retained overall responsibility for the Civil Service, but functions relating to conditions of service and pay were transferred to the Treasury, and other matters of management and efficiency to a new Management and Personnel Office, which is run on a day-to-day basis by another Cabinet minister.

Choosing a Prime Minister

As a matter of constitutional theory the choice of Prime Minister is that of the Queen alone in the exercise of the Sovereign's personal prerogative. In practice the person in whose favour that prerogative must be exercised is known in advance by the Sovereign. Generally, in appointing a Prime Minister, the Queen should choose that person who is able to command the support of the majority in the House of Commons – usually the leader of the party with the majority of seats. The Sovereign no longer has a personal discretion as to whom she appoints except in certain unusual circumstances.

The office of Prime Minister may become vacant on the dismissal, death or resignation of the holder. In modern constitutional practice the dismissal of a Prime Minister is unlikely to arise except in the most extreme circumstances. Since the Victorian era all new appointments have been made necessary by death or resignation. Resignation may be personal, for example, on grounds of ill-health where it is akin to death in office or the entire executive or ministry may resign with the Prime Minister, when the governing party is defeated on a motion of non-confidence or at a General Election.

Before the Conservative Party adopted a ballot system for the election of its leader in 1964, the resignation or death of a Conservative Prime Minister left some discretion to the Sovereign in the choice of a successor. All the major parties now elect their leader by ballot, although the electoral colleges which make the choice are differently constituted. Conservative MPs alone elect their leader, whereas the Labour leader is elected on a 'one member one vote' basis. It seems that the proper course for the Sovereign to take on the death or resignation of a Prime Minister is to wait until the governing party has elected its new leader and then invite that person to take office. This is what happened in 1976 when Wilson announced his intention to resign and Callaghan was elected as the new leader of the Labour Party.

The appointment of John Major as Prime Minister in 1990 arose as a result of Margaret Thatcher's resignation, following her decision not to contest the election for the Conservative Party leadership beyond its second round. As she later pointed out, even though she lost the leadership contest, she remained Prime Minister until her resignation was accepted by the Queen. An interesting situation would have arisen had she declined to offer her resignation despite her defeat at the hands of her own party.

In the event of a Prime Minister's death it might be necessary to appoint someone to carry out his duties until a leadership election could be held.

Following defeat on a motion of no confidence, the proper course is for the Prime Minister and the entire Government to resign. The Prime Minister may then either advise the monarch to invite the Leader of the Opposition, which is a recognised position having a statutory salary, to form a Government or request a dissolution. The latter cause was favoured by Callaghan when his minority Labour Government was defeated on an Opposition motion of no confidence in 1979.

If the Prime Minister judges that the time is advantageous he may request a dissolution with a view to causing a general election to be held. If the Government is defeated decisively at the subsequent election, modern constitutional convention requires the Prime Minister and entire Government to resign before the new Parliament meets. The Leader of the Opposition will usually have an overall majority in the Commons if the Government has been defeated, and will be the person invited to form a new ministry. Where no one party secures an overall majority at a General Election the Prime Minister need not resign immediately, but may wait to see if he can obtain a majority in the new House with support from another party.

Functions of the Prime Minister
Formation of the Government. The primary function of a Prime Minister is the formation of a Government or ministry. A list of proposed ministerial appointments is presented to the Queen for her approval. The Queen may make observations,

suggestions and objections, but she cannot disapprove the appointment of a particular minister if the Prime Minister insists on that choice. Junior ministers are chosen by the Prime Minister without consulting the Sovereign.

In appointing ministers the Prime Minister is bound by certain conventions. A minister must be or become a member of one or other House of Parliament, each department must have a ministerial spokesman in the Commons and the Chancellor of the Exchequer must be a member of the House of Commons. Under the House of Commons Disqualification Act 1975, s2, there may be up to 95 holders of ministerial office in the Commons. Additional ministers may be appointed from the House of Lords. The Prime Minister may require a minister to resign at any time.

Formation of the Cabinet. The choice of a Cabinet is entirely in the Prime Minister's discretion, although his choice will be influenced by political expediency. Normally the Cabinet will include the senior ministers who head the principal Government departments and, by convention, the Chancellor of the Exchequer, Secretary of State for Foreign and Commonwealth Affairs, Secretary of State for Defence, Lord Chancellor and Home Secretary must always be in a peacetime Cabinet.

Presiding over Cabinet meetings. The Prime Minister presides over meetings of the full Cabinet and its most important committees. He decides the agenda for Cabinet meetings and controls discussion. At the end of a meeting no formal vote is taken on the policy decided; it is for the Prime Minister to sum up the consensus. Cabinet decision making may therefore be dominated by the Prime Minister. The Cabinet secretariat is directly responsible to the Prime Minister and the allocation of functions between Cabinet, committees of the Cabinet and individual departments is controlled by him or her.

The organisation and control of central Government. The Prime Minister decides how Government functions should be allocated between departments and may create, amalgamate or abolish departments. He may take an active interest in the affairs of particular departments, especially the Treasury and Foreign and Commonwealth Office, intervene personally in major issues, and take decisions without consulting Cabinet.

Powers of patronage. By convention the Prime Minister enjoys substantial powers of patronage. He advises the Queen on the granting of peerages and other honours and on appointments to certain high offices of State, including bishops, Lords of Appeal and senior members of the armed forces. Senior appointments in the Civil Service must be approved by the Prime Minister.

Advising the Sovereign. The Sovereign, as titular head of the Executive, must act on the advice tendered by ministers and in particular the Prime Minister. The latter is the main channel of communication between the Cabinet and the Sovereign and keeps her informed on matters of State at a weekly audience. He has responsibility for advising the Queen on the dissolution of Parliament and may do so without consulting other members of the Cabinet.

Presentation and defence of Government policy. Prime Minister's Question Time in the House of Commons, speeches and interventions in debate always attract media attention. The Prime Minister controls Government communications and the dissemination of information.

The Cabinet

The origins and development of the Cabinet

At the close of the seventeenth century, Trenchard wrote in his *Short History of Standing Armies*:

> 'Formerly all matters of State and discretion were debated and resolved in Privy Council, where every man subscribed his opinion and was answerable for it. The late King Charles II was the first who broke this most excellent part of our constitution by setting up a cabal or cabinet council, where all matters of consequence were debated and resolved, and then brought to the Privy Council to be confirmed.'

A cabal was a club or association of intriguers; cabinet was a French word for a small private room or closet. Both words were derogatory and the whole passage illustrates the misgivings which surrounded the emergence of this new political institution, at the end of the seventeenth century.

At the restoration of the monarchy in 1660 the Privy Council was involved in a large volume of political and administrative business. Charles II become frustrated with the delays occasioned by debate and began to weaken the Council by removing political power from it, preferring to consult with a small number of trusted advisers. He was able to justify this to some extent by alleging that the size of the Privy Council made it unable to act in secrecy and with sufficient speed to meet the exigencies of great affairs. Yet it was he who increased the number of Privy Councillors so as to make it unwieldy and unworkable.

The use of a Cabinet vested real power in the hands of a small group of ministers who were not accountable to Parliament. Parliament complained that the Privy Council was not being consulted regularly and did not know who was responsible for the formulation of policy. Attempts were made to restore the Privy Council to its former status and in 1679 it was remodelled and the membership reduced from 50 to 30. Charles II promised to be guided by its advice but that promise was soon broken and a Cabinet, cabal or 'jurba' reappeared.

Clause 4 of the Act of Settlement 1700 would have imposed a statutory duty to govern by Council and not Cabinet. It provided that:

> '... all matters and things relating to the well governing of this country which are properly cognisable in the Privy Council by the bias and customs of this Realm shall be transacted

there, and all resolutions thereupon shall be signed by such of the Privy Council as shall consent to the same.'

This clause was a response to the alarm which the use of the Cabinet device had provoked, but it was repealed during the reign of Queen Anne before it came into effect. It is argued in Taswell-Longmead's *Constitutional History* that the last example of spontaneous and independent action by the Privy Council is to be found at the very end of the reign of Queen Anne, when the Council met and secured the Hanoverian succession against the Jacobites, as she lay on her death-bed.

By the middle of the eighteenth century the Cabinet had become a recognised institution, but its precise status was still uncertain. The relationship between the Cabinet and the party system was undefined as was the broader relationship of the Cabinet with Parliament. The process which eroded the right of the King to choose his ministers was a lengthy one.

Several factors taken together indicate the manner in which political power shifted away from the monarch to the Cabinet, until eventually the effective choice of ministers passed to the Prime Minister. Firstly, the eighteenth century saw a gradual decline in the prestige of the monarchy. George I did not attend Cabinet meetings after 1717 and both he and George II were frequently absent from Britain. This shifted the emphasis within the Cabinet towards the formulation of policy as well as its execution. A period of personal direction of national policy by George III between 1763 and 1782 culminated in the loss of the American colonies and the fall of Lord North's Government. This severe blow to the prestige of the monarchy was exacerbated by the onset of George III's mental illness in 1788. During his reign the Cabinet established the right to consider matters without the King's request that they should do so.

The party system was also developing in the eighteenth century and where, as under Walpole, who presided at Cabinet meetings between 1721 and 1742, the Cabinet was relatively homogeneous, its members met not only as advisers to the King, but as leaders of a party. Such a Cabinet was in a position to initiate policy and gain parliamentary support for it.

Gradually it became accepted that the Cabinet and Prime Minister needed the support of a majority in Parliament, and therefore must have the same political views as that majority. After the Reform Act of 1832, which extended the franchise and reformed abuses, it became clear that influence and patronage would no longer be sufficient to secure the election of that majority. The reliance of the Cabinet on the support of a majority in the Commons meant that the choice of ministers had been greatly narrowed, if it had not yet passed completely from the monarch's hands. The increased power of the electorate meant that the Executive had to be more responsive to its views. The chain of responsible Government, the Executive being responsible to Parliament and ultimately through the process of election of MPs to the electorate, was established.

Composition of the Cabinet

The number of ministers in the Cabinet is in the sole choice of the Prime Minister. Attlee thought 16 was the ideal, Churchill preferred a larger Cabinet of 22. Heath favoured a small Cabinet of 18 members while Labour Cabinets have fluctuated between 20 and 23. Prior to the General Election of 1992 Mr Major's Cabinet had 22 members. By convention and custom certain ministers are always members of the Cabinet. They include: the Lord Chancellor, Secretary of State for Foreign and Commonwealth Affairs, Home Secretary, Chancellor of the Exchequer, Secretary of State for Defence, Lord President of the Council, Leader of the House of Commons, Secretary of State for Scotland, together with the other Secretaries of State and ministers in charge of the major departments. In addition every Cabinet includes two or three ministers without portfolio who have no department of State but instead undertake special duties and often co-ordinate Government policy.

During wartime the normal Cabinet is usually replaced by a small War Cabinet to oversee the conduct of the war. During the First World War the War Cabinet had six members. The Second World War Cabinet had between seven and ten members. During the South Atlantic Campaign Mrs Thatcher formed an inner War Cabinet of five members: the Prime Minister, Foreign Secretary, Home Secretary, Secretary of State for Defence and the chairman of the Conservative Party.

Conventions relating to Cabinet Government

The main conventions of Cabinet Government are:

1. The Queen must act on the advice of her ministers.
2. The Cabinet must always tender unanimous advice.
3. The Cabinet must obtain and maintain a majority in the House of Commons on all major matters of policy.
4. The Cabinet must produce a 'Queen's Speech' at the opening of each session, stating the legislation which it proposes during that session.
5. The mandate doctrine requires the Government's statement in the Queen's Speech to be consistent with the policy on which they were elected. Latitude is allowable only in respect of issues that are unforeseeable, such as foreign affairs. Here the Government must offer policies consistent with its general political philosophy.

Cabinet committees

Since the end of the First World War a complicated Cabinet committee system has been established to facilitate the discussion and formulation of policy options and to co-ordinate the activities of the various Government departments, with regard to policy. The existence, composition and functions of these Cabinet committees has always been highly secret. However, intelligence suggested that Mrs Thatcher had some 25 standing Cabinet committees and about 110 ad hoc groups. In May 1992,

John Major broke with tradition by making public the existence of the Cabinet committees and naming the members of the committees.

It is now known that there are, in total, 26 main committees and sub-committees, not including the so-called 'Star Chamber' which resolves disputes between spending ministries and the Treasury.

The committee structure as of July 1994 was:

Economic and Domestic Policy (EDP)
Chairman: Prime Minister
Terms of reference: to consider strategic issues relating to the Government's economic and domestic policies.

Defence and Overseas Policy (OPD)
Chairman: Prime Minister
Terms of reference: to keep under review the Government's defence and overseas policy.

The Gulf (OPDG)
Chairman: Prime Minister
Terms of reference: to keep under review developments in the Gulf region and to co-ordinate any necessary action.

Nuclear Defence Policy (OPDN)
Chairman: Prime Minister
Terms of reference: to keep under review the Government's policy on nuclear defence.

European Security (OPDSE)
Chairman: Prime Minister
Terms of reference: to keep under review arrangements for defence and security in Europe.

Hong Kong and Other Dependent Territories (OPDK)
Chairman: Prime Minister
Terms of reference: to keep under review the implementation of the agreement with the Chinese on the future of Hong Kong and the implications of that agreement for the Government of Hong Kong and the well-being of its people; and to keep under review as necessary the Government's policy towards other Dependent Territories.

Northern Ireland (NI)
Chairman: Prime Minister
Terms of reference: to oversee the Government's policy on Northern Ireland issues and relations with the Republic of Ireland on these matters.

Science and Technology (EDS)
Chairman: Prime Minister
Terms of reference: to review science and technology policy.

The Intelligence Services (IS)
Chairman: Prime Minister
Terms of reference: to keep under review policy on the security and intelligence services.

Industrial, Commercial and Consumer Affairs (EDI)
Chairman: Chancellor of the Duchy of Lancaster
Terms of reference: to consider industrial, commercial and consumer issues including questions of competition and deregulation.

The Environment (EDE)
Chairman: Chancellor of the Duchy of Lancaster
Terms of reference: to consider questions of environmental policy.

Home and Social Affairs (EDH)
Chairman: Lord President of the Council
Terms of reference: to consider home and social policy issues.

Local Government (EDL)
Chairman: Chancellor of the Duchy of Lancaster
Terms of reference: issues affecting local government including the annual allocation of resources.

Regeneration (EDR)
Chairman: Chancellor of the Duchy of Lancaster
Terms of reference: regeneration policies and their co-ordination.

Public expenditure (EDX)
Chairman: Chancellor of the Exchequer
Term of reference: allocation of public expenditure control totals; makes recommendations to the Cabinet.

The Queen's Speeches and Future Legislation (FLG)
Chairman: Lord President of the Council
Terms of reference: to prepare and submit to the Cabinet drafts of the Queen's speeches to Parliament and proposals for the government's legislative programme for each session of Parliament.

Legislation (LG)
Chairman: Lord President of the Council
Terms of reference: to examine all draft Bills; to consider the parliamentary handling of government Bills, and European Community documents and private members' business and related matters; reviews government's policy in relation to issues of parliamentary procedures.

Sub-Committee on Health Strategy (EDH (H))
Chairman: Lord President of the Council
Terms of reference: to oversee the development, implementation and monitoring of the government's health strategy, to co-ordinate the government's policies on United

Kingdom-wide issues affecting health, and report as necessary to the Ministerial Committee on Home and Social Affairs.

Sub-Committee on Public Sector Pay (EDI (P))
Chairman: Chancellor of the Duchy of Lancaster
Terms of reference: to co-ordinate the handling of pay issues in the public sector, and report as necessary to the Ministerial Committee on Industrial, Commercial and Consumer Affairs.

Sub-Committee on European Questions (OPD (E))
Chairman: Secretary of State for Foreign and Commonwealth Affairs
Terms of reference: to consider questions relating to Britain's policy of assisting change in the former Soviet republics and other former communist countries in Europe and report as necessary to the Ministerial Committee on Defence and Overseas Policy.

Sub-committee on Eastern Europe
Chairman: Secretary of State for Foreign and Commonwealth Affairs
Terms of reference: Britain's policy of assisting change in the former Soviet republics and other former communist countries in Eastern Europe; reports to the committee on defence and overseas policy.

Sub-Committee on Terrorism (OPD (T))
Chairman: Secretary of State for the Home Department
Terms of reference: to keep under review the arrangements for countering terrorism and for dealing with terrorist incidents and their consequences; reports as necessary to the Ministerial Committee on Defence and Overseas Policy.

Sub-Committee on London (EDL (L))
Chairman: Secretary of State for the Environment
Terms of reference: to co-ordinate the government's policies on London.

Sub-Committee on Drug Misuse (EDH (D))
Chairman: Lord President of the Council
Terms of reference: to co-ordinate the government's national and international policies for tackling drugs misuse, and report as necessary to the Ministerial Committee on Home and Social Affairs.

Sub-Committee on Women's Issues (EDH (W))
Chairman: Secretary of State for Employment
Terms of reference: to review and develop the government's policy and strategy on issues of special concern to women; to oversee their implementation; and to report as necessary to the Ministerial Committee on Home and Social Affairs.

It can be seen from the above that the Prime Minister exercises considerable control over policy discussion by chairing nine of the committees.

The Cabinet secretariat
Before 1917 there was no machinery for recording Cabinet decisions. In 1917 a Secretary to the Cabinet was appointed to service Cabinet and Cabinet committee meetings, take minutes and circulate details of conclusions. The secretariat is headed by the Permanent Secretary to the Cabinet Office who is directly responsible to the Prime Minister.

Prime Minister's policy unit
The Prime Minister maintains a policy unit in Downing Street, independent of the Cabinet Office. There are at present nine members with the following responsibilities: home policy, law and order and environmental pollution; jobs, privatisation, tax and public sector; export credits, Scottish and Welsh affairs; education and science, employment, local government; housing, parliamentary affairs; defence, competition, agriculture, Civil Service; deregulation, pay, trade and industry; health and social security, Treasury affairs; energy, transport, the financial management initiative.

Cabinet secrecy
As all ministers must support Government policy it is desirable that the process by which such policy decisions are made be kept secret. Unless the Prime Minister decides otherwise, secrecy attaches to discussions in Cabinet, Cabinet papers and the proceedings of Cabinet committees.

Prime Ministerial or Cabinet Government

Cabinet Government was described by L S Amery in *Thoughts on the Constitution* 1953, as follows:

> 'The central directing instrument of government, in legislation as well as in administration, is the Cabinet. It is in Cabinet that administrative action is co-ordinated and that legislative proposals are sanctioned. It is the Cabinet which controls Parliament and governs the country.'

The special position enjoyed by the Prime Minister has led some authorities to the conclusion that Cabinet Government has now given way to Prime Ministerial Government. As Richard Crossman wrote: 'The post-war epoch has seen the final transformation of Cabinet Government into Prime Ministerial Government.' Certainly, if a Prime Minister took full advantage of the conventional powers available he could dominate Cabinet and policy formulation. But the power of the Prime Minister relative to the Cabinet depends upon a number of factors, including his personality and his strength and standing in Parliament and in the party.

10.2 Ministerial responsibility

Introduction

Democracy requires that those who govern should be responsible to those whom they govern. The convention of ministerial responsibility seeks to achieve this aim. It has two aspects:

1. The collective responsibility of the Government to Parliament and in particular to the House of Commons.
2. The individual responsibility of ministers to Parliament for decisions taken in their departments, whether by themselves or by their civil servants.

Collective responsibility

The doctrine of collective responsibility involves two rules:

1. The Government must resign if it loses the support of the House of Commons. The Prime Minister and his ministers are collectively responsible to Parliament for the conduct of national affairs. If he loses support in Parliament he must resign or seek a dissolution of Parliament.

   The rule does not mean that the Government must resign whenever it is defeated; there has to be a clear-cut defeat on a matter of policy. The Government may choose to treat an issue as a matter of confidence indicating that it will resign if defeated. The Opposition can move a motion of no confidence which if carried would mean the resignation of the Government.

   The resignation rule is not always regarded as part of collective responsibility, but as a separate convention. This is because collective responsibility is seen as the day-to-day answerability of the Government for policy, rather than its obligation to resign when it loses the confidence of the House. It seems more natural to treat resignation for lack of the confidence of the House as the ultimate threat which gives answerability its substance.

2. That the Government must speak with one voice. All members of the Government share in the collective responsibility of the Government, and ministers may not publicly criticise or dissociate themselves from Government policy. The essence of collective responsibility is that the Cabinet should be seen to be in agreement. A Cabinet minister who feels unable to agree with his colleagues should resign.

   The constitutional justification for the rule is that the answerability of the Government to Parliament would be much impaired if individual ministers were able to say that they personally did not agree with decisions taken in Cabinet. ministers, including non-Cabinet members, are normally bound therefore not to differ publicly from Cabinet decisions nor to speak or vote against the Government in Parliament.

The rule is closely related to that of Cabinet secrecy. As all ministers must support Government policy, it is desirable that the process by which such policy decisions are made be kept secret. Unless the Prime Minister decides otherwise therefore, secrecy attaches to discussions in Cabinet, Cabinet papers and the proceedings of Cabinet committees.

The rule increases party discipline and unity within the Government, strengthens the Government in Parliament and reinforces the secrecy of decision making within the Cabinet thereby minimising public disagreement between both ministers and Departments of State. It also serves to strengthen the authority of the Prime Minister in relation to his colleagues.

Agreements to differ

Occasionally it may be politically impossible for the Cabinet to maintain a collective front.

The National Government 1932
In 1932 the Liberal members of the National Government only agreed to remain on condition that they were allowed to speak and vote against it on the question of the imposition of tariffs. The Opposition attacked the Government for abandoning the convention of Cabinet responsibility but the Government defended itself on the ground that the National Government was a constitutional phenomenon to which new considerations applied. This episode became known as the 'agreement to differ'.

The Labour Government 1975
In 1975, the Labour Cabinet 'agreed to differ' on the question of the United Kingdom's continued membership of the EEC. A referendum was to be held and the Cabinet, by a majority of 16:7, decided to recommend continued membership of the EEC to the electorate. But it was agreed that ministers who opposed the Government's policy should be free to speak and campaign against it outside Parliament.

Individual responsibility

Ministers are responsible to Parliament for their own actions, omissions and mistakes as well as for those of the officials in their departments. Normally, criticism should be directed at the minister rather than at any civil servant who may be at fault. This principle is said to help preserve the anonymity and therefore the objectivity and efficiency of the Civil Service.

Ministerial responsibility for departmental maladministration

Two questions arise from the minister's departmental responsibility:

1. Is the minister obliged to accept responsibility for every piece of mal-administration within his department?
2. If maladministration is found to have occurred, is the minister under a duty to resign?

Situations in which a minister must accept responsibility

The Crichel Down affair 1954. Crichel Down was an area of farmland in Dorset which had been compulsorily acquired by the Air Ministry in 1939. After the war the land was transferred to the Ministry of Agriculture. The previous owner asked to re-purchase it, but was refused. The refusal was accompanied by misleading replies and assurances from the Ministry of Agriculture and was largely based upon an inaccurate report prepared by a civil servant. Members of Parliament raised the case with the Minister of Agriculture and an inquiry found that there had been 'muddle, inefficiency, bias and bad faith' on the part of certain officials. The report of the inquiry led to the resignation of the Minister of Agriculture, Sir Thomas Dugdale.

In the debate, the Home Secretary, Sir David Maxwell-Fyfe, stated his views as to when a minister must accept responsibility and not blame his civil servants.

1. A minister must protect a civil servant who has carried out his explicit orders.
2. Equally, a minister must defend a civil servant who acts properly in accordance with policy.
3. Where an official makes a mistake or causes some delay, but not on an important issue of policy and not where a claim to individual rights is seriously involved, the minister acknowledges the mistake and accepts responsibility although he is not personally involved. He states that he will take corrective action in the department.
4. Where action has been taken by a civil servant of which the minister disapproves and has no previous knowledge, and the conduct of the official is reprehensible, there is no obligation on a minister to endorse what he believes to be wrong or to defend what are clearly shown to be errors of his officers. He remains, however, constitutionally responsible to Parliament for the fact that something has gone wrong, but this does not affect his power to control and discipline his staff.

   While civil servants cannot usually be blamed by the minister, they are employed at the pleasure of the Crown and can be dismissed at any time.

Is there a duty to resign? There is no suggestion that a minister has to resign if he does accept responsibility. As Professor Finer concluded, there can be no rule of resignation because of the irregularity and unpredictability of the sanction. He divided 'delinquent ministers' into the 'fortunate' who go to other ministries, the 'less fortunate' who go to another place (the House of Lords), the 'unfortunate' who simply go, and the 'plain unlucky' who have to write resignation speeches or letters. Whether a minister has to resign or not depends upon a variety of political factors including the temperament of the minister, the attitude of the Prime Minister, the mood of the Party and the tone of the Opposition.

The courts and ministerial responsibility

While the courts cannot enforce the convention of ministerial responsibility they do, from time to time, cite it as a reason for not intervening to quash a minister's decision. In particular the courts will recognise the fact that ministers will frequently have to delegate their decision-making functions. Whilst, strictly, this would be a breach of the rule against sub-delegation, the courts accept that ultimately the minister is responsible to Parliament for the actions carried out on his behalf and with his authority by senior civil servants.

10.3 Government departments

Government departments, sometimes known as ministries, are, in law, part of the Crown. They are involved in the everyday process of assisting in the formulation of Executive policy and executing the law. In general constitutional terms, each department is headed by a minister, sometimes known as a Secretary of State, who is answerable to Parliament for all the operations of his department. These departments are staffed by civil servants, full-time paid employees who owe their position to appointment not election and who do not lose their position when one Government falls and is replaced by another.

The creation of Government departments: fission, fusion and transfer

Except for periods of wartime emergency, it is difficult to find an example of the creation of a new department in direct response to the discovery of a new need. Needs become gradually evident and at first are usually provided for through an existing department dealing with matters which are in some way similar.

For example, the nineteenth century saw the growth of the social service functions of Government. Some of these functions were attached at first to the Home Office (itself set up in 1782) or Board of Trade. Others were performed by a committee of the Privy Council set up to perform the particular functions concerned. When the administrative duties of these committees became more complicated it was felt necessary that they should be entrusted to a separate department. The relevant committee of the Privy Council developed into what was called a board and eventually into a fully fledged ministry or department. Thus, a new department is created at a point where a function becomes sufficiently important and sufficiently complex to require separate departmental organisation. It has been said by Hanson and Walles in their book *Governing Britain* that as regards Government departments and their spheres of responsibility there has been 'a continuous process of creation, fission, fusion and transfer'.

Fusion and fission

An illustration of fusion and fission is provided by the functions originally vested in the Ministry of Health when it was set up in 1918. The Ministry of Health took over from other authorities various functions concerned with the relief of poverty and the improvement of the conditions of life. Thus the ministry:

1. Took over the powers of the Local Government Board.
2. Replaced the English and Welsh Insurance Commissioners.
3. Acquired the Privy Council's powers over the midwifery service.
4. Acquired the powers of the Home Office over infant life protection, the practice of anatomy and the treatment of lunacy and mental deficiency.

In addition, a variety of other functions were transferred to the Ministry of Health from the Board of Trade, the Ministry of Agriculture and Fisheries and the Board of Education. It was also responsible in the 1920s for operating the then very rudimentary town and country planning legislation.

It seemed like good policy to gather together such services in one ministry in order to ensure their proper co-ordination but the functions of the Government in these fields increased, especially after the Second World War, and the ministry became unwieldy, with the danger that certain of its functions would be neglected. So the process of fission (splitting up) was put into operation and the responsibilities of the former Ministry of Health became divided between three ministries: Health; Housing and Local Government; and Ministry of Social Security.

The process is illustrated by the following diagram:

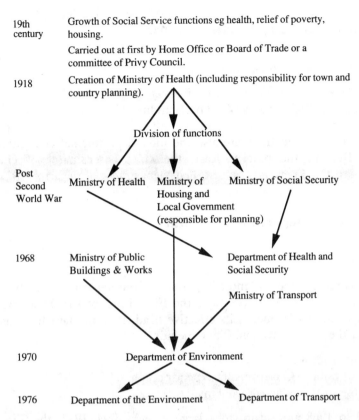

19th century   Growth of Social Service functions eg health, relief of poverty, housing.

Carried out at first by Home Office or Board of Trade or a committee of Privy Council.

1918   Creation of Ministry of Health (including responsibility for town and country planning).

Division of functions

Post Second World War   Ministry of Health   Ministry of Housing and Local Government (responsible for planning)   Ministry of Social Security

1968   Ministry of Public Buildings & Works   Department of Health and Social Security

Ministry of Transport

1970   Department of Environment

1976   Department of the Environment   Department of Transport

However, change occurred again in 1970 when housing, local government and planning became part of the new Department of the Environment, which also until 1976 had responsibility for transport. In 1968 health and social security were fused to form the Department of Health and Social Security, a 'super department' which became too unwieldy for one secretary of state. From June 1987 the two parts were again separated into two departments, the Department of Health and the Department of Social Security.

Transfer

In addition to this fusion and fission process there has been, over the years, an almost continuous process of functions being transferred from one department to another. Excluding instances of creation and transfer made for purely political reasons, for example, to please a particular interest group by giving recognition to their interest by the creation of a new department, or to increase the status of one minister at the expense of another, the aim is to produce departments with what has been described as 'coherent missions'. Of course, it is impossible today to divide Government functions into a series of neatly defined blocks each to be occupied by one Government department, and so the boundaries between the Government departments are blurred, and continually changing.

Co-ordination of Government activities

The ultimate responsibility for the co-ordination of Government activities lies with the Cabinet and the Prime Minister. The Standing Committees of the Cabinet on defence and overseas policy and economic affairs may also have a particularly important role to play, and there are also the inter-departmental committees at civil service level. But, in the past at least, the chief co-ordinator of Government activities has been the Treasury, the so-called 'department of departments'.

10.4 The principal departments of State

The Treasury

The Treasury is regarded as the most important of the departments of State and the Prime Minister is always, by convention, the First Lord of the Treasury, although the Chancellor of the Exchequer is its effective head. Its important functions place it at the centre of the Administration. They include:

1. the raising of revenue;
2. the control of public (Government) expenditure; and
3. the overseeing of the national economy.

From 1920 to 1968 and again, to a large extent, since 1982, the Treasury also managed the Civil Service. This involved the control of Civil Service promotion and appointments, especially at the highest levels, the direction of organisation and methods, and the overseeing of discipline. In 1968 the Government adopted the Fulton Committee's recommendation for a Civil Service Department, and this was established, headed by the Prime Minister. It was disbanded at the end of 1981.

Departmental estimates of their spending for the coming year have to be approved by the Treasury before presentation to Parliament. Whenever a department proposes action involving new expenditure or new distribution of existing expenditure the consent of the Treasury is, in effect, necessary.

The Home Office

While the functions of the Treasury are all closely inter-related, the Home Office, by contrast, has many very different duties involving an enormous volume of work. They include the organisation of the prison service, race relations, immigration and nationality, together with important responsibilities for the fire service, the police and internal security. The Home Office has a large staff: about 25,000 compared with 1,000 in the Treasury. However, the Treasury's tasks are regarded as particularly important and so it has 25 per cent more senior civil servants than the Home Office. Ambitious civil servants covet posts in the Treasury and this would seem to be a recognition of its influential position in Government structure and the power of its officials. The head of the Home Office is the Home Secretary.

The Department of Health

This department is responsible for health services. The National Health Service Reorganisation Act 1973 provided for the establishment of 14 regional health authorities and 90 area health authorities, and smaller district authorities were also set up. In 1980 the area authorities were disbanded so that the pattern now is one of regional and district authorities only.

The Department of Social Security

This department, separated from that of Health in 1987, is responsible for social security services such as war pensions, sickness benefit, maternity allowance and supplementary benefit.

The Department of the Environment

This department, headed by the Secretary of State for the Environment, was formed in 1970 from the former Ministries of Housing and Local Government, Transport, and Public Buildings and Works. It no longer has responsibility for transport, which was transferred to a separate Department of Transport in 1976. The functions of the Department of the Environment include:

1. Local government and development, covering local government, land use and town and country planning, countryside and conservation, water, sewerage and refuse disposal.
2. Housing and construction, dealing with housing programmes, home improvements, building regulations, building research and development, government accommodation at home and overseas, and maintenance of royal parks, palaces, and museums.

The Foreign and Commonwealth Office

The Foreign Office and the Commonwealth Office merged in 1968 under a Secretary of State for Foreign and Commonwealth Affairs. In 1975 the Ministry of Overseas Development lost its identity as a separate Government department and became a part of the Foreign and Commonwealth Office. The then Minister of Overseas Development, Mrs Judith Hart, was highly critical of this move, regarding it as an indication of the Government's increasing lack of commitment to providing overseas aid to developing countries. Since the present Conservative Government came to power this part of the Foreign and Commonwealth Office has been known as the Overseas Development Administration.

The Foreign and Commonwealth Office is staffed, as are overseas missions, consular posts and delegations, by members of the Diplomatic Service. This is a body separate from the Civil Service which was formed in 1965, although even before that date the Foreign Service had an identity which was separate from the Home Civil Service.

In 1977, the Central Policy Review Staff produced a report on the Diplomatic Service, which caused considerable controversy in Government circles, and which on the whole, has not been acted upon. The guiding premise was that Britain's power and influence in the world had declined considerably since the Second World War but that Government servants and ministers alike had failed to recognise this. The report stressed that more emphasis should be placed on British exports and on Britain's commercial and economic interests. It urged greater inter-action and exchange between those in Government posts overseas and in key departments concerned with exports, such as the Department of Trade and Industry. In this way diplomats would not lose touch with change in the country they represented and civil servants in departments like Trade and Industry, part of whose job was to generate an export drive, would not lose track of changing markets at which they were supposed to be aiming.

The report favoured the establishment of a 4,000 strong Foreign Service Group drawing its staff from the Department of Trade and Industry, the Ministry of Overseas Development (as it then was) and the Foreign and Commonwealth Office. This group was to co-ordinate and handle the most important economic negotiations at home and overseas, and the adoption of the scheme would have meant that some of the main diplomatic posts, particularly in key trade countries, would no longer go to Foreign Office diplomats but to young 'high fliers' from the Department of Trade and Industry. This scheme was not adopted. But it has been quite a long-standing practice for members of the Department of Trade to serve at overseas posts on loan or attachment, and since the 1977 report the practice has increased of diplomatic staff being seconded, for perhaps two years at a time, to the Department of Trade and Industry, the Department of Energy, the Treasury, or the Ministry of Defence.

The Ministry of Defence

A unified Ministry of Defence was established in 1964 by the merger of four separate departments: the Ministry of Defence, the Admiralty, the War Office, and the Air Ministry. Its responsibilities include:

1. the formulation of defence policy; and
2. control and administration of the armed forces.

The political head of the ministry is the Secretary of State for Defence.

Other departments

Other Government departments include the Departments of Agriculture, Fisheries and Food; Education and Science; Employment; Energy; Trade and Industry; and Transport. In addition there are the Northern Ireland, Scottish, Welsh and Privy Council Offices, the Paymaster General's Department and the Department of the Duchy of Lancaster.

10.5 The Civil Service

What is a civil servant?

A civil servant may be defined as a servant of the Crown employed in a civil capacity who is paid wholly and directly out of money voted by Parliament. This definition excludes the armed services who are employed in a military and not in a civil capacity and police officers. It also excludes public servants in local government and the public corporations who are not servants of the Crown, and are not paid directly from money voted by Parliament. The term 'civil' also implies a distinction from the 'political' service consisting of ministers responsible to Parliament.

Pre-nineteenth century organisation of the Civil Service

Before the nineteenth century it was not possible to speak of a Civil Service since each department head had almost complete independence in the matter of recruitment, which was generally by patronage or purchase of a sinecure, and there were no general rates of pay applicable across department boundaries, nor indeed possibilities for movement from one department to another.

The Northcote-Trevelyan Report and late nineteenth century reforms

In 1854 Sir Stafford Northcote and Sir Charles Trevelyan presented a commissioned *Report on the Organisation of the Permanent Civil Service*. Four main points were made in the report:

1. For recruitment, open competitive examinations should be introduced, standardised throughout the service and conducted by a central board.
2. There should be a distinction between the 'intellectuals' and the 'mechanicals', namely, those destined for 'superior situations' and those who were to occupy 'the lower class of appointments', and the two classes should be recruited at two quite distinct educational levels.
3. The service should be unified by the introduction of uniform salary grades and the principle of free transferability of a civil servant from one department to another.

4. Promotion should be by merit rather than by seniority and safeguards should be introduced to prevent abuses in the promotion system.

In 1855 Civil Service Commissioners were appointed by Order in Council and given the task of organising a system of examinations for recruitment. By Orders in Council in 1870, a system of open competitive examinations was introduced for all departments except the Home Office (which has now come within the system) and the Foreign Office, with separate examination for Class 1 and Class 2, the Northcote-Trevelyan intellectuals and mechanicals. The staff of all departments were unified into one Civil Service and certain general rates of pay and pensions were laid down.

It will be seen that the fundamentals laid down by Northcote and Trevelyan have remained virtually unchallenged until very recent times.

The Fulton Report 1968: its criticisms and recommendations

There have been, since the Northcote-Trevelyan Report, several reviews of the organisation of the Civil Service. Perhaps the most important in terms of actually bringing about change was the Fulton Report of 1968. The Fulton Commission, set up in 1966, saw six major defects in the organisation. These included:

1. The service was too much based on the philosophy of the amateur, the generalist or all-rounder, rather than emphasising the need for particular skills for particular jobs.
2. After 1920 the Northcote-Trevelyan divisions into intellectuals and mechanicals was replaced by a four-fold division of administrative class, executive class, clerical class, and clerical assistant class. Each class was recruited at distinct educational levels and class to class promotion was extremely difficult. The Fulton Committee, considering this, concluded that the system of classes, each with a separate pay and career structure, impeded the most efficient use of individuals.
3. The 'specialists', for example the medical officer and legal classes, as opposed to the 'generalist' classes, were denied opportunities for full administrative responsibility. They never took the top positions.
4. Personnel management and career planning were inadequate.

The post-Fulton reforms

In 1971 the administrative, executive and clerical classes merged to form one administrative group. Recruitment to each of the three classes is still at three distinct educational levels and promotion from one class to another can still prove difficult.

In 1968 a special Civil Service Department was set up to take over responsibility for the management and recruitment functions of the Treasury and the Civil Service

Commissions, although the commission still exists to deal with the actual task of recruitment. At the end of 1981 the Civil Service Department ceased to exist as a separate department. Its responsibility for pay and conditions was handed back to the Treasury, while responsibility for management of the service and personnel matters was transferred to the Cabinet Office.

The continuing need for reform

The effect of the amateur tradition is still felt in the Civil Service. For the generalist classes, the main requirement seems to be that recruits should have a broad general education, a 'good mind', and the ability to examine matters, technical or otherwise, from the viewpoint of the intelligent amateur. Leading figures in the Treasury and the Department of Trade and Industry do not need to have degrees or training in economics. Officials in the Ministry of Agriculture, Fisheries and Food do not need degrees in agriculture or similar qualifications. The theory behind this approach is that the more specifically technical information can be obtained through the advisory committee system which is partly staffed by experts from outside the Civil Service, or can be supplied by its own specialist classes. It is suggested by some that it is necessary to recruit more graduates for their specific qualifications in languages, economics, science and technology, rather than for their general abilities as revealed by academic achievement in arts subjects and classics. It is also suggested that there is no reason why some of the top management posts should not go to those in the specialist rather than the generalist classes.

Promotion from the top clerical grades to the lower executive grades and from the top executive to the lower administrative grades still presents greater difficulties than it should.

Over the last decade there has been an increasing trend towards quasi-privatisation of civil service functions, with the devolution of power to nearly 100 semi-independent agencies under the 'Next Steps' programme. Amongst the functions re-allocated were passports, prisons and social security benefits. On the basis of the White Paper 'Continuity and Change' published in July 1994, it would appear that the trend towards de-centralisation is set to continue. Among its key proposals are the following: performance-related pay for senior civil servants; increased flexibility in pay structures for senior staff; overall staffing levels to decline further. In 1979 there were 732,000 civil servants, the figure for 1994 was 533,000. The White Paper envisages the total dropping to below 500,000 by 1998. The White Paper does not address the implications for the working relationship between senior civil servants and ministers, and the provision of information for parliamentary questions.

In a separate Cabinet Office report, also published in July 1994, the government confirmed its support for the 'fast track' stream under which the most able graduates would be able to rise quickly to senior positions within the service.

10.6 The relationship between ministers and civil servants

The theory

The theoretical position is that ministers, who are elected representatives, make policy decisions under the influence of a variety of factors, and civil servants, who are paid employees and non-representative, execute those decisions. However, it has long been accepted that the reality may be very far from this theoretical concept and that civil servants may play an important part in determining Government policy and activity. Nevertheless, the doctrine of ministerial responsibility whereby the minister is responsible to Parliament and ultimately to the public for all that happens within his ministry still exists, since it is accepted as an essential foundation of British democracy that those who govern the people should be answerable through Parliament to the people.

The reality

In real terms the importance of the Civil Service in the formulation of policy in any particular case is dependent upon various factors. However, the following points may be considered:

1. Ministers are Members of Parliament as well as heads of Government departments and will have parliamentary and constituency duties as well as ministerial responsibilities. By contrast, the civil servant spends all his working time in the department. Inevitably, some decision taking of lesser importance will fall upon the top civil servants in the department.
2. Ministers frequently move from department to department and, when newly arrived, a minister is inevitably very reliant on his civil servants for some things.
3. The very extent of Government activities today means that some decision-taking will rest with higher civil servants.
4. Civil servants are expected to supply the minister with the information he needs in order to come to a decision on any particular matter. Obviously his decision can be influenced by the way in which the information is presented and, indeed, by what information is omitted. A minister may ask top civil servants for advice, and even if he requests an outline of the possible alternatives with the pros and cons, there are clearly plenty of opportunities for the civil servants to influence the minister's decision.
5. An enormous amount of law today takes the form of statutory instruments. These are actually drafted by the civil servants in the relevant department, unlike Acts of Parliament which are drafted by parliamentary counsel.

On the other hand

One of the main qualities of a politician must be an ability to influence people and that should be a considerable weapon in the hands of the minister, particularly if he chooses to have contact with his department through the permanent secretary only, on a one-to-one basis.

Policy decisions have to be acceptable to the Cabinet, the Treasury, the party and Parliament. There is a strong incentive for the minister to have the last word since he will have to defend the decisions before these bodies.

It is difficult to come to any clear conclusion as to how much influence lies with the civil servants. Perhaps the most that may be said is that it varies from situation to situation depending on factors such as:

1. Whether the Government and ministers are clear in their own minds as to precisely what they wish to achieve. Are they clear as to the policies they wish to adopt? A Government newly coming to power with pre-determined policies to carry into effect may be contrasted here with a Government that has been in power for a long time and has perhaps executed such of its manifesto pledges as it wishes to carry out.
2. Whether the policy concerned is one on which the Government party has taken a strong line. If so the opportunities for 'sabotage' by civil servants are fewer and the minister has a strong incentive to ensure the policy's execution.
3. The strength of personality of minister and permanent secretary.

Some politicians and political scientists have taken a much stronger line than that indicated above and have insisted in very strong terms on the independence of mind of civil servants and on their ability to sabotage a minister's scheme. The Labour Party politician and former senior minister, Mr Tony Benn, has expressed this view, and Mrs Barbara Castle, another former senior Labour minister, has spoken of the lack of enthusiasm of civil servants in executing socialist policies. It is argued that there would never be a truly effective thorough-going socialist Government in this country whilst the present organisation of the Civil Service exists.

10.7 Rules affecting the political activities of civil servants

In order to preserve the appearance of political neutrality, civil servants are limited as to the political activities they may undertake. No civil servant may become a Member of Parliament: House of Commons Disqualification Act 1975. A civil servant is required to resign his position before his nomination as a parliamentary candidate can be accepted: Servants of the Crown (Parliamentary Candidature) Order 1960.

Beyond this, political activity is restricted according to which of three groups a civil servant is a member of:

1. *The restricted category.* Civil Servants in senior administrative grades, and staff in executive or clerical grades whose work is associated with those in the position of giving advice to ministers, or whose work involves direct contact with the public, are barred from participation in political activities at national level. Although they may be members of a political party, they may not hold office in the party, and may not express in public any views on matters of national political controversy. With permission they may take part in local politics, associated with the work of the local council, but are obliged to act with discretion, particularly where a matter concerns the department where they are employed. In practice, it is unlikely that those in senior administrative grades would seek permission to associate themselves publicly with any particular political party.

2. *The intermediate category.* Civil servants in this category may, with the permission of their departments, take part in all political activity both local and national, except parliamentary candidature. However, they must observe a code of discretion, for example, they may discuss in public national policies, but are to avoid personal attacks on ministers, or causing embarrassment to the departments which employ them.

3. *The politically free category.* This includes industrial civil servants – for example, those working in Royal Ordnance factories – and those non-industrial civil servants in the most minor grades. They may engage in all political activities whether at national or local level, other than parliamentary candidature, unless they are on duty, wearing uniform or on Government premises at the time.

It must be remembered, of course, that all civil servants are subject to the provisions of the Official Secrets Acts 1911 to 1989, which prohibit the passing on by a civil servant of any confidential information gained by him by virtue of his employment.

10.8 Tenure of appointment of civil servants

Unless statute provides otherwise, all civil servants are employed at the pleasure of the Crown. They may therefore, in law, be dismissed at pleasure and civil servants have no common law remedy for wrongful dismissal or breach of contract of employment. The civil service staff associations and the Crown have negotiated procedures for disciplining and dismissing staff, and the Employment Protection (Consolidation) Act 1978 (as amended) now gives civil servants a statutory right to appeal to an industrial tribunal in respect of unfair dismissal. In practice civil servants enjoy one of the most secure tenures of employment in the country.

10.9 The Privy Council

Introduction

Today the Privy Council has more than 380 members. Appointments are made by the Sovereign on the advice of her ministers. By convention all Cabinet ministers must be sworn as members of the Privy Council. Holders of certain high offices, such as the Archbishops of Canterbury and York, the Speaker of the House of Commons, the Lords of Appeal in Ordinary, the Lords Justices of Appeal, the Master of the Rolls, the Lord Chief Justice, the President of the Family Division, senior non-Cabinet ministers, distinguished politicians and eminent judges from the Commonwealth, and others who have rendered high public or political service, may also be appointed. Members must be British subjects or citizens of the Republic of Ireland. Appointment is for life. All members of the Privy Council are entitled to the prefix 'the Right Honourable'.

The Privy Councillors' oath

On appointment new Privy Councillors must swear on oath not to disclose anything said or done in Council. It was thought that this oath preserved Cabinet secrecy, but following the decision in *Attorney-General* v *Jonathan Cape Ltd* (*The Crossman Diaries Case*) [1976] QB 752 this is now doubtful.

Meetings of the Privy Council

Meetings of the Privy Council are held in the presence of the Queen. The Lord President of the Council, a senior minister, is responsible for summoning the members and drafting the agenda. For a quorum at least three members must be present. Usually four are summoned and they will be the ministers most concerned with the business to be transacted. All formal acts of the Council are expressed either as Orders in Council which are authenticated by the signature of the Clerk of the Council, or as proclamations which are signed by the Queen personally. It is customary to make the more important executive orders by way of Order in Council, as it is felt that this gives to them an added dignity. Although the Orders issued by the Council are still expressed to be made by the Queen with the advice of her Privy Council, the Council has in fact lost its advisory role and merely records formal assent to the documents already deliberated and decided upon by Cabinet, committee of the Council or the various ministers and Government departments.

The Privy Council Office

Business for the Privy Council and its committees is prepared by the Privy Council Office for which the Lord President of the Council is responsible. The Clerk of the

Privy Council in Ordinary is the permanent head of this office and both he and the deputy head are appointed by the Sovereign on the Lord President's recommendation.

Committees of the Privy Council

Several standing committees of the Privy Council exist. These include the Political Honours Scrutiny Committee which advises on the suitability of persons to receive titles and honours at CBE level and above; the Baronetage Committee which reports on claims to baronetcies; the Universities Committee which advises on the Statute of the Universities of Oxford and Cambridge; and committees on the Isle of Man and the Channel Islands which report on Bills passed by the island legislatures. Ad hoc committees of the Privy Council may also be appointed by the Crown at any time to advise upon particular questions. In 1982 for example, members of the Privy Council, under the chairmanship of Lord Franks, were appointed to conduct an inquiry into the apparent failure of the Government to respond to intelligence information in such a way as to prevent an invasion of the Falkland Islands occurring.

The Judicial Committee of the Privy Council

In 1641 the Act for Abolishing Arbitrary Courts was passed, abolishing the prerogative jurisdiction of the monarch through the Privy Council to hear civil and criminal cases which fell within the jurisdiction of the ordinary courts of equity and common law. The Privy Council was still able to hear appeals from the overseas possessions of the Crown, and as the British Empire expanded throughout the 18th century it became usual to provide for appeal from the decisions of the colonial courts to His Majesty's Privy Council. With the growth of the Empire the amount of judicial business coming before the Privy Council from the Colonies increased to the extent that in 1833 it became necessary for the Judicial Committee Act to be passed. This Act 'for the better administration of justice in his Majesty's Privy Council' constituted a committee of the Privy Council to be known as the Judicial Committee. Together with the Judicial Committee Act 1844, this is still the principal United Kingdom enactment regarding the Judicial Committee.

The Judicial Committee comprises the Lord President of the Council (who never sits), persons who hold or have held high judicial office in the United Kingdom and are Privy Councillors, and senior members of the judiciary from certain Commonwealth countries which retain the right of appeal to the Privy Council. The quorum of the Judicial Committee is three, but usually five members sit to hear an appeal.

The Judicial Committee hears appeals from the Superior Courts of the Isle of Man, the Channel Islands, Colonies, associated States, and such independent Commonwealth countries as have retained the right of appeal from their own courts.

Appeals may lie as of right, with leave of the court below, or by special leave of the Judicial Committee. The committee will only give special leave to appeal in a criminal case if there has been such disregard of the forms of legal process or the principles of natural justice as to involve a substantial and grave injustice to the accused. Special leave will only be granted in civil cases where important points of law, matters of public importance, or substantial property are in issue.

The Judicial Committee does not deliver a judgment. Its decision is still delivered in the form of an advice and the Government issues an Order in Council to give effect to that advice. The Judicial Committee (Dissenting Opinions) Order 1966 now permits dissenting opinions to be delivered. The committee is not strictly bound by its own decisions.

The Judicial Committee of the Privy Council also exercises a number of functions within the United Kingdom legal system:

1. It hears appeals from various professional disciplinary bodies including the General Medical Council and other professions ancillary to medicine. It also hears some appeals from the ecclesiastical courts.
2. Under s4 of the Judicial Committee Act 1833 the Crown may refer any matter to the Judicial Committee for an advisory opinion.
3 Under s7 of the House of Commons Disqualification Act 1975 any member of the public may apply to the Judicial Committee for a declaration that a member of the House of Commons is disqualified under the Act.

11

The Crown

11.1 Introduction

11.2 Title to the Crown

11.3 Royal finance

11.4 Duties of the Sovereign

11.5 The Queen as head of the Established Church

11.6 Act of State

11.1 Introduction

Historically the greater part of the machinery of central Government emanates from the Crown. It is for that reason that from very early days the central government has been exercised in the name of the Sovereign. In the United Kingdom the legal Sovereign is the monarch (Queen Elizabeth II). But the monarch is not an absolute ruler. The United Kingdom has a constitutional monarchy, sovereignty being vested in the Queen in Parliament. In this respect a distinction must be made between the Sovereign and the Crown. When referring to the Queen's personal executive functions one speaks of the Sovereign. When referring to the function of the central Government generally, one speaks of the Crown.

There has been some confusion as to how the distinction between the Crown and the Government should be delineated. In *Town Investments* v *Department of the Environment* [1978] AC 359 Lord Diplock observed that:

'Where ... [the courts] are concerned with the legal nature of the exercise of executive powers of government, I believe that some of the more Athanasian-like features of the debate in your Lordships' House could have been eliminated if instead of speaking of "the Crown" we were to speak of the "government" – a term appropriate to embrace both collectively and individually all of the ministers of the Crown and parliamentary secretaries under whose direction the administrative work of government is carried on by the civil servants employed in the various Government departments. It is through them that the executive powers of Her Majesty's Government in the United Kingdom are exercised, sometimes in the more important administrative matters in Her Majesty's name, but most often under their own official designation. Executive acts of government that are done by

164

any of them are acts done by 'the Crown' in the fictional sense in which that expression is now used in English public law.'

As H W R Wade points out:

'... the case did not concern statutory powers and it should presumably not be taken to alter the rule that powers conferred upon ministers belong to them personally and not to the Crown. Otherwise the system of remedies would be gravely weakened.' (*Administrative Law* 6th ed p52 n2)

The reasoning behind this comment is that the Crown has historical immunities in litigation that it can choose to waive, or agree to limit by way of legislation. Coercive remedies, particularly prerogative orders, cannot lie against the Crown, in the proper sense of that phrase. Thus a minister purporting to act on behalf of the Crown would enjoy similar immunities. The essential question, therefore, is when are ministers acting as the Crown, and when are they acting as administrative agents? The solution may lie in distinguishing between the exercise of prerogative and statutory power. In the case of the former, the minister is acting as the agent of the Crown, the only form of 'control' being the declaratory judgment. In the latter case the minister is a 'body of limited jurisdiction' subject to the full range of controls provided by way of judicial review. It is for this reason that certain aspects of Lord Diplock's analysis, extracted above, should be approached with caution.

The discussion is important because the Crown (if one can use that expression in the light of the foregoing) enjoys considerable immunities and privileges at law; if these were to extend to ministers then legal challenge to the exercise of their powers would be severely curtailed. Where a minister, or other statutory body, exercises statutory powers in his, or its, own name, normal legal controls, in particular judicial review, will be available. Problems still arise, however, where persons enter into contracts with the Crown, or are injured by the negligence of Crown servants.

11.2 Title to the Crown

The title to the Crown was originally elective and the notion of an hereditary monarchy grew gradually. At common law the title to the Crown of England was governed by the feudal rules of hereditary descent formerly applicable to land, except that in the case of a Sovereign dying and leaving no son but several daughters, the Crown descends to the eldest alone. She who holds the Crown in her own right as Queen of England has the same powers, prerogatives, rights and dignities as if she had been a King.

Ever since the Glorious Revolution of 1688 title to the Crown has been a matter which Parliament may regulate by statute. Today the Queen derives her title to the Crown from the Act of Settlement 1700, the Union with Scotland Act 1706, which constituted one Kingdom of Great Britain, and the Union with Ireland Act 1800 (as varied by the Government of Ireland Act 1920 and the Royal and Parliamentary

Titles Act 1927), whereby the United Kingdom means Great Britain and Northern Ireland. By the Act of Settlement 1700 the Crown of England, France and Ireland was settled on Princess Sophia, Electress of Hanover and granddaughter of James I, 'and the heirs of her body being Protestant'.

The Act of Settlement therefore disqualifies from the succession Roman Catholics and those who marry Roman Catholics. The Sovereign must also swear to maintain the Established Churches in England and Scotland, and must be in communion with the Church of England. His Majesty's Declaration of Abdication Act 1936 altered the hereditary succession to the Crown in that it provided that Edward VIII, his issue, if any, and the descendants of that issue should not thereafter have any right to the succession.

The royal titles

By Royal Proclamation under the Great Seal issued under the Royal Titles Act 1953, the present royal title is:

Elizabeth II by the Grace of God of the United Kingdom of Great Britain and Northern Ireland and of Her other Realms and Territories Queen, Head of the Commonwealth, Defender of the Faith.

The forms of royal title adopted by other member States of the Commonwealth for the Queen vary.

Royal marriages

Under the Royal Marriages Act 1772, the marriage of a descendant of George II (other than the issue of princesses who have married into foreign families) shall be void unless the Sovereign has signified formal consent. Such a person may marry without the Sovereign's consent if he is over 25, provided 12 months' notice is given to the Privy Council and Parliament does not object.

Regency and Counsellors of State

The Regency Acts 1937–53 make provision for a regency in the event of the Sovereign being under the age of 18 years on his accession and in the event of the incapacity of the Sovereign through illness. They also make provision for the performance of certain of the royal functions in the Queen's name by Counsellors of State appointed by letters patent whenever she is absent or intends to be absent from the United Kingdom.

In the case of regency, normally the regent will be the next person in the line of succession who is not disqualified by the Act of Settlement and is a British subject domiciled in the United Kingdom and of full age. The regent may exercise all royal functions except the granting of assent to a Bill to alter the succession to the throne, or to repeal the Scottish Act of 1706 securing the Scottish religion and Church.

Counsellors of State may exercise those functions conferred upon them by letters patent. They may not, however, dissolve Parliament, except on the Sovereign's express instructions, nor grant any title or dignity of the peerage. The Counsellors of State must be the wife or husband of the Sovereign, the four persons next in line of succession to the Crown (unless disqualified from being regent or absent from the realm) and Queen Elizabeth, the Queen Mother.

Demise of the Crown

'... the death of the Sovereign ... signifies merely a transfer of property; for when we say the demise of the Crown, we mean only that in consequence of the disunion of the Sovereign's natural body from his body politic, the Kingdom is transferred to his successor and so the royal dignity remains perpetual.' (Paraphrase of I Plowdens Reports 1550–80, page 177a.)

The paraphrase above explains as well as it is possible to do so the saying that 'the King never dies'. There may be a demise of the Crown on the death, abdication or deposition of the Sovereign. When any such event occurs the member of the Royal Family next in succession to the throne immediately accedes to the rights, privileges, and dignities of the monarch. The meeting of an Accession Council and the coronation are little more than public affirmations of the fact of the accession of the new monarch.

Formerly public business and tenure of public office were affected by a demise of the Crown, but this is no longer the case. Sections 4 and 5 of the Succession to the Crown Act 1707 and s51 of the Representation of the People Act 1867 provide that Parliament shall continue for its normal term despite the death of the reigning Sovereign, unless sooner prorogued or dissolved by his successor.

The Demise of the Crown Act 1901, s1 provides that:

'The holding of any office under the Crown, whether within or without His Majesty's dominions, shall not be affected, nor shall any fresh appointment thereto be rendered necessary, by the demise of the Crown.'

11.3 Royal finance

Since the reign of George III it has been customary at the beginning of each reign for the Sovereign to surrender to Parliament for his life all the hereditary revenues of the Crown, including the Crown estates. In return Parliament grants the Civil List which is an annual sum to meet the salaries and other expenses of the royal household (Civil List Act 1952 as amended in 1972 and 1975), including sums for the use of those members of the Royal Family who undertake official duties on behalf of the Sovereign; other expenses are met by certain Government departments. The royal yacht is maintained by the Ministry of Defence, for example, and the royal palaces by the Department of the Environment. The Prince of Wales receives the revenues of the Duchy of Cornwall. The Queen is personally exempt from taxation unless Parliament expressly or by necessary implication provides otherwise, or she consents to such taxation.

11.4 Duties of the Sovereign

Many activities of Government require the participation of the Sovereign. Apart from her more public and ceremonial duties the Queen has a very full 'private' work schedule. She receives Cabinet papers and minutes, Foreign Office dispatches and telegrams and other State papers, and receives the Prime Minister at a weekly audience at which she is kept informed of matters of State policy. The Queen presides over meetings of the Privy Council and receives visiting heads of State and foreign diplomatic representatives. She holds investitures to present honours and awards and gives her formal consent to major Crown appointments, including bishops and the senior Judiciary. The Queen is head of the armed forces. Many State documents require her signature.

By convention, the Queen exercises her formal legal powers only upon and in accordance with the advice of her ministers. However, because of her long and wide experience of government, her guidance may prove invaluable. As Bagehot said, the Queen has 'the right to be consulted, the right to encourage, the right to warn'.

11.5 The Queen as head of the Established Church

The Act of Supremacy 1534 declared Henry VIII supreme head of the Church in England and gave him control over its organisation. Queen Mary repealed that Act in the first year of her reign, but the Act of Supremacy 1558 passed in the first year of Elizabeth's reign re-asserted the Church of England's independence from Rome and emphasised the monarch's ultimate authority over matters spiritual and ecclesiastical. It was originally entitled:

> 'An Act restoring to the Crown the ancient jurisdiction over the State ecclesiastical and spiritual and abolishing all foreign power repugnant to the same.'

It enacted that:

> 'Such jurisdictions, privileges, superiorities and pre-eminences spiritual and ecclesiastical as by any spiritual or ecclesiastical power or authority had therefore been or might lawfully be exercised or used for the visitation of the ecclesiastical state and persons and for the reformation, order, and correction of the same and of all manners of errors, heresies, schisms, abuses and offences, contempts and enormities, should for ever by authority of Parliament be annexed to the Imperial Crown of this realm.'

An oath of allegiance was included, and failure to take it debarred a person from holding office in Church and State. It was not until the Roman Catholic Relief Act

1829 that members of the Catholic faith were rehabilitated to the extent of being entitled to sit and vote in Parliament. The Act of Supremacy 1558 is still the foundation of the Queen's ultimate authority over all which are spiritual and ecclesiastical.

11.6 Act of State

Professor Wade defined an Act of State as:

> '... an act of the executive as a matter of policy performed in the course of its relations with another State, including its relations with the subjects of that State, unless they are temporarily within the allegiance of the Crown.'

This definition was cited with approval by Lord Wilberforce in *Nissan* v *Attorney-General* [1968] 1 QB 327. His Lordship observed however that this is less a definition than a construction put together from the decided cases, as he felt the doctrine of Act of State could not really be put in terms of principle. According to Lord Wilberforce the doctrine incorporates two rules.

The first provides a defendant, normally a servant of the Crown, with a defence to acts otherwise tortious or criminal committed abroad provided that the act was authorised or subsequently ratified by the Crown.

The second rule is one of justifiability; it prevents British municipal courts from taking cognisance of certain acts. The class of each so protected has not been accurately defined.

Where the Crown pleads the defence of Act of State, the mere fact of the plea does not oust the court's jurisdiction. The court must examine all the circumstances to determine whether the act in question is in the nature of an Act of State. No test has been laid down to assist in such a determination, but today it is probable that only acts which are part of or necessarily incidental to high policy decisions will be treated as Acts of State; see further *Littrell* v *United States of America (No 2)* [1994] 4 All ER 203.

Requirements for a successful plea of Act of State

The act must be authorised or subsequently ratified by the Crown
Buron v *Denman* (1848) 2 Ex 167. The Royal Navy were given general instructions to suppress the slave trade. Captain Denman exceeded these instructions by setting fire to a slave enclosure belonging to a Spaniard in West Africa, outside British territory. The British Government subsequently ratified his action. The Court of Exchequer held that the ratification had the same effect as a prior command would have done, and that consequently Act of State was a complete defence to an action by the slave owner for damages arising from the trespass.

Act of State may not be pleaded against British subjects within the territories of the Crown

Walker v *Baird* [1892] AC 491. The British owners of a lobster factory in Newfoundland (then British territory) brought an action for trespass against the officers of a British warship who had, with the authority of the Government, seized it. It was held that because the action had been against British subjects within British territory, the Crown could not plead Act of State as a defence.

Act of State and friendly aliens

The temporary allegiance owed to the Crown by a friendly alien who is resident can deprive the Crown of the defence of Act of State in an action brought by a friendly alien.

Johnston v *Pedlar* [1921] 2 AC 262. An ex-Irish citizen of the United States who had taken part in the Dublin Rebellion of 1916 was arrested in 1921 while resident in Ireland. He sued for recovery of money and a cheque book taken from him on his arrest. The House of Lords held that as he was a friendly alien owing allegiance to the Crown, Act of State could not be pleaded as a defence. The fact that the Crown could have chosen to expel him did not mean that instead it could simply deprive him without remedy of his property. The House also observed that the Crown could have chosen to prosecute the friendly alien for high treason.

Viscount Finlay said that the doctrine of *Buron* v *Denman* 'has no application to any case in which the plaintiff is a British subject'.

He then went on to equate the position of the British subject to that of the friendly alien resident in British territory for the purpose of the rule. The deciding factor is allegiance to the Crown. If the litigant owes allegiances to the Crown, Act of State may not be pleaded. But such a person may be subject to the royal prerogative.

Act of State and enemy aliens

The defence of Act of State may be available in respect of executive acts taken against enemy aliens within the territories of the Crown.

R v *Bottrill, ex parte Kuechenmeister* [1947] KB 41. This case concerned a German national, long resident in the United Kingdom, who was interned during the war and who applied for a writ of habeas corpus in 1946. The Crown argued, inter alia, that whether hostilities had ceased (as in fact they had) or not was irrelevant since the Crown could certify conclusively that a state of war continued. This was accepted by the Court of Appeal, together with the general proposition that the Crown may expel or intern an enemy alien in time of war unfettered by the jurisdiction of the courts. The judgment of Lord Justice Scott is almost entirely in terms of the royal prerogative, but the phrase 'Act of State' is used as if there were no distinction.

'In the British constitution, which is binding in all British Courts, the King makes both war and peace, and nonetheless so, in the eyes of the law, that he does so as a constitutional monarch upon the advice of his democratic cabinet. If the King says by an

Act of State that the Commonwealth of countries over which he reigns is at war with a particular foreign state, it is at war with that state, and the certificate of the Secretary of State is conclusive.'

However, as this case is probably based more on the prerogative power of the Crown in relation to enemy aliens, the position regarding the availability of the defence Act of State is still less than clear.

Act of State and aliens outside territories of the Crown

As in *Buron* v *Denman* authorised acts of the executive in relation to aliens outside the territories of the Crown are Acts of State and are outside the jurisdiction of the courts. Aliens who suffer injury as a result of such acts must seek redress through diplomatic channels.

Act of State and British subjects outside Crown territories

The position regarding the availability of the plea of Act of State against British subjects outside the territories of the Crown is unclear.

Nissan v *Attorney-General* [1970] AC 179. Nissan was a citizen of the United Kingdom and Colonies. He wanted compensation for damage caused by the occupation of his hotel on Cyprus, an independent republic within the Commonwealth, by British troops acting as part of an international peace-keeping force. The House of Lords held that Nissan was not prevented from bringing an action for compensation by the defence of Act of State, because the occupation of the hotel was not an act in the nature of an Act of State. Regarding the question whether the defence of Act of State could succeed against a British subject abroad, Lord Reid considered that Act of State could not be pleaded as a defence where the plaintiff is a British subject. The rest of the court reserved their views on this or expressed doubt. Lord Wilberforce found it 'impossible to accept the broad proposition that in no case can the plea of act of state ... be raised against a British subject'. The legal position therefore remains unclear.

The relationship between Act of State and the Royal Prerogative

The true relationship between these two concepts is a vexed question. One view is that Act of State is simply the Royal Prerogative in foreign affairs. It is not difficult to find dicta in which the terms are used interchangeably. However, this view gives rise to certain difficulties.

A plea of Royal Prerogative is an assertion that lawful authority exists to take the action in question. The court may then determine whether the prerogative claimed does in fact exist and if so whether the act in question is within its scope. A plea of Act of State on the other hand is an assertion not that an act is lawful but that the particular act is outside the jurisdiction of the courts:

'The court does not come to any decision as to the legality or illegality, or the rightness or wrongness, of the act complained of: the decision is that because it was an Act of State the court has no jurisdiction to entertain a claim in respect of it.' (Lord Pearson: *Nissan* v *Attorney-General* [1970] AC 179.)

However, in *Nissan*'s case the majority of the House of Lords took the view that the question whether an act was or was not an Act of State is for the court to decide. It has been argued that this leaves Act of State in the same position as the rest of the royal prerogative; the courts cannot question the propriety of the royal prerogative, nor the propriety of an Act of State, but it is for the court to decide whether or not an act falls within these categories. An act cannot be extra-legal if it is for the court to decide whether or not it has jurisdiction.

There is no doubt that an Act of State may take place in foreign territory; yet it may be doubted whether the common law allows that the royal prerogative may be exercised outside the territory of the Crown.

Act of State may not be pleaded as a defence against a British subject, at least when the act takes place within the territory of the Crown. If the defence of Act of State is simply part of the prerogative, it is difficult to see why a connection with the territory of the Crown nullifies its effect, when the same act, if performed abroad and against an alien, would give rise to it.

12

Organisation and Accountability of the Police

12.1 The constitutional position of police officers

One of the better known truisms in English law is that a police constable is simply 'a citizen in uniform'. While it is true that private citizens enjoy powers of arrest, and that in exercising those powers a police constable is not above the law, there are many powers relating to law enforcement that can only be exercised by police constables. Most writers agree with the assertion that a police officer is a Crown servant, although not a servant of the Government. For certain purposes a police officer is expressly stated to be a Crown servant. An example is Official Secrets legislation; see *Lewis* v *Cattle* [1938] 2 KB 454. Police officers are appointed by the Chief Constable and paid out of local police authority funds. In this sense they are analogous to local government employees. See the judgment of McCardie J in *Fisher* v *Oldham Corp* [1930] 2 KB 364; [1930] All ER Rep 96.

173

12.2 The organisation of police forces outside London

The origins of the modern police force can be traced back to the County and Borough Police Act 1856, which placed local authorities under a duty to provide such a force. A local police force was supervised by a watch committee consisting either of councillors, or councillors and magistrates, possessing the power to dismiss the Chief Constable if it saw fit; see *Ridge* v *Baldwin* [1964] AC 40. Today the police forces outside London are governed by the Police Act 1964, s1, which provides for the maintenance by local authorities of county and combined police forces. The supervisory body is now known as the local police authority.

12.3 The role of the chief constable

Appointment

Under s4(2) of the 1964 Act, the chief constable is appointed by the local police authority, the power of appointment being exercised with reference to criteria such as rank, experience, and qualifications. Under s6(4) any appointment is subject to the approval of the Home Secretary.

Jurisdiction

By virtue of s5(1) the chief constable is given a very wide discretion as to the organisation and disposition of his officers. The police force is 'under his direction and control'.

Dismissal

The police authority may, subject to the approval of the Home Secretary, call upon the chief constable to retire 'in the interest of efficiency'. Under s29(1) of the 1964 Act, the Home Secretary can, of his own volition, call upon the chief constable to resign, but is required to conduct an inquiry into the matter where representations are made to him to do so.

The unique constitutional position of a chief constable was usefully summarised by Lord Denning MR in *R* v *Metropolitan Police Comr, ex parte Blackburn* [1968] 2 QB 118 at 135 where he stated:

> 'The office of Commissioner of Police within the metropolis dates back to 1829 when Sir Robert Peel introduced his disciplined force. The commissioner was a justice of the peace specially appointed to administer the police force in the metropolis. His constitutional status has never been defined either by statute or by the courts. It was considered by the Royal Commission on the Police in their report in 1962 (Cmnd 1728). I have no hesitation, however, in holding that, like every constable in the land, he should be, and is,

independent of the executive. He is not subject to the orders of the Secretary of State, save that under the Police Act 1964 the Secretary of State can call on him to give a report, or to retire in the interests of efficiency. I hold it to be the duty of the Commissioner of Police, as it is of every chief constable, to enforce the law of the land. He must take steps so to post his men that crimes may be detected: and that honest citizens may go about their affairs in peace. He must decide whether or not suspected persons are to be prosecuted; and, if need be, bring the prosecution or see that it is brought; but in all these things he is not the servant of anyone, save of the law itself. No Minister of the Crown can tell him that he must, or must not, keep observation on this place or that; or that he must, or must not, prosecute this man or that one. Nor can any police authority tell him so. The responsibility for law enforcement lies on him. He is answerable to the law and to the law alone. That appears sufficiently from *Fisher* v *Oldham Corporation* ([1930] 2 KB 364, [1930] All ER Rep 96), the Privy Council case of *A-G for New South Wales* v *Perpetual Trustee Co Ltd* ([1955] 1 All ER 846, [1955] AC 457).'

12.4 The police authorities

County police forces

County police forces have a police committee which, by virtue of s2, exists as a statutory body in its own right. It is a committee of the local authority. Two-thirds of its members are local councillors, the remainder being magistrates appointed by the Crown Court.

Proposals currently before Parliament in the Police and Magistrates' Courts Bill would, if enacted in their current form, involve a reform of the police committee system. The membership of 17 would be comprised of three magistrates, nine local councillors and five independent members appointed from a short-list drawn up by the Secretary of State. Not surprisingly the proposals have attracted criticism as regards the degree of central government influence that would be brought to bear over what has, historically, been an independent body.

Combined police forces

For geographical reasons, certain police forces are amalgamated to form combined police forces, as in the case of Thames Valley police. Section 3 of the 1964 Act provides for appropriate police authorities to oversee such forces.

Metropolitan county police authorities

The metropolitan county police authorities oversee the metropolitan county police forces, replacing the police authorities that existed under the old metropolitan county council structures. Members are nominated by the relevant district councils. Under s33 of the 1964 Act, the balance of appointments should reflect the political balance of the district councils.

Powers and duties

Police authorities are under a duty to maintain an adequate and efficient police force in the areas for which they are responsible: s4 1964 Act. The authorities are responsible for determining the overall budget of the local force (see s4(3)), and supplying equipment to police forces, under s4(2). The power of supply is not a monopoly power, but exists alongside the statutory and prerogative powers possessed by the Home Secretary; see *R* v *Secretary of State for the Home Department, ex parte Northumbria Police Authority* [1988] 1 WLR 356.

The role of the Home Secretary

The Home Secretary has the power to dismiss a chief constable (s29), request reports on policing matters (s30), make grants to police forces (s31), order local inquiries into police matters, such as the Scarman Report on the Brixton riots (s32), make regulations concerning the administration of the police force (s33), and appoint Inspectors of Constabulary who investigate the efficiency of forces and report back to the Home Secretary. More generally, the Home Secretary may, from time to time, issue circulars to police forces.

The residual prerogative power of the Home Secretary to supply equipment to Chief Constables, possibly against the wishes of the local police authority, was confirmed in *R* v *Secretary of State for the Home Department, ex parte Northumbria Police Authority* [1988] 1 WLR 356.

12.5 The Police and Magistrates' Courts Act 1994

The Act, when it comes into force, will largely give effect to the proposals for reform of the police service set out in the *White Paper Police Reform: the Government's Proposals for the Police Service in England and Wales* (Cm 2881). Part 1 of the Act will effect substantial amendments to the Police Act 1964. Sections 1 and 2 will replace s1–3 of the 1964 Act by providing for 37 police areas in England (excluding the Metropolitan District) and four in Wales, each with its own police authority. Police authorities will comprise 17 members (s3), each being subject to a statutory duty to secure the maintenance of an efficient and effective police force for its area, with reference to objectives determined by the Secretary of State, objectives determined by the authority itself, performance targets determined by the authority for itself, and any local policing plan issued by the authority. Prior to the commencement of each financial year each police authority will be under a statutory duty to determine policing objectives for the year ahead, following consultation with the chief constable and steps taken to ascertain views on community policing under s106 of the Police and Criminal Evidence Act 1984. In addition, each authority will be required to issue a local policing plan (prepared by the chief constable for its consideration), which should include a statement of the authority's priorities for the year ahead, resource requirements and resource allocation. If an authority proposes to issue a plan that differs from that submitted for consideration by the chief constable it must consult him first. At the end of each financial year each police authority will be required to submit an annual report, which must include an assessment of the extent to which the local policing plan has been carried out (s4).

Under Schedule 2 of the 1994 Act, where a police authority consists of 17 members, nine will be members of the relevant local authority appointed by that authority, five will be independent members appointed by the police authority from a short-list prepared by the Secretary of State and three will be magistrates appointed by the relevant panel. Appointment will normally be for four years, with retirement at 70 years of age.

Section 5 of the 1994 Act will replace s5 of the 1964 Act, and provides that each force shall have a chief constable, appointed by the police authority and subject to the approval of the Home Secretary. In discharging his functions, the chief constable will have to have regard to the local policing plan issued by the police authority. The police authority, acting with the approval of the Home Secretary, will be able to call upon the chief constable to retire in the interests of efficiency, but not before it has provided the chief constable with an opportunity to make representations.

Section 15 of the 1994 Act will add to s28 of the 1964 Act by providing that the Home Secretary may determine objectives for the policing of all police areas having consulted those who represent both police authorities and chief constables. The Home Secretary may further require police authorities to establish performance targets to be aimed at in seeking to achieve his objectives.

12.6 The Metropolitan Police

The Metropolitan Police was established by the Metropolitan Police Act 1829. It was run by magistrates until 1866 when the first Commissioner was appointed, answerable to the Home Secretary. The Commissioner of the Metropolitan Police is not subject to the provisions of the Police Act 1964, and can be dismissed at will by the Home Secretary, who also determines the budget for the Metropolitan Police. Note that the City of London has its own police force for which the Common Council of the City of London is the police authority. When the London County Council was created in 1888, moves to introduce a police authority, similar to those that exist outside London, were resisted on the grounds that it was more desirable for the policing of the capital to be under the control of central government. Note also that the Inspectors of Constabulary do not have powers to investigate and report on the efficiency of the Metropolitan Police.

12.7 A national police force?

The idea of a national police force has traditionally been rejected for fear that it could create the beginnings of a police state, with officers under the direction of politicians. The Royal Commission on the Police (1962) (Cmnd 1728) considered the issue, concluding that the ideal solution was local forces accountable to local bodies, with a degree of central control over standards. Provision does exist for co-operation between local forces on the basis of what is known as 'mutual aid'. Under s14(1) of the Police Act 1964 a chief constable can supply manpower and equipment to another force, regardless of the view of his police authority. In addition, the Association of Chief Police Officers (ACPO), is a powerful lobby group co-ordinating the views of chief constables. The president of the association normally has some direction over the national reporting centre which helps to co-ordinate mutual aid. There was evidence of a high level of co-operation during the miners' strikes of the 1980s.

12.8 Judicial control of police forces

As public officers, chief constables are in theory subject to control by the courts through the process of judicial review. In reality, however, the courts have shown themselves overwhelmingly reluctant to intervene and order a chief constable to exercise his discretion in respect of police policy in a particular way. In *R v MPC, ex parte Blackburn* (above), Raymond Blackburn sought an order of mandamus compelling the Commissioner to enforce the law against illegal gambling. The Court of Appeal held that while there might be extreme cases where the courts would issue orders of mandamus directed at the Commissioner, as a general rule day to day policing policies were a matter for the police alone. By the time this matter reached the Court of Appeal the policy of the Metropolitan Police had been altered.   As Lord Denning commented (at p136):

> '... it is for the Commissioner of Police of the Metropolis, or the chief constable, as the case may be, to decide in any particular case whether inquiries should be pursued, or whether an arrest should be made, or a prosecution brought. It must be for him to decide on the disposition of his force and the concentration of his resources on any particular crime or area. No court can or should give him direction on such a matter. He can also make policy decisions and give effect to them, as, for instance, was often done when prosecutions were not brought for attempted suicide. But there are some policy decisions with which, I think, the courts in a case can, if necessary, interfere.'

A similar non-interventionist approach was taken, again by a Court of Appeal led by Lord Denning MR in *R v Chief Constable of Devon and Cornwall, ex parte CEGB* [1981] 3 WLR 807. The case arose because the Electricity Board were unable to carry out a survey of farm land as a possible site for a nuclear power station, due to the continuing activities of objectors. In a written reply to complaints from the

Board, the chief constable stated that he was unwilling to act against the objectors in the absence of stronger evidence of illegal action on their part. The Board applied for an order of mandamus to compel the chief constable to act, but this was refused by the Divisional Court. The Board appealed to the Court of Appeal. In upholding this decision Lord Denning MR stated:

> 'Notwithstanding all that I have said, I would not give any orders to the chief constable or his men. It is of the first importance that the police should decide on their own responsibility what action should be taken in any particular situation ... The decision of the chief constable not to intervene in this case was a policy decision with which I think the courts should not interfere.'

The Master of the Rolls did, however, express the hope that the chief constable would 'decide to use his men to clear the obstructors off the site or at any rate help the Board to do so.' Reluctance has also been shown as regards intervening in matters of internal management. In *Vince and Another* v *Chief Constable of Dorset Police* [1993] 1 WLR 415, the plaintiffs sought a declaration that the chief constable of Dorset was, by virtue of s36(1) of the 1984 Police and Criminal Evidence Act, under a duty to appoint a sufficient number of custody officers so as to ensure that there would always be one available at each designated station. The plaintiffs also sought a declaration that it would be unlawful for the chief constable to appoint an acting sergeant as a custody officer under s36(3) of the 1984 Act. At first instance the first declaration in relation to s36(1) was granted, but not that in relation to s36(3). On appeal by the chief constable and cross-appeal by the plaintiffs, the Court of Appeal held, allowing the appeal and (by a majority) dismissing the cross-appeal, that whilst s36(1) created a duty to appoint a custody officer at each designated station, the chief constable had a discretion as to the number of additional officers to be appointed. The cross-appeal was dismissed on the ground that the plaintiffs had not produced evidence of an acting sergeant being appointed as a custody officer, hence the question was academic, and the court would not express a final opinion. Steyn LJ (dissenting) expressed the view that the Royal Commission on Criminal Justice ought to consider the implications of the decision given the crucial role played by custody officers. In particular he felt that the court should have indicated its view that acting sergeants should not be appointed to such a position. See further *R* v *Oxford, ex parte Levey* (1986) The Times 1 November; *Hill* v *Chief Constable of West Yorkshire* [1988] 2 All ER 238.

12.9 Complaints against the police

Prior to the enactment of the Police and Criminal Evidence Act 1984, complaints against the police were dealt with by the Police Complaints Board, a system subject to heavy criticism in light of the extent to which it empowered the police to adjudicate upon the merits of complaints made against them; see further comments made by Sir Robert Mark, former Commissioner of Police for the Metropolis, in his autobiography *In the Office of Constable*, pp214–5.

Under the 1984 Act, the role previously undertaken by the Police Complaints Board is now discharged by the Police Complaints Authority (PCA). The PCA is essentially a supervisory body, in that it oversees the investigation of complaints by officers unconnected with the complaint. PCA members are appointed by the Home Secretary, are entirely independent of the police, and will not have ever served in the police force.

Complaints are made, in the first instance, to the chief officer of police for the area where the alleged misconduct occurred. He must initiate an investigation and preserve evidence of the subject matter: s84. He may deal with the complaint himself if it concerns any member of his own force below the rank of chief superintendent; for senior ranks he must pass the complaint to the police authority for his area. Unless passed on in this way, the complaint may be disposed of informally, without full hearing and evidence. A complaint is not suitable for informal resolution unless the complainant consents and the chief officer is satisfied that the conduct complained of, even if proved, would not justify criminal or disciplinary proceedings: s85(10). If this informal procedure fails to satisfy the complainant, the case may be referred for a fuller investigation by an officer of at least the rank of the one against whom the complaint was raised, and his report is submitted to the chief officer of police for the area.

The PCA will supervise a complaint if it is referred to it by a chief officer of police, or by a police authority, or if the PCA itself requests to have the matter referred to it. Certain complaints must be referred to the PCA, notably those arising out of death or serious injury to a person, including fractures of bones, damage to internal organs or deep lacerations of the skin. A matter may be referred to the PCA by a police authority or chief officer of police, even though no complaint has been made, if it appears that an officer may have committed a criminal offence or acted in a manner that may justify disciplinary proceedings if it appears that such a reference is justified by the exceptional circumstances involved: s88. When seized of the case the authority can, in effect, choose which police officer is to conduct the investigation, and disciplinary charges may follow the PCA's report on the complaint. The PCA is under a statutory duty to prepare an annual report to the Home Secretary.

In his foreword to the 1993 report the PCA chairman, Sir Leonard Peach, rejected criticisms to the effect that the system was still not sufficiently independent of the police, noting that most investigations were carried out by experienced complaints teams specialising in that one task. He did, however, observe that problems were caused by complaints having to be proved beyond all reasonable doubt, and suggested that in less serious cases the civil standard of proof might be more appropriate.

In 1986, 6,646 complaints were received (including supervised and unsupervised investigations). By 1992, this had risen to 9,200.

In 1993, 9,047 were received, of which 4,139 were referred to the PCA for possible supervision. Although this represents a drop of 7 per cent on the previous year, the number accepted for supervision increased by 25 per cent, to 951. A total of 1,092 complaints resulted in some form of disciplinary action, and there were 27 instances of criminal charges being brought as a result of investigations. The average time taken for the PCA to deal with a case fell to 29 days in 1993.

12.10 Civil remedies

Section 48(1) of the Police Act 1964 provides that the chief constable shall in certain circumstances be vicariously liable for the acts of police constables under his direction and control.

Negligence

A plaintiff pursuing an action in negligence in respect of police action may encounter the argument that the action complained of was essentially the result of a policy decision, rather than one that is operational. If action is characterised as being within the sphere of policy the courts are unlikely to recognise the existence of a private law duty of care: see the speech of Lord Diplock in *Home Office* v *Dorset Yacht* [1970] AC 1004. An example of this problem is provided by the decision of the court in *Rigby* v *Chief Constable of Northamptonshire* [1985] 1 WLR 1242. The plaintiff's gun shop was broken into by a psychopath who had armed himself and refused to leave. The police laid siege to the shop, eventually firing a canister of CS gas to smoke out the intruder. The canister set the shop ablaze. The plaintiff sought damages for negligence on the grounds that the police had used CS gas canisters known to have a propensity to burst into flames, without having on hand the necessary fire fighting equipment. There was evidence that the police had not been equipped with the less dangerous 'Ferret' CS gas canisters. The courts held that the decision not to provide the local police force with the 'Ferret' CS gas equipment was one falling into the category of policy, and could not be attacked on the ground of negligence. In any event, it would not have been negligent to decide not to equip the local police force with such equipment. Note, however, that the court did find the police to have been negligent in firing the CS gas cylinders in the absence of adequate fire fighting equipment. Decisions concerning the allocation of resources for the investigation of particular crimes are more clearly within the 'policy' sphere, and thus unlikely to give rise to a successful claim for damages.

In *Hill* v *Chief Constable of West Yorkshire* (above), the plaintiff sought damages on behalf of her daughter who had been murdered by a serial killer, Peter Sutcliffe. The plaintiff's daughter had been Sutcliffe's last victim, and the plaintiff's claim was based on the assertion that, but for negligence in the way the hunt for Sutcliffe had been organised, he would have been apprehended before killing her daughter.

The House of Lords rejected the contention that the police owed any member of the public a private law duty of care. Referring to Lord Diplock's speech in *Dorset Yacht*, Lord Keith observed:

> '... if there is no general duty of care owed to ... the public ... to prevent the escape of a known criminal ... there cannot reasonably be imposed upon any police force a duty of care similarly owed to identify and apprehend an unknown one.'

Lord Keith went on to express the view that regardless of the issue of liability in negligence as an issue of private law, it was contrary to public policy to impose such liability in relation to the conduct of investigations, since it was to be assumed that police officers used their best endeavours to prevent crime in any event. It would be undesirable for the courts to be placed in a situation of having to judge whether or not a particular line of enquiry ought to have been pursued by the police during an investigation. *Hill* was followed in *Ancell* v *McDermott* (1993) The Times 4 February, where the court refused to accept the contention that police officers, who had reported a spillage of diesel oil on the highway, were under a duty to remain at the scene and warn other road users of the hazard: see further *Hughes* v *National Union of Mineworkers* [1991] 4 All ER 278.

13

Freedom of Assembly and Association

13.1 Freedom of association

13.2 Freedom of assembly

13.3 Martial law

13.4 Emergency powers in time of war

13.5 Statutory emergency powers in time of peace

13.1 Freedom of association

As a general principle, individuals are free to associate with each other for political purposes under English law. Typically, however, a number of significant legal limitations have been created. The Public Order Act 1936 s1 places a general prohibition on the wearing of political uniforms in any public place or at any public meeting except for uniforms worn on ceremonial, anniversary or other special occasions where public disorder is not likely to be provoked. (The Prevention of Terrorism (Temporary Provisions) Act 1989 contains a similar prohibition in respect of proscribed organisations). Section 2 of the 1936 Act creates an offence of controlling, managing, organising or training an association of persons for the purpose of usurping the functions of the police or the armed forces or for the use or display of physical force in promoting any political object. In 1963, for example, the leaders of 'Spearhead', a neo-Nazi organisation, were convicted under s2. Similarly the Unlawful Drilling Act 1819 prohibits assemblies for the purpose of training or drilling in the use of arms or practising military exercises without lawful authority.

The Prevention of Terrorism (Temporary Provisions) Act 1989, as amended by the Criminal Justice Act 1993, contains, in Part 1 of the Act, a series of offences which may be committed by persons supporting proscribed organisations. Two organisations are proscribed under the Act: the Irish Republican Army and the Irish National Liberation Army. By s1 of the Act it is an offence to belong or profess to belong to such an organisation, to solicit or invite financial or other support for it, to make or receive contributions to its resources, or to arrange, assist in the arrangement of, or address its meetings.

Members of the armed forces, the police and senior civil servants may be prevented by their conditions of service from engaging in political activities and may not therefore join political associations.

13.2 Freedom of assembly

As indicated above, the starting point is that anyone is free to assemble provided that no law is breached. The law in this area consists in essence of the restrictions that Parliament and the courts have felt necessary over the years to impose on the freedom to assemble in public, in the interests of maintaining order.

The right to hold meetings

Meetings on private and public property

There is no legal right to hold a meeting on private premises without the consent of the owner or occupier. Unless permission has been granted, a person holding such a meeting becomes a trespasser and the owner or occupier of the premises may use reasonable force in evicting the trespasser.

Meetings in public places are subject to a number of limitations. Places such as Hyde Park Corner or Trafalgar Square which are traditionally used for public meetings are Crown property and there is no right to hold meetings there. The permission of the Secretary of State for the Environment is needed, and he can impose restrictions on any meeting.

Many local authority premises are also subject to regulations governing meetings. If there are by-laws which require permission to be obtained for a meeting on local authority property, then holding one without permission will be a criminal offence. Local authorities have a wide discretion to stop meetings being held in their parks or buildings but their decisions are open to judicial review. A decision to refuse permission for any meeting, or a meeting by a particular organisation, may be unreasonable under the principles laid down in *Associated Provincial Picture Houses* v *Wednesbury Corporation* [1948] 1 KB 223.

There is, however, a statutory right under the Representation of the People Act 1983 for candidates in general or local elections to have access to local authority premises for the purpose of holding election meetings. It has been argued that this statutory right ought to be extended to all meetings, following recent decisions by some local authorities to refuse the National Front permission to hold meetings on their premises.

Imposing conditions on public assemblies. The Public Order Act 1986 s14 (as amended by ss70 and 71 of the Criminal Justice and Public Order Act 1994) provides that a senior police officer may impose conditions in relation to public assemblies if, having regard to the time or place at which and the circumstances in which any public assembly is being held or is intended to be held, he reasonably believes that: (1) it may result in serious public disorder, serious damage to property or serious disruption to the life of the community, or (2) the purpose of the persons organising it is the intimidation of others with a view to compelling them not to do an act they have a right to do, or to do an act they have a right not to do. The section states that he may give directions imposing on the persons organising or taking part in the assembly such conditions as to the place at which the assembly may be (or continue to be) held, its maximum duration, or the maximum number of persons who may constitute it, as appears to him necessary to prevent such disorder, damage, disruption or intimidation. Section 16 defines public assembly as an assembly of 20 or more persons in a public place which is wholly or partly open to the air. Under ss14A, B and C (added by the 1994 Act) a chief officer of police is empowered to apply to the relevant local authority for an order prohibiting trespassory assemblies on land to which the public does not normally have a right of access, provided that there are grounds to reasonably believe that the owner of the land has not granted permission for the assembly and that the trespassory assembly may result in either serious disruption to the life of the community, or significant damage to land or buildings of historical, archaeological or scientific importance. It is an offence to organise or participate in any such trespassory assembly in the knowledge that a banning order has been granted. Under s14C a police constable has the power to intercept and stop those reasonably believed to be proceeding to a trespassory assembly, and direct them not to proceed to the assembly. Disobedience to an order under this provision is a summary offence in relation to which a constable may exercise a power of arrest without a warrant. A fairly obvious occasion for the use of these powers would appear to be in respect of summer solstice celebrations at Stonehenge.

'Raves'

Section 63 of the Criminal Justice and Public Order Act 1994 seeks to address the use of open land for so-called 'raves', defined as a gathering on land in the open air of 100 or more persons at which amplified music is played during the night and is such that by reason of its loudness and duration and the time at which it is played likely to cause serious distress to the inhabitants of the locality. 'Music' is further defined as '... sounds wholly or predominantly characterised by the emission of a succession of repetitive beats'. An officer of at least the rank of superintendent may give directions to those gathering for a rave, or taking part in one, to leave the land in question and remove any property brought onto the land. Failure to comply with any such direction constitutes a summary offence, and any constable who reasonably suspects that such an offence is being committed can arrest without a warrant. Section 64 provides the police with the power to seize sound equipment, and s65 provides a further power to intercept those reasonably believed to be proceeding to a rave and direct them not to proceed.

'Mass trespass'

Criminal liability for involvement in so-called mass trespass upon land, originally introduced by s39 of the Public Order Act 1986, is now provided for by ss61 and 62 of the Criminal Justice and Public Order Act 1994. The provisions, which seem to be specifically targeted at the activities of persons leading a nomadic lifestyle ('new age travellers' etc), state that a police constable is empowered to order the removal of trespassers (ie two or more persons) from land where he reasonably believes that (1) they are present with the common purpose of residing there for any period; and (2) reasonable steps have been taken by or on behalf of the occupier to ask them to leave; and either (3) any of the persons has caused damage to the land or property on the land or used threatening or abusive or insulting words or behaviour towards the occupier, his family or agents; or (4) the trespassers have between them six or more vehicles (a reduction from 12 under the 1986 Act) on the land. For these purposes 'land' does not include land forming part of a highway other than footpaths, bridleways, by-ways or cycle tracks. Subject to certain statutory defences, failure to comply with a constable's direction under this section is an offence in relation to which a person can be arrested without a warrant, and in relation to which a constable has the power to seize vehicles involved. A person removed from land under these provisions is prohibited from returning for the following three months.

Aggravated trespass

Section 68 of the Criminal Justice and Public Order Act 1994, primarily aimed at the activities of groups such as hunt saboteurs, animal rights protesters attempting to prevent the transport of live animals, or demonstrators attempting to disrupt road-building programmes, provides the police with the power to deal with those committing aggravated trespass on open land. Aggravated trespass arises where a person is present on land (excluding highways other than footpaths, bridleways, by-ways or cycle tracks) without the owner's permission, and he commits acts intended to intimidate others present on the land so as to deter them from engaging in any lawful activity, or intended to obstruct or disrupt such activities. The section creates a summary offence for which a person can be arrested by a constable without a warrant if the constable reasonably suspects that such an offence is being committed. A senior police officer may, under s69, direct persons to leave land if he reasonably believes that they have committed or intend to commit the offence of aggravated trespass, or if he reasonably believes that two or more persons are trespassing on land in the open air and are present there with the common purpose of intimidating persons so as to deter them from engaging in a lawful activity or of obstructing or disrupting a lawful activity. Again, failure to comply with such a direction is, subject to certain statutory exceptions, a summary offence in relation to which a constable in uniform may exercise a power of arrest without a warrant.

Meetings on the highway

At common law, the highway is land dedicated to the public use for the primary purpose of passing and repassing of pedestrians and traffic. If either exceed this function then they will be using the highway unreasonably and will be subject to a number of sanctions.

The owners of the highway can sue anyone in trespass who uses the highway for an improper purpose. The surface of the highway is usually vested in the local authority, but adjacent landowners have an interest in the subsoil and can also sue in trespass and nuisance. In *Hickman* v *Maisey* [1900] 1 QB 752 a racehorse trainer successfully sued in trespass a person who stood on the highway to time the trainer's racehorses. Similarly, in *Harrison* v *Duke of Rutland* [1893] 1 QB 142 a person who objected to the Duke shooting grouse walked up and down a highway across the grouse moor opening and closing his umbrella so as to frighten the birds. He was held to be an unreasonable user of the highway and therefore a trespasser who could not complain when the Duke's gamekeeper used reasonable force to eject him from the moor.

Under the Highways Act 1980 s137(1), it is a criminal offence wilfully to obstruct the free passage along a highway. If the highway is obstructed then a constable can arrest those causing the obstruction. Obstruction, in this context, is a very flexible term. In *Gill* v *Carson* (1917) it was held that there was no necessity to show that anyone was actually obstructed. In *Homer* v *Cadman* (1866) 55 LJMC 110 it was held that it is no defence to show that there was a way around the obstruction, a street stall, erected on a wide pavement, leaving plenty of room for people to pass, would still constitute an obstruction. In *Arrowsmith* v *Jenkins* [1963] 2 QB 561, Arrowsmith was arrested for obstructing the highway under s121 of the Highways Act 1959. She argued that the prosecution had to show that she had an intention to obstruct the highway. Lord Parkes rejected this argument and refused to introduce mens rea into the Act, stating that 'if a person does an act according to their free will which results in an obstruction, it will be sufficient for the offence of obstruction'.

Processions

Processions along the highway, being mobile, will generally be lawful at common law since the highway is being used for passage. However, if the procession goes beyond reasonable use, then it may constitute a public nuisance. This offence is rare but it was used in the case of *R* v *Clarke (No 2)* [1964] 2 QB 315. Clarke was charged with inviting others to obstruct the highway around Whitehall. The police had blocked the path of the demonstration and Clarke was said to have told the crowd to go around the blockade. It was argued that this amounted to an incitement to commit a public nuisance. The accused was convicted and given a sentence of 18 months' imprisonment. The conviction was quashed on appeal. The court held that the question that must be asked was whether there had been an unreasonable use of the highway. It was held to be irrelevant that some obstruction had occurred if the use of the highway was reasonable.

The Public Order Act 1986, ss11, 12 and 13. Under the Public Order Act 1986 advance notice of public processions must be given in certain circumstances. Section 11 provides that proposals to hold a public procession must be notified to the police if it is a procession intended to demonstrate support for or opposition to the views or actions of any person or body of persons; or publicise a cause or campaign; or mark or commemorate an event. Written notice must be given to the police not less than six clear days before the date of the procession, or as soon as is practicable. The organisers commit an offence if they fail to satisfy these requirements or, if in general the conduct of the procession differs from that indicated in the notice.

The Public Order Act 1986, ss12 and 13, replaces the provisions first enacted in s3 of the Public Order Act 1936. The 1936 Act was enacted following disorder caused by Fascist marches in the East End of London. Powers to control the route of processions had long existed, in the Metropolitan Police Act 1839 and the Town Police Clauses Act 1847, but s3 of the 1936 Act introduced for the first time the power to ban processions. These provisions are now contained in ss12 and 13 of the 1986 Act. They are directed to preventing serious public disorder rather than dealing with it when it has occurred. The framework of control has two stages, in order to ensure that banning orders are used only as a measure of last resort.

Section 12 provides that:

'If the senior police officer, having regard to the time or place at which and the circumstances in which any public procession is being held or is intended to be held and to its route or proposed route, reasonably believes that –
(a) it may result in serious public disorder, serious damage to property or serious disruption to the life of the community, or
(b) the purpose of the persons organising it is the intimidation of others with a view to compelling them not to do an act they have a right to do, or to do an act they have a right not to do,
he may give directions imposing on the persons organising or taking part in the procession such conditions as appear to him necessary to prevent such disorder, damage, disruption or intimidation, including conditions as to the route of the procession or prohibiting it from entering any public place specified in the directions.'

If, however, it is considered that these powers will not be sufficient to prevent serious disorder, then the second stage of the process is used.

Section 13 provides that:

'If at any time the chief officer of police reasonably believes that, because of particular circumstances existing in any district or part of a district, the powers under section 12 will not be sufficient to prevent the holding of public processions in that district or part from resulting in serious public disorder, he shall apply to the council of the district for an order prohibiting subject to the consent of the Home Secretary (s13(2)) for such period not exceeding 3 months as may be specified in the application the holding of all public processions (or of any class of public procession so specified) in the district or part concerned.'

In the City of London or the metropolitan police district, the Commissioner of Police for the City of London or the Commissioner of Police of the Metropolis may make such orders with the consent of the Home Secretary (s13(3),(4)).

The only way to appeal against such a ban is to show that it was unreasonable.

Metropolitan Police Act 1839, s52. Under s52 of the Metropolitan Police Act 1839 the Commissioner of Police of the Metropolis may make regulations for preventing obstruction of the streets within the vicinity of Parliament. Any contravention of those regulations is a criminal offence. Although this is a wide power there are some limits to it. In *Papworth* v *Coventry* [1967] 1 WLR 633, the accused was convicted of ignoring a s52 order that the streets around Parliament should be kept clear. He appealed on the grounds that the seven protesters could not have caused an obstruction. The appeal was upheld.

The police also have the power to stop potential disorderly processions by bringing the possible demonstrators before the magistrates before the demonstration. They may then be bound over to keep the peace. Should they refuse to be bound over they can be imprisoned for up to six months.

Responsibility for causing disorder

The general principle is that a lawful act does not become unlawful just because it may cause others to act unlawfully.

Beatty v *Gillbanks* (1882) 9 QBD 308. The Salvation Army regularly held processions through the town of Weston-super-Mare. These processions were regularly confronted by a group called the Skeleton Army. The confrontations frequently resulted in violence and general disorder. The local magistrates purported to ban marches by the Salvation Army. The Salvation Army ignored the ban and violence occurred. Members of the Salvation Army were convicted of unlawful assembly by the magistrates, but this was reversed on appeal. The Divisional Court held that as the disorder had been caused by the Skeleton Army, and the Salvation Army did not incite the counter-demonstration, the disorder was not a natural consequence of the procession.

Per Field J:

'The present decision of the justices ... amounts to this, that a man may be punished for acting lawfully if he knows that his so doing may induce another man to act unlawfully – a proposition without any authority to support it.'

However, the general principle laid down in *Beatty* v *Gillbanks* is today subject to certain qualifications:

1. The Public Order Act 1986, s13, refers to processions which may result in serious public disorder. Innocent marchers may be stopped if their march is likely to be the occasion for serious disorder caused by others.
2. If the police reasonably apprehend an imminent breach of the peace they may take any action necessary to control or prevent it, including arresting those responsible. They may also limit numbers in any particular place to prevent breaches of the peace. See *Duncan* v *Jones* (below).

    In *O'Kelly* v *Harvey* (1883) 15 Cox CC 435, a magistrate was held to be justified in dispersing a lawful meeting on the basis that he had reasonable grounds for supposing that those opposed to the meeting would use violence and that there was no other way in which the peace could be preserved.

    In *Moss and Others* v *McLachlan* (1984) 149 JP 167, the police were held to be entitled to stop and turn back pickets otherwise lawfully on the highway during the miners' dispute.
3. The principle in *Wise* v *Dunning* [1902] 1 KB 167 that if the speakers or demonstrators use insulting language which is likely to cause a breach of the peace, they can be successfully prosecuted for 'disturbing the peace'. This case is in keeping with the general principle in *Beatty* v *Gillbanks*. In that case the disorder was not the natural or probable consequence of the procession, but in *Wise* v *Dunning* it was.

Public order offences and police powers

The police have a wide range of powers at their disposal, both statutory and common law, to deal with outbreaks of public disorder, or indeed, the threat of disorder. The most significant common law power is that related to action taken to deal with a breach of the peace, a concept of considerable antiquity. Breach of the peace is not, in England and Wales, a substantive offence, but it forms the basis of important police powers. If the police reasonably apprehend an imminent breach of the peace they may take any action which is necessary to control or prevent it, including arresting those who are responsible. The police may also limit numbers in any particular place in order to prevent breaches of the peace. The common law power to disperse an unlawful assembly also derives from the general power of the police to control breaches of the peace. The police may also bring anyone who threatens the peace before the courts to enter into a recognisance and find sureties to keep the peace or to be of good behaviour, or in default to be imprisoned for up to six months. This preventative power to bind someone over to be of good behaviour is traced back to the Justices of the Peace Act 1361, and is still frequently used in public order cases. Thus a police officer acting to deal with a reasonably apprehended breach of the peace will be acting in the execution of his duty. The significance of this lies in the fact that s51(1) of the Police Act 1964 creates the offence of assaulting a police officer in the execution of his duty, while s51(3) makes it an offence to wilfully obstruct a constable in the execution of his duty.

In *Duncan* v *Jones* [1936] 1 KB 218 Duncan intended to hold a meeting outside a government training centre. At a previous meeting there had been a disturbance. As she was about to start speaking a police officer asked her to move about 150 yards down the road. She refused to move and was arrested and charged with obstructing a police officer in the execution of his duty. She was convicted and appealed. The Divisional Court upheld the conviction. They found that Duncan must have realised that a probable consequence of holding the meeting was a disturbance, and that the police officer had reasonable grounds for believing that a breach of the peace might ensue and therefore was under a duty to stop the meeting taking place. It could be argued that the case was wrongly decided on the basis that Mrs Duncan committed no offence other than the obstruction of the officer. She did not incite anyone to commit a breach of the peace, nor was she causing an obstruction. It would seem that in such a case the court could have followed *Beatty* v *Gillbanks* (above) and adhered to the principle that a lawful act does not become unlawful merely because other people act unlawfully. The issue continues to create difficulties for the courts. In *R* v *Morpeth Ward Justices, ex parte Ward and Others* [1992] Crim LR 497, the applicants, anti-blood sports demonstrators who had entered a field where a shooting party had gathered and engaged in noisy disruptive behaviour intending to impede the shoot, were subsequently summoned for breach of the peace and bound over to keep the peace. Their challenge to the magistrates' order, on the basis that the elements of the offence of breach of the peace contrary to common law had not been made out, and thus the magistrates had not had jurisdiction to make the orders in question, was rejected by the court on the ground that magistrates could exercise their powers of bindover provided there was evidence that the Queen's peace was threatened by the conduct of the defendant. The court felt that it was not necessary to show that any other person had been put in bodily fear by the conduct, provided that a natural consequence of the conduct was that it would provoke others to violence. In the present case the applicants may not have actually committed the offence of breach of the peace, but their conduct had come close to provoking it. Note that the applicants were entitled to protest against blood sports, but presumably not in a manner that was likely to provoke violence. Had they acted lawfully and provoked the shooting party to violence, members of the party could themselves have been dealt with for breaching the peace; refer again to *Beatty* v *Gilbanks* (above), and see further *R* v *Howell* [1982] QB 416, *R* v *Chief Constable of Devon and Cornwall, ex parte CEGB* [1982] QB 458.

The Public Order Act 1986

The Public Order Act 1986 introduces several new offences and abolishes or repeals several common law and statutory offences. The ancient common law offences of riot, rout, unlawful assembly and affray have been abolished. Three offences have been created as replacements: riot, violent disorder and affray.

Section 1 redefines the offence of riot. Where 12 or more persons who are present together use or threaten unlawful violence and the conduct of them, taken together, is such as would cause a person of reasonable firmness present at the scene to fear for his personal safety, each of the persons using unlawful violence for the common purpose is guilty of riot. A person guilty of riot is liable on conviction on indictment to imprisonment for a term not exceeding ten years or a fine or both.

Section 2 creates the offence of violent disorder. Where three or more persons who are present together use or threaten unlawful violence and the conduct of them, taken together, is such as would cause a person of reasonable firmness present at the scene to fear for his personal safety, each of the persons using or threatening unlawful violence is guilty of violent disorder. A person guilty of violent disorder is liable on conviction on indictment to imprisonment for a term not exceeding five years or a fine or both, or on summary conviction to imprisonment for a term not exceeding six months or a fine or both. See *R* v *McGuigan* [1991] Crim LR 719; *R* v *Worton* [1990] Crim LR 124.

Section 3 redefines the offence of affray. A person is guilty of affray if he uses or threatens unlawful violence towards another and his conduct is such as would cause a person of reasonable firmness present at the scene to fear for his personal safety. The test is objective. Even if the only witness to an incident is a police officer, the test is still that of how a person of reasonable firmness would have reacted: *R* v *Davison* [1992] Crim LR 31. Sub-section 3(3) provides that for the purposes of the offence of affray, a threat cannot be made by the use of words alone. In *R* v *Dixon* [1993] Crim LR 579, the appellant had been involved in a domestic argument with his common law wife. The police were called and the appellant made off, accompanied by his dog. When eventually cornered by the police, the appellant ordered the dog, which was in an agitated state, to attack the officers. Two officers suffered bites in an attack by the dog. The dog returned to the appellant who then ordered it to kill the officers. At this point the officers retreated awaiting reinforcements. The appellant was convicted of affray, and appealed on the grounds that his words alone could not constitute the affray; that there was insufficient evidence to show that the dog had been responding to his commands; and that the trial judge may have given the jury the impression that passivity on the part of the appellant might be sufficient actus reus for the offence.

Dismissing his appeal, the Court of Appeal held that, whilst the offence could not comprise the use of words alone, in the instant case the prosecution had relied upon the actions of the appellant in deliberately setting the dog on the officers and the words he had uttered at the time. The prosecutor was not required to prove that the dog had responded to the commands uttered by the appellant. The actus reus of the offence comprised the words spoken to the dog, coupled with the dog being in a highly agitated state. The decision perhaps raises the question as to whether the mere presence of the dog should have been regarded as sufficient to convert what would otherwise have been words alone into an affray, where the instructions given might cause fear in the reasonable bystander. The requirement of something more than words alone is further confirmed in *R* v *Robinson* [1993] Crim LR 581: see also

R v *Davies* [1991] Crim LR 469. A person guilty of affray is liable on conviction on indictment to imprisonment for a term not exceeding three years or a fine or both, or on summary conviction to imprisonment for a term not exceeding six months or a fine or both.

Section 4 largely replaces s5 of the Public Order Act 1936 with an offence of causing fear or provocation of violence. A person is guilty of an offence if he uses towards another person threatening, abusive or insulting words or behaviour, or distributes or displays to another person any writing, sign or other visible representation which is threatening, abusive or insulting, with intent to cause that person to believe that immediate unlawful violence will be used against him or another by any person, or to provoke the immediate use of unlawful violence by that person or another, or whereby that person is likely to believe that such violence will be used or it is likely that such violence will be provoked. *Atkin* v *DPP* (1989) 89 Cr App R 199 holds that the words must be used in the presence of, and earshot of, the person to whom they are directed. No offence is committed under s4 where the behaviour complained of occurs in a dwellinghouse; *R* v *Va Kun Hua* [1990] Crim LR 518. In *R* v *Horseferry Road Justices, ex parte Siadatan* [1990] Crim LR 598, the Divisional Court refused to allow an application for judicial review of the decision not to prosecute the publishers of Salman Rushdie's *Satanic Verses* under s4(1). The court felt that as the 1986 Act created criminal liability it was to be construed narrowly, and that in any event the disturbances created by the book's publication did not amount to the provocation of 'immediate violence'. *R* v *Afzal* [1993] Crim LR 791, confirms that, in relation to the charge of threatening behaviour contrary to s4, the trial judge should, where appropriate, direct the jury to consider whether or not the violence might have been lawful, for example, where it was threatened by way of self-defence, since actual violence by way of reasonable self-defence would not be unlawful.

When s154 of the Criminal Justice and Public Order Act 1994 comes into force it will have the effect of creating a further offence, namely causing intentional harassment alarm or distress, by the addition of a s4A to the 1986 Act. Under s4A a person will be guilty of the offence if he, with intent to cause another harassment, alarm, or distress, uses threatening, abusive or insulting words or behaviour or disorderly behaviour, or displays any writing, sign or other visible representation which is threatening, abusive or insulting, thereby causing another person harassment, alarm or distress. The offence can be committed in a public or private place, except where both parties are in private dwellings. A constable may arrest without a warrant anyone he reasonably suspects to be guilty of committing the offence. The offence is likely to be charged in cases of racial harassment, although it is clearly not limited to such activities.

The new offence will be effectively an aggravated form of the offence created by s5 of the 1986 Act, ie causing harassment, alarm or distress, and shares many of its features. Under s5 a person is guilty of an offence if he uses threatening, abusive or insulting words or behaviour, or disorderly behaviour, or displays any writing, sign or other visible representation which is threatening, abusive or insulting, within the hearing or sight of a person likely to be caused harassment, alarm or distress thereby. It is a matter of fact for the court to determine whether or not this has occurred. For the purposes of s5, a police officer may be the person harassed or alarmed by the defendant's words: as Glidewell LJ observed in *DPP v Orum* (1989) 88 Cr App R 261:

'I find nothing in the context of the 1986 Act to persuade me that a police officer may not be a person who is caused harassment, alarm or distress by the various kinds of words and conduct to which section 5(1) applies. I would therefore answer the question in the affirmative, that a police officer can be a person who is likely to be caused harassment and so on. However, that is not to say that the opposite is necessarily the case, namely, it is not to say that every police officer in this situation is to be assumed to be a person who is caused harassment. Very frequently, words and behaviour with which police officers will be wearily familiar will have little emotional impact on them save that of boredom. It may well be that in appropriate circumstances, justices will decide ... as a question of fact that the words and behaviour were not likely in all the circumstances to cause harassment, alarm or distress to either of the police officers. That is a question of fact for the justices to be decided in all the circumstances: the time, the place, the nature of the words used, who the police officers are and so on.'

See further *R v Ball* (1990) 90 Cr App R 378. A constable may arrest a person without warrant if he engages in offensive conduct which the constable warns him to stop, and he engages in further offensive conduct immediately or shortly after the warning. The maximum penalty on summary conviction is a fine.

Section 5 provides for three specific defences. First, that the defendant had no reason to believe that there was anyone within hearing or sight of his conduct who was likely to be harassed, alarmed or distressed; second, that he was inside a dwelling and had no reason to believe that the conduct would have been seen or heard by anyone outside; third, that his conduct was reasonable. These are all objective tests: see *DPP v Clarke and Others* [1992] Crim LR 60; and *DPP v Fidler and Morgan* [1992] Crim LR 62. In relation to the issue of reasonableness see further *Kwasi Poku v DPP* [1993] Crim LR 705.

Sections 17–23 of the 1986 Act deal with racial hatred and replace s5A of the 1936 Act. The Act creates six offences all of which require the consent of the Attorney General to institute proceedings. All of these offences concern conduct which is threatening, abusive or insulting and which is intended or which is likely, having regard to all the circumstances, to stir up racial hatred. They are: using such words or behaviour or displaying such materials (s18); distributing or directing such materials (s19); presenting or directing a public play which involves such words or behaviour (s20); distributing, showing or playing a recording of such visual images or sounds (s21); certain participation in a broadcast or cable programme service which includes such images or sounds (s22); possessing such material or recordings with a view to its being displayed, published, distributed, broadcast or included in a cable broadcast service (s23).

Section 30 empowers a court by or before which a person is convicted of an offence connected with football to make an exclusion order prohibiting him from entering premises to attend a prescribed football match.

Section 38 creates various offences connected with contamination of or interference with goods.

Police powers of entry to private meetings

Following *Thomas* v *Sawkins* [1935] 2 KB 249 it appears that the police have a power to enter a public meeting even though it is held on private premises and permission has been withheld, if they reasonably apprehend a breach of the peace. In that case a meeting was held against the Incitement to Disaffection Bill. Two police officers entered the meeting and the organiser asked them to leave. One police officer grabbed him and then 30 other officers entered the meeting. Thomas prosecuted the police officer for battery. The magistrate held that the police had a right to enter the meeting, and therefore there was no battery.

The view of the Divisional Court was that if the police apprehended both the possibility of seditious speeches and a breach of the peace, they had a power of entry. Section 17(6) of the Police and Criminal Evidence Act 1984 expressly retains the constable's common law power to enter premises to deal with a breach of the peace. The power is not limited to entry of premises open to the public. In *McLeod* v *Commissioner of the Metropolitan Police* [1994] 4 All ER 553, the plaintiff's husband, from who she was divorced, obtained a court order, concerning the division of chattels that were matrimonial property, under which he was entitled to seize them from the house that the plaintiff shared with her mother. The plaintiff's husband arrived to collect the property in several vans, accompanied by a number of police officers. The plaintiff arrived home from work whilst the vans were being loaded and remonstrated with the police officers, who indicated that the operation was to proceed and that the vans would not be unloaded. The plaintiff sought unsuccessfully to recover damages for trespass to goods and property against the police, the court confirming that, at common law, police officers had the power to enter private premises if they reasonably believed that a breach of the peace was likely to occur in the near future. The contention that the case of *Thomas* v *Sawkins* should be limited to entry into private property where a public meeting was being held was expressly rejected. See further *McConnell* v *Chief Constable of Greater Manchester* [1990] 1 WLR 364; and *Lamb* v *DPP* [1990] Crim LR 58.

Pickets and picketing

Picketing by strikers usually involves a few of them standing at the works gate and informing their fellow workers that a strike is taking place. Mass picketing is simply picketing in large numbers. There are three ways in which pickets can become involved with the law. Firstly, if the picketing is unlawful then the employer can use the civil law to obtain an injunction ordering the pickets to stop. Secondly, the pickets may be prosecuted for breaches of the criminal law. Finally, anyone can obtain an injunction to stop pickets who are 'unreasonable users' of the highway. (*Hubbard* v *Pitt* [1976] 1 QB 142.)

The civil law

Generally there is no 'right' to picket because it will not be a reasonable use of the highway unless for passing and repassing. However, under s15 of the Trade Union and Labour Relations Act 1974, picketing is lawful if it is in 'contemplation or furtherance of a trade dispute' and at or near the strikers' own workplace 'for the purpose only of peacefully obtaining or communicating information or peacefully persuading any person to work or to abstain from working'. It follows from this that picketing someone else's place of work is illegal and the employer can obtain an injunction to stop it. This is so-called secondary picketing. For the picketing to be legal it must fall within each of the following categories:

1. The people picketing must be employees, their trade union officials or those sacked during the dispute.
2. The only places that can be picketed are the entrances to the premises, or if there is more than one place of work or it is impracticable to picket the workplace (for example seamen), then they can picket 'those offices of their employer from which they receive their instructions or pay packets, or depot or garage from which their vehicles operate'.
3. The picketing is only lawful if it is peaceful. The Code of Practice states: 'The main cause of violence and disorder on the picket line is excessive numbers ... Accordingly, pickets and their organisers should ensure that in general the numbers of pickets do not exceed six at any entrance to a workplace ...' The Code is not law. It is, therefore, not legally binding but the courts must take it into account when considering whether to grant an injunction.
4. Unless the picketing is in 'furtherance of a trade dispute' it is unlawful. In *Hubbard* v *Pitt* [1976] 1 QB 142, it was held that consumers picketing an estate agent could be stopped by an injunction.

The practice of stopping vehicles in order to persuade their occupants not to cross the picket line is not allowed by s15 of the Trade Union and Labour Relations Act 1974. In *Hunt* v *Broome* [1974] AC 587 it was held that if pickets seek to compel a person to refrain from work and seek to prevent him from attending his place of work he may use force if necessary to cross the picket line.

The criminal law

Section 15 of the Trade Union and Labour Relations Act 1974 does not provide protection from the criminal law. Pickets can be protected from the civil law and yet be prosecuted under the criminal law. For example, more than 10,000 charges were brought in England and Wales for offences committed in connection with the miners' dispute in 1984–85. More than 4,000 were brought under s5 of the Public Order Act 1936: 1,500 for obstructing the police; 1,000 for criminal damage; 640 for obstructing the highway and 360 for assaulting a police officer. Other offences committed included murder, riot, unlawful assembly and affray.

13.3 Martial law

The status of this concept in the United Kingdom law is unclear. Many writers emphasise its ambiguity. It is sometimes used to denote an extreme form of the situation discussed above in which the military aid the civil authorities to maintain order. Martial law can be defined as the suspension of the ordinary law, and the substitution therefor of discretionary government by the executive exercised by the military. The 'suspension of the ordinary law' in this context means that the ordinary courts of the land are suspended or otherwise unable to sit.

Martial law certainly does not mean military law, which is a special branch of the law applying to members of the armed forces. During a period of martial law, military courts may be set up to administer justice while the ordinary courts are unable to function, but this is quite different from the ordinary function of courts martial applying military law subject to appeal in the civil courts.

Military administration of occupied enemy territory in time of war is also sometimes called martial law. Where a true state of martial law obtains, the actions of the military are immune from interference by the civil courts.

Whether martial law is recognised by the common law is uncertain. Writers did not usually distinguish between martial law and military law. Martial law is lawful only in time of war, being illegal in time of peace under the Petition of Rights 1628, but war may have a different meaning in this context from the usual one of armed conflict between states. Apparently, it is for the civil courts to decide whether at any particular time insurrection has given rise to a state of war so that, for example, military courts could be set up (see *R* v *Allen* (1921) 2 IR 241). This is in contrast to the conclusiveness of a ministerial certificate declaring that at a certain time the United Kingdom is at war with another state (see *R* v *Bottrill, ex parte Kuechenmeister* [1947] KB 41).

There is no standard procedure whereby authority is handed over by the Government to the military to commence a period of martial law.

It is not the case that martial law obtains at all times during which the United Kingdom is at war with another state.

DF Marais v *GOC Lines of Communication, ex parte Marais* [1902] AC 109 was a decision of the Judicial Committee of the Privy Council on a petition for special leave to apply from a decision of the Supreme Court of the colony of the Cape of Good Hope. Marais had been arrested by the military in an area in which martial law had been declared. It was argued for him that his detention was unlawful because the ordinary courts were still functioning, that if he were guilty of any crime he should be prosecuted in the ordinary way, and that his detention by the military was therefore illegal and he should be forthwith released. The petition was refused. Lord Halsbury LC said:

> '[Their Lordships] are of opinion that where actual war is raging acts done by the military authorities are not justifiable by the ordinary tribunals, and that war in this case was actually raging, even if their Lordships did not take judicial notice of it, is sufficiently evidenced by the facts disclosed by the petitioner's own petition and affidavit ...
>
> The fact that for some purposes some tribunals had been permitted to pursue their ordinary course is not conclusive that war was not raging ... The truth is that no doubt has ever existed that where war actually prevails the ordinary courts have no jurisdiction over the action of the military authorities.'

The idea that the ordinary courts may be 'allowed' to sit by the military seems very doubtful; see for example Molony CJ in *R (Garde)* v *Strickland* (1921) 2 IR 317 at p326. The better view seems to be that the fact of the ordinary courts continuing to sit is no more than a factor in answering the real question as to whether a state of war exists.

In *R* v *Allen* (1921) 2 IR 241 the court of the King's Bench in Ireland refused writs of prohibition, habeas corpus and certiorari against the decision of a military court which had passed a sentence of death on a person convicted of being found in possession of arms and ammunition. The authority for this trial and the sentence was a proclamation of martial law in certain parts of South Ireland and a proclamation that persons found in possession of arms and ammunition would be liable to suffer death on conviction by such a court.

The court accepted the point in *Marais* that the fact of the ordinary courts continuing to sit is not conclusive of the question whether a state of war exists. It also decided, in line with most modern authority, that military courts set up under martial law are not truly courts at all, but only committees set up to carry into execution the discretionary powers assumed by the Government. See also Lord Halsbury in *Tilonko* v *Attorney-General of Natal* (1907) AC 93–95 and Viscount Cave in *Re Clifford and O'Sullivan* [1921] 2 AC 570.

Molony CJ said:

> 'The proceedings of a military court derive their sole justification for authority from the existence of actual rebellion, and the duty of doing whatever may be necessary to quell it and to restore peace and order ...'

This does not mean that the court will inquire into the necessity for each act: the rule appears to be that once it recognises the necessity of martial law, it will not claim jurisdiction, at any rate until after the war is over. In *Egan* v *Macready* (1921) 1 IR 265, O'Connor MR decided that habeas corpus should be issued on facts similar to those in *R* v *Allen*. He based his decision on the Restoration of Order (Ireland) Act 1920 which he said governed the existing situation and therefore made recourse to a military court unnecessary and illegal. He said:

> 'The argument based on military necessity was pressed strongly and I fully recognise that in a case not touched by special legislation it is not for the civil court to decide whether a

military act was necessary or not. That must be left to the military authority. But I think that it should at least appear that there may have been the necessity. Now, the evidence offered by the military in this case seems to me to negative the bringing the prisoner before a military court rather than a court-martial ...'

If, apart from the act, the second last sentence is meant to assert that, for example, if no reasonable man could have found the act necessary, the court intervene, it is contrary to the proposition in *Marais* that the court simply has no jurisdiction during the war.

After the war, it is not clear to what extent there can be redress for action taken under martial law. Usually Parliament passes Acts of Indemnity. It may be that acts which no reasonable man could have found necessary will be punishable, even if the military commander is alone liable at least where his orders were not patently illegal.

13.4 Emergency powers in time of war

Most of the special powers taken by the Government in time of war are nowadays conferred by statute. During the First World War the Government acted under the Defence of the Realm Acts 1914–15. Section 1(1) of the 1914 Act provided that:

'His Majesty in Council has power during the continuance of the present war to issue regulations for securing the public safety and defence of the realm.'

It also said that such regulations could authorise the trial and punishment of persons committing offences against them. This was a very wide power to pass delegated legislation, though its exercise was limited by the doctrine of ultra vires. See, for example, *Chester* v *Bateson* [1920] 1 KB 829. In *R* v *Halliday, ex parte Zadig* [1917] AC 260 a regulation made under the 1914-15 Acts was held not to be ultra vires in purporting to give to the Secretary of State unrestricted powers to detain a person – even a British subject – on security grounds. After the First World War, most acts done in the prosecution of the war were protected from legal action by the Indemnity Act 1920.

Emergency powers were again taken by the Government during the Second World War under the Emergency Powers (Defence) Acts 1939 and 1940. Regulations which could be made under the 1939 Act included those which appeared to His Majesty:

'... to be necessary or expedient for securing the public safety, the defence of the realm, the maintenance of public order and the efficient prosecution of any war in which His Majesty may be engaged, and for maintaining supplies and services essential to the life of the community.'

Various matters were expressly specified as proper subjects for these regulations, such as dealing with offenders against them, detention of people for security reasons, taking possession of property and entering and searching premises. The imposition of charge was authorised. Provision was made by the Emergency Powers (Defence)

Act 1940 (No 2) for the making of regulations for the trial of persons whether or not members of the armed forces in special military courts, should the military situation require it. Such regulations were never in fact made. Some of the regulations were interpreted by the courts in ways very favourable to the Executive. The most famous instance, perhaps, is *Liversidge* v *Anderson* [1942] AC 206 in which regulation 18B(1) on the internment of certain persons was taken to be satisfied by honesty and good faith on the part of the Secretary of State, even though it expressly required him to have 'reasonable cause to believe' in the hostile origin or associations of the person to be detained, and in the necessity of detaining him for those reasons. The Acts expired in 1946.

13.5 Statutory emergency powers in time of peace

Emergency Powers Act 1920

The Act of 1920 permits the proclamation of a state of emergency to last no more than a month (renewable) if at any time it appears to Her Majesty that there have occurred, or are about to occur, events of such a nature as to be calculated, by interfering with the supply and distribution of food, water, fuel or light, or with the means of locomotion, to deprive the community, or any substantial portion of the community, of the essentials of life. Provision is made for the communication of the proclamation to Parliament, even when it is not sitting. During the emergency the Act authorises the making of regulations for securing the essentials of life to the community. As the powers given are very wide, and intended to be used during very disruptive strikes, it is expressly provided that no regulations under the Act shall make it an offence to take part in a strike or peacefully to persuade others to do so.

The Prevention of Terrorism (Temporary Provisions) Act 1989

The Prevention of Terrorism (Temporary Provisions) Act 1989, conferring extraordinary powers to deal with acts of terrorism in Great Britain and Northern Ireland, is a re-enactment and enlargement of the Prevention of Terrorism (Temporary Provisions) Act 1984, which in turn had its origins in the Prevention of Violence (Temporary Provisions) Act 1939. That Act conferred powers on the Secretary of State to make 'expulsion', 'prohibition' and 'registration' orders against persons reasonably suspected of involvement in 'acts of violence designed to influence public opinion or Government policy with respect to Irish affairs', and enabled the police to arrest and detain such persons. Although stated to be temporary these provisions were regularly renewed until 1954 when they were allowed to lapse.

The 1939 Act formed the basis for the Prevention of Terrorism (Temporary Provisions) Act 1974 enacted immediately after the IRA bombing campaign in

Birmingham. The 1974 Act was replaced, with modifications and additions, by the Prevention of Terrorism (Temporary Provisions) Act 1976. The working of both Acts was reviewed by Lord Shackleton in 1978, and by Lord Jellicoe in 1983. The 1984 Act incorporated 12 of the 44 recommendations for change contained in the Jellicoe Report. The operation of the 1984 Act was, in turn, considered by Lord Colville, (1987) Cm 264. Most of the 1989 Act, which represents the fruits of that review, came into effect on 22 March 1989.

Part I of the 1989 Act retains, with minor modifications, the provisions of the earlier legislation, creating a series of offences which may be committed by persons supporting a proscribed organisation. Two organisations are proscribed under the Act, the Irish Republican Army and the Irish National Liberation Army.

Section 1 outlines the meaning of 'proscribed organisation' and s2 makes it an offence to belong or profess to belong to such an organisation, or to solicit or invite non-financial support for it. Under ss2 and 3 it is an offence for any person in a public place to wear any item of dress or to wear, carry or display any article in such a way or in such circumstances as to arouse reasonable apprehension that he is a member or supporter of a proscribed organisation.

Part II gives power to the Secretary of State to make exclusion orders from Great Britain, from Northern Ireland and from the United Kingdom in specified circumstances.

By s5, an order excluding persons from Great Britain may be made where the Secretary of State is satisfied that any person is or has been concerned in the commission, preparation or instigation of acts of terrorism or is attempting or may attempt to enter Great Britain with a view to being concerned in the commission, preparation or instigation of such acts of terrorism.

Section 6 gives power in similar terms to make orders excluding persons from Northern Ireland. A s5 order cannot be made in respect of a person who is the subject of a s6 order and vice versa. A British citizen who has been ordinarily resident in the area concerned throughout the last three years cannot be the subject of such an exclusion order.

Section 7 gives the Secretary of State power to make orders excluding persons from the United Kingdom. Such orders shall not be made against British citizens.

The power to make exclusion orders is expressed to be available to the Secretary of State to be exercised by him in such a way as appears to him expedient to prevent acts of terrorism designed to influence public opinion or Government policy with respect to affairs in Northern Ireland. An exclusion order shall, unless revoked earlier, expire at the end of the period of three years beginning with the day on which it is made.

A person subject to an exclusion order has seven days from service of the notice to make representation objecting to it either in writing to the Secretary of State or in person to persons nominated by the Secretary of State.

Section 8 creates offences concerned with the failure to comply with an exclusion order.

Part III of the Act creates offences relating to the provision of financial assistance to terrorists.

Section 9 makes it an offence to solicit or invite any other person to give, lend or otherwise make available any money or other property or to receive or accept any money or other property, intending that it shall be used for or in connection with acts of terrorism. Section 10 relates more specifically to proscribed organisations. Sections 11 and 12 create offences relating to the 'laundering' of terrorist funds. The Criminal Justice Act 1993 introduces new offences concerning the financing of terrorism.

Part IV of the Act deals with arrest, detention and port powers.

Section 14 provides that a constable may arrest without warrant a person whom he has reasonable grounds for suspecting to be a person guilty of an offence under ss2, 8, 9, 10 or 11 of the Act or a person who is or has been concerned with acts of terrorism, or a person subject to an exclusion order. A person arrested under s14 may be detained for up to 48 hours in right of the arrest. However, the Secretary of State may extend the period of detention up to a further five days. In *Brogan* v *United Kingdom* [1989] 11 EHRR 117 it was held that detention without charge for more than four days was in breach of Article 5(3) of the European Convention on Human Rights. The United Kingdom's response to that ruling was not to alter domestic law so as to ensure conformity, but to seek permission to derogate from Article 5. Regardless of the criticisms directed at that response, it does now seem to have been vindicated to some extent by the subsequent decision in *Brannigan and McBride* v *United Kingdom* (Case No 5/1992/350/423-424) (1993) The Times 28 May. The European Court of Human Rights held that the detention of the applicants, without charge, for a number of days under what is now s14(5) of the Prevention of Terrorism (Temporary Provisions) Act 1989, was not a contravention of Article 5 of the European Convention on Human Rights. The United Kingdom relied on Article 15 of the Convention, which permits signatory states to derogate from their obligations under the Convention in time of war or other public emergency threatening the life of the nation. Given the evidence of the terrorist threat in Northern Ireland, the court held that the derogations from Article 5 were justified in the circumstances, and there were sufficient safeguards to prevent abuse.

Section 15 provides for the issuing of related search warrants.

Section 16 provides for the examination of persons arriving in or leaving Great Britain or Northern Ireland to determine their involvement in terrorism, including the power of arrest and search.

Part V of the Act contains general provisions relating to the investigation of terrorism. Section 18 creates an offence of failing to disclose information about terrorist activities.

Part VI details further provisions relating to Northern Ireland. As regards anti-terrorist legislation for the Province see further the Northern Ireland (Emergency Provisions) Act 1978, as amended by the 1989 Act.

Section 81 of the Criminal Justice and Public Order Act 1994 provides additional powers of stop and search in relation to terrorism by adding a s13A to the Prevention of Terrorism (Temporary Provisions) Act 1989. A senior officer, ie Commander in the Metropolitan Police or assistant chief constable elsewhere, may authorise the use of powers to stop and search persons and vehicles for articles that could be used in connection with acts of terrorism. A constable may exercise these powers whether or not he has reasonable grounds for suspecting that a stop and search of a person or vehicle may reveal such articles. The 1989 Act is further amended by the insertion of s16A, which makes it an offence to possess articles reasonably suspected of being for use in connection with terrorist activities, to collect or record information likely to be of use to terrorists (without lawful authority or reasonable excuse), or to possess any such record or document.

14

Freedom of Expression

14.1 Introduction

14.2 The Government and the media

14.3 The law relating to privacy

14.4 Criminal law restraints upon freedom of expression

14.5 Contempt of court

14.1 Introduction

The numerous laws restricting freedom of expression are an attempt to balance competing rights – the right to say and write anything, and other people's rights not to be offended, abused or scandalised. The State has a right to protect itself from betrayal or subversion, but the individual members of the State have a right to know what it is doing on their behalf. The balance between these rights is the subject of this chapter. There are two ways in which the law attempts to balance these rights: first, by imposing restraints on what is said or written before it has been communicated, and second, by punishing those who have already written or said something.

As Lord Goff of Chieveley observed in *Attorney-General* v *Guardian Newspapers Ltd (No 2)* [1990] 1 AC 109 at pp283–284:

'... we may pride ourselves on the fact that freedom of speech has existed in this country perhaps as long as, if not longer than, it has existed in any other country in the world ... we in this country (where everybody is free to do anything, subject only to the provisions of the law) proceed rather upon an assumption of freedom of speech, and turn to our law to discover the established exceptions to it.'

For a positive right to free speech one would have to turn to Article 10 of the European Convention on Human Rights which provides:

10(1) 'Everyone has the right to freedom of expression. This right shall include freedom to hold opinions and to receive and impart information and ideas without interference by public authority and regardless of frontiers. This article shall not prevent states from requiring the licensing of broadcasting, television and cinema enterprises.'

10(2) 'The exercise of these freedoms, since it carries with it duties and responsibilities, may be subject to such formalities, conditions, restrictions or penalties as are prescribed by law and are necessary in a democratic society, in the interests of national security, territorial integrity or public safety, for the prevention of disorder or crime, for the protection of health or morals, for the protection of the reputation or rights of others, for preventing the disclosure of information received in confidence, or for maintaining the authority and impartiality of the judiciary.'

The Convention does not form part of English law, and thus cannot give right to enforceable rights in the domestic courts, but there is evidence to suggest that the courts regard its enactment as unnecessary on the grounds that domestic law already meets the Convention's requirements. In *Derbyshire County Council* v *Times Newspapers Ltd and Others* [1993] 2 WLR 449, the defendant newspaper published articles that were severe in their criticism of the plaintiff local authority's management of its pension funds. The local authority sought to bring proceedings for libel against the defendants, who responded by applying to have the proceedings struck out as disclosing no known cause of action. At first instance the application to strike out was dismissed. The Court of Appeal allowed the appeal on the basis that, whilst a trading corporation could, in certain circumstances sue for defamation, a local authority could not do so in respect of its reputation in respect of administrative or governmental functions. The House of Lords, dismissing the appeal, held that it was not in the public interest to permit democratically elected local government bodies to bring actions for defamation. The threat of a civil action might inhibit legitimate public comment on, or criticism of, the activities of a local authority. Although the point was obiter, Lord Keith indicated that this prohibition on the right to sue for defamation would extend equally to central government bodies. Any individual councillor, who felt that his reputation had been damaged by a publication that allegedly defamed the council of which he was a member, would still be able to maintain an action for defamation in his own right. Note that Lord Keith arrived at this conclusion without reliance on the European Convention on Human Rights, expressing the view that '... the common law of England is consistent with obligations assumed by the Crown under the Treaty in this particular field'.

Similarly in *Rantzen* v *Mirror Group Newspapers* (1986) Ltd. [1993] 3 WLR 953, where the Court of Appeal considered the argument that to permit an allegedly excessive award of damages for defamation would amount to an infringement of Article 10, it was held that the right of a jury to award unlimited damages was difficult to reconcile with the wording of Article 10, as it required any limitation on freedom of expression, such as the law of defamation, to be necessary in a democratic society. The court doubted whether such large awards were necessary to protect the reputation of plaintiffs. In order to show that the award of damages was a restriction on free speech 'prescribed by law', it was essential that the jury be given guidance on the basis of previous decisions. As s8(2) of the Courts and Legal Services Act 1990 empowered the Court of Appeal to reduce a jury's award of damages where it considered the award to be excessive, the award in the instant case was reduced from £250,000 to £110,000.

14.2 The Government and the media

Press

There is no censorship of the press in peacetime although in time of war the Executive have the power to censor or stop publication of a newspaper. This is very rarely used. Perhaps the most usual form of censorship, if one can call it that, is news management, in other words feeding to the press only such information as the Government wants to be reported. Two further areas will be considered later: offences committed by virtue of the subject matter of the publication; and those matters that cannot be reported by virtue of the law of contempt of court.

'D' Notices

The Defence, Press and Broadcasting Committee is a non–statutory body which has as its function the issuing of 'D' Notices. The committee has no legal status but it is made up of some senior civil servants, and its full-time secretary is paid by the Ministry of Defence.

The function of the committee is to give informal confidential advice to the editors of newspapers on whether or not they should publish any article concerning defence or security matters. If clearance has been given then a newspaper should be safe from prosecution under the Official Secrets Acts 1911 to 1989. However, this is not always the case, as the *Sunday Telegraph* discovered to its cost when publishing an article concerning the war in Biafra. Merely disregarding a 'D' Notice is not itself an offence but it can leave a newspaper or publisher open to prosecution under the Official Secrets Act. As the 'D' Notices themselves say, their 'success depends on goodwill' and in effect upon very little else. As James Michael wrote in *The Politics of Secrecy*, 1982:

> 'The "D" Notice system is the most explicit example of what is either self-censorship or responsible journalism, depending on who is speaking.'

Broadcasting

The British Broadcasting Corporation (BBC) is a body constituted by royal charter and its powers to broadcast are to be found in the licence and agreement statutory instruments. It is controlled by nine governors appointed on advice from the Prime Minister.

The crucial person is the Home Secretary, who grants the licence and who sets the broadcasting receiving licence fee upon which the BBC depends for its income.

Under the licence and agreement the BBC is required to broadcast impartial reports on the proceedings of both Houses of Parliament and to refrain from broadcasting programmes which might offend against good taste and decency or promote violence. The Home Secretary also has the ultimate power to revoke the BBC's broadcasting licence at any time if the BBC does not comply with a request from him to refrain from broadcasting any matter, so long as that request complies with clause 14(3) of the licence and agreement.

The Independent Broadcasting Authority (IBA) established under the Independent Broadcasting Act 1973, as amended, provides all broadcasts not provided by the BBC. It is the body which controls the commercial broadcasting services. Like the BBC, the IBA has a duty not to broadcast anything which could offend against good taste or decency or lead to crime or violence. Both broadcasting services have a duty to provide politically impartial programmes. This requires balanced reporting of current affairs, and a balanced number of 'party political broadcasts'. The balance for these is usually agreed on the basis of the number of seats and votes each party received at the previous General Election. Small parties do get occasional 'party political broadcasts'. Finally, the BBC and the IBA are required to allow the Government the right to broadcast any announcement so long as it is an official statement not a policy statement.

There are no actual safeguards against this being abused but the BBC and the IBA can announce that the broadcast is at the request of the Government.

Theoretically these duties and obligations could be enforced by the courts, but private individuals may require the consent of the Attorney-General if they want to try to enforce the regulations.

14.3 The law relating to privacy

At present there is no legally enforceable right to privacy in English law. It is not one of the recognised torts to invade the privacy of another. An individual seeking legal redress for what they perceive to have been an invasion of their privacy will have to resort to some collateral legal remedy, such as trespass, defamation, or breach of confidence, or indeed seek a remedy before the European Commission, or Court, of Human Rights. A central difficulty lies in attempting to define the concept of privacy.

If one approaches the problem from the perspective of the victim, it is perhaps possible to diagnose two different, although not mutually exclusive, types of complaint. On the one hand an invasion of privacy can involve attention being drawn to the victim so that he becomes the subject of speculation and comment amongst the press and public, and may as a result be unable to go freely about his business or enjoy the unfettered use of his property. Alternatively, an invasion of privacy can arise from an unauthorised disclosure of information, raising the issue of when, if ever, an individual has the right in law to have sensitive information suppressed.

The right to be left alone

If a person enters upon the private property of another without permission, he commits the tort of trespass and can be removed, prevented from committing further trespass by way of injunction, and sued for damages in respect of any harm caused to the property. Thus in theory privacy could be protected, where someone enters the grounds of a house to spy upon its occupants, by invoking the tort of trespass. Arguably the same rules apply if this surveillance is conducted from the public highway, as it is dedicated for users to pass and repass, not to watch and beset neighbouring properties, see *Hickman* v *Maisey* [1990] 1 QB 752. This case concerned the defendant loitering on a road owned by the plaintiff in order to watch the plaintiff's racehorses at the gallops. A highway authority may not necessarily be as eager to help the victim of a voyeur stationed on a public road. In any event, once information has been obtained as a result of a trespass, the law of trespass itself cannot be used to prevent publication. In *Baron Bernstein of Leigh* v *Skyviews and General Ltd* [1978] QB 479, the court rejected the plaintiff's claim for trespass to his property arising out of the defendant's flying over the property and taking aerial photographs. As Griffiths J observed: '... the mere taking of a photograph cannot turn an act which is not a trespass into ... a trespass.'

If a person is physically manhandled by others, notably reporters and photographers, the possibility of a civil action for assault and battery or trespass to the person might be sustainable, although the damages are likely to be small. In *Kaye* v *Robertson* [1991] FSR 92 (see below) the court rejected a claim that to take flash photographs at close range without the consent of the subject could constitute a trespass to the person, although to deliberately cause harm to another's eyesight, albeit temporarily, might constitute a battery. Beyond this there is no general right in law not to be photographed: see *Sports and General Press Agency* v *Our Dogs Publishing Co Ltd* [1916] 2 KB 880.

As the law stands, therefore, a journalist would not commit any criminal offence by gaining unauthorised access (assuming no damage is caused to property) to the house of a well known actress, entering her bathroom and photographing her bathing. It would be too late to restrain the trespass and the photographs could be published provided they did not constitute a libel (see below). The only risk created by such an enterprise is the award of punitive damages for the trespass: see *Rookes* v *Barnard* [1964] AC 1129.

The tort of nuisance could be invoked in extreme cases, but only where the plaintiff can show that the defendant's activities are interfering with the normal use of the property. Cases of surreptitious surveillance would almost certainly fail the relevant test. Thus, it is submitted that the person who wishes to take action against a neighbour who observes them from behind net curtains, or constantly watches them in the garden from an upstairs window, would fail to obtain any legal remedy.

To use a photograph or image of a person, without their consent, in order to advertise a product or promote some cause, or indeed to boost the circulation of a newspaper may amount to defamation if the inference that the person had endorsed the use of their name or image would have the effect of lowering the reputation of that person in the minds of right thinking people. In *Tolley* v *Fry* [1931] AC 333 the defendants had, without obtaining his consent, published an advertisement showing the plaintiff, an amateur golfer, sporting a bar of their chocolate in his back pocket. The plaintiff was successful in recovering damages for defamation on the basis that the advertisement created an innuendo that he had forfeited his amateur status by agreeing to be featured for reward. Greer LJ was, however, at pains to point out that in such cases, no remedy will be available unless the plaintiff can establish that the association is defamatory. Hence if Tolley had been a professional golfer he might not have succeeded. Similarly in *Charleston and another* v *News Group Newspapers Ltd* (1994) The Times 12 January, the defendants published the faces of the plaintiffs (who were both actors appearing in the television serial *Neighbours*) superimposed on to the naked bodies of models engaged in pornographic activities. The article accompanying the photographs claimed that they were evidence of a type of computer pornography that was, unknown to the plaintiffs, available to children. The plaintiffs sought damages alleging that the publication of the photograph was defamatory. The Court of Appeal held that the publication was not capable of having the defamatory meaning for which the plaintiff contended, as the publication had to be considered in its totality. As the law stood it could offer no protection to the plaintiffs. The court remained unpersuaded by arguments drawing attention to the nature of tabloid journalism and the likely reaction of tabloid newspaper readers, ie that they were likely to concentrate on the photographs rather than note the contents of the accompanying article: see further *Sim* v *Heinz* [1959] 1 WLR 313.

Even if defamation is established, the remedy is likely to lie in damages. A plaintiff seeking to prevent publication will only be granted an interlocutory injunction in a very clear case where any properly directed jury would conclude that the matter complained of was libellous: see *Bonnard* v *Perryman* [1891] 2 Ch 269, and *Francombe* v *Mirror Newspapers* [1984] 2 All ER 408. See further *Corelli* v *Wall* (1906) 22 TLR 532, and *Dockerell* v *Dougall* (1899) 80 LT 556.

In *Kaye* v *Robertson* [1991] FSR 62, the plaintiff, a leading actor in a popular television comedy series, had been hospitalised following an accident necessitating brain surgery. Photographers and a journalist from the *Sunday Sport* newspaper entered his hospital room without permission, photographed the plaintiff, and purported to interview him. At first instance the plaintiff obtained an injunction preventing publication on the basis that such publication would constitute a libel. On appeal, however, the court narrowed the injunction, holding that it could not be granted on the basis of libel as it was not 'inevitable' that the plaintiff would be defamed by the publication. The court did agree to the maintenance of an injunction to prevent publication on the basis that, if permitted, the publication could be a malicious falsehood as the journalists concerned knew that to claim that the plaintiff had consented to the interview would be a deliberately false claim. The result was something of a Pyrrhic victory for the plaintiff as the revised injunction allowed the newspaper to publish some of the photographs, provided it did not claim that the plaintiff had in any way consented to the publication. Note that the hospital, unlike the plaintiff, could have proceeded against the journalists for trespass.

Where the copyright in photographs or film is owned by the person featured, he or she can invoke the laws relating to copyright in order to prevent unauthorised publication, although these rights may be waived by contract: see further Copyright, Designs and Patents Act 1988, ss85 and 87; *Williams* v *Settle* [1960] 1 WLR 1072. It may be possible for celebrities, particularly pop stars, to argue that they have copyright in their image if, for example, it forms part of some distinctive logo. In the United States the law has been developed to protect the so-called right of publicity, which perhaps should be renamed as the right to self-publicity: see *Carson* v *Here's Johnny Portable Toilets Inc* 698 F 2d 831 (1983). The American courts have recognised that celebrity status has commercial value from a marketing perspective, and that the celebrity concerned should be able to control the use of his name and image, even where the associations are not defamatory or such as to amount to malicious falsehood.

The European Convention on Human Rights

Article 8 of the European Convention on Human Rights provides:

> 1. Everyone has the right to respect for his private and family life, his home and his correspondence.
> 2. There shall be no interference by a public authority with the exercise of this right except such as is in accordance with the law and is necessary in a democratic society in the interests of national security, public safety or the economic well-being of the country, for the prevention of disorder or crime, for the protection of health or morals, or for the protection of the rights and freedoms of others.

Although the application of Article 8 has resulted in some significant changes to domestic law, it is submitted that it could not be used to curb some of the more intrusive press activities that are the subject of many complaints by those who feel that their privacy has been invaded. Most of the cases that have come before the European Court of Human Rights have been concerned with the right to pursue a particular lifestyle without being harassed or suffering undue embarrassment.

Article 8 was successfully invoked against the United Kingdom in *Malone* v *United Kingdom* (1985) 7 EHRR 14, the European Court of Human Rights ruling unanimously that the then current law relating to interception of communications was insufficiently precise. The Court accepted that such interception might be necessary in order to investigate crime, but again stressed that this should be in accordance with the law and, in the absence of any clear law, the United Kingdom was unable to satisfy this condition. The consequence of this ruling was the introduction of the Interception of Communications Act 1985 (see below).

In *Dudgeon* v *United Kingdom* (1981) 4 EHRR 149, the European Court of Human Rights upheld (by a majority) a claim that the Northern Ireland laws prohibiting buggery between consenting adult males amounted to a violation of the right to privacy under Article 8, as the police had relied upon the law to justify questioning the applicant about his sex life. The Homosexual Offences (Northern Ireland) Order 1982 was introduced to meet the requirements of the court's ruling.

Applicants claiming that their right to privacy has been violated because their changed sexual status has not been recorded by variations to their birth certificates have met with less success. In *Rees* v *United Kingdom* (1986) 9 EHRR 56 (woman having sex change operation to become a man), and *Cossey* v *United Kingdom* (1990) Eur Court HR, Series A, Vol 184 (man having sex change operation to become a woman) the Court recognised that the margin of appreciation allowed to signatory states permitted them to insist on a system of recording births that identified the sex of a child when born. In *Rees* the Court noted that the register of births recorded '... facts of legal significance and ... the establishment of family ties in connection with succession, legitimate descent and the distribution of property'.

It is somewhat ironic that applications designed to assert the right to privacy should be of a nature likely to attract a high degree of press and public interest.

On the European Convention on Human Rights generally, see Chapter 15.

Press reporting

Under English law the press is free to report facts that can be substantiated, subject to restrictions such as those imposed by the legislation governing contempt of court and official secrets. Thus previous convictions or other salacious facts about the lives of both famous and previously unheard of persons can be 'dredged up' by the press. Justification would be the defence to any action for defamation. An individual whose previous convictions are made public may bring proceedings in defamation if the provisions of the Rehabilitation of Offenders Act 1974 apply. Under the Act a conviction becomes 'spent' if the sentence imposed was less than 30 months imprisonment, and provided it was imposed between five and ten years previously. A defamation action will fail if the person revealing the 'spent' conviction can show that he did not act with malice, and it should be borne in mind that the plaintiff in such a case will not be eligible for legal aid.

The Press Council, established in 1953, dealt with many complaints about intrusive reporting by newspapers, but was the subject of much criticism for its failure to curb the excesses of the press, particularly the tabloid newspapers. Following the recommendations of the Calcutt Committee (Report of the Committee on Privacy and Related Matters Cm 1102 (1990)), the Press Complaints Commission was introduced, reflecting a desire on the part of newspaper owners, in particular, to be seen to be taking self-regulation seriously. Like its predecessor, however, the Commission has no coercive power, and cannot award compensation. It can merely censure errant journalists and editors, and ask for any adverse adjudications to be given appropriate publicity by the publisher found to be at fault.

The Press Commission Code of Practice provides as follows:

'The Press Complaints Commission is charged with enforcing the following Code of Practice which was framed by the newspaper and periodical industry

All members of the Press have a duty to maintain the highest professional and ethical standards. In doing so, they should have regard to the provisions of this code of practice and to safeguarding the public's right to know.

Editors are responsible for the actions of journalists employed by their publications. They should also satisfy themselves as far as possible that material accepted from non-staff members was obtained in accordance with this code.

While recognising that this involves a substantial element of self-restraint by editors and journalists, it is designed to be acceptable in the context of a system of self-regulation. The code applies in the spirit as well as in the letter.

1. Accuracy
(i) Newspapers and periodicals should take care not to publish inaccurate, misleading or distorted material.
(ii) Whenever it is recognised that a significant inaccuracy, misleading statement or distorted report has been published, it should be corrected promptly and with due prominence.
(iii) An apology should be published, whenever appropriate.
(iv) A newspaper or periodical should always report fairly and accurately the outcome of an action for defamation to which it has been a party.

2. Opportunity to reply
A fair opportunity for reply to inaccuracies should be given to individuals or organisations when reasonably called for.

3. Comment, conjecture and fact
Newspapers, while free to be partisan, should distinguish clearly between comment, conjecture and fact.

4. Privacy
Intrusions and enquiries into an individual's private life without his or her consent are not generally acceptable and publication can only be justified when in the public interest. This would include:
(i) Detecting or exposing crime or serious misdemeanour.
(ii) Detecting or exposing seriously anti-social conduct.
(iii) Protecting public health and safety.
(iv) Preventing the public from being misled by some statement or action of that individual.

5. Hospitals
(i) Journalists or photographers making enquiries at hospitals or similar institutions should identify themselves to a responsible official and obtain permission before entering non-public areas.
(ii) The restrictions on intruding into privacy are particularly relevant to enquiries about individuals in hospitals or similar institutions.

6. Misrepresentation

(i) Journalists should not generally obtain or seek to obtain information or pictures through misrepresentation or subterfuge.

(ii) Unless in the public interest, documents or photographs should be removed only with the express consent of the owner.

(iii) Subterfuge can be justified only in the public interest and only when material cannot be obtained by any other means.

In all these clauses the public interest includes:

(a) Detecting or exposing crime or serious misdemeanour.

(b) Detecting or exposing anti-social conduct.

(c) Protecting public health or safety.

(d) Preventing the public being misled by some statement or action of an individual or organisation.

7. Harassment

(i) Journalists should neither obtain information nor pictures through intimidation or harassment.

(ii) Unless their enquiries are in the public interest, journalists should not photograph individuals on private property without their consent; should not persist in telephoning or questioning individuals after having been asked to desist; should not remain on their property after having been asked to leave and should not follow them.

The public interest would include:

(a) Detecting or exposing crime or serious misdemeanour.

(b) Detecting or exposing anti-social conduct.

(c) Protecting public health and safety.

(d) Preventing the public from being misled by some statement or action of that individual or organisation ...

9. Intrusion into grief or shock

In cases involving personal grief or shock, enquiries should be carried out and approaches made with sympathy and discretion.

10. Innocent relatives and friends

The Press should generally avoid identifying relatives or friends of persons convicted or accused of crime unless the reference to them is necessary for the full, fair and accurate reporting of the crime or legal proceedings.

11. Interviewing or photographing children

(i) Journalists should not normally interview or photograph children under the age of 16 on subjects involving the personal welfare of the child, in the absence of or without the consent of a parent or other adult who is responsible for the children.

(ii) Children should not be approached or photographed while at school without the permission of the school authorities.

12. Children in sex cases

The Press should not, even where the law does not prohibit it, identify children under the age of 16 who are involved in cases concerning sexual offences, whether as victims, or witnesses or defendants.

13 Victims of crime

The Press should not identify victims of sexual assault or publish material likely to contribute to such identification unless, by law, they are free to do so.

14. Discrimination

(i) The Press should avoid prejudicial or pejorative reference to a person's race, colour, religion, sex or sexual orientation or to any physical or mental handicap.

(ii) It should avoid publishing details of a person's race, colour, religion, sex or sexual orientation, unless these are directly relevant to the story ...'

In January 1994 the Press Complaints Commission appointed Professor Robert Pinker as its Privacy Ombudsman. He can act, without a complaint actually being received, to ensure that the press complies with its own code of practice. Despite the existence of the Code of Practice, however, the second *Calcutt Report* indicates that this system of self-regulation may now be discredited to the point where statutory control is the only remedy (see below '*Proposals for Reform*').

Broadcast media

The Broadcasting Complaints Commission, created by the Broadcasting Act 1990, is empowered, under s143 of that Act, to adjudicate upon complaints of '... unwarranted infringement of privacy in, or in connection with, the obtaining of material included in ... programmes'. The breadth of this jurisdiction was considered by the Court of Appeal in *R* v *Broadcasting Complaints Commission* (1994) The Times 16 December. The appellants were responsible for the broadcasting of two programmes, both of which contained details of tragic deaths. One concerned a child who had been raped and murdered, the other of a young woman who had died as a result of an allergy. The parents of the deceased did not consent to the broadcasts and suffered distress as a result of having seen them by chance. In both cases the parents complained to the Broadcasting Complaints Commission that the broadcasts amounted to an invasion of privacy, and the Commission upheld the complaints. The appellants contended that there could be no invasion of privacy where the material broadcast was already in the public domain and did not relate to the complainants themselves. Confirming the correctness of the Commission's decision, the Court held that, as the Broadcasting Act 1990 Act did not contain a definition of privacy, it could be inferred that Parliament intended that the question of whether or not an infringement of privacy had occurred should be dealt with as one of fact and degree by the Commission itself. Whilst the court would be willing to intervene in an extreme case where the Commission's interpretation of privacy could not be substantiated on any grounds, the present case was not regarded as falling within that category. The fact that the details had been in the public domain did not prevent their republication from amounting to an invasion of privacy, and it was unacceptably narrow to argue that the fact had to concern the complainant personally. Once the Commission concluded that an invasion of privacy had occurred it had jurisdiction to determine whether or not that invasion had been warranted. On the facts the Commission's determination could not be impeached.

The Commission has been held to have jurisdiction to consider complaints on the grounds of infringement of privacy even where material concerning the complainant is not actually broadcast. In *R* v *Broadcasting Complaints Commission, ex parte BBC* (1992) The Times 16 October, the Court held that the Commission had been right to uphold a complaint about invasion of privacy raised by the proprietor of a dating agency, about whom the BBC had been trying to produce an investigative film item. The complainant had been subjected to persistent attempts to interview and to photograph himself and his family by those compiling material for the programme, and claimed that these activities amounted to an invasion of his privacy. The court ruled that the fact that none of the material was eventually used in the programme was irrelevant to the issue of the Commission's jurisdiction, provided there was a nexus between the material broadcast and the matter complained of.

Security of communications

The Interception of Communications Act 1985, enacted following the ruling of the European Court of Human Rights in the *Malone* case (considered above) creates the offence of intercepting a communication in the course of its transmission by post or by a public telecommunications system unless a warrant has been issued by the Secretary of State to permit the interception, or the person making the interception reasonably believes that the sender or the receiver of the communication consented to it (s1). The Secretary of State may issue a warrant to intercept in this way only if it is necessary; in the interests of national security; for the purpose of preventing or detecting serious crime; or for the purpose of safeguarding the economic well-being of the United Kingdom (s2). In considering if there is such a necessity the Secretary of State must consider whether he could obtain the information by other means and, in the case of a warrant issued on the grounds of safeguarding the economic well-being of the United Kingdom, the condition of necessity will only be satisfied where the information sought relates to the acts or intentions of those outside the British Isles.

Section 7 of the 1985 Act creates a tribunal to investigate complaints by persons who believe their postal or telephone communications have been intercepted. If the tribunal believes the interception to have been unjustified in accordance with the principles of judicial review then it must not only report to the Prime Minister but may also quash any warrant, direct destruction of copies of intercepted mail, and order compensation to be paid by the Secretary of State. The tribunal is to be staffed by five independent lawyers. Section 8 of the Act creates the post of Commissioner, to be held by the serving holder or past holder of high judicial office. His function is to supervise the Secretary of State and assist the tribunal.

The House of Lords was invited to consider the ambit of the restrictions on telephone-tapping created by the 1985 Act in *R* v *Effick; R* v *Mitchell* [1994] 3 WLR 583. The appellants, who had been charged with conspiracy to supply controlled drugs, sought, during the course of their trial, to challenge the admission of prosecution evidence comprising tape recordings of telephone conversations. The recordings had been made by police officers, engaged in surveillance activities, who had occupied premises adjoining the house of a Ms Sumer (who was involved in the plan to supply drugs), and had been able to record her telephone conversations, which had taken place on her cordless telephone, on a domestic radio-cassette recorder. The trial judge rejected the appellants' contention that the evidence was inadmissible on the basis that it had been obtained in contravention of s1(1) of the 1985 Act, and this ruling was upheld by the House of Lords, where it was held that the term 'public telecommunications system' applied to the British Telecom system up to the point where the signal was applied to the first terminal socket in Ms Sumer's house. The cordless telephone unit was a privately operated system connected to the public British Telecom system. Applying *R* v *Ahmed* (1994 unreported Court of Appeal 28 March), Lord Oliver cited with approval the four-stage approach adopted in that case by Evans LJ where he held that: (1) the interception of communications took place when and at the place that the electrical impulse or signal is in fact intercepted; (2) if there is interception of a private system it cannot be regarded as the interception of a transmission made by means of a public telecommunications system; (3) the fact that later or earlier signals will either have formed part of, or will form part of, the same communication or message does not mean that the interception takes place at some other place or time; (4) communication refers to the telephonic communication that is actually intercepted, and not the whole of the transmission process.

The use of surveillance equipment, for example 'bugging' devices that can relay private conversations, falls outside the scope of the 1985 Act, although the placing of such items in a person's property would be likely to involve a trespass, and possibly criminal damage. Where the device is one that can be used to pick up conversations taking place in public from some distance away, it may be the case that no offence is involved at all in the actual act of surveillance. In the absence of any liability arising from the way in which an individual's conversations are overheard, attention would have to shift to the use that could be made of such information. It seems unlikely that an injunction could be obtained to prevent publication of the conversations overheard as the information is not given in confidence. In *R* v *Khan (Sultan)* (1994) The Times 1 June, the Court of Appeal ruled that evidence against the appellant, primarily in the form of tape-recorded conversations that had taken place whilst he had visited a private address in Sheffield, was admissible under s78 of the Police and Criminal Evidence Act 1984, despite the fact that it had been obtained by police officers who had attached a surveillance device to the exterior of the premises. The court felt that the invasion of privacy that this method of surveillance had involved was outweighed by the public policy considerations regarding the seriousness of the activity under investigation, ie the large-scale importation of heroin. The only regulation that currently exists is in the form of the Home Office guidelines: *Covert Listening Devices and Visual Surveillance (Private Places)* 1984, under which the chief constable of the relevant force must be satisfied that, where devices are to be used to record conversations in places where a citizen would normally be entitled to presume privacy, such surveillance is required because the investigation concerns major organised crime, particularly violence. The guidelines assume that such evidence would be admissible in court.

The right to secrecy

The law recognises that there are situations where an individual can claim a legal right not to divulge information. In some cases this can be seen as an aspect of privacy, where the information is of a sensitive nature and its disclosure would cause embarrassment and distress to the person concerned, or their close family. In many cases, however, the right to maintain secrecy is invoked by those who seek some tactical advantage in litigation, or who wish to ensure a supply of information from informants who do not wish to be identified.

In litigation, communications between lawyer and client attract legal professional privilege, which effectively prevents the court from ordering their disclosure. The rationale for this privilege is clearly that individuals should be able to discuss their cases freely with their legal advisers. In order to determine whether or not the privilege will apply, a 'dominant purpose' test is applied. In *Waugh* v *British Railways Board* [1980] AC 521, the widow of a man who had been killed in a railway accident sought production of a report compiled for the safety inspectorate to assist them in determining the cause of the accident. The report stated that it was to be passed on to British Rail's solicitors to enable them to advise British Rail. The court held the report had principally been drawn up to assist in accident prevention, hence it could order disclosure. See also *Peach* v *Commissioner of the Metropolis* [1986] 2 A11 ER 129.

A subpoena duces tecum can compel a third party to attend trial with any relevant documents. Generally, mere witnesses cannot be compelled to reveal what they have seen, or provide information. The exceptions where the production of documents in the possession of non-parties before the trial can be ordered are:

1. Personal injury litigation/fatal accident claims, eg to obtain hospital records where the health authority is not a party to the litigation. In *Paterson* v *Chadwick* [1974] 2 A11 ER 772, the plaintiff sued the defendant solicitor for allowing a personal injury action to become statute barred. Even though the action appeared to be one based on a claim of professional negligence, the court held that the hospital should be required to disclose its records relevant to the injury, since the matter arose out of a personal injuries case.
2. Banks can be required to allow inspection of books.
3. Where a third party has inadvertently assisted in the wrongdoing complained of. In *Norwich Pharmacal Ltd* v *Customs and Excise Commissioners* [1974] AC 133, the Customs and Excise was ordered to disclose information on who was importing fertiliser in breach of the plaintiff's patent.

As to the effect of s10 of the Contempt of Court Act 1981 on the confidentiality of journalistic sources, see below.

Breach of contract and confidence

The law has, for many years, recognised that in certain relationships an obligation of confidence can arise between the parties. The obligation may arise as the result of an express or implied contractual term, but the existence of a contract is not a pre-condition of a duty of confidentiality. In *Argyll* v *Duke of Argyll* [1967] Ch 302, details of dealings between a husband and wife were held to be protected by a duty of confidence, and this has since been extended to details of the sexual relationships of unmarried partners, including homosexual relationships. Although damages may in some cases be an adequate form of compensation, in the vast majority of cases the confider will be seeking an injunction to prevent a threatened breach of confidence. Once information has been disclosed there is clearly little that can be done to prevent its wider publication.

What is the situation where the confider is the State? Can the Government of the day resort to breach of confidence to prevent its servants, be they ministers or civil servants, from revealing information? It may be thought that in such situations the Official Secrets Act 1989 might be invoked, but its use may not always be appropriate or possible. Where the disclosures are threatened by a serving or recent holder of ministerial office there would be considerable political discomfort caused by resorting to criminal sanctions to 'gag' a senior figure. Where the disclosures are threatened by a civil servant, he may be beyond the jurisdiction of the criminal courts. A trial in his absence would invoke adverse comment. Even where the civil servant is brought to trial, the jury may refuse to convict, as was the situation in the case of Clive Ponting.

Hence the civil remedy of injunction to restrain a breach of confidence has its attractions where the Government seeks to prevent an embarrassing disclosure. Although no injunction was granted in *Attorney-General* v *Jonathan Cape Ltd* [1976] QB 752, Lord Chief Justice Widgery re-affirmed the existence of the equitable doctrine that no man should be allowed to profit from his own wrongdoing, namely the unauthorised publication of material received in confidence. In that case the court ruled that there was insufficient evidence that the workings of government would be damaged by the publication of Richard Crossman's diaries, but the court clearly indicated that in an appropriate case it would not hesitate to act. The Attorney-General had won on the point of principle.

Following the case the report of the Radcliffe Committee (1976 Cmnd 6386) led to much stricter guidelines being laid down concerning ministerial disclosures. Note that Cabinet papers are not normally made public for 30 years, under the terms of the Public Record Acts 1958 and 1967. The ruling in *Attorney-General* v *Jonathan Cape Ltd* served as a prelude to the most celebrated case of a government seeking refuge in the civil remedy of an action for breach of confidence, the so-called *Spycatcher* litigation.

A former member of MI5, Peter Wright, became disturbed by what he saw as foreign infiltration of the secret services. He approached a House of Commons Select Committee with his evidence, but his complaints were not taken up. He retired to Australia from where he proposed to publish his memoirs, in the form of the book *Spycatcher* which revealed much about the workings of the security services. Whilst the Government sought an injunction to prevent its publication in Australia, several newspapers in the United Kingdom sought to publish extracts from the book. The Attorney-General was granted an injunction to prevent the publication of extracts by *The Observer* newspaper, even though the nature of the revelations in the extracts was becoming well known. The basis for the injunction was not so much that confidentiality had to be maintained, but more that no disclosure had been authorised by the Government. Other newspapers moved to publish the extracts from *Spycatcher* on the basis that they were not prevented from doing so by the injunction, as this was directed at *The Observer*. The courts ruled, however, that publication in any other newspaper would amount to a contempt of court as it would have had the effect of undermining the injunction already granted.

By July 1987 *Spycatcher* had been published in the United States, and *The Observer* returned to court in an attempt to have the interim injunction prohibiting publication of extracts discharged, on the basis that there was nothing left to protect. At first instance the court agreed, noting that British citizens returning from the United States were able to purchase the book at any airport bookstall. This ruling was reversed by the Court of Appeal, however, subject to the relaxation on restrictions which would have prevented accurate reporting of the debates on the issue in Parliament. Ultimately the question of whether the interim injunction should be discharged reached the House of Lords: *Attorney-General* v *Guardian Newspapers Ltd and Others* [1987] 3 All ER 316. By a majority of three to two, it was held that, pending a trial of the main issue, the interim injunction would remain. Lord Brandon thought the maintenance of the injunction might serve to deter further disclosures, whilst Lord Ackner, referring to the fact that the Attorney-General had been unable to prevent publication in the United States, felt that to lift the injunction now would be seen as surrendering to the American constitutional right to free speech. Lord Bridge and Lord Oliver, dissenting, expressed grave misgivings as regards the implications of maintaining the injunctions. Lord Oliver, in particular, pointed out that in the absence of a constitutional right to freedom of expression, the liberty of the press was of paramount importance.

By the time the matter came to trial, international publication of *Spycatcher* had become much more widespread, and the High Court and the Court of Appeal recognised that granting a final injunction to prevent publication in the United Kingdom would be futile: [1988] 3 All ER 545. The Attorney-General nevertheless appealed to the House of Lords: *Attorney-General* v *Observer Ltd and Others* [1988] 3 WLR 776. It was held (Lord Griffiths dissenting in part) that no final injunction to restrain a breach of confidence would be granted unless it could be shown to be in the public interest to do so. Where the information had already been published abroad, little further damage would be prevented by an injunction.

It is interesting to note that the Attorney-General had attempted to obtain an injunction to prevent any future publication of confidential material divulged by

Peter Wright. The House of Lords refused to grant any such general prohibition, declaring that each incident would have to be dealt with in its own right.

Data protection

In its White Paper of 1984 the Government recognised the need for some legislation controlling the use of personal information stored in computers:

> 'First, because of the threat to privacy posed by the rapid growth in the use of computers, with their ability to process and link at high speed information about individuals. There have been few reported instances in this country of information held on computers being misused so as to threaten the personal privacy of individuals. But the ease and scale of misuse which the versatility of computers makes possible is significantly greater than with manual records. Secondly, without legislation firms operating in the United Kingdom may be at a disadvantage compared with those based in countries which have data protection legislation. When the Council of Europe Data Protection Convention [in force 1985, the United Kingdom is a signatory] comes into force it will confirm the right of countries with data protection legislation to refuse to allow personal information to be sent to other countries which do not have comparable safeguards.'

The resultant legislation was the Data Protection Act 1985. Subject to the exceptions created by the Act, any person storing such data on a computer must register as a 'user'. Unauthorised disclosure of information so held is a criminal offence, as is a failure to register. Section 161 of the Criminal Justice and Public Order Act 1994 creates additional offences by adding to s5 of the 1985 Act a new sub-section (6) 'procuring disclosure of computer-held personal information'; and new sub-sections (7) and (8) 'selling, or offering for sale, personal data'. These additional offences are triable either way and are punishable by fine only. The provisions of the Act are administered by a registrar, who can reject applications to register, issue enforcement notices for non–compliance, and even inspect premises and records. Appeal from his decisions lies to the Data Protection Tribunal. Within the limitations imposed by the Act, individuals can, upon payment of a fee, request details of the information that is held on them.

Proposals for reform

The issue of privacy has been the subject of four post-war reports: the 'Justice' Report *Privacy and the Law* (1970); the Younger Committee *Report of the Committee on Privacy* (1972), Cmnd 5012; the Calcutt Committee *Report of the Committee on Privacy and Related Matters* (1990) Cm 1102; and the second Calcutt Report (1993).

Like its predecessors the first Calcutt Report came out against the introduction of a new tort of infringement of privacy, chiefly because of the practical difficulties this would involve. As the Report states (para 12.34):

> 'Any form of legal action in tort suffers from a number of limitations. The individual who has been wronged has the daunting task of mounting and pursuing an action in the courts.

Many find the financial risks a deterrent. One of the main shortcomings of a tort of infringement of privacy would be that it would not provide a readily accessible remedy. Even if legal aid were made available, which we would consider essential, many would still fall outside its scope ... we set ourselves the test of asking whether any proposed remedy would satisfy the criteria of speed, cheapness and readiness of access. We are not persuaded that a tort of infringement of privacy would perform very well against such criteria. We consider this a major weakness.'

The committee felt that the introduction of a new self-regulatory body, in the form of the Press Complaints Commission (see above) would provide a procedure for complaint which

'... would undoubtedly be less daunting to many people than having to use a new tort. The people whose privacy we consider most needs protecting should they, for example, become the victim of a crime or a disaster, or suffer from a disfiguring illness, are precisely those who hold no office, play no prominent role in society, have no publicity agent and also probably lack the means to sue. Thus, while we have not based our rejection of a general tort of infringement of privacy on accessibility alone, it is, nevertheless, an important factor in deciding whether the case for a tort has been made out ...' (para 12.36)

The committee went on to recommend (inter alia) the introduction of a new criminal offence of surreptitious unlawful surveillance by means of a technical device; a tort related to such unlawful surveillance; and a tort of disclosure of unlawfully obtained information.

The second Calcutt Report, published in January 1993, was highly critical of the Press Complaints Commission, claiming that it had been an ineffectual self-regulatory body, dominated by those with the interests of the Press at heart.

The second report contains two significant proposals. First, it recommends new criminal offences outlawing unauthorised entry into private property, photography, placing a surveillance device, or telephone tapping, conducted with the intention of obtaining information. Liability might extend to editors and proprietors of newspapers who instructed reporters to gather information by these means. Defendants would be able to rely on defences that they had acted to prevent crime, protect public safety or to prevent the public from being misled. Individuals who had suffered such intrusions would be able to invoke the civil courts in order to obtain an injunction to prevent disclosure of illegally obtained information.

The second major proposal is the replacement of the Press Complaints Commission with a statutory press tribunal, funded by the Crown, empowered to apply a code of practice. The tribunal would have the power to prevent the publication of material in breach of the code, investigate complaints, aid conciliation, award compensation and impose fines, enforce publication of retractions, apologies, and adjudications. Under the proposals the tribunal would be empowered to impose a fine of up to one per cent of a publication's net annual revenue. Individuals would face a maximum fine of £5,000. There are, at present, no plans to give these latest proposals legislative effect.

In July 1993 the Lord Chancellor's Department published its consultation paper on the law relating to privacy. The paper proposes a new cause of action that could be invoked in cases of infringement of privacy causing substantial distress to the plaintiff in circumstances where a person of ordinary sensibilities would have similarly suffered substantial distress. Privacy would be taken to include details concerning an individual's health, communications, family life and relationships. The proposals also envisage a right to be free from harassment or molestation. A defendant would be permitted to raise defences that he had lawful authority for his actions, had the consent of the plaintiff, that the disclosure was protected by privilege, or that the disclosure was in the public interest. The paper envisages actions being brought in the county courts, with awards of damages up to £10,000. A major weakness of the proposals,however, is the absence of any provision of legal aid.

14.4 Criminal law restraints upon freedom of expression

Sedition

At common law it is an offence to publish a seditious libel or to utter seditious words. In *R* v *Burns* (1886) 16 Cox CC 355, a definition of sedition was given:

> 'An intention to bring into hatred or contempt, or to excite disaffection against the person of Her Majesty, or the Government and constitution of the United Kingdom as by law established, or either House of Parliament, or the administration of justice, or to excite Her Majesty's subjects to attempt, otherwise than by lawful means, the alteration of any matter in Church or State by law established, or to raise discontent or disaffection amongst Her Majesty's subjects, or to promote feelings of ill-will and hostility between different classes of such subjects.'

In *R* v *Caunt* (1948) Birkett J directed the jury that proof of an intention to promote violence was an essential part of the offence. Therefore today the prosecution will probably have to show 'an intention to promote violence and disorder over and above the strong criticism of public affairs'.

Many activities which would previously have been regarded as coming within the scope of sedition are now covered by other, more appropriate, offences, for example under the Public Order Act 1986.

Incitement to disaffection

Section 53 of the Police Act 1964 prohibits acts calculated to cause disaffection among police officers or to induce them to withhold their services or commit breaches of discipline.

Similarly it is an offence under the Incitement to Disaffection Act 1934 maliciously and advisedly to endeavour to seduce a member of the armed forces from his duty or allegiance to the Crown, or for any person, with intent to commit or aid, counsel or procure the commission of the main offence, to have in his possession or under his control any document of such a nature that the distribution of copies among members of the forces would constitute that offence.

In *R* v *Arrowsmith* [1975] QB 678, Pat Arrowsmith was convicted under this Act of possessing, and distributing near army barracks, leaflets which might seduce soldiers from their duty of serving in Northern Ireland.

Racial hatred

Offences related to stirring up racial hatred are contained in ss17–23 of the Public Order Act 1986. Section 17 defines racial hatred as hatred against a group in Great Britain defined by reference to colour, race, nationality, or ethnic origin. The use of words, or behaviour, or the displaying of written material, in a public place, which is intended to, or is likely to, stir up racial hatred is prohibited by s18. The publication or distribution of such material is prohibited by s19. The possession of racially inflammatory material is prohibited by s23.

Sections 20 to 22 deal with the issues arising from plays and other public performances which may stir up racial hatred.

Blasphemy

Blasphemy is a common law offence consisting of the publication of matter which denies the truth of the Christian religion, or which vilifies Christ. In *Bowman* v *Secular Society* [1917] AC 406, Lord Sumner stated that such acts were criminal because they tended to 'shake the fabric of society generally'.

In *R* v *Lemon* [1979] AC 617, Mrs Mary Whitehouse prosecuted the editor of a homosexual newspaper, *Gay News*, which published a poem in which a Roman soldier expressed homosexual 'love' for Christ. His conviction for blasphemous libel was upheld by the House of Lords. Their Lordships stated:

1. it is not necessary that a breach of the peace is a likely or intended result of the publication; and
2. it is not necessary that the accused should intend to blaspheme; it is enough that he intends publication.

In *R* v *Bow Street Magistrates, ex parte Choudbury* (1990) The Times 9 April, the Divisional Court refused an application for judicial review of the magistrates' refusal to issue a summons for blasphemy in respect of the Salman Rushdie book *Satanic Verses*. The court noted that the Law Commission had recommended the abolition of the offence, and accepted that in the light of this it might not have been desirable to extend the ambit of the existing offence to other religions.

Criminal libel

Criminal libel covers those serious cases of libel where mere damages are not appropriate as a remedy. It is very rare and not encouraged by the courts. Leave of a High Court judge is required before a prosecution can be commenced.

In *Goldsmith* v *Pressdram Ltd* [1976] 3 WLR 191 a judge granted an order enabling a private prosecution for criminal libel to be brought by Sir James Goldsmith against *Private Eye* in respect of repeated allegations that Goldsmith was involved in a conspiracy to obstruct the course of justice, concerning the disappearance of Lord Lucan. The judge stated:

> '... the press does not have licence to publish scandalous or scurrilous matter which is wholly without foundation.'

Obscenity

The law of obscenity comprises both statutory and common law offences. In regulating this area the law distinguishes between performance art and the written word. Obscenity in films to be shown in cinemas may be regulated in two ways.

The first of these is statutory. Cinemas are licensed by local authorities under the Cinematograph Act 1952, and local authorities are allowed to attach conditions to the grant of licences. These can refer to the type of films shown and the courts have held that the conditions attached can apply to the morality of the films. A usual condition is that no film can be shown unless it has been approved by the British Board of Film Censors.

This body constitutes the second non-statutory form of cinema censorship. The Board has no power to stop a film being shown or to enforce any cuts or to impose and enforce its classification. However, it is very influential and local authorities usually follow the Board's recommendations.

As regards theatres, it was not until the Theatres Act 1968 that censorship was finally ended. There is still a need for premises used for showing plays to be licensed by the local authority, but no conditions as to the content of the performances can be attached.

The law relating to obscenity, incitement to racial hatred and breaches of the peace still applies to theatrical performances, but for a prosecution to be commenced the permission of the Attorney-General is required. Under the civil law any defamatory statements made in plays are libellous.

Statutory offences relating to obscenity

Obscene Publications Act 1959. Section 1 of the 1959 Act defines the meaning of obscene. It follows the definition laid down in *R* v *Hicklin* (1868) LR 3 QB 360.

An obscene article is one whose effect, if taken as a whole, is such as tends to deprave and corrupt persons who are likely, having regard to all relevant circumstances, to read, see or hear the matter contained or embodied in it.

The book or article must be taken as a whole so that it is no longer possible to select parts of the article. Prosecuting counsel in the case concerning the book *Lady Chatterley's Lover* attempted selectively to read out the most infamous parts of it, but was stopped by the judge. However, a magazine which has many articles in it can be within the definition even if only one article is held to be obscene: *R* v *Anderson* [1972] 1 QB 304.

The most difficult part of the definition of obscene is the meaning of the words 'to deprave and corrupt'. Mr Justice Byrne in the *Lady Chatterley* case gave this definition of the phrase to the jury:

'... to deprave means to make morally bad, to pervert, to debase, or corrupt morally. The words "to corrupt" mean to render morally unsound or rotten, to destroy the moral purity or chastity of, to pervert, to ruin a good quality, to debase, to defile ... just as loyalty is one of the things which is essential to the well-being of the nation, so some sense of morality is something that is essential to the well-being of a nation, and to the healthy life of the community ... and accordingly, anyone who by his writing tends to corrupt that fundamental sense of morality is guilty of an obscene libel.'

The difficulty with this definition is that juries have not been able or willing consistently to apply it. Modern-day jurors are likely to be much more liberal in their views. As de Smith puts it:

'Nowadays a judge, magistrate or jury is unlikely to be persuaded that anything less than an explicit portrayal or description of sexual activity ... is obscene in this sense.'

The 1959 Act requires that, for the material in question to be regarded as obscene, the prosecution must satisfy the court that it will tend to deprave and corrupt those who are likely to read, see or hear it, as the case may be. Hence in *R* v *Clayton and Halsey* [1963] 1 QB 163, where a police officer was shown obscene material, the court decided he was unlikely to be depraved and corrupted. However, it is no defence that the sort of people likely to obtain particular material are already depraved and corrupted. In *R* v *O'Sullivan* [1994] NLJ 635 the appellant was observed by police whilst delivering and collecting pornographic material from a garage, and working behind the counter of a sex shop where the items were sold. He was also found to have pornographic video cassettes in his possession. The appellant was convicted of having obscene articles for gain contrary to s2(1) of the Obscene Publications Act 1959, and he appealed on the ground that the material in question was not obscene. In particular, he contended that the trial judge should have directed the jury to consider whether the publications would tend to deprave and corrupt those likely to see the material (ie customers of the sex shop) as opposed to those who might possibly see the material. Dismissing the appeal the Court of Appeal held that for a conviction the jury had to: (1) be satisfied beyond all reasonable doubt that the defendant had the relevant articles in his possession with a view to publication for gain; (2) decide what publication the defendant had in contemplation; (3) consider what further publication, for example by giving, lending, or selling, could reasonably be expected to follow from the original contemplated publication; and (4) be satisfied that the effect of any of those contemplated publications would be to deprave and corrupt a more than negligible proportion of those likely to see the relevant matter.

'Publishing' includes distributing, circulating, selling, hiring, showing pictures or playing records.

Obscenity is not limited to sexual matters. In *John Calder (Publishers) v Powell* [1965] 1 QB 509, the Lord Chief Justice held that a book advocating drug-taking was obscene.

Section 2 gives a publisher a defence if he can show that he 'had not examined the article ... and had no reasonable cause to suspect' that what was published was obscene.

Section 4 gives those charged with the offence of publishing an obscene article a defence if it can be shown that the publication was for the public good, 'in the interests of science, literature, art or learning, or other objects of general concern'. Evidence can be given on the literary, artistic or scholastic merits of a piece of work but evidence cannot be given of whether the publication is for the public good: that is for the jury to decide. In *R v Calder and Boyars Ltd* [1969] 1 QB 15, the Court of Appeal held that the jury had two questions to answer: Was the book obscene? And:

'... they should assess the strength of the literary, sociological or ethical merit which they consider the book to possess. They should then weigh up all these factors and decide whether on balance the publication is proved to be justified as being for the public good.'

The Obscene Publications Act 1964. This was a response to the growing importation of pornography. Under the 1959 Act the police could only search for and seize an obscene publication if it was for a 'publication for gain' (s3). If no publication took place then no seizure, search or prosecution could take place. The 1964 Act changed the law so that the police could get warrants to search for and seize obscene material if the material was 'in possession for gain'. This means the Act becomes effective before publication.

Customs Consolidation Act 1876. Section 42 grants the power to seize and destroy indecent or obscene books and articles imported into the United Kingdom.

Post Office Act 1953. Section 11 makes it an offence to send indecent or obscene articles through the post.

Vagrancy Act 1824. Section 4 makes it an offence to expose to view in any public place 'any obscene print, picture or other indecent exhibition'.

Children and Young Persons (Harmful Publications) Act 1955. The Act makes it an offence to publish horror comics: 'stories told in pictures which portray the commission of crimes, acts of violence or cruelty, or incidents of a repulsive or horrible nature'.

Protection of Children Act 1978. This Act creates offences of taking, permitting to be taken, possessing or publishing indecent photographs of children under the age of 16. Section 84 of the Criminal Justice and Public Order Act 1994 Act extends the scope of the offence to include 'pseudo-photographs' which extends to data stored on a computer disk or by other electronic means, thereby encompassing the growing field of computerised child pornography.

Common law offences relating to obscenity

Conspiracy to corrupt public morals. Shaw v *Director of Public Prosecutions* [1962] AC 220. Shaw published the *Ladies Directory* which advertised prostitutes and their services. The House of Lords upheld Shaw's conviction for the offence of conspiracy to corrupt public morals. It was not realised before this decision that there was such a crime. Lord Simonds stated:

> '... there remains in the courts of law a residual power to enforce the supreme and fundamental purpose of the law, to conserve not only the safety and order but also the moral welfare of the State.'

Shaw was also convicted under the Obscene Publications Act 1959. The effect of *Shaw*'s case was that prosecutions could be brought at common law for conspiracy as well as for breaches of the 1959 Act. Viscount Simmonds suggested that such prosecutions for common law conspiracy could be used where doubt existed as to whether a conviction of obscenity under the Act could be obtained.

Conspiracy to outrage public decency. Knuller Ltd v *Director of Public Prosecutions* [1973] AC 435. The appellant published a magazine containing advertisements by homosexuals seeking to meet other homosexuals. The House of Lords upheld a conviction for conspiracy to corrupt public morals thereby affirming the decision in *Shaw*'s case. It was no defence that under the Sexual Offences Act 1967 homosexual acts between consenting males in private had ceased to be an offence. A second conviction for conspiracy to outrage public decency was quashed on the ground of misdirection. Nevertheless a majority of their Lordships held that at common law it was an offence to outrage public decency and also to conspire to outrage public decency.

Official Secrets Acts 1911 to 1989

Section 1(1) of the Official Secrets Act 1911 provides that it is an offence punishable with 14 years imprisonment:

> '... if any person for any purpose prejudicial to the safety or interest of the State:
> 'a) approaches, inspects, passes over or is in the neighbourhood of, or enters any, prohibited place within the meaning of this Act; or
> 'b) makes any sketch, plan, model, or note which ... might be or is intended to be directly or indirectly useful to an enemy; or

'c) obtains, collects, records, or publishes or communicates to any other person any secret official code word or any sketch, plan, model, article, or note, or other document or information which ... might be or is intended to be directly or indirectly useful to an enemy.'

In *Chandler* v *DPP* [1964] AC 763, anti-nuclear demonstrators sought to enter an RAF base and sit on the runway in order to prevent nuclear bombers taking off. As they approached the base they were arrested and charged with conspiracy to enter a prohibited place for a purpose prejudicial to the safety or interests of the State, contrary to s1 of the 1911 Act. The House of Lords unanimously upheld the conviction. Thus the 1911 Act is not restricted to spying but includes acts of sabotage and other acts of physical interference.

Section 2 of the Official Secrets Act 1911 was for many years the subject of severe criticism for creating more than 2,000 offences and being a 'catch-all'. It was not consistently enforced and a number of well-publicised prosecutions, such as those of Clive Ponting and Sarah Tisdall, both civil servants, lent strength to calls for its reform. Broadly the section made it an offence for a person receiving information in confidence from the Government to communicate it to anyone who was not authorised to receive it unless it was in the interests of the State for him to do so. Even information which was not confidential was protected by the section and there were many difficulties of interpretation.

Section 2 was eventually replaced by the Official Secrets Act 1989 which came into force in March 1990. The 1989 Act is designed to protect more limited classes of official information. It also clarifies the position of members of the security and intelligence services.

Section 1 of the Act imposes a stringent duty on members or retired members of the security and intelligence services and those notified that they are subject to the section. It provides that such a person commits an offence if without lawful authority he discloses any information or document he has received in the course of such work or while such notification is in force.

Other Crown servants or government contractors working in the security or intelligence fields are only guilty of an offence if they make a damaging disclosure of information or documents. A damaging disclosure is defined as one which causes damage to the work of or any part of the security and intelligence services or would be likely to do so.

It is a defence to any of these charges if the defendant had no reasonable cause to believe that the information related to security and intelligence and, in the case of Crown servants or government contractors only, that they did not know the disclosure would be damaging. Note the heavier liability placed on members of the security and intelligence services.

Sections 2 and 3 of the 1989 Act respectively make it an offence for a Crown servant or government contractor without lawful authority to make a damaging disclosure' in the field of defence and international relations. The phrase 'damaging disclosure' is precisely defined in the context of defence and international relations by the respective sections.

Similar defences to charges under ss2 and 3 are provided as those for s1 (see above).

Section 4 of the Official Secrets Act 1989 makes it an offence for a Crown servant or government contractor or such retired employees to disclose information the disclosure of which results in the commission of an offence, facilitates escape from legal custody or impedes the prevention or detection of offences or the apprehension or prosecution of suspected offenders. Again similar defences are provided.

A person who receives a disclosure which is outlawed by the Act himself commits an offence if he discloses the information without lawful authority where he had reasonable grounds for belief that the information would be protected by the Act. A defence is provided if the defendant did not have reasonable cause to believe the disclosure would be damaging or if it is not in fact damaging.

The new provisions of the 1989 Act have been criticised since there is no public interest defence and there is a sufficient protection for the press. It makes no headway in the continuing attempts to persuade the Government to enact a Freedom of Information Act.

14.5 Contempt of court

Contempt of court tends to fall into one of four categories, namely, outraging the court, disobedience, undermining the Judiciary, and contempts likely to interfere with the fairness of the trial.

Outraging the court

Contempt in the face of the court relates to unacceptable behaviour whilst the court is sitting. This may involve insulting or unseemly behaviour, a refusal to comply with the trial judge's directions, or even physical assault on others present. The trial judge has a common law power to regulate such behaviour and can deal with contemners summarily: see *Balogh* v *St Albans Crown Court* [1975] QB 73.

Disobedience

Where a trial judge has been given an undertaking by one of the parties that certain action will or will not be taken, it is a contempt of court for that undertaking to be ignored. In *Harman* v *Home Secretary* [1984] 2 WLR 338 the House of Lords considered the case of a solicitor who had been granted access to Home Office documents on the undertaking that they would only be used by her in the preparation of her client's case against the Home Office. A number of these documents were subsequently read in open court during the trial of the action. Harman then made the documents available to a journalist from *The Guardian* newspaper, who subsequently wrote an article based on the information provided. The House of Lords held (Lords Simon and Scarman dissenting) that Harman was in contempt of court in making the documents available to the press, notwithstanding their disclosure in court. The undertaking that they should only be used for the purposes of the trial was still effective.

Undermining the Judiciary

Proceedings for contempt may be brought where a publication imputes bias on the part of a judge, although such cases are rare. The leading authority is the Privy Council decision in *Ambard* v *Attorney-General for Trinidad and Tobago* [1936] AC 322, in which Lord Aitken laid down the standard test for the commission of the offence and its limits:

> 'But whether the authority and position of an individual judge, or the due administration of justice, is concerned, no wrong is committed by any member of the public who exercises the ordinary right of criticising, in good faith, in private or public, the public act done in the seat of justice. The path of criticism is a public way; the wrong-headed are permitted to err therein; provided that members of the public abstain from imputing improper motives to those taking part in the administration of justice, and are genuinely exercising a right of criticism, and not acting in malice or attempting to impair the administration of justice, they are immune. Justice is not a cloistered virtue; she must be allowed to suffer the scrutiny and respectful, even though outspoken, comments of ordinary men.'

The Judiciary have generally not used this power, but it still remains even though the Phillimore Committee recommended that it should be abolished.

Contempts likely to interfere with the fairness of the trial

There are two rights or freedoms which have to be balanced; first the freedom of the mass media, and second, the right to a fair trial. It is readily agreed by most people that the right of an accused to a fair trial outweighs the freedom of the mass media. The questions that remain are whether the law of contempt weighs too heavily against the media, and secondly whether it is precise enough to enable the media to know when it is allowed to publish material.

This area is now governed by the Contempt of Court Act 1981 which was enacted following the unfavourable judgment given by the European Court of Human Rights in *The Sunday Times* case, regarding the House of Lords definition of contempt laid down in *Attorney-General* v *Times Newspapers* [1974] AC 273.

In the 1960s, many children were born with gross deformities due to their mothers having taken the drug thalidomide during pregnancy. Numerous negligence actions were commenced. *The Sunday Times* newspaper ran a campaign on behalf of the children calling for them to receive more compensation. During the campaign they intended to publish an article which furnished further proof of the negligence of the manufacturers, Distillers.

The House of Lords granted an injunction to stop the publication of the article, despite admitting that neither the court nor the witnesses would have been prejudiced. The decision was criticised as introducing a 'new wider test that prejudgments of issues in pending proceedings should not be permitted'. Such a sweeping rule naturally received a hostile reception and *The Sunday Times* appealed to the European Court of Human Rights. The court found that the test was drawn much too widely and had the effect of unlawfully silencing a newspaper's right to freedom of expression contrary to Article 10 of the European Convention on Human Rights. The Government had already established the Phillimore Committee to examine the law of contempt and its final report was highly critical of the House of Lords' decision. Their report was an extensive and thorough examination of the law and many of its recommendations were enacted in the Contempt of Court Act 1981.

The Contempt of Court Act 1981

The law of contempt only applies to courts or tribunals which exercise judicial functions. It does not apply to commissions or committees of inquiry or the members of such commissions or committees in their capacity as such.

In *Attorney-General* v *BBC* [1981] AC 303, the House of Lords held that the law of contempt did not apply to the activities of a local valuation court because (per Viscount Dilhorne, Lord Fraser and Lord Scarman) it was a court which discharged administrative functions and not a court of law. According to Lord Salmon, while a local valuation court has some of the attributes of the long established 'inferior courts' such as county courts, magistrates' courts, courts martial, coroner's courts and consistory courts, public policy required that in the interests of freedom of speech and freedom of the press, the principles relating to contempt of court should not apply to it or to the host of other modern tribunals which might be regarded as inferior courts.

Viscount Dilhorne, in attempting to state a general rule, commented:

' ... I do not think that the Divisional Court's jurisdiction extends to all courts created by the State for I think that a distinction has to be drawn between courts which discharge judicial functions and those which discharge administrative ones; between courts of law which form part of the judicial system of the country on the one hand and courts which are constituted to resolve problems which arise in the course of administration of the government of this country. In my opinion a local valuation court comes within the latter category. It discharges functions formerly performed by assessment committees. It has to resolve disputes as to the valuation of hereditaments. While its decisions will affect an occupier's liability for rates, it does not determine his liability. It is just part of the process of rating ...'

The courts have been willing to recognise situations where tribunals need the protection of the 1981 Act. In *Pickering* v *Liverpool Daily Post and Echo* [1991] 2

WLR 513, the House of Lords accepted that the 'novel jurisdictions' of the Mental Health Tribunal, and the need for privacy in its proceedings, justified its classification as a 'court' for the purposes of the Act.

The strict liability rule

The test for contempt laid down in the Act refers to that which tends 'to interfere with the course of justice in particular legal proceedings regardless of intent to do so' (s1).

The test itself is fairly clear but the time at which it applies is rather more complicated.

Section 2 of the Act refers to works which are published. Section 2(3) provides that the strict liability rule does not apply to any publication unless the 'proceedings in question are active'. The first schedule of the Act gives some guidance, but whether newspapers can be any more certain about when they can publish an article on a possible crime with impunity is to be doubted.

The Act is supposed to come into operation when a person is charged or summoned or at the time of his arrest. The issue of a warrant for a person's arrest is also taken as a relevant starting point for the Act. As far as civil proceedings are concerned the Act applies only after the case has been set down for trial. A related point deals with the status of the Act regarding appeals. Here the starting point is the granting of leave to appeal by the court. Therefore newspapers are free to comment on trials once they have been decided.

There are a number of defences to the 'strict liability rule'. Firstly, s3 of the Act gives a publisher a defence of 'innocent publication or distribution ... if he does not know or has no reason to suspect that the relevant proceedings are active'. The same applies if he has no reason to suspect that the contents of a publication contain a contempt. The crucial test is whether the publisher or distributor could not reasonably have discovered either that proceedings were active or that a book or magazine contained within it a contempt. For example, in *R* v *Griffiths* [1957] 2 QB 192, when W H Smith's pleaded innocence as to the content of *Newsweek*, an American magazine, which contained a very prejudicial article concerning someone on trial. The court held that W H Smith's ought to have known that *Newsweek* specialised in sensationalism and also that American papers were far more open in their statements about trials, because of the Bill of Rights protecting press freedom. The courts would probably still have convicted in this case because W H Smith's had not taken all reasonable care.

The second defence provided in the Act is the contemporaneous reporting of proceedings. The court, however, retains the power to postpone any report if it is 'necessary for avoiding a substantial risk of prejudice to the administration of justice' (ss4(1) and 4(2)).

Thirdly, s5 of the Act provides:

'A publication made as or as part of a discussion in good faith of public affairs or other matters of general interest is not to be treated as a contempt of court under the strict liability rule if the risk of impediment or prejudice to particular legal proceedings is merely incidental to the discussion.'

The effect of s5 was considered at length by the House of Lords in *Attorney-General v English* [1982] 2 WLR 278. Proceedings under the Act were initiated against the editor and publishers of the *Daily Mail* newspaper in respect of an article entitled 'The Vision of Life that Wins My Vote'. It was an article written in support of a candidate in a parliamentary by-election. The candidate, Ms Carr, had been born without arms and was standing as an independent 'Pro-Life' candidate; the main basis of her election campaign was the stopping of the practice which she alleged had been developed in some British hospitals of killing newborn handicapped babies. Public interest in the question of whether severely handicapped babies should be allowed to die had been aroused by a Court of Appeal decision two months earlier ordering a surgeon to carry out a life-prolonging operation on a 'Down's syndrome' baby despite the refusal of the parents to give their consent to the operation. Shortly before the publishing of the article in question, a Sunday newspaper had published an article asserting that the termination of life of unborn, hopelessly handicapped babies was morally justifiable. Ms Carr published her election address three days later and the article in question in the present case was published nine days later on 15 October. Coincidentally, on 13 October, there commenced the trial of Dr Arthur, a consultant paediatrician on a charge of murdering a three-day-old Down's syndrome baby by giving instructions that a drug should be administered that caused the baby to die of starvation. Dr Arthur pleaded not guilty.

The article in question made no mention of Dr Arthur's trial. However, apart from passages such as:

> 'Are human beings to be culled like livestock? No more sick or misshapen bodies, no more disturbed or twisted minds, no more hereditary idiots or mongoloid children. Babies not up to scratch to be destroyed, before or after birth, as would also the old beyond repair ...'

The article also contained the following:

> 'Today the chances of such a baby surviving would be very small indeed. Someone would surely recommend letting it die of starvation or otherwise disposing of it.'

Clearly the article was a 'publication' within s2(1) of the Contempt of Court Act 1981. Since an intention to prejudice the trial was not alleged, the issues in question were, firstly, whether or not the nature and circumstances of the publications were such as to satisfy s2(2) of the 1981 Act so that the strict liability rule might apply, and, secondly whether or not the publication escaped the strict liability rule by virtue of coming within s5.

The Divisional Court had held that the article did create a substantial risk of seriously impeding Dr Arthur's fair trial as required by s2(2) for the strict liability rule to apply. It further held that the onus of proving that the conditions of s5 applied lay on the defendants and that they had not discharged this burden since the article contained accusations – that babies were killed or allowed to die – which were 'unnecessary' and not therefore merely incidental to the 'discussion in good faith of public affairs or other matters of general public interest' which alone was protected by s5. 'Discussion' was, in the court's view, limited to 'the airing of views and the propounding and debating of principles and arguments' and did not include the making of 'accusations'. On appeal the House of Lords held that the nature and circumstances of the publication satisfied s2(2). If a publication put at risk the outcome of a trial or the need to discharge the jury without proceeding to a verdict, that was risking serious prejudice to the legal proceedings. The adjective 'substantially' was meant to exclude risks which were remote only. The publication of the article in question on the third day of Dr Arthur's trial did involve a more than remote risk that the jury verdict might be affected. The House of Lords went on to hold, however, that the onus of proving that the conditions of s5 were satisfied did not necessarily lie on the defendants and in the present case, s5 applied. 'Discussion' should not be regarded as limited only to the 'airing of views and the propounding and debating of principles and arguments' but could include also assertions of fact. Indeed in the absence of any assertion of fact that 'mercy killing' did take place, the article in question would be no more than a contribution to the discussion of a purely hypothetical problem which would be quite remote from all public affairs and devoid of any general public interest to readers of the *Daily Mail*. The risks to Dr Arthur's fair trial were merely incidental to the bona fide discussion of Ms Carr's election policy and of the wider question of the justifiability of mercy killing. To hold otherwise would have prevented Ms Carr from gaining publicity for her election campaign and prevented all public discussion of the issue of mercy killing between February and November 1981 whilst the proceedings in Dr Arthur's case were active. Section 5 was intended to prevent the 'gagging' of just such bona fide public discussion. Lord Diplock observed:

> 'There is, of course, no question that the article in the *Daily Mail* of which complaint is made by the Attorney-General was a 'publication' within the meaning of s2(1). That being so, it appears to have been accepted in the Divisional Court by both parties that the onus of proving that the article satisfied the conditions stated in s2(2) lay upon the Attorney-General and that, if he satisfied that onus, the onus lay upon the appellants to prove that it satisfied the conditions stated in s5. For my part, I am unable to accept that this represents the effect of the relationship of s5 to s2(2). Section 5 does not take the form of a proviso or an exception to s2(2). It stands on an equal footing with it. It does not set out exculpatory matter. Like s2(2) it states that publications shall not amount to contempt of court despite their tendency to interfere with the course of justice in particular legal proceedings.'

Having agreed that the article fell within s2(2) of the Act he continued:

> 'The article, however, fell also within the category dealt with in s5. It was made, in undisputed good faith, as a discussion in itself of public interest, viz [Ms Carr's] candidature as an independent Pro-Life candidate. It was also part of a wider discussion on a matter of general public interest that had been proceeding intermittently over the last three months, upon the moral justification of mercy killing and in particular of allowing newly born hopelessly handicapped babies to die. So it was for the Attorney-General to

show that the risk of prejudice to the fair trial of Dr Arthur, which I agree was created by the publication of the article at the stage the trial had reached when it was published, was not "merely incidental" to the discussion of the matter with which the article dealt.'

The protection of journalistic sources

The Act also gives journalists a limited defence if they wish to withhold their sources of information. The meaning of this section was examined in the case of *Secretary of State for Defence* v *Guardian Newspapers Ltd* [1984] 3 WLR 986.

A document entitled 'Deliveries of Cruise Missiles to RAF Greenham Common – Parliamentary and Public Statements' was prepared in the Ministry of Defence on or about 20 October 1983. It was classified 'secret'. Only seven copies left the ministry.

The next day a photocopy of one of the copies arrived at the news-desk of *The Guardian*. No one on the staff knew whence it came or who delivered it. The editor, after inquiries, decided that it was authentic. He also concluded that the national interest would not be damaged by its publication. On 31 October he published it.

On 11 November the Treasury Solicitor wrote to the editor asking him to deliver up the document. On 17 November *The Guardian*'s solicitors replied saying that certain markings on the document might disclose, or assist in the identification of, the source of the information, although the editor did not know the source and that in accordance with the well-established convention of journalism which had statutory force by s10 of the Contempt of Court Act 1981 he was not prepared to take any steps which might lead to the disclosure.

Section 10 of the Contempt of Court Act 1981 provides:

> 'No court may require a person to disclose, nor is any person guilty of contempt of court for refusing to disclose, the source of information contained in a publication for which he is responsible, unless it be established to the satisfaction of the court that disclosure is necessary in the interests of justice or national security or for the prevention of disorder or crime.'

The reply stated that the editor was only concerned to protect his sources and was prepared to hand over the document with the markings excised. That was unacceptable and proceedings were begun on 22 November.

The Court of Appeal held that by virtue of s18(1) of the Copyright Act 1956 the Crown had a strong prima facie right to be treated as the owner of the copy document. The interests of justice and those of national security required the immediate return of the document in the defendant's possession and, accordingly, those exceptions to the operation of s10 of the Contempt of Court Act 1981 regarding the immunity from disclosure of a source of information had been established.

On appeal, the House of Lords was unanimous in its view that the protection offered by s10 of the 1981 Act applied in all judicial proceedings, regardless of their nature, or the course of action, but (Lords Fraser and Scarman dissenting) in this particular case the Crown had adduced sufficient evidence to establish that the delivery up of the document was required in the national interest.

15

The European Convention on Human Rights

15.1 Introduction

While the protection of fundamental rights and freedoms on the international plane has proved a slow and difficult process, the protection of human rights on the regional level among groups of states sharing common ideals and standards has been more effective. One of the most highly regarded of the regional conventions for the protection of human rights is the European Convention on Human Rights (hereinafter the 'ECHR'). The United Kingdom was one of the original signatories of the ECHR, on 4 November 1950, and its First Protocol, on 8 March 1952. The instruments of ratification of the ECHR and its First Protocol were deposited with the Secretary-General of the Council of Europe on 8 March 1951 and 3 November 1952 respectively. The ECHR entered into force on 3 September 1953. On 23 October 1953 a declaration was made under Article 63(1) extending the ECHR's force to certain territories for whose international relations the United Kingdom was responsible. On 14 January 1966, the United Kingdom recognised the competence of the European Commission of Human Rights (hereinafter 'the Commission') to receive individual applications, and recognised the compulsory jurisdiction of the European Court of Human Rights.

15.2 The rights protected under the ECHR

The ECHR seeks to provide the following fundamental rights:

Article 2 – the right to life – 'No one shall be deprived of life intentionally, save in the execution of a sentence of death by a court.'

Article 3 – 'No one shall be subject to torture or inhuman or degrading treatment.'

Article 4 – 'No one shall be held in slavery or servitude, or be required to perform forced labour.'

Article 5 – the right to liberty and security of person; see further *Wynne* v *United Kingdom* (Case No 26/1993/421/500) and *Murray* v *United Kingdom* (Case No 13/1993/408/487).

Article 6 – the right to a fair and public hearing within a reasonable time before an independent and impartial tribunal established by law. In *Bonner* v *UK; Maxwell* v *UK* (1994) The Times 1 November, the European Court of Human Rights held that the rights guaranteed by this provision extended to the provision of legal aid to everyone charged with a criminal offence where the interests of justice so required, in light of the importance of the hearing (as regards the sentences imposed on the applicants), the limited scope for the unrepresented applicant to present his case competently, the nature of the proceedings, and clear evidence that the applicants lacked the financial resources to pay for their own lawyers.

Article 7 – prohibition on retrospective legislation creating any criminal offence or increasing the penalty for an offence.

Article 8 – the right to respect for private and family life, home and correspondence.

Article 9 – the right to freedom of thought, conscience and religion.

Article 10 – the right to freedom of expression.

Article 11 – the right to freedom of peaceful assembly and freedom of association, including the right to form and join trade unions.

Article 12 – the right of men and women of marriageable age to marry and found a family.

Article 13 – the right to an effective remedy before a national authority where the rights and freedoms set forth in the ECHR are violated.

Article 14 provides that: 'The enjoyment of the rights and freedoms set forth in this Convention shall be secured without discrimination on any ground such as sex, race, colour, language, religion, political or other opinion, national or social origin, association with a national minority, birth or other status.'

Limitations, restrictions and derogations

A number of articles contain express exemption provisions. For example, Article 11(2) provides: 'No restrictions shall be placed on the exercise of these rights other than such as are prescribed by law and are necessary in a democratic society in the interests of national security or public safety, for the prevention of disorder or crime, for the protection of health or morals or for the protection of the rights and freedoms of others'. Similar provisions are contained in Articles 8(2), 9(2) and 10(2).

As regards derogation in time of war or public emergency, Article 15 provides:

'(1) In time of war or other public emergency threatening the life of the nation any High Contracting Party may take measures derogating from its obligations under this Convention to the extent strictly required by the exigencies of the situation, provided that such measures are not inconsistent with its other obligations under international law. But: (2) No derogation from Article 2, except in respect of deaths resulting from lawful acts of war, or from Articles 3, 4(1) and 7 shall be made under this provision.'

In *Brannigan and McBride* v *United Kingdom* (Case No 5/1992/350/423-424) (1993) The Times 28 May, the European Court of Human Rights accepted the contention of the United Kingdom that the situation in Northern Ireland justified a derogation under Article 15 in respect of the provisions of the ECHR relating to detention without charge. Hence, the detention of the applicants under the Prevention of Terrorism (Temporary Provisions) Act 1984 did not amount to a violation of the ECHR. The decision vindicates, to some extent, the refusal of the United Kingdom government to alter the law relating to the detention of suspected terrorists following the ruling in *Brogan* v *United Kingdom* (1989) 11 EHRR 117, in which it was held that detention without charge for more than four days was in breach of Article 5(3) of the ECHR.

Article 16 provides that nothing in Article 10 (freedom of expression), Article 11 (freedom of assembly) and Article 14 (non-discrimination) shall be regarded as preventing the High Contracting Parties from imposing restrictions on the political activities of aliens.

The protocols to the ECHR

The First Protocol to the ECHR 1952 provides: Article 1 – right to peaceful enjoyment of possessions; Article 2 – right to education; Article 3 – right to free elections by secret ballot. The Fourth Protocol to the ECHR 1963 provides: Article 1 – no one shall be deprived of his liberty for failure to fulfil a contractual obligation; Article 2 – right to liberty of movement and freedom of residence; Article 3 – freedom from expulsion and right to enter the State of which he is a national; Article 4 – prohibition on collective expulsion.

15.3 Machinery for enforcement

Article 1 of the ECHR provides that the High Contracting Parties shall secure to everyone within their jurisdiction the rights and freedoms defined in the ECHR. To help achieve compliance with this objective the ECHR establishes a procedure for enforcement (Article 19) which provides for a European Commission of Human Rights and a European Court of Human Rights.

The Commission

Article 20 of the ECHR provides that the Commission shall consist of a number of members equal to that of the High Contracting Parties. No two members of the Commission may be nationals of the same State. Members are elected by the Committee of Ministers of the Council of Europe for a period of six years. Article 24 provides for inter-State applications under which any High Contracting Party may refer to the Commission, through the Secretary-General of the Council of Europe, any alleged breach of the provisions of the ECHR by another High Contracting Party.

Several applications have been made by States under Article 24. For example, in 1956 and 1957 two cases were brought against the United Kingdom by Greece, alleging breach of the ECHR by the British authorities in Cyprus. In 1967 Denmark, Norway, Sweden and the Netherlands brought an application against Greece in respect of alleged violations of the ECHR by the military Government. In 1971 and 1972 Ireland brought two actions against the United Kingdom in respect of breaches of the ECHR by the security forces in Northern Ireland.

Article 25 provides for the right of individual petition. The Commission may receive petitions addressed to the Secretary-General of the Council of Europe from any person, non-governmental organisation or group of individuals claiming to be the victim of a violation by one of the High Contracting Parties of the rights set forth in the ECHR, provided that the High Contracting Party against which the complaint has been lodged has declared that it recognises the competence of the Commission to receive such petitions. Those of the High Contracting Parties who have made such a declaration undertake not to hinder in any way the effective exercise of this right.

The practice of most States has been to make declarations under Article 25 valid for a specific period, usually three to five years. The Commission will not accept an individual petition unless satisfied that the applicant has exhausted all domestic remedies. The application must be referred to the Commission within six months from the date on which the final decision complained of was taken (Article 26).

Under Article 27 the Commission shall not deal with any petition submitted under Article 25 which is anonymous; or is substantially the same as a matter which has already been examined by the Commission or has already been submitted to another procedure of international investigation or settlement and if it contains no relevant new information. The Commission will consider inadmissible any petition submitted under Article 25 which it regards as incompatible with the provisions of the ECHR, manifestly ill-founded, or an abuse of the right of petition. Approximately 90 per cent of the petitions submitted by individuals under Article 25 are declared inadmissible by the Commission at this stage, which suggests that there is still widespread misunderstanding of the scope and purpose of the ECHR.

In the event of the Commission accepting a petition referred to it, then under Article 28 it will, with a view to ascertaining the facts, undertake, together with the representatives of the parties, an examination of the petition and, if need be, an investigation, for the effective conduct of which the States concerned shall furnish all necessary facilities, after an exchange of views with the Commission. The Commission will place itself at the disposal of the parties concerned with a view to securing a friendly settlement of the matter on the basis of respect for human rights as defined in the ECHR. The examination and investigation under Article 28 are conducted on the basis of written and oral pleadings by the parties.

If the Commission succeeds in effecting a friendly settlement in accordance with Article 28, it will draw up a report which will be sent to the States concerned, to the Committee of Ministers of the Council of Europe and to the Secretary-General of the Council of Europe for publication (Article 30). If a solution is not reached, then under Article 31 the Commission will draw up a Report on the facts and state its opinion as to whether the facts found disclose a breach by the State concerned of its obligations under the ECHR. The report will be forwarded to the Committee of Ministers together with such proposals as the Commission thinks fit. Article 32(1) provides that if the question is not referred to the Court of Human Rights within three months of the transmission of the report to the Committee of Ministers, the Committee shall decide by a two-thirds majority whether there has been a violation of the ECHR.

If it decides that there has been a violation, the Committee shall prescribe a period during which the High Contracting Party concerned must take the measures required by the decision of the Committee of Ministers. If the party concerned does not comply with this decision the Committee shall decide by a two-thirds majority what effect shall be given to its original decision and shall publish the report. Under Article 32(4) the High Contracting Parties undertake to regard as binding on them any decision which the Committee of Ministers may take.

The European Court of Human Rights

Article 38 provides that the European Court of Human Rights shall consist of a number of judges equal to that of the Members of the Council of Europe. No two judges may be nationals of the same State. Under Article 39 the members of the Court are elected by the Consultative Assembly by a majority of the votes cast from a list of persons nominated by the members of the Council of Europe. The candidates must be of high moral character and must either possess the qualifications required for appointment to high judicial office or be jurists of recognised competence. Members of the Court are elected for nine years. Article 43 provides that for the consideration of each case brought before it the Court shall consist of a chamber composed of seven judges. There shall sit as an ex-officio member of the chamber, the judge who is a national of any state party concerned, or, if there is none, a person of its choice who shall sit in the capacity of judge. Only the High Contracting Parties and the Commission have the right to bring a case before the Court. An individual applicant cannot initiate proceedings or plead his case. Under Article 45 the jurisdiction of the Court extends to all cases concerning the interpretation and application of the ECHR which the High Contracting Parties or the Commission refer to it, providing that the High Contracting Parties have declared that they recognise as compulsory the jurisdiction of the Court in all matters concerning the interpretation and application of the ECHR. If a case is brought before the Court by a High Contracting Party, that party must be one whose national is alleged to be a victim; or the party which referred the case to the Commission; or the party against which the case has been lodged.

Under Article 50 of the ECHR the European Court of Human rights has the power to afford just satisfaction to an injured party. The judgment of the Court is final and execution of the judgment is supervised by the Committee of Ministers. The parties undertake to abide by the decision of the Court in any case to which they are parties.

The future

The number of States accepting the right of individual petition under the ECHR has now reached 26. There is evidence to suggest that the effective protection offered by the Commission and the Court may be undermined by its inability to deal with the ever-growing caseload. Current figures indicate that 5,000–6,000 applications are received each year, of which approximately 1,600 are registered, and approximately 200 declared admissible. The backlog of unconsidered cases has reached 1,500. The average time taken for an application to reach the European Court of Human Rights is five years.

In 1990 changes were introduced to the way in which the Commission handled applications, with committees being used to rule on admissibility, and chambers determining routine cases, with a resultant improvement in processing rates, but concerns about the system being overwhelmed continue. A more radical reform has been agreed at the Council of Europe in the form of Protocol 11 ECHR, which provides for a new permanent European Court of Human Rights that will replace the current structure of the Commission and the Court. The new Court, a two-tier structure comprising a Chamber of seven judges and a Grand Chamber of 17 judges, will also take over the role, currently discharged by the Committee of Ministers, of determining whether or not the ECHR has been violated. The right of individual petition to the new court will become mandatory upon Member States.

The new procedure will involve an applicant submitting his application with the court's registry, which will assign it to a Chamber and a judge *rapporteur* who will have responsibility for overseeing the progress of the application. A tribunal of judges will consider the admissibility of the application, and provided at least one of the three consider it to be admissible, the ruling will be communicated to the member state against whom the application has been made. If a friendly settlement cannot be reached the Chamber (seven judges) will give its judgment. It is envisaged that this procedure would also apply to applications between States. The authors of these reforms envisage that an application would only need to be referred to the Grand Chamber in exceptional cases, and a panel of five Grand Chamber judges will decide whether there are grounds for re-examination, unless the case is one where the Chamber itself has relinquished jurisdiction. It may be a number of years before this new single-tier system becomes operational.

In addition, the incorporation of the ECHR into the domestic law of all signatory States would help to relieve this pressure by ensuring that all cases are dealt with by domestic courts in the first instance, applying the principles of the ECHR, thus increasing the likelihood of the complainant obtaining a remedy in a meritorious case.

15.4 The place of the ECHR in English law

Although the ECHR and its First Protocol have been signed and ratified by the United Kingdom, as yet they have not been incorporated by legislation into English law. Whilst the Crown has power to enter into treaty obligations on the international plane, such treaties can only resound in domestic law if incorporated by Act of Parliament. The ECHR cannot, therefore, be relied upon in domestic courts as a binding source of law. Typical of the approach of the courts are cases such as *Uppal* v *Home Office* (1978) The Times 11 November. The applicants, illegal immigrants, applied for declarations that they should not be deported from the United Kingdom until the Commission had determined whether deportation would contravene the applicants' right to respect for family life under Article 8 of the ECHR. The applicants argued that their deportation would hinder the effective exercise of the right of individual petition. In his judgment, Sir Robert Megarry doubted the validity of this argument; but in any event he held that obligations in international law which were not enforceable as part of English law could not be the subject of declaratory judgments or orders. Subsequently, when considering the legality of telephone-tapping in *Malone* v *Metropolitan Police Commissioner* [1979] Ch 344, he reaffirmed his decision in *Uppal* after full argument on the point.

Against this is the view that, whilst the domestic courts are not bound by the ECHR, it is persuasive, in that the courts are entitled to presume that Parliament, in enacting legislation, does not intend to contravene international obligations contained in treaties unless express words are used to this effect. Hence, in *R* v *Home Secretary, ex parte Bhajan Singh* [1976] QB 198, Lord Denning observed that the executive should have regard to the ECHR in exercising its discretion because the articles were, in his view, only a statement of the principles of fair dealing.

The argument that the fundamental principles reflected in the ECHR should be reflected in the reviewing function of the court when entertaining an application for judicial review received a severe setback, however, in the House of Lords' decision in *R* v *Secretary of State for the Home Department, ex parte Brind* [1991] 2 WLR 588. An application for judicial review was brought by journalists seeking a declaration that the restrictions imposed by the Home Secretary, acting pursuant to powers conferred upon him by s29(3) of the Broadcasting Act 1981 in regard to the IBA, and clause 13(4) of the licence and agreement with the BBC, ordering both organisations to refrain from broadcasting interviews with members and representatives of certain named terrorist organisations, were ultra vires the minister's powers. The applicants also sought an order of certiorari to quash the restrictions. They contended that Parliament could not have intended to empower the minister to issue restrictions that were, in their submissions, in breach of Article 10 of the ECHR. The Divisional Court had dismissed the application, holding that the 1981 Act appeared to provide the minister with a very wide power to censor the output of the IBA, without any formal parliamentary control. The Court felt, however, that it was entitled to consider the extent to which the minister's action had complied with the requirements of Article 10 of the ECHR, notwithstanding that it was not part of English law. Having examined Article 10, the Court held that, prima facie, the restrictions imposed by the minister did not conflict with Article 10. The Court of Appeal held that the contention that any ministerial directives prohibiting the broadcasting of any matter had to be construed so as to ensure their compliance with the ECHR must be rejected as being an attempt to introduce the ECHR into English law by 'back door' means. The Court of Appeal's decision was upheld by the House of Lords.

In holding that a local authority could not use the law of defamation against a newspaper that had been critical of its conduct in certain financial matters, the House of Lords appeared to regard any argument based on Article 10 of the ECHR as redundant. Whilst Balcombe LJ, in the Court of Appeal, had felt that domestic law was uncertain on the point and observed that:

> '... where the law is uncertain, it must be right for the court to approach the issue before
> it with a predilection to ensure that our law should not involve a breach of Article 10 ...',

Lord Keith expressed the view that he had reached his conclusion based on the common law of England, adding only that it was '... consistent with obligations assumed by the Crown under the Treaty in this particular field.'; see *Derbyshire County Council* v *Times Newspapers Ltd and Others* [1993] 2 WLR 449. A more positive approach to reliance on the ECHR was expressed in *Rantzen* v *Mirror Group Newspapers (1986) Ltd* [1993] 3 WLR 953, where the Court of Appeal held that to allow juries to award unlimited amounts of damages to successful plaintiffs in defamation actions could amount to a breach of Article 10, in the sense that as a restriction on free speech the threatened sanction of a large award of damages had to be shown to be necessary in a democratic society, and 'prescribed by law'. Like the House of Lords in the *Derby* case, the Court expressed the view that Article 10 reflected the rules of the common law in relation to freedom of expression.

The ECHR and European Union law

Where appropriate the European Court of Justice has been influenced in its decisions by the content of the ECHR and other general principles of international law relating to the protection of human rights. To some extent this situation has been formalised by reference to the ECHR in the preamble to the Single European Act, and the inclusion of Article F in the Treaty on European Union (the 'Maastricht Treaty') which states:

> '... the Union shall respect fundamental rights, as guaranteed by the [ECHR] and as they result from the constitutional traditions common to the Member States, as general principles of Community law.'

Note that an individual would not be able to take a case against the European Union to the Commission under the ECHR, as the European Union is not a party to the ECHR.

Where the application of a European Union law having direct effect has been held, by the European Court of Justice, to require reference to, and conformity with, provisions of the ECHR (see for example *R* v *Kirk* [1984] CMLR 522), there is a possibility that the provisions of the ECHR could be relied upon in the UK courts; see further Chapter 5.

15.5 Incorporation into English law

Those who advocate the incorporation into English law of the ECHR argue that it could be simply achieved by a single Act of Parliament, with the text of the ECHR appendicised. Litigants would then be able to cite the Act in domestic courts, rather than having to petition the Commission because no remedy was available before domestic courts. Putting aside the question of whether the protection of individual rights under domestic law is sufficiently domestic to warrant incorporation, a number of key questions arise regarding enforcement. Without some entrenchment provisions, a Bill of Rights would be at the mercy of any given parliamentary majority. It could be argued that legislation purporting to deal with fundamental constitutional rights ought to be protected in some way from subsequently being repealed on the basis of a simple majority vote in Parliament. The problem with this view, of course, is that the British constitution has, historically, never recognised an especially protected or enshrined 'higher' type of legislation. The doctrine of express and implied repeal ensures that Parliament cannot bind its successors.

One way of countering this problem would be the introduction of a written constitution, replete with a Constitutional Court, along the lines of the Supreme Court in the United States, which would be empowered to adjudicate upon the extent to which legislation conformed with the ECHR. A more modest measure would be to include in any incorporating legislation a provision similar to that found in s2(4) of the European Communities Act 1972 (see Chapter 6), with the effect that any subsequent legislation would be applied so as to ensure compliance with the terms of the ECHR. This alternative model could incorporate the concept of a Constitutional Court to which cases could be referred for preliminary rulings, as is the case with references to the ECJ under Article 177 EC Treaty.

Questions would still remain as to who the ECHR would apply to. To borrow the terminology of the ECJ, the ECHR would presumably have vertical direct effect, in that it could be invoked against organs of the State, but would it have horizontal direct effect, ie could it be invoked by one private party against another? This latter issue does not arise at present because applications to Strasbourg can only be made against Member States. If the ECHR is incorporated, however, its ambit will have to be reconsidered.

The issue of remedies would also have to be addressed. The tradition in English public law is that actions are brought by individuals to vindicate the rule of law, not to obtain personal financial compensation. The remedy for a breach of the ECHR could be purely declaratory, although this would deter many litigants unless there was a guarantee that costs would follow the event. If a right to damages were created, interesting problems could arise regarding the appropriate measure of damages.

A more fundamental objection to the incorporation of the ECHR is that, as a human rights' document, it is now somewhat dated, concentrating as it does on individual rights, rather than collective rights, such as, for example, freedom from pollution.

16

Arrest, Search and Seizure and Interrogation

16.1 Introduction

In the majority of criminal cases, the defendant's first involvement in the criminal process will be his contact with the police. It is with these first stages of the criminal process that this chapter is primarily concerned.

Police powers to stop, search, detain and arrest persons were developed piecemeal across many decades. There were wide variations between rural and metropolitan areas, and several anomalies, for example, that there was no power to issue a warrant for search of premises where vital evidence of a suspected murder might lie: see *Ghani* v *Jones* [1970] 1 QB 693. Rights to stop and search were often conferred in wide and uncertain terms, such as the much-criticised and now repealed 'sus' laws, and different conditions attached to the exercise of those rights according to the particular statutes creating them. Much has now been placed upon a more consistent footing with the introduction of the Police and Criminal Evidence Act 1984 (PACE) and the Codes of Practice issued thereunder.

The Codes of Practice, issued by the Home Secretary, aim to provide guidelines as to how the discretion given to police officers by the 1984 Act should be exercised. The desire of the Home Office was to produce a document that reiterated provisions of the Act in non-technical terms. A breach of the code may not affect the legality of an officer's action, but as s67(8) states: 'A police officer shall be liable to disciplinary proceedings for a failure to comply with any provision of such a code …'. Although a failure on the part of a police officer to comply with any provision of a code will not of itself render him liable to any criminal or civil proceedings, the codes are admissible in evidence in civil and criminal and must be taken into account where relevant. Although the codes are not law in the strict sense, a trial judge can recognise non-compliance on the part of the police by excluding evidence obtained in breach of the codes. Thus in *R* v *Saunders* [1988] Crim LR 521, where D was not shown a record of her statements made so that she could attest to their accuracy, and was not cautioned in terms that made clear her right to remain silent, the trial judge ruled the evidence inadmissible under s78. Note, however, the obiter statements of Lord Lane CJ in *R* v *Delaney* [1989] Crim LR 39, to the effect that the courts should not punish police officers for non-compliance by excluding evidence obtained in breach of the codes. His view was that judges should only exclude evidence where it has been obtained after substantial and significant breaches that make it good sense to exclude evidence. Useful guidance is provided by the Court of Appeal in *R* v *Keenan* [1989] 3 All ER 598. D was charged with possession of an offensive weapon. Shortly before his trial defence counsel were served with copies of statements allegedly made by D to police officers in which he admitted knowledge that the weapon was in his car. D, who denied ever having made the statement, had not been invited to read and sign the statement. On appeal following conviction, the Court of Appeal held that the evidence of the statement should not have been admitted. The test to be adopted was whether, if the other evidence was compelling, the police would still secure a conviction, despite the exclusion of evidence obtained in breach of the code. If the other evidence was weak, then it was right that the 'vital' evidence obtained in breach of the code should be excluded since the safeguards designed to ensure its reliability had not been complied with.

16.2 Police powers to stop and search

Traditionally police officers have not possessed a common law power to detain suspects for questioning, short of first exercising a power of arrest. Whilst cases such as *Donnelly* v *Jackman* [1970] 1 All ER 987 confirm that a constable can commit a trivial interference with an individual's liberty, for example tapping him on the shoulder to attract his attention, without exceeding the scope of his duty, *Rice* v *Connolly* [1966] 2 QB 414 is still authority for the proposition that a citizen is not required to stop and answer police enquiries per se. In that case D refused to answer a constable's questions concerning his activities and refused to provide him with his address. D's conviction for obstructing a police officer in the execution of his duty, contrary to s51(3) of the Police Act 1964 was allowed, on the ground that D had been under no legal duty to provide the police with information. (Note that to provide deliberately misleading information could give rise to liability.) Similarly in *Kenlin* v *Gardner* [1967] 2 QB 510, where the defendants, two schoolboys going from house to house to remind fellow members of their rugby team of a fixture, were stopped by a constable who produced a warrant card in order to hold the boys for questioning. The defendants struggled and assaulted the officer. The question arose as to the availability of the defence of self defence on a charge under s51(1) of the Police Act 1964 – assaulting an officer in the execution of his duty. The court held that the defence was available, as the constable had no power short of arrest to physically detain the boys for questioning.

In theory the 1984 Act does not invalidate any of these decisions, but, as indicated below, a constable can now detain a suspect in order to conduct a search under s1, and failure to provide personal details may give rise to a power to arrest without a warrant under s25. Part 1 of PACE confers general powers of stop and search, not restricted to metropolitan areas, and provides for the keeping of records of searches.

Section 1(2) creates a general power in constables to search a person or a vehicle or anything which is in or on a vehicle, and to detain the person or vehicle for the search. The power may only be exercised if the police constable 'has reasonable grounds for suspecting that he will find stolen or prohibited articles' as a result of the search: s1(3).

In addition, the search may only be carried out if the person or vehicle is (s1(1)):

'a) in any place to which at the time when he proposes to exercise the power the public or any section of the public has access, on payment or otherwise, as of right or by virtue of express or implied permission; or

b) in any other place to which people have a ready access at the time when he proposes to exercise the power but which is not a dwelling.'

So far as concerns searches of persons or vehicles on land adjacent to a dwelling house, the Act provides by s1(4) and (5):

'(4) If a person is in a garden or yard occupied with and used for the purposes of a dwelling or on other land so occupied and used, a constable may not search him in the exercise of the power conferred by this section unless the constable has reasonable grounds for believing –
a) that he does not reside in the dwelling; and
b) that he is not in the place in question with the express or implied permission of a person who resides in the dwelling.
(5) If a vehicle is in a garden or yard occupied with and used for the purposes of a dwelling or on other land so occupied and used, a constable may not search the vehicle or anything in or on it in the exercise of the power conferred by this section unless he has reasonable grounds for believing –
a) that the person in charge of the vehicle does not reside in the dwelling;
b) that the vehicle is not in the place in question with the express or implied permission of a person who resides in the dwelling.'

The purpose of the search is to locate stolen goods or 'prohibited articles'. The definition of the former may be analogous to s24(2) of the Theft Act 1968, so that goods are 'stolen goods' if they are goods originally stolen, or which directly or indirectly represent or have at any time represented stolen goods, or are the proceeds of any disposal or realisation of stolen goods, or are goods obtained by blackmail or by deception. With respect to 'prohibited articles', the Act provides by s1(7), (8) and (9):

'(7) An article is prohibited for the purposes of this Part of this Act if it is –
a) an offensive weapon; or
b) an article –
c) made or adapted for use in the course of or in connection with an offence to which this sub-paragraph applies; or
d) intended by the person having it with him for such use by him or by some other person. [Section 40 of the Criminal Justice Act 1988 extends the meaning of offensive weapon to include any article with a blade or point carried in a public place, except a folding pocket knife.]
(8) The offences to which subsection (7)(b)(i) above applies are:
a) burglary;
b) theft;
c) offences under s12 of the Theft Act 1968 (taking a motor vehicle or other conveyance without authority); and
d) offences under s15 of that Act (obtaining property by deception).
(8A) This subsection applies to any article in relation to which a person has committed or is committing or is going to commit an offence under section 139 of the Criminal Justice Act 1988.
(9) In this Part of this Act "offensive weapon" means any article –
a) made or adapted for use for causing injury to persons; or
b) intended by the person having it with him for such use by him or by some other person.'

If a search results in the discovery of stolen or prohibited articles, s1(6) confers a power to seize them upon the constable conducting the search:

'If in the course of ... a search a constable discovers an article which he has reasonable grounds for suspecting to be a stolen or prohibited article, he may seize it.'

In Part I of the Act particularly, and elsewhere in the powers of arrest and search, the phrase 'reasonable grounds' for suspecting or believing appears frequently. Ultimately the existence of such grounds much be a question of fact, but Annex B of Code A of the Codes of Practice for the Exercise by Police Officers of Statutory Powers of Stop and Search (as amended), issued under s66 of the Act and of general application in its interpretation, gives guidance on its meaning:

'1. Reasonable suspicion does not require certainty that an unlawful article is being carried; nor does the officer concerned have to be satisfied of this beyond reasonable doubt. Reasonable suspicion, in contrast to mere suspicion, must be founded upon fact. There must be some concrete basis for the officer's suspicion, related to the individual person concerned, which can be considered and evaluated by an objective third person. Mere suspicion, in contrast, is a hunch or instinct which cannot be explained or justified to an objective third person. An officer who has such a hunch or instinct may well be justified in continuing to keep the person under observation or speak to him, but additional grounds which bring up mere suspicion to the level of reasonable suspicion are needed before he may exercise the powers dealt with in this code.

2. Reasonable suspicion may arise from the nature of the property observed or being carried or suspected of being carried, coupled with other factors including the time, the place and the suspicious behaviour of the person concerned or those with him. The decision to search must be based on all the facts which, to a careful officer, bear on the likelihood that an article of a certain kind will be found, and not only on what can be seen at the time. So an officer with prior knowledge of the behaviour of someone he sees in a certain situation, or acting on information received (such as a description of a suspected offender) may have reasonable grounds for searching him although another officer would not.

3. Reasonable suspicion cannot be supported on the basis simply of a higher than average chance that the person has committed or is committing an offence, for example because he belongs to a group within which offenders of a certain kind are relatively common, or because of a combination of factors such as these. For example, a person's colour of itself can never be a reasonable ground for suspicion. The mere fact alone that a person is carrying a particular kind of property or is dressed in a certain way or has a certain hair style is likewise not of itself sufficient. Nor is the fact that a person is known to have a previous conviction for unlawful possession of an article ...

5. Paragraph 4 above is subject to the principle that where a police officer has reasonable grounds to suspect that a person is in innocent possession of a stolen or prohibited article, the power of stop and search exists notwithstanding that there would be no power of arrest. However every effort should be made to secure the voluntary production of the article before the power is resorted to.'

16.3 Conduct of searches under s1 of the 1984 Act

Once satisfied that the conditions of s1 are met, and that there are the required 'reasonable grounds' for exercising the stop and search power, a constable must in carrying out the search follow the procedure laid down by s2, and must usually make a record of it in accordance with s3. If, having stopped a person or vehicle for the purpose of search, the constable thinks it unnecessary actually to make the search, he need not do so; s2(1), but that decision does not affect the lawfulness of his initial act in detaining that person or vehicle.

If the constable wishes to search a person, or a vehicle which is 'attended' (which presumably means that there is a person in it or appearing to be in charge of it nearby), s2(2) and (3) ensure that the intended object of the search is made aware of the identity of the searcher and the reasons for the search:

> '(2) If a constable contemplates a search, other than a search of an unattended vehicle, in the exercise –
> a) of the power conferred by s1 above; or
> b) of any other power, except the power conferred by s6 below and the power conferred by s27(2) of the Aviation Security Act 1982 –
> i) to search a person without first arresting him; or
> ii) to search a vehicle without making an arrest,
> it shall be his duty, subject to subsection (4) below, to take reasonable steps before he commences the search to bring to the attention of the appropriate person –
> i) if the constable is not in uniform, documentary evidence that he is a constable; and
> ii) whether he is in uniform or not, the matters specified in subsection (3) below;
> and the constable shall not commence the search until he has performed that duty.
> (3) The matters referred to in subsection (2)(ii) above are –
> a) the constable's name and the name of the police station to which he is attached;
> b) the object of the proposed search;
> c) the constable's grounds for proposing to make it; ...'

'Appropriate person' in s2(2) means the person to be searched or the person in charge of the vehicle to be searched, as the case may be. The Act does not state what is to be done when the constable is unable to determine which of several persons is 'in charge' of a vehicle: presumably all should be told the matters in s2(3). The extent of the search is governed by s2(9) which provides:

> 'Neither the power conferred by s1 above nor any other power to detain and search a person without first arresting him or to detain and search a vehicle without making an arrest is to be construed –
> a) as authorising a constable to require a person to remove any of his clothing in public other than an outer coat, jacket or gloves; or
> b) as authorising a constable not in uniform to stop a vehicle.'

The ambiguous wording of this subsection could be taken to mean that a constable can require a person to remove *other* articles of clothing provided such removal is not made 'in public'. Thus if the constable asked the subject of the search to remove his trousers, and offered to allow him to do so in the privacy of a closed police van, or inside a nearby house, it may well be that the power exists to compel the subject to comply. The code issued under s66 clearly contemplates that such power is implied into s2(9) in that it states:

'Where on reasonable grounds it is considered necessary to conduct a more thorough search (eg by requiring someone to take off a T-shirt or headgear), this should be done out of public view (eg in a police van or a nearby police station if there is one).'

Any such search may only be conducted by an officer of the same sex as the person searched.

Unattended vehicles. Provided the conditions in s1 are met, vehicles which are not 'attended' may be searched even though there is no person during the search who is in charge of the vehicle or otherwise responsible for it. In such a case, s2(6) and (7) provide for the fact of the search to be brought to the attention of the vehicle's owner, driver or other person responsible for it:

'(6) On completing a search of an unattended vehicle or anything in or on such a vehicle in the exercise of any such power as is mentioned in subsection (2) above a constable shall leave a notice –
a) stating that he has searched it;
b) giving the name of the police station to which he is attached;
c) stating that an application for compensation for any damage caused by the search may be made to that police station;
d) stating the effect of s3(8) below.
(7) The constable shall leave the notice inside the vehicle unless it is not reasonably practicable to do so without damaging the vehicle.'

Duration of detention. So as to avoid excessive delay in the carrying out of a search of persons or vehicles, s2(8) imposes a statutory (if rather vague) duty upon the police:

'(8) The time for which a person or vehicle may be detained for the purposes of such a search is such time as is reasonably required to permit a search to be carried out either at the place where the person or vehicle was first detained or nearby.'

How much time is 'reasonably required' must of course depend upon the facts of each case, but it is to be hoped that the subsection will encourage the police to make the search quickly, rather than risking a civil action for unlawful detention for a period beyond what a court could later find to have been adequate.

16.4 Other powers to stop and search

The 1984 Act significantly tidies up a confused morass of varying general and local powers. Nonetheless, several powers peculiar to particular offences, places or persons survive the Act, and of these the most notable are:

1. To stop and search for prohibited drugs. The conditions for search remain those stated in s23 of the Misuse of Drugs Act 1971.
2. To search persons in public places for unlicensed firearms, or for firearms used or suspected of being intended for use in the course of crime. This power is still governed by s47 of the Firearms Act 1968.

3. To stop and search persons suspected of terrorist offences. The very wide rights given the police by the Prevention of Terrorism (Temporary Provisions) Act 1989 take priority over any of the requirements of the present Act.

4. Under s60 of the Criminal Justice and Public Order Act 1994, a police officer of or above the rank of superintendent may, if he reasonably believes that incidents involving serious violence may take place in any locality in his area, and it is expedient to prevent their occurrence, authorise the use of stop and search powers in the area for which he is responsible for a period of up to 24 hours. The period may be extended by a further six hours where it appears to the officer who gave the initial authorisation that it is expedient to do so. The stop and search powers conferred by this section extend to stopping any pedestrian, or vehicle and searching him or the occupants of any such vehicle, or the vehicle itself, for offensive weapons or dangerous instruments (ie bladed or pointed), whether or not a constable has any grounds for suspecting that he might find such articles. If any such articles are found they may be seized by a constable.

5. Section 81 of the Criminal Justice and Public Order Act 1994 provides additional powers of stop and search in relation to terrorism by adding a s13A to the Prevention of Terrorism (Temporary Provisions) Act 1989; see further Chapter 14, section 14.5.

Constables employed by certain statutory undertakers are also given a power of stop and search wider than that conferred on the police in general, and by s6 of the 1984 Act they may stop, detain and search any vehicle before it leaves a 'goods area' included in the premises of their employers. There is no need in such cases for the holding of 'reasonable grounds' for any suspicion of carriage by the vehicle of stolen or prohibited articles – the power is almost unlimited, though it applies only to searches of vehicles and not to searches of persons, so that any search of a person may be carried out only if the conditions mentioned in s1 of the Act are met. 'Goods area' is defined by s6(2) as 'any area used wholly or mainly for the storage or handling of goods'. The principal beneficiaries of the s6 power will be railway, dock, canal and other transport police forces, which are in theory not a part of the police force of the county in which they operate.

16.5 Road checks

Where a serious crime has been committed, it is of great assistance to the police to be able to establish roadside stations through which motor vehicles must pass and be checked to see whether they are carrying the suspect criminal or someone who may be a witness to the offence. The example of an armed raid upon an armoured security van springs first to mind; the police must act quickly if the villains are to be identified and caught before their trail becomes cold. To help in this case, and in a wide variety of others, s4 of the 1984 Act provides for short-term local powers of stop and search of vehicles:

'(1) This section shall have effect in relation to the conduct of road checks by police officers for the purpose of ascertaining whether a vehicle is carrying –

a) a person who has committed an offence other than a road traffic offence or a vehicles excise offence;

b) a person who is a witness to such an offence;

c) a person intending to commit such an offence; or

d) a person who is unlawfully at large.

(2) For the purposes of this section a road check consists of the exercise in a locality of the power conferred by s159 of the Road Traffic Act 1972 in such a way as to stop during the period for which its exercise in that way in that locality continues all vehicles or vehicles selected by any criterion.

(3) Subject to subsection (5) below, there may only be such a road check if a police officer of the rank of superintendent or above authorises it in writing.

(4) An officer may only authorise a road check under subsection (3) above –

a) for the purpose specified in subsection (1)(a) above, if he has reasonable grounds –

i) for believing that the offence is a serious arrestable offence; and

ii) for suspecting that the person is, or is about to be, in the locality in which vehicles would be stopped if the road check were authorised;

b) for the purpose specified in subsection (1)(b) above, if he has reasonable grounds for believing that the offence is a serious arrestable offence;

c) for the purpose specified in subsection (1)(c) above, if he has reasonable grounds –

i) for believing that the offence would be a serious arrestable offence; and

ii) for suspecting that the person is, or is about to be, in the locality in which vehicles would be stopped if the road check were authorised;

d) for the purpose specified in subsection (1)(d) above, if he has reasonable grounds for suspecting that the person is, or is about to be, in that locality.

(5) An officer below the rank of superintendent may authorise such a road check if it appears to him that it is required as a matter of urgency for one of the purposes specified in subsection (1) above.

(6) If an authorisation is given under subsection (5) above, it shall be the duty of the officer who gives it –

a) to make a written record of the time at which he gives it; and

b) to cause an officer of the rank of superintendent or above to be informed that it has been given ...

(10) An officer giving an authorisation under this section shall specify the locality in which vehicles are to be stopped.

(11) An officer giving an authorisation under this section, other than an authorisation under subsection (5) above –

a) shall specify a period, not exceeding seven days, during which the road check may continue; and

b) may direct that the road check –

i) shall be continuous; or

ii) shall be conducted at specified times, during that period.

(12) If it appears to an officer of the rank of superintendent or above that a road check ought to continue beyond the period for which it has been authorised he may, from time to time, in writing specify a further period, not exceeding seven days, during which it may continue.

(13) Every written authorisation shall specify –

a) the name of the officer giving it;

b) the purpose of the road check; and

c) the locality in which vehicles are to be stopped.

(14) The duties to specify the purposes of a road check imposed by subsections (9) and (13) above include duties to specify any relevant serious arrestable offence.

(15) Where a vehicle is stopped in a road check, the person in charge of the vehicle at the time when it is stopped shall be entitled to obtain a written statement of the purpose of the road check if he applies for such a statement not later than the end of the period of twelve months from the day on which the vehicle was stopped.

(16) Nothing in this section affects the exercise by police officers of any power to stop vehicles for purposes other than those specified in subsection (1) above.'

Though rather long, the section is at least relatively clear. Its purpose is to allow, not a full search of vehicles, but rather a cursory inspection and interrogation to determine whether any of the persons specified in s4(1) is driving or being carried in the vehicle. The phrase 'serious arrestable offence' occurs elsewhere in the Act and its definition appears in s116:

'(1) This section has effect for determining whether an offence is a serious arrestable offence for the purposes of this Act.

(2) The following arrestable offences are always serious –

a) an offence (whether at common law or under any enactment) specified in Part 1 of Schedule 5 of this Act; and

(aa) any of the offences mentioned in paragraphs (a)–(dd) of the definition of "drug trafficking offences" in section 38(1) of the Drug Trafficking Offences Act 1986; and

b) an offence under an enactment specified in Part II of that Schedule.

(3) Subject to subsections (4) and (5) below, any other arrestable offence is serious only if its commission –

a) has led to any of the consequences specified in subsection (6) below; or

b) is intended or is likely to lead to any of those consequences.

(4) An arrestable offence which consists of making a threat is serious if carrying out the threat would be likely to lead to any of the consequences specified in subsection (6) below.

(5) An offence under ss2, 8, 9, 10 or 11 of the Prevention of Terrorism (Temporary Provisions) Act 1984 is always a serious arrestable offence for the purposes of ss56 or 58 above, and an attempt or conspiracy to commit any such offence is also always a serious arrestable offence for those purposes.

(6) The consequences mentioned in subsections (3) and (4) above are –

a) serious harm to the security of the State or to public order;

b) serious interference with the administration of justice or with the investigation of offences or of a particular offence;

c) the death of any person;

d) serious injury to any person;

e) substantial financial gain to any person; and

f) serious financial loss to any person.

(7) Loss is serious for the purposes of this section if, having regard to all the circumstances, it is serious for the person who suffers it.

(8) In this section 'injury' includes any disease and any impairment of a person's physical or mental condition.'

Part I of Schedule 5 lists those offences conclusively regarded as serious arrestable offences; these include murder, rape, buggery, treason, manslaughter, kidnapping, incest with a girl under the age of 13 and so on. Part II provides details of other specific offences to be treated as serious arrestable offences, and is subject to amendment as new offences are created; see for example the offences added to Part II by s85 of the Criminal Justice and Public Order Act 1994. Other offences will fall within the definition only if they are 'arrestable' in the meaning given by s24 of PACE, but have also caused or were intended to cause harm classified as 'serious' by s116(6). For example, theft contrary to s1 of the Theft Act 1968 is an arrestable offence, but can qualify as a 'serious arrestable offence' only if it has caused or was intended to cause one of the s116(6) consequences, notably '... substantial financial gain to any person or serious financial loss to any person'. These phrases unfortunately lack precision, and all must be a question of fact and degree in each case. In *R* v *Neil McIvor* [1987] Crim LR 409 (a Crown Court decision), the trial judge ruled that access to a solicitor under s58 should not have been denied as the theft alleged, 28 hunt dogs valued at £800, was not a serious arrestable offence as it did not involve a substantial loss to the victim. Similarly, in *R* v *Eric Smith* [1987] Crim LR 579, the theft of two video recorders from Woolworths plc was not regarded as involving substantial loss.

As will be seen further in this chapter the concept of 'serious arrestable offence' also has a key part to play in determining the extent of police powers to detain, isolate and interrogate arrested persons.

Stop and search statistics

Home Office figures for 1993 indicate that police officers carried out 442,000 stop and search operations in respect of drugs, stolen property and offensive weapons, a fourfold increase since PACE came into force. Over half the searches were conducted in London. Searches for stolen property accounted for 40 per cent of cases, and drugs 31 per cent. Approximately 12 per cent of all stop and search incidents were followed by an arrest. The number of road checks totalled 3,560, an eightfold increase on the previous year.

16.6 Powers of entry, search and seizure on premises

The powers of stop, search and seizure thus far discussed have all related to persons or vehicles in public places, whether they be roads or pavements, or the gardens and yards provided for by s1(4) and (5). It now falls to consider the powers to enter buildings and other premises for the purpose of search or seizure. As Part I of the Act has clarified and consolidated rights to stop and search in public places, so Part II substantially amends the powers of entry and search of premises, and several anomalous lacunae have been closed in the process.

The police are now authorised to enter and search premises on the authority of a warrant issued by a Justice of the Peace if they suspect the commission of a 'serious arrestable offence' (see section 16.5 above) and the presence on those premises of evidence relevant to that suspected offence. Specifically, s8 provides:

'If on an application made by a constable a Justice of the Peace is satisfied that there are reasonable grounds for believing –
a) that a serious arrestable offence has been committed; and
b) that there is material on premises specified in the application which is likely to be of substantial value (whether by itself or together with other material) to the investigation of the offence; and
c) that the material is likely to be relevant evidence; and
d) that it does not consist of or include items subject to legal privilege, excluded material or special procedure material; and
e) that any of the conditions specified in subsection (3) below applies,
he may issue a warrant authorising a constable to enter and search the premises.'

The references to items 'subject to legal privilege', 'excluded material' and 'special procedure material' mean that no warrant may be issued by a magistrate which gives authority to enter and search for any of the following classes of evidence:

1. Documents subject to legal professional privilege according to the principles of the law of evidence and s10 of the Act. Such items are excluded from the right to search so as to preserve the defendant's right not to be compelled to incriminate himself by disclosure of anything he may have told to or been told by his legal advisers in connection with some legal matter, even though it is not the matter raised in the warrant.
2. 'Excluded material' includes personal records of any person's physical or mental health or personal welfare acquired or created in confidence, and any human tissue or tissue fluid taken for the purposes of diagnosis or medical treatment and held in confidence, and also journalistic material held in confidence. The precise definitions of this phrase appear in s11, and a right of access to excluded material arises only on the order of a circuit judge made in an application by the police under Schedule 1 of the Act. Thus there is a safeguard against unjustified invasion of privacy.
3. 'Special procedure material' includes certain journalistic material other than that in the definition of 'excluded material', together with certain business records held in confidence or subject to an obligation by statute not to disclose them. Such material can once again only be made the lawful object of police search and seizure on the authority of a circuit judge: s14.

Given that none of the evidence sought falls into the categories of 'legal privilege', 'excluded' or 'special procedure' material, a justice's warrant may issue to enter and search premises for it. Nonetheless, such a warrant may not issue unless, as s8(1)(e) provides, one of the conditions in s8(3) applies. These conditions are designed to ensure that the draconian weapon of warrant operates only where it is impracticable or undesirable to gain access to evidence by request to the person who holds the right to grant access to it, perhaps because the evidence might be destroyed if the police are compelled to await an occupier's permission to enter, or cannot find out who has the right to allow them entry. The subsection provides:

'(3) The conditions mentioned in subsection (1)(e) above are –
a) that it is not practicable to communicate with any person entitled to grant entry to the premises;
b) that it is practicable to communicate with a person entitled to grant entry to the premises but it is not practicable to communicate with any person entitled to grant access to the evidence;
c) that entry to the premises will not be granted unless a warrant is produced;
d) that the purpose of a search may be frustrated or seriously prejudiced unless a constable arriving at the premises can secure immediate entry to them.'

The application to a Justice of the Peace for issue of the warrant must be made in the form prescribed by s15, which is intended to ensure that there is good reason for its grant, and that it clearly specifies the suspected offence and, so far as is possible, the evidence sought:

'(2) Where a constable applies for ... a warrant, it shall be his duty –
a) to state –
i) the ground on which he makes the application; and
ii) the enactment under which the warrant would be issued;
b) to specify the premises which it is desired to enter and search;
c) to identify, so far as is practicable, the articles or persons to be sought ...
(4) The constable shall answer on oath any question that the justice of the peace or judge hearing the application asks him.
(5) A warrant shall authorise an entry on one occasion only.
(6) A warrant –
a) shall specify –
i) the name of the person who applies for it;
ii) the date on which it is issued;
iii) the enactment under which it is issued;
iv) the premises to be searched; and
b) shall identify, so far as is practicable, the articles or persons to be sought.'

Once issued, the search warrant remains in force for only one month, and if it has not been executed within that period it lapses and must be returned to the court office from which it issued; s16(3) and (10). It must be executed at a 'reasonable hour' unless it appears to the constable executing it that the purpose of a search may be frustrated on an entry at a reasonable hour: 16(4). This test seems to be wholly subjective, so that the constable's honest even though unreasonable belief will be conclusive. The occupier or apparent occupier of the premises to be searched must be shown the warrant, provided with a copy of it, and given documentary evidence that the person seeking to execute it is a constable: s16(5). The courts appear to be taking a strict line in requiring compliance by the police with the search warrant safeguards. In *R* v *Chief Constable of Lancashire, ex parte Parker* [1993] 2 WLR 428, the applicants' premises were entered by police officers purporting to act under search warrants and items were seized. The officers carrying out the searches provided the occupiers with warrants comprising photocopies of the authorisations unaccompanied by the schedules that would have detailed the articles sought. The applicants sought judicial review seeking orders of certiorari to quash the warrants and a declaration to the effect that the entries and searches had been unlawful. The Divisional Court, granting the declarations sought, held that a search warrant comprised two documents, the authorisation and the schedule of articles to be seized. Sub-sections 15(7) and (8) of the Police and Criminal Evidence Act 1984 required that two certified copies should be made of any warrant, so that one might be given to the occupier, or left at the premises. The certification was required so that the occupier did not have to rely on the word of the police as to the warrant's validity. Showing the occupier a copy of the warrant would not suffice. As Nolan LJ observed:

> 'It seems to us clear beyond argument that when the Act refers to a warrant issued by a judge it means the whole of the original document seen and approved and put forth by him ... It would be wholly contrary to the purpose of the legislation if a judge could authorise the police to replace the whole or a part of the original warrant, for the purposes of its execution, by an uncertified photocopy which he has not seen.'.

Hence the original warrant had been valid, and certiorari would not be granted to quash it, but the subsequent searches were unlawful given the failure to comply with the statutory requirements concerning authentification an completeness of copies.

Provided the documents are in order, *R* v *Longman* [1988] Crim LR 534 suggests that the police can gain entry to premises before informing the occupants as to who they are. In that case a female officer, posing as an 'Interflora' delivery woman, gained entry and then produced her warrant card. The court declared such a procedure lawful, provided the police could show that providing information prior to entry would render the subsequent search nugatory.

If the constable finds the evidence connected with the suspected offence for which the warrant issued, he may seize it: s8(2).

16.7 Entry, search and seizure without warrant

The powers to enter and search premises thus far discussed have concerned the grant of a justices' warrant (or, if the search is for 'excluded' or 'special procedure' material, on the authority of a circuit judge), without the arrest of any suspect. It is now necessary to consider the police powers of entry and search of premises without such a warrant. These are contained in general terms in ss17 and 18. They are in addition to any other statutory powers of entry and search, and to the sole remaining such power at common law, that of entry to deal with or prevent a breach of the peace: s17(6).

So far as is material, s17 provides:

'(1) Subject to the following provisions of this section, and without prejudice to any other enactment, a constable may enter and search any premises for the purpose –
a) of executing –
i) a warrant of arrest issued in connection with or arising out of criminal proceedings; ...
b) of arresting a person for an arrestable offence;
c) of arresting a person for an offence under –
i) section 1 (prohibition of uniforms in connection with political objects), of the Public Order Act 1936;
ii) any enactment contained in ss6 to 8 or 10 of the Criminal Law Act 1977 (offences relating to entering and remaining on property);
iii) section 4 Public Order Act 1986 ...
d) of recapturing a person who is unlawfully at large and whom he is pursuing; or
e) of saving life or limb or preventing serious damage to property.
(2) Except for the purpose specified in paragraph (e) of subsection (1) above, the powers of entry and search conferred by this section –
a) are only exercisable if the constable has reasonable grounds for believing that the person whom he is seeking is on the premises; and
b) are limited, in relation to premises consisting of two or more separate dwellings, to powers to enter and search –
i) any parts of the premises which the occupiers of any dwelling comprised in the premises' use in common with the occupiers of any other such dwelling; and
ii) any such dwelling in which the constable has reasonable grounds for believing that the person whom he is seeking may be ...
(4) The power of search conferred by this section is only a power to search to the extent that is reasonably required for the purpose for which the power of entry is exercised.'

Note that the power to enter under s17(1)(b) is exercisable by a constable who seeks to arrest a suspect in relation to an arrestable offence. For the power of arrest to exist, and hence the power to enter without warrant, the constable will have to have reasonable grounds to suspect that an arrestable offence has been committed. The matter was considered in *Chapman* v *DPP* (1989) 89 Cr App R 190. A Constable Sneller was called to assist an officer who was being assaulted by a number of youths. Sneller saw a youth he suspected of being involved in the attack run into the flat occupied by his father, the defendant. Sneller sought entry to the defendant's premises, but the defendant resisted, and was arrested for obstructing a constable in the execution of his duty. Sneller purported to be exercising his power of arrest under s24(6) of the Police and Criminal Evidence Act 1984, in relation to the defendant's son. The defendant's submission of no case to answer, in relation to the obstruction charge, was rejected by the justices, and he appealed by way of case stated, the question for the court being: 'whether the justices were right to conclude that [Sneller] at the time of the assault was exercising a statutory power of entry and so was a constable acting in the execution of his duty'. The court felt compelled to allow the appeal on the ground that the common assault on a fellow officer was not an arrestable offence, hence no power of arrest existed under s24(6), and in turn no power to enter under s17(1)(b). As Bingham LJ commented:

'What is ... inescapable and fatal to this conviction is that the justices have not found as a fact that Constable Sneller reasonably suspected ... any ... arrestable offence, to have been committed, or any facts amounting to an arrestable offence to have occurred. Such a reasonable suspicion is the source from which all a police constable's powers of summary arrest flow and the justices have felt unable to make the   crucial finding which the prosecutor required. This was plainly not the result of oversight or inadvertence. Had the justices found that Constable Sneller reasonably suspected an arrestable offence to have been committed, it would have been incumbent on them to identify, at least in general terms, the arrestable offence which the police constable suspected and this, it is plain, the evidence adduced did not enable them to do. It is not of course to be expected that a police constable in the heat of an emergency, or while in hot pursuit of a suspected criminal, should always have in mind specific statutory provisions, or that he should mentally identify specific offences with technicality or precision. He must, in my judgment, reasonably suspect the existence of facts amounting to an arrestable offence of a kind which he has in mind. Unless he can do that he cannot comply with section 28(3) of the Act by informing the suspect of grounds which justify the arrest.'

It seems clear, following the House of Lords' decision in *D'Souza* v *DPP* [1992] 1 WLR 1073, that the power to enter without a warrant under s17(1)(d) is only to be used in cases of 'hot pursuit'. In that case the appellant's mother had left a hospital where she was being detained for psychiatric assessment without leave being granted as required under s17 of the Mental Health Act 1983. Several hours later uniformed officers arrived at the house where the appellant lived with her parents in order to take her mother back to the hospital. The appellant and her father refused the police officers entry as they did not have a warrant to enter the premises, but the officers nevertheless exercised a forced entry and were attacked by the appellant and her father, who were subsequently convicted of assaulting police officers in the execution of their duty contrary to s51(1) of the Police Act 1964. Allowing their appeals against conviction, the House of Lords held that s17(1)(d) of the 1984 Act could only be used by officers seeking to enter premises where they sought to apprehend a person who was unlawfully at large, and at the time of entering the premises the police officers were in 'hot pursuit' of the said person. Whilst a person absconding from a hospital in breach of the Mental Health Act would be a person 'unlawfully at large', in the present case there was no evidence that the police had entered the dwelling in question whilst in hot pursuit of the appellant's mother. It would appear from this ruling that if the officers had spotted the appellant's mother entering her house and had chased after her, they would have had the power of entry without warrant provided for by s17(1)(d). As a consequence of this decision it must be the case that the subsection cannot be relied upon by a constable who, acting upon information received that a person unlawfully at large is at a particular dwelling, then proceeds to visit and enter the premises to effect the recapture of such a person. Whether a constable is in 'hot pursuit' will inevitably be a question of fact to be determined in each case.

Further powers of entry and search are conferred by s18, which permits a search of premises following the arrest of a suspect for an 'arrestable' offence, if the suspect arrested occupies or controls the premises to be searched. Nonetheless, the section creates safeguards against ill-considered searches and invasions of privacy:

'(1) Subject to the following provisions of this section, a constable may enter and search any premises occupied or controlled by a person who is under arrest for an arrestable offence, if he has reasonable grounds for suspecting that there is on the premises evidence, other than items subject to legal privilege, that relates –
a) to that offence; or
b) to some other arrestable offence which is connected with or similar to that offence.
(2) A constable may seize and retain anything for which he may search under subsection (1) above.
(3) The power to search conferred by subsection (1) above is only a power to search to the extent that is reasonably required for the purpose of discovering such evidence.
(4) Subject to subsection (5) below, the powers conferred by this section may not be exercised unless an officer of the rank of inspector or above has authorised them in writing.
(5) A constable may conduct a search under subsection (1) above –
a) before taking the person to a police station; and
b) without obtaining an authorisation under subsection (4) above,
if the presence of that person at a place other than a police station is necessary for the effective investigation of the offence ...'

16.8 Powers of seizure

Certain powers to seize evidence have already been examined, for instance that permitting seizure of evidence specified in a search warrant under s8(2). A general power of seizure is conferred upon constables who are 'lawfully on any premises' by s19. This will include not only lawful presence following entry to effect an arrest, or following arrest of a suspect, or on the authority of a search warrant, but also cases where the constable has been allowed into the premises by a person with the power to give him permission to enter, even though he is not there pursuant to any statutory or common law right of entry. For example, where the constable visits a suspect to question him, and the suspect invites the constable into his house. In all these instances, s19 provides:

'(2) The constable may seize anything which is on the premises if he has reasonable grounds for believing –
a) that it has been obtained in consequence of the commission of an offence; and
b) that it is necessary to seize it in order to prevent it being concealed, lost, damaged, altered or destroyed.
(3) The constable may seize anything which is on the premises if he has reasonable grounds for believing –
a) that it is evidence in relation to an offence which he is investigating or any other offence; and
b) that it is necessary to seize it in order to prevent the evidence being concealed, lost, altered or destroyed.

(4) The constable may require any information which is contained in a computer and is accessible from the premises to be produced in a form in which it can be taken away and in which it is visible and legible if he has reasonable grounds for believing –
a) that –
i) it is evidence in relation to an offence which he is investigating or any other offence; or
ii) it has been obtained in consequence of the commission of an offence; and
b) that it is necessary to do so in order to prevent it being concealed, lost, tampered with or destroyed.
(5) The powers conferred by this section are in addition to any power otherwise conferred.
(6) No power of seizure conferred on a constable under any enactment (including an enactment contained in an Act passed after this Act) is to be taken to authorise the seizure of an item which the constable exercising the power has reasonable grounds for believing to be subject to legal privilege.'

Where the s19 power is invoked, and articles seized, those articles may be retained 'so long as is necessary in all the circumstances', for instance for use at the trial of an accused, or to allow a forensic examination of them or to find out who is their lawful owner, but must be released to the person from whom they were seized – unless there is reason to believe that they have been obtained in consequence of the commission of an offence – if a photograph or copy of them would be sufficient for the purpose for which retention is desired. These matters are governed by s22.

16.9 Powers of arrest

Where time permits, the arrest of a suspect will often be made on the authority of a warrant issued by a justice of the peace under s1 of the Magistrates' Courts Act 1980. Such a warrant may issue in respect of any offence known to law, and is obtained by deposing to the facts of the alleged offence on oath. In addition to its use as a means of taking a suspect into custody before any charge has been made, the warrant procedure also aids in detaining those who have absconded while on bail awaiting trial, or who have failed to appear at court to answer to a summons.

In many cases, however, there is not sufficient time to apply for a warrant, and the statutory powers to arrest without it will now be considered. The 1984 Act significantly simplifies the law in this area, though several powers of arrest without warrant remain in other legislation, for example s7(3) of the Public Order Act 1936 and s28(2) of the Children and Young Persons Act 1969. These preserved additional powers of arrest are listed in Sch 2 of the 1984 Act. The Act draws a distinction between 'arrestable offences', for which a power of arrest without warrant exists in every case, subject to certain conditions, regardless of the seriousness of the harm or damage done in the actual offence, and other offences which become arrestable without warrant only if the gravity of the harm, or risk of further harm, or of the suspect's absconding without having given a true name and address, call for immediate detention.

16.10 Arrestable offences

By virtue of s24, a power to arrest without warrant exists where an offence of the following kinds is suspected:

'(1) The powers of summary arrest conferred by the following subsections shall apply –
a) to offences for which the sentence is fixed by law;
b) to offences for which a person of 21 years of age or over (not previously convicted) may be sentenced to imprisonment for a term of five years (or might be so sentenced but for the restrictions imposed by s33 of the Magistrates' Courts Act 1980); and
c) to the offences to which subsection (2) below applies, and in this Act 'arrestable offence' means any such offence.
(2) The offences to which this subsection applies are –
a) offences for which a person may be arrested under the Customs and Excise Acts, as defined in s1(1) of the Customs and Excise Management Act 1979;
b) offences under the Official Secrets Act 1920 that are not arrestable offences by virtue of the term of imprisonment for which a person may be sentenced in respect of them;
bb) offences under any provision of the Official Secrets Act 1989 except s8(1), (4) or (5).
c) offences under s14 (indecent assault on a woman), 22 (causing prostitution of women) or 23 (procuration of girl under 21) of the Sexual Offences Act 1956;
d) offences under s12(1) (taking motor vehicle or other conveyance without authority etc) or 25(1) (going equipped for stealing etc) of the Theft Act 1968; and
e) any offence under the Football (Offences) Act 1991;
f) an offence under section 2 of the Obscene Publications Act 1959 (publication of obscene matter);
g) an offence under section 1 of the Protection of Children Act 1978 (indecent photographs and pseudo-photographs of children);
h) an offence under section 166 of the Criminal Justice and Public Order Act 1994 (sale of tickets by unauthorised persons);
i) an offence under section 19 of the Public Order Act 1986 (publishing etc material intended or likely to stir up racial hatred);
j) an offence under section 167 of the Criminal Justice and Public Order Act 1994 (touting for car hire services).
(3) Without prejudice to s2 of the Criminal Attempts Act 1981, the powers of summary arrest conferred by the following subsections shall also apply to the offences of –
a) conspiring to commit any of the offences mentioned in subsection (2) above;
b) attempting to commit any such offence
c) inciting, aiding, abetting, counselling or procuring the commission of any such offence;
and such offences are also arrestable for the purposes of this Act.'

The offences made arrestable by s24(1)(a) include murder, genocide and high treason. Section 24(1)(b) covers all the more serious offences such as robbery, rape, grievous bodily harm, theft, blackmail, obtaining property by deception and malicious wounding. The offences in s24(1)(c) are those which would not be arrestable within the definition of (a) or (b) but which are deemed sufficiently serious by s24(2) to merit immediate arrest without warrant. Section 24(3) confirms that inchoate offences of the types mentioned in s24(2) are also arrestable. Inchoate offences of the types covered by s24(1)(a) and (b) are arrestable because they carry the same maximum penalty as the full offence.

16.11 Power to arrest for arrestable offences

Given that the offence suspected falls within s24, to whom is a power of arrest allowed, and in what circumstances? There are differences between the powers of constables and those of private citizens. Section 24(4) and (5) detail the powers available to both:

'(4) Any person may arrest without a warrant –
a) anyone who is in the act of committing an arrestable offence;
b) anyone whom he has reasonable grounds for suspecting to be committing such an offence.
(5) Where an arrestable offence has been committed, any person may arrest without a warrant –
a) anyone who is guilty of the offence;
b) anyone whom he has reasonable grounds for suspecting to be guilty of it.'

It can be seen that a power to arrest arises against anyone who is in the act of committing an arrestable offence, or who is suspected on reasonable grounds to be committing such an offence, that is, someone who is still committing and has not yet completed the suspected crime, by s24(4). The power to arrest after the event given by s24(5) requires that an arrestable offence has been committed. If a private citizen arrests someone he suspected of having committed an arrestable offence, but it emerges that no arrestable offence was committed, the private citizen is liable in damages for false arrest. Such was the law prior to 1968, as enshrined in decisions such as *Walters* v *WH Smith* [1914] 1 KB 595, and it has since been confirmed in relation to s24(5) by the Court of Appeal in *R* v *Self* [1992] 1 WLR 476. The appellant, who was believed to have stolen a bar of chocolate, was arrested by a store detective and another member of the public. During the course of the arrest the appellant assaulted those trying to apprehend him. The appellant, who was ultimately acquitted of theft, but convicted of assault with intent to resist or prevent lawful apprehension, contrary to s38 of the Offences Against the Person Act 1861, contended that as he had been acquitted on the theft charge, neither the store detective nor any other member of the public could have been empowered to arrest him under s24(5) of the 1984 Act, since this required proof that an arrestable offence had been committed. It followed, therefore, that the detention had not been lawful, and thus he should not have been convicted under s38. Allowing the appeal, the court confirmed that a condition precedent to the exercise of the citizen's power of arrest under s24(5) was that an arrestable offence had already been committed, and hence the contention in relation to s38 had to succeed. As Garland J observed:

'Subsection (5) makes it abundantly clear that the powers of arrest without a warrant where an arrestable offence has been committed require as a condition precedent an offence committed. If subsequently there is an acquittal of the alleged offence no offence has been committed. The power to arrest is confined to the person guilty of the offence or anyone who the person making the arrest has reasonable grounds for suspecting to be guilty of it ... If it is necessary to go further, one contrasts the words of subsection (5) with subsection (6), the very much wider powers given to a constable who has reasonable grounds for suspecting that an arrestable offence has been committed.'

Powers of arrest in wider terms are conferred on constables, in addition to those they possess in their capacity as citizens, by s24(4) and (5). These allow arrest even where no arrestable offence has in fact been committed. Section 24(6) and (7) provides:

'(6) Where a constable has reasonable grounds for suspecting that an arrestable offence has been committed, he may arrest without a warrant anyone whom he has reasonable grounds for suspecting to be guilty of the offence.
(7) A constable may arrest without a warrant –
a) anyone who is about to commit an arrestable offence;
b) anyone whom he has reasonable grounds for suspecting to be about to commit an arrestable offence.'

What constitutes reasonable grounds to suspect? In *Shaabin Bin Hussein* v *Chong Fook Kam* [1970] AC 492, an action against the Malaysian police for false imprisonment, the Privy Council held that reasonable grounds to suspect was not to be equated with prima facie proof based on admissible evidence, it was a much wider concept that could be based on inadmissible evidence; eg hearsay. In *Holgate-Mohammed* v *Duke* [1984] 1 All ER 1054, Lord Diplock expressed the view that a constable was exercising an executive discretion, hence the test expounded in *Associated Provincial Picture Houses* v *Wednesbury Corporation* [1948] 1 KB 223, was to be applied. Hence in *Castorina* v *Chief Constable of Surrey* (1988) 138 NLJ 180, the court held that the existence of reasonable cause was to be determined objectively – it was not necessary to consider whether the arresting constable had an honest belief that D had committed an offence, merely whether a reasonable person (officer) would have similarly suspected. The courts appear to be willing to grant the arresting officer a margin of appreciation, given that he may have been acting in the heat of the moment: see *G* v *Superintendent of Police, Stroud* (1985) The Times 29 November. *Holtham* v *Commissioner of Police for the Metropolis* (1987) The Times 28 November, reaffirms the approach in a number of earlier authorities to the effect that suspicion was a state of conjecture or surmise where actual proof was lacking.

The 1984 Act does not contain a definition of arrest. However in *R* v *Brosch* [1988] Crim LR 743, the court held, following *Alderson* v *Booth* [1969] 2 All ER 271, that an arrest might be effected by any action or words indicating to D that he is under a compulsion and is no longer at liberty.

16.12 Power to arrest for offences which are not arrestable

Where the suspected offence does not fall within the definition of arrestable given by s24, a power to arrest without warrant is conferred upon constables – but not upon private citizens – where it is thought undesirable to follow the normal procedure of leaving the suspected offender at large and proceeding against him by simple summons to appear at court later. The general purpose of this power is to prevent the suspect's avoiding prosecution by giving false particulars, or by refusing to give any particulars at all, or to remove the risk of further harm to the suspect himself or to the public or to property. Section 25 provides:

'(1) Where a constable has reasonable grounds for suspecting that any offence which is not an arrestable offence has been committed or attempted, or is being committed or attempted, he may arrest the relevant person if it appears to him that service of a summons is impracticable or inappropriate because any of the general arrest conditions are satisfied.

(2) In this section 'the relevant person' means any person whom the constable has reasonable grounds to suspect of having committed or having attempted to commit the offence or of being in the course of committing or attempting to commit it.

(3) The general arrest conditions are –

a) that the name of the relevant person is unknown to, and cannot be readily ascertained by, the constable;

b) that the constable has reasonable grounds for doubting whether a name furnished by the relevant person as his name is his real name;

c) that –

i) the relevant person has failed to furnish a satisfactory address for service; or

ii) the constable has reasonable grounds for doubting whether an address furnished by the relevant person is a satisfactory address for service;

d) that the constable has reasonable grounds for believing that arrest is necessary to prevent the relevant person –

i) causing physical injury to himself or any other person;

ii) suffering physical injury;

iii) causing loss of or damage to property;

iv) committing an offence against public decency; or

v) causing an unlawful obstruction of the highway;

e) that the constable has reasonable grounds for believing that arrest is necessary to protect a child or other vulnerable person from the relevant person.

(4) For the purposes of subsection (3) above an address is a satisfactory address for service if it appears to the constable –

a) that the relevant person will be at it for a sufficiently long period for it to be possible to serve him with a summons; or

b) that some other person specified by the relevant person will accept service of a summons for the relevant person at it.

(5) Nothing in subsection (3)(d) above authorises the arrest of a person under subparagraph (iv) of that paragraph except where members of the public going about their normal business cannot reasonably be expected to avoid the person to be arrested.'

In *Edwards and Others* v *DPP* (1993) 97 Cr App Rep 301, two men, Fox and Sumner, were observed by police officers who believed them to be using cannabis. When challenged, the men appeared to try to dispose of certain substances. They were informed that they were being arrested for obstructing the officers in the execution of their duties under the Misuse of Drugs Act 1971. A woman named Prendergast intervened to prevent the arrest of Fox and was arrested for obstruction contrary to s51(3) Police Act 1964. Edwards intervened to prevent the arrest of Prendergast and was similarly arrested for obstruction contrary to s51(3). The defendants submitted that there was no case to answer since there was no power to arrest without warrant for obstruction under the Misuse of Drugs Act 1971. The magistrates found that in the circumstances there was a power to arrest under s25 of the 1984 Act as, on the facts now known, the arresting officer would have every reason to doubt the truth of any name he was given by the suspect, hence the arrests were lawful. On appeal by way of case stated, the Divisional Court considering the question of whether or not the arresting officer, in the circumstances of the case, had had the power to arrest Fox under s25(3)(a) and (b) and/or s25(3)(d)(i) of the 1984 Act, held that, as the power to arrest without warrant for obstruction of a police officer in the execution of his duty contrary to the Misuse of Drugs Act 1971 had been abolished by s26 of the Police and Criminal Evidence Act 1984, the only power to arrest for such obstruction would be that now arising under s25 of the 1984 Act, ie the power of summary arrest in relation to a non-arrestable offence. By simply telling Fox that he was '... nicked for obstruction ...', the officer had failed to give s25(1) of the 1984 Act or any of the general arrest conditions detailed in s25(3) as justification. The court confirmed that, by virtue of s28(5) of the 1984 Act, an arrest was not lawful unless the arrestee was informed of the grounds of arrest. In the instant case the court felt that there were no circumstances that precluded the giving of that information; it had obviously practicable for the officer to give reasons for the arrest, because that was precisely what he had done, although they were invalid. The arrest might have been valid if the general arrest conditions under s25 had been given as the reason for arrest, but the arrest could not be retrospectively validated. As Evans LJ observed:

> 'It may seem unrealistic that the court should be concerned after the event with the precise words that were used ... Nevertheless, it has to be borne in mind that giving correct information as to the reasons for an arrest is a matter of the utmost constitutional significance in a case where a reason can be and is given at the time.'

16.13 Information on arrest

Section 28 of the 1984 Act codifies certain established principles of common law relating to the duty of the police to inform an arrested person of the fact of and reason for his arrest. It provides:

> '(1) Subject to subsection (5) below, where a person is arrested, otherwise than by being informed that he is under arrest, the arrest is not lawful unless the person arrested is informed that he is under arrest as soon as is practicable after his arrest.
>
> (2) Where a person is arrested by a constable, subsection (1) above applies regardless of whether the fact of the arrest is obvious.
>
> (3) Subject to subsection (5) below, no arrest is lawful unless the person arrested is informed of the ground for the arrest at the time of, or as soon as is practicable after, the arrest.
>
> (4) Where a person is arrested by a constable, subsection (3) above applies regardless of whether the ground for the arrest is obvious.
>
> (5) Nothing in this section is to be taken to require a person to be informed –

a) that he is under arrest; or

b) of the ground for the arrest,

if it was not reasonably practicable for him to be so informed by reason of his having escaped from arrest before the information could be given.'

It would appear that even though reasons for an arrest are not given at the time of the arrest, the arrest can become lawful once those reasons are supplied. In *Lewis v Chief Constable of the South Wales Constabulary* [1991] 1 All ER 206, the plaintiffs had been arrested on suspicion of burglary and taken to a police station. One had been told the reason for the arrest 10 minutes after it had occurred, the other some 23 minutes after arrest. They were detained for about five hours and then released. In an action for false arrest and wrongful imprisonment, they were awarded damages for unlawful detention of only 10 and 23 minutes respectively. The plaintiffs were unsuccessful in challenging these decision in the Court of Appeal. Balcombe LJ rejected the contention of counsel for the plaintiffs to the effect that, if at the moment of initial apprehension the arrest was unlawful, the act was a nullity. His Lordship expressed the view that arrest was a situation; a matter of fact, citing *Spicer v Holt* [1976] 3 All ER 71. Whether a person has been arrested depended not on the legality of his arrest but on whether he has been deprived of his liberty to go where he pleased. There was no doubt that, on the facts of this case, the plaintiffs had been deprived of their liberty at the moment that they were arrested, and that that act was not a nullity. Arrest was a continuing act, and in his Lordship's view there was nothing inconsistent with the wording of s28(3) to say that from that moment when reasons were given the arrest became lawful, or the continued deprivation of liberty became lawful, or the continued custody became lawful. Hence the trial judge had been correct in the ruling that the period in respect of which the plaintiffs were entitled to damages was that between the arrest and the giving of reasons. The decision confirms the earlier case of *DPP v Hawkins* (1988) The Times 9 June.

Decisions such as *Abbassy v MPC* [1990] 1 WLR 385, confirm that a constable exercising his powers of arrest need not use technical language to indicate the offence for which D is being arrested. It is sufficient that the type of offence is identified, so that D may volunteer information which would render the arrest unnecessary. Where the arrest is made pursuant to s25, *DPP v Nicholas* [1987] Crim LR 474 suggests that a constable telling D that he is being arrested because of his failure to provide a name and address is enough.

16.14 Voluntary attendance at police station

At common law, the status of someone who was 'helping the police with their inquiries', but without having been formally arrested, was never very clear. It was repeatedly stated that a person was either under arrest or at liberty to leave the police station, and that the law did not recognise any form of detention as legal unless it was a lawful arrest. For the avoidance of doubt, and following the recommendations of the 1981 Royal Commission on Criminal Procedure, s29 of the 1984 Act now provides:

> 'Where for the purposes of assisting with an investigation a person attends voluntarily at a police station or at any other place where a constable is present or accompanies a constable to a police station or any such other place without having been arrested –
> a) he shall be entitled to leave at will unless he is placed under arrest;
> b) he shall be informed at once that he is under arrest if a decision is taken by a constable to prevent him from leaving at will.'

16.15 Procedure following arrest

Once a suspect has been arrested, whether with or without a warrant, he must be taken to a police station as soon as is practicable after his arrest, unless the arrest was made at such a station: s30(1). Provision is made by that section for conveying the suspect to a 'designated police station', defined by s35 as being one specified by the Chief Officer of Police for the detention of arrested persons, unless it is impracticable to do so in the short term. The suspect may be searched at the time of his arrest if there is reason to believe that he may present a danger to himself or to others, or may have upon him anything which he might use to escape from lawful custody, or which might be evidence relating to an offence: s32(1) and (2). These latter words are wide enough to allow a search for evidence of an offence other than that for which the arrest has been made. The search may also extend to premises in which the suspect was arrested, or in which he was present, immediately before his arrest, in order to discover evidence relating to the offence for which the arrest was made, if the arresting constable has reasonable grounds for believing that such evidence exists: s32(2) and (6): see further, *R v Badham* [1987] Crim LR 202.

On arrival at a designated police station, the suspect will come under the supervision of a 'custody officer' of at least the rank of sergeant, whose duties are prescribed by Part IV of the 1984 Act; see also *Vince v Chief Constable of Dorset Police* [1993] 1 WLR 415, considered in Chapter 13. In brief, an arrested person should not be kept in detention, but should be released either without charge or on bail, at the earliest reasonable opportunity. The custody officer must first decide, if the arrest has been without warrant, whether there is sufficient evidence to justify a charge against the suspect: s37(1). If insufficient evidence exists, the suspect must be released, either on bail or not, unless the officer has reasonable grounds for believing that continued detention is necessary to secure or preserve evidence relating to an offence, or to obtain evidence by questioning the suspect: s37(2). Records must be kept throughout the suspect's detention, detailing the decisions and reasons of the custody officer. If there is sufficient evidence to justify a formal charge, the suspect must be charged or released with or without bail: s37(7). Suspects who are not in a fit state to allow the custody officer to make a charge under subs (7) or to be released under that subsection, for example, through drunkenness or the influence of drugs, may be detained until they are fit: s37(9).

Once a charge has been made against the suspect and entered in the charge book, there is a presumption that the suspect will be released. He may be detained further only if he is an adult, his name or address cannot be ascertained or is reasonably suspected by the custody officer to be false, the custody officer has reasonable grounds for believing that the person arrested will fail to appear in court to answer to bail; in the case of a person arrested for an imprisonable offence the custody officer has reasonable grounds for believing that the detention of the arrested person is necessary to prevent him from committing an offence; in the case of case of a person arrested for a non-imprisonable offence the custody officer has reasonable grounds for believing that the detention of the arrested person is necessary to prevent him from causing physical injury to any other person or from causing loss of or damage to property; the custody officer has reasonable grounds for believing that the detention of the arrested person is necessary to prevent him interfering with the administration of justice or with the investigation of offences; or the custody officer has reasonable grounds for believing that continued detention is necessary for the protection of the suspect; (s38(1) as amended by s28 of the Criminal Justice and Public Order Act 1994).

Whether or not a charge has been made, the continued detention of every suspect depends upon a review made at intervals by the custody officer or, in the case of a suspect not yet charged, an officer of at least the rank of inspector who has not been directly involved in the investigation of the offence for which the arrest was made: s40(1). The first review must be made not later than six hours after detention was first authorised under s37 or s38, the second review not later than nine hours after the first, and subsequent reviews at intervals of not more than nine hours: s40(3). There is power to postpone a review if it is 'not practicable' to carry it out by the stated time, for instance if the review would interrupt a period of interrogation and the review officer is satisfied it would prejudice the investigation subject of the interrogation, or if no review officer is available at the stated time: s40(4). In such a case, the review must take place as soon as is practicable: s40(5).

The purpose of the review is to decide whether the reason for which detention was first authorised still holds good, for example, that the suspect was a source of harm to himself or others, or that evidence for use against him might be destroyed if he were to be released. If it does not, the suspect must be released. In deciding whether detention remains justified, s40(12) requires the officer to consider any representations made by the suspect himself or by any solicitor acting for him and available at the time of the review, though he need not consider what the suspect may have to say if the latter is asleep, or unfit to make representations by reason of his condition or behaviour: s40(14).

Where the suspect has been arrested and is being detained without charge, s41 imposes a maximum period for which he can be detained in police custody without being brought before a court. The general maximum is 24 hours, calculated from the time of his arrival at the first police station to which he is taken after his arrest: s41(1) and (2)(d). The period is calculated from the time of arrest if he voluntarily attended at a police station and was subsequently arrested there or if he is arrested in a police area other than that in which he has been sought – for instance, the suspect who is wanted by the Metropolitan Police but who is arrested by a different police force – and has not been questioned by the arresting police force with a view to discovering evidence of the offence. Other special provisions for calculating the 24-hour period are made in the cases of suspects who are removed from police detention for medical treatment in hospital, or who are arrested outside England and Wales.

Where the 24-hour period has expired and no charge has been made, the suspect must be released, with or without bail, unless detention beyond the 24 hours has been authorised by a superintendent under s42 or has been allowed by a magistrate's warrant of further detention under s43. Section 42 allows detention up to a total of 36 hours without charge on reasonable grounds for belief that it is necessary to secure or preserve evidence, and that the offence for which the investigation is continuing is a 'serious arrestable offence' and that the investigation is being conducted diligently and expeditiously. A warrant under s43 is issued on very similar grounds to the superintendent's authority under s42, and permits detention in police custody and without charge beyond 36 hours and up to a maximum total of 96 hours, in periods of not more than 36 hours at a time before further application to the court is necessary. The detailed contents of ss42–44 are beyond the scope of this manual, and the Act should be consulted for procedure at the hearing and the grounds for warrants of further detention.

The courts will construe the requirements as extension of detention as mandatory, unless the Act expressly provides for some discretion. Hence in *R* v *Slough Justices, ex parte Stirling* [1987] Crim LR 576, where the police arrived after 38 hours with an application to extend detention, the application was refused, on the basis that, under s43(7), it would have been reasonable for the police to apply in good time for an extension. Similarly in *In the matter of an application for a warrant of further detention* [1988] Crim LR 296, where detainees were not given the opportunity to make representations via a solicitor before a superintendent extended detention from 24 to 36 hours, and a brief note was placed on custody record to the effect that the superintendent considered detention necessary because the detainees might impede the course of justice if released, the justices accepted the detainees' contentions that the police had failed to comply with the mandatory requirements under s42. Detention beyond 24 hours had, therefore, been unlawful. Either the justices therefore had no jurisdiction to consider an application for further detention, or if they did they would decline to exercise it. Note that under s14 of the Prevention of Terrorism (Temporary Provisions) Act 1989, a person suspected of involvement in terrorist activities can be detained for up to five days without charge. See further *Brannigan and McBride* v *United Kingdom* (Case No 5/1992/350/423–424) (1993) The Times 28 May.

16.16 Appearance before magistrates following charge

An arrested person who has been charged but who, pursuant to ss38–40 of the 1984 Act, has been detained in police custody, must be brought before a magistrates' court as soon as is practicable after charge, and not later than the first sitting of the court after he has been charged with the offence: s46(2). This will usually be on the day of the charge or the day after, but in cases where no court sitting is to be held for either of those days, detention in police custody is permitted until the next sitting, provided the clerk to the justices is informed of the fact that the suspect is in custody and awaiting appearance at the next sitting. It is then the duty of the clerk to arrange for a hearing not later than the day on which the charge was made, or, if a public holiday or weekend intervenes, the day after that holiday or weekend: s46(3)–(9). The obligation to bring the suspect before the court does not apply if he is not well enough: s46(9).

16.17 The use of force

In exercising the powers of stop, search, entry, seizure and arrest, an unwilling suspect presents problems. The Act therefore provides, by s117, for the use of force by a constable:

'Where any provision of this Act –
a) confers a power on a constable; and
b) does not provide that the power may only be exercised with the consent of some person, other than a police officer,
the officer may use reasonable force, if necessary, in the exercise of the power.'

16.18 Interrogation of suspects and the right to legal advice

Persons arrested, whether by warrant or not, and held at a police station, are given by the Act rights to have someone named by them informed of the fact and place of their detention, and are to be allowed access to legal advice from a solicitor, in most cases. Although these rights are not absolute, and can be denied for a period of time in certain circumstances, the intent of the Act is clearly that they be respected and granted in all but the clearest cases calling for their denial.

So far as concerns notification to an outside person of the fact and place of arrest, s56 provides:

'(1) When a person has been arrested and is being held in custody in a police station or other premises, he shall be entitled, if he so requests, to have one friend or relative or other person who is known to him or who is likely to take an interest in his welfare told, as soon as is practicable except to the extent that delay is permitted by this section, that he has been arrested and is being detained there.

(2) Delay is only permitted –
a) in the case of a person who is in police detention for a serious arrestable offence; and
b) if an officer of at least the rank of superintendent authorises it.
(3) In any case the person in custody must be permitted to exercise the right conferred by subsection (1) above within 36 hours from the relevant time, as defined in s41(2) above.
(4) An officer may give an authorisation under subsection (2) above orally or in writing but, if he gives it orally, he shall confirm it in writing as soon as is practicable.
(5) [subject to subsection (5A) ...] An officer may only authorise delay where he has reasonable grounds for believing that telling the named person of the arrest –
a) will lead to interference with or harm to evidence connected with a serious arrestable offence or interference with or physical injury to other persons; or
b) will lead to the alerting of other persons suspected of having committed such an offence but not yet arrested for it; or
c) will hinder the recovery of any property obtained as a result of such an offence.
(5A) An officer may also authorise delay where the serious arrestable offence is a drug trafficking offence ...
(6) If a delay is authorised –
a) the detained person shall be told the reason for it; and
b) the reason shall be noted on his custody record.
(7) The duties imposed by subsection (6) above shall be performed as soon as is practicable.
(8) The rights conferred by this section on a person detained at a police station or other premises are exercisable whenever he is transferred from one place to another; and this section applies to each subsequent occasion on which they are exercisable as it applies to the first such occasion.
(9) There may be no further delay in permitting the exercise of the right conferred by subsection (1) above once the reason for authorising delay ceases to subsist.'

The provision governing access to legal advice is s58. It is in terms similar to s56:

'(1) A person arrested and held in custody in a police station or other premises shall be entitled, if he so requests, to consult a solicitor privately at any time.
(4) If a person makes such a request, he must be permitted to consult a solicitor as soon as is practicable except to the extent that delay is permitted by this section.
(5) In any case he must be permitted to consult a solicitor within 36 hours from the relevant time, as defined in s41(2) above.
(6) Delay in compliance with a request is only permitted –
a) in the case of a person who is in police detention for a serious arrestable offence; and
b) if an officer of at least the rank of superintendent authorises it.
(7) An officer may give an authorisation under subsection (6) above orally or in writing but, if he gives it orally, he shall confirm it in writing as soon as is practicable.
(8) [Subsection to subsection (8A) ...] An officer may only authorise delay where he has reasonable grounds for believing that the exercise of the right conferred by subsection (1) above at the time when the person detained desires to exercise it –
a) will lead to interference with or harm to evidence connected with a serious arrestable offence or interference with or physical injury to other persons; or
b) will lead to the alerting of other persons suspected of having committed such an offence but not yet arrested for it; or
c) will hinder the recovery of any property obtained as a result of such an offence.'

Thus a person held in custody at a police station shall be entitled to consult a solicitor at any time, if he so requests. The detainee may consult a solicitor of his own choice, but if he knows of none he should be informed by the police of the availability of the 'duty solicitor'. [Section 8A relates to drug trafficking offences]

The Criminal Justice Act 1988 extends the power to delay access where serious drug trafficking offences are involved.

Under the Codes of Practice accurate records must be made of each interview and interrogation, and in some circumstances tape-recordings of interviews will be permitted under s60. The suspect must be cautioned that he has a right of silence, and that caution must be administered as soon as the constable has grounds for believing that he has committed an offence. A further caution must be given before the arrested person is interviewed, and if the interview is interrupted for more than one hour, yet another caution is to be given before it is continued. Interviews of arrested persons can be carried out only with the agreement of the custody officer responsible for them and they must be allowed at least eight hours continuous rest in any period of 24 hours. No form of oppressive conduct is to be used in questioning, and the suspect may make a written statement if he wishes. The Code also details the records to be kept, and provides for the conduct of identification parades and interrogation of those who are physically or mentally ill or who are under the age of 17.

The revised Code C: 'Detention Treatment and Questioning of Persons by Police Officers' (paragraph 3.1(ii)) provides that detainees must now be informed of their right to free legal advice, and must be reminded of this right before any interview takes place.

A frequently voiced criticism of PACE and the original Code on interrogation was the absence of any explicit prohibition on interviews with suspects prior to their arrival at the police station. The revised Code C goes some way to meeting these objections by providing that interviews can only be held outside a police station in certain specified circumstances. Under paragraph 11.1 exceptions can only be made where no decision to arrest the interviewee has been taken; or, the interchanges do not amount to the questioning of a person regarding his involvement or suspected involvement in criminal activity; or, delaying the interview would be likely to lead to endangering others or enabling other suspects to flee or hinder the return of any property. In *R* v *Khan* [1993] Crim LR 54, the Court of Appeal upheld the decision of the trial judge not to exclude, under s78 of PACE, evidence obtained by police asking D. questions whilst they were searching his dwelling. The court confirmed that the proper venue for any interrogation was the police station, where the safeguards provided by s58 and the Codes would apply, but was satisfied that, on the facts, the main thrust of the police questioning had related to the whereabouts of property.

In what circumstances, if any, will the courts permit the police to rely on evidence obtained during interrogations at a police station, where D has not been permitted to exercise his right to consult with a solicitor?

In *R v Samuel* [1988] 2 WLR 920, the appellant was interviewed by the police on four occasions about a robbery and two burglaries. The appellant denied any involvement. During the second interview he asked for access to a solicitor, but his request was refused on the ground of likelihood of other suspects involved in the robbery being inadvertently warned. At the fourth interview the appellant confessed to the two burglaries and he was charged with those offences at 4.30 pm. At 4.45 pm a solicitor was informed of the charges, but denied access. Shortly afterwards the appellant confessed to the robbery and the solicitor was allowed to see him one hour later. At the trial, the appellant contended that evidence of the latter confession should be excluded, but it was admitted and he was convicted of robbery. On appeal the Court of Appeal held that the conviction should be quashed as, in the circumstances, the refusal of access to a solicitor had been unjustified and the interview in question should not have taken place. The court held that the crucial aspect of an interrogating officer's decision to exclude access to a solicitor under s58 was that, at the time of exclusion he has reasonable grounds to believe that access *will* lead to or hinder one or more of the things set out in paras (a) to (c) of s58(8). As Hodson J observed:

> 'The use of the word "will" is clearly of great importance. There were available to the draftsman many words or phrases by which he could have described differing nuances as to the officer's state of mind, for example "might", "could", "there was a risk", "there was a substantial risk" etc. The choice of "will" must have been deliberately restrictive. Of course, anyone who says that be believes that something will happen, unless he is speaking of one of the immutable laws of nature, accepts the possibility that it will not happen, but the use of the word "will" in conjunction with belief implies in the believer a belief that it will very probably happen.
>
> What is it that the officer has to satisfy the court he believed? The right denied is a right "to consult a solicitor privately". The person denied that right is in police detention. In practice, the only way that the person can make any of the matters set out in paras (a) to (c) happen is by some communication from him to the solicitor. For the matters set out in paras (a) to (c) to be made to happen the solicitor must do something. If he does something knowing that it will result in anything in paras (a) to (c) happening he will, almost inevitably, commit a serious criminal offence. Therefore, inadvertent or unwitting conduct apart, the officer must believe that a solicitor will, if allowed to consult with a detained person, thereafter commit a criminal offence. Solicitors are officers of the court. We think that the number of times that a police officer could genuinely be in that state of belief will be rare. Moreover it is our view that, to sustain such a basis for refusal, the grounds put forward would have to have reference to a specific solicitor. We do not think they could ever be successfully advanced in relation to solicitors generally ...'

It is submitted that to deny access to a specified solicitor may be tantamount to defamation, unless the police can produce evidence justifying the decision. As the above extract indicates, this will have to be evidence that the solicitor is likely to be duped by the suspect, or will help him pervert the course of justice. The former is perhaps possible. In *Re Walters* [1987] Crim LR 577, the court accepted that access to a solicitor could be denied where there was evidence that the suspects had been using 'Delphic phrases' to communicate with each other. A solicitor could be used in such a case to convey an apparently innocent message that could alert other gang members. To suggest that a solicitor would knowingly engage in such activities would obviously be a very grave allegation indeed. *Samuel* was followed in *R* v *Alladice* (1989) 88 Cr App R 332.

Where the interrogating officers fail to inform D of his right to consult with a solicitor, or fail to act upon his request for such consultation, the trial judge will have to assess the extent to which the failure to follow the provisions of the Act and the codes vitiates any subsequent interrogations.

In *R* v *Dunford* (1990) 91 Cr App R 150, where the Court of Appeal upheld the trial judge's decision to admit D's statement made in the absence of a solicitor on the basis that a solicitor's advice would not have added anything to the appellant's knowledge of his rights, Neill LJ expressly approved of the approach taken in *R* v *Walsh* (1989) Cr App R 161, 163, where it was stated that, whilst a breach of s58 would prima facie have an adverse effect on the fairness of proceedings:

> 'This does not mean, of course, in every case of a significant or substantial breach of s58 or the code of practice the evidence concerned will automatically be excluded. The task of the court is not merely to consider whether there would be an adverse effect on the fairness of the proceedings, but such an adverse effect that justice requires the evidence to be excluded ... Breaches which are in themselves significant and substantial are not rendered otherwise by the good faith of the officers concerned.'

This decision, and others, suggests that the courts are willing to adopt a causation based approach, assessing what difference access to legal advice might have had on D's conduct. Thus in *R* v *Absolam* (1989) 88 Cr App R 322, the Court of Appeal allowed D's appeal against conviction where the trial judge had allowed in evidence statements made before access to a solicitor was submitted. Bingham LJ noted that the interrogating officers should have informed D of his right to consult a solicitor when it became apparent to them that an offence had been committed, even though the series of questions and answers taking place between the officers and D was not in any formal sense a conventional interview. He continued:

> '... it seems to us that if the learned judge had been persuaded that there were here significant and substantial breaches of the Code he would, in all probability, have excluded the answers given by the appellant ... he would, we think, had he taken the same view of the Code as we have, have formed the opinion that this was a case in which, as a result of a line of questioning initiated in remarkable circumstances but with no warning to the appellant of his right, the appellant would not have given the answers that he did, and that the prosecution would not have been in receipt of these admissions if the appropriate procedures had been followed.'

Complications can arise in cases such as *R* v *Anderson* [1993] Crim LR 448, where D does not request access to a solicitor, later changes his mind, but due to a breakdown in communications, the interviewing officer is unaware that D has made such a request. In that case the Court of Appeal upheld the trial judge's decision to permit in evidence D's confession, under s78, on the basis that there was insufficient evidence that 'but for' the failure to provide legal advice D would not have made the statement, and further because there was no evidence to suggest the police had acted in any way to make the statement unreliable. See further *R* v *Parris* (1989) 89 Cr App R 68, and *R* v *Silcott* (1991) The Times 9 December.

Note that in *R* v *Chief Constable of South Wales, ex parte Merrick* [1994] 1 WLR 663, the Divisional Court ruled that whilst the statutory right to consult privately with a solicitor created by s58(1) did not extend to a prisoner held in custody at a court following a refusal of bail, such a prisoner did have a common law right to consult with a legal adviser as soon as was reasonably practicable, bearing in mind the other demands on police officers responsible for the custody of prisoners being held at the court. On this basis the policy adopted at Cardiff Magistrates' Court (of not permitting interviews between prisoners and solicitors after 10.00 am, unless there were good reasons for the interview not having taken place earlier) was declared to be unlawful.

16.19 Searches and fingerprinting following arrest

The general power to search an arrested person at the time of arrest has already been considered. Once at the police station, a search may be conducted on the authority of the custody officer, and what is found may be seized in the circumstances provided for by s54(3) and (4):

'(3) ... a custody officer may seize and retain any (item found in a search) or cause any such thing to be seized and retained.
(4) Clothes and personal effects may only be seized if the custody officer –
a) believes that the person from whom they are seized may use them –
i) to cause physical injury to himself or any other person;
ii) to damage property;
iii) to interfere with evidence; or
iv) to assist him to escape; or
b) has reasonable grounds for believing that they may be evidence relating to an offence.'

In certain situations it will be necessary for the search carried out upon an arrested person to go beyond a simple inspection of his outer clothing and personal effects. Section 55 of PACE thus provides for the carrying out of an intimate search (ie a search of the bodily orifices other than the mouth) where an officer of at least the rank of superintendent has reasonable grounds to believe that a person who has been arrested and is in police detention may have concealed on him anything which he could use to cause physical injury to himself or others; and he might so use while he is in police detention or in the custody of a court; or that such a person may have a Class A controlled drug concealed on him and was in possession of it with the appropriate criminal intent before his arrest. An intimate search may only be carried out at a police station, hospital, doctor's surgery or other place used for medical purposes: s55(8); and may not be made by a person of the sex opposite to the person searched. Intimate searches for evidence of drugs offences may not be made at a police station: s55(9).

Samples of hair other than pubic hair, from a nail or under a nail, from body swabs (other than body orifices), saliva and footprints or similar impressions of the body other than a part of the hand, may be taken from an arrested person without his consent under conditions very similar to those allowing intimate searches: s63; except that the power to take intimate and non-intimate sample extends to all recordable offences, and not merely serious arrestable offences. Intimate samples, meaning a sample of blood, semen or other body tissue, fluid, urine, pubic hair, dental impression, or a swab from a body orifice, may not be taken against the arrested person's will. An intimate sample, other than one of urine or a dental impression, may be taken only by a registered medical practitioner, and a dental impression may only be taken by a registered dentist. A court may draw such inferences as seem justified from a person's refusal to consent to the taking of an intimate sample.

A significant new power, resulting from the amendment to s62 of PACE by s54 of the Criminal Justice and Public Order Act 1994, will permit the taking of intimate samples from persons not in police detention, provided such action is authorised by an officer of at least the rank of superintendent and the consent of the person is given (although adverse inferences can be drawn from a failure to grant such consent). The criteria to be satisfied are that two or more non-intimate samples must have been provided by the person in question, in the course of the investigation into an offence, which have proved insufficient (for the purposes of DNA analysis). Alternatively, non-intimate samples can be taken from a person not in detention, regardless of his consent, if he has been charged with a recordable offence or informed that he will be reported for such an offence and either he has not had a non-intimate sample taken from him in the course of the investigation of that offence, or if he has, it has not proved suitable for analysis.

Fingerprints may normally be taken from an arrested person only with his consent, but s61 provides for them to be taken without consent, on the authority of an officer of at least the rank of superintendent if he has reasonable grounds for suspecting the involvement of the person whose fingerprints are to be taken in a criminal offence; and for believing that his fingerprints will tend to confirm or disprove his involvement.

16.20 Confessions: general

Confessions are an important form of evidence in that they will presumably tend to produce a plea of guilty at trial, and hence are the best evidence that the accused has actually committed the offence with which he is charged. A defendant may, however, make a confession for a number of reasons other than guilt. For example, he may be attempting to shield the truly guilty party; he may be one of those whose psychological condition or state of mind makes him a compulsive confessor – police investigations are beset with those who invent confessions to prominent crimes which they could not possibly have committed – he may confess because he is intimidated or induced to make a statement by promises; he may feel that, if the offence is not serious, a confession and even a guilty plea is preferable just to 'get things over'.

In such circumstances it is clear that confessions should be treated with care and not admitted in evidence as they are unreliable as evidence of the truth. The police may wish to obtain evidence by questioning a suspect and they are allowed to do so by virtue of the notes for guidance issued under the Code of Practice for the Detention, Treatment and Questioning of Persons by Police Officers:

> '1B This Code does not affect the principle that all citizens have a duty to help police officers to prevent crime and discover offenders. This is a civic rather than a legal duty; but when a police officer is trying to discover whether, or by whom, an offence has been committed he is entitled to question any person from whom he thinks useful information can be obtained, subject to restrictions imposed by this Code. A person's declaration that he is unwilling to reply does not alter this requirement.'

This means that the police can ask anyone questions despite that person's unwillingness to answer them. It is possible that those questions may lead to a confession. Leaving aside the special requirements regarding juveniles and the mentally ill or handicapped, paragraph 11 of the code says:

> '11.1 No police officer may try to obtain answers to questions or to elicit a statement by the use of oppression, or shall indicate, except in answer to a direct question, what action will be taken on the part of the police if the person being interviewed answers questions, makes a statement or refuses to do either. If the person asks the officer directly what action will be taken in the event of his answering questions, making a statement or refusing to do either, then the officer may inform the person what action the police propose to take in that event provided that that action is itself proper and warranted.
> 11.2 As soon as a police officer who is making inquiries of any person about an offence believes that a prosecution should be brought against him and that there is sufficient evidence to succeed, he shall without delay cease to question him.'

The first part of this leads back to s76 of the Act. The second shows it is not intended that, where the police have decided there is sufficient evidence to succeed in a prosecution, they should press on to secure a confession. It is perhaps unfortunate that in a number of cases a confession is the only substantial piece of evidence the police have. The confession will, after all, be a valuable constituent towards the element of the defendant's mens rea. In theory, the defendant wants to confess in order to clear his conscience and to unburden himself of guilt. Arguably, this is a very powerful compulsion. The problem in the courts is that some defendants recant and seek to withdraw their confessions. In this situation it is up to the judge to decide in the absence of the jury whether or not the confession should be admitted in evidence; this is known as a 'voir dire' or a 'trial within a trial'.

16.21 The right to silence

The position at common law

Historically, the position at common law has been that a defendant is innocent until proven guilty, and that it is the task of the prosecution to convince the court of the defendant's guilt. A particular aspect of the criminal process has been the right to silence, whereby the courts have not been permitted to draw any adverse inferences from the defendant's failure to provide an exculpatory answer when taxed with the details of the offence he is alleged to have committed. The rationale for the common law right to silence was that the suspect and interrogator were not on equal terms, given that the interrogator would inevitably be a police officer. Exceptions were recognised where the defendant could be regarded as being on equal terms with his accuser, for example in *Parkes* v *R* (1976) 64 Cr App R 25, where the defendant was accused by his landlady of murdering her daughter.

The right to silence is reflected in the form of the caution to be administered by a police officer conducting an investigation into alleged offences, the wording being as follows: 'You do not have to say anything unless you wish to do so, but what you say may be given in evidence.' Minor deviations are permitted provided the sense of the caution is preserved.

Under the guidelines contained in Code C, a caution must be given before any questions are put to a suspect for the purpose of obtaining evidence which may be given in a court in a prosecution. The defendant, therefore, need not be cautioned if questions are put for other purposes, for example, to establish his identity, his ownership of, or responsibility for, any vehicle, or the need to search him in the exercise of powers of stop and search. A person must be cautioned upon arrest for an offence unless (a) it is impracticable to do so by reason of his condition or behaviour at the time; or (b) he has already been cautioned immediately prior to his arrest. When there is a break in questioning under caution the interviewing officer must ensure that the person being questioned is aware that he remains under caution. If there is any doubt on this matter the caution should be given again in full when the interview resumes.

The pressure for change

The view expressed in some quarters was that the right to silence was open to abuse by more sophisticated and experienced criminals and was partly responsible for some allegedly guilty defendants escaping conviction. The criticisms of the right to silence rest to a large extent on the assertion that any innocent person would seek to exculpate himself at the earliest possible moment if he has nothing to hide. Such research as has been conducted suggests that relatively few suspects choose to remain silent when interrogated by the police, although the percentage exercising this right has substantially increased since the enactment of the Police and Criminal Evidence Act 1984.

Given the right of a detained person to consult privately with a solicitor under s58 of PACE, questions have been raised as to the extent to which it remains true to say that detainee and interrogator are not on equal terms. Lawton LJ in *R* v *Chandler* [1976] 1 WLR 585, suggested that this might be the case, but went on to observe that once a detainee had been cautioned no adverse inferences were to be drawn from his silence. Curiously, the effect of this view suggests that the police would be better off allowing a detainee to have access to a solicitor but not to caution him, although such a practice would undoubtedly involve a breach of the Codes. Some, such as Lord Lane CJ, commenting in *R* v *Alladice* (above), have called for a re-assessment of the position. He stated:

'Paragraph 6.3 of the Code provides that a person who asks for legal advice may not be interviewed or continue to be interviewed until he has received it unless delay has been lawfully authorised ... The result is that in many cases a detainee who would otherwise have answered proper questioning by the police will be advised to remain silent. Weeks later at his trial such a person not infrequently produces an explanation of, or a defence to, the charge the truthfulness of which the police have had no chance to check. Despite the fact that the explanation or defence could, if true, have been disclosed at the outset and despite the advantage which the defendant has gained by these tactics, no comment may be made to the jury. The jury may in some cases put two and two together, but it seems to us that the effect of s58 is such that the balance of fairness between prosecution and defence cannot be maintained unless proper comment is permitted on the defendant's silence in such circumstances. It is high time that such comment should be permitted together with the necessary alteration to the words of the caution.'

In July 1993 the Royal Commission on Criminal Justice, chaired by Lord Runciman, produced its report (Cm 2263). A majority of its members proposed no change to the common law position on the 'right to silence' at a police station, but recommended that once the prosecution case was fully disclosed, it should be possible to draw adverse inferences from the introduction of any new defence or departure from any previously disclosed defence.

As a prelude to reform of the law in England and Wales, the law in Northern Ireland has been amended, by virtue of the Criminal Evidence (Northern Ireland) Order 1988, to permit the trial judge to direct the jury (or himself where the case involves a 'Diplock' court), that adverse inferences can be drawn from the defendant's failure to give evidence.

Such inferences are permitted, if D is silent, if:

a) he offers an explanation for his conduct for the first time at his trial which he could reasonably have been expected to produce when being questioned;

b) the prosecution satisfies the court that there is a case to answer and D declines to give evidence;

c) he gives no explanation in relation to certain facts such as substances found, or marks on clothing;

d) he gives no explanation for his presence in a particular place.

The House of Lords confirmed, in *R* v *Murray* [1994] 1 WLR 1, that the Order has the effect of changing the law and practice relating to the defendant who fails to give evidence, thus permitting the jury to infer guilt from his silence where the prosecution has established a prima facie case against him. An application designed to question the extent to which the abolition of the right to silence in Northern Ireland constitutes a breach of Article 6.1 of the European Convention on Human Rights has been declared admissible by the European Commission on Human Rights, and a judgment is awaited.

The changes introduced by the Criminal Justice and Public Order Act 1994

Section 34 of the 1994 Act provides that if a suspect fails to mention any fact relied on in his defence (being something that he could reasonably be expected to have mentioned) either when being questioned after cautioning by a constable, or after having been charged with an offence or officially informed that he might be prosecuted, the court or jury may draw such inferences from the failure as appear proper. Section 36 provides similarly in relation to an arrested person's failure to account for any object in his possession, or any substance or mark on his person, clothing or article in his possession, when required to do so by a constable investigating an offence, and s37 applies similarly to an arrested person's failure to account for his presence at a particular location.

A consequence of this change in the law is the amendment to the police caution that has been in use for over 30 years. In place of the current wording (see above) the Home Secretary has proposed (The Times 19 August 1994):

> 'You do not have to say anything. But if you do not mention now something which you later use in your defence, the court may decide that your failure to mention it now strengthens the case against you. A record will be made of anything you say and it may be given in evidence if you are brought to trial.'

This new form of caution has been criticised as being unduly lengthy and confusing, the fear being that the vulnerable and those of limited intellect (possibly those most likely to make false confessions) may not fully appreciate its implications. Critics have also questioned why the suspect's silence should actually be regarded as *strengthening* the case against him. It may also be the case that police officers, acting in the heat of the moment, find it difficult to repeat the exact wording of the caution accurately. Should a jury be entitled to draw adverse inferences from a defendant's statement that he is remaining silent on the advice of his solicitor?

The provisions contained in ss34–39 of the Criminal Justice and Public Order Act 1994 are due to come into effect during 1995, along with a revised Code C, containing guidelines on cautioning and the conduct of questioning.

16.22 Challenging the admissibility of evidence

A confession made by an accused person may be given in evidence against him at the trial provided it is relevant and has not been excluded by the court in pursuance of s76. This initial requirement is laid down because a confession is essentially an out-of-court statement and would normally be excluded by the rule against hearsay, that only testimony given under oath by a witness as to what he directly heard or otherwise experienced is to be regarded as good evidence. A confession is admitted as an exception to the hearsay rule and is tendered by the prosecution as evidence of the truth of its contents because it is thought that a person would not make a statement against himself unless it were true.

According to s82 the term 'confession':

'... includes any statement wholly or partly adverse to the person who made it, whether made to a person in authority or not and whether made in words or otherwise.'

A statement made by the accused which serves to exculpate him may be excluded as a 'self-serving' statement. It may, of course, be that a statement contains material of both an inculpatory and an exculpatory nature. Both elements would then have to be put before the court.

Section 76(2) contains the vital provision with regard to the exclusion of confessions. This states that:

'If, in any proceedings where the prosecution proposes to give in evidence a confession made by an accused person, it is represented to the court that the confession was or may have been obtained –
a) by oppression of the person who made it; or
b) in consequence of anything said or done which was likely, in the circumstances existing at the time, to render unreliable any confession which might be made by him in consequence thereof,
the court shall not allow the confession to be given in evidence against him except in so far as the prosecution proves to the court beyond reasonable doubt that the confession (notwithstanding that it may be true) was not obtained as asaforesaid.'

Thus where D alleges that the confession has been improperly obtained it is for the prosecution to prove beyond all reasonable doubt that this is not the case. Section 76(3) provides that, in any event, the court may require of its own motion that the prosecution should prove that the confession was not obtained as mentioned in s76(2). One effect of the subsection is that if there has been oppression the resulting confession so obtained can be excluded even though it is true, presumably to deter the police from using oppression. In this sense police impropriety is to be deprecated more than the obtaining of what may be a true confession. 'Oppression' is defined by s76(8) as including 'torture, inhuman or degrading treatment, and the use or threat of violence (whether or not amounting to torture).' In *R* v *Fulling* [1987] 2 WLR 923, Lord Lane CJ commented:

' "Oppression" in s76(2)(a) should be given its ordinary dictionary meaning. The Oxford English Dictionary as its third definition of the word runs as follows: "Exercise of authority or power in a burdensome, harsh, or wrongful manner; unjust or cruel treatment of subjects, inferiors, etc; the imposition of unreasonable or unjust burdens." One of the quotations given under that paragraph runs as follows: "There is not a word in our language which expresses more detestable wickedness than oppression." We find it hard to envisage any circumstances in which such oppression would not entail some impropriety on the part of the interrogator.'

Fulling was applied in *R* v *Paris, Abdullahi and Miller* (1993) 97 Cr App R 99 (the 'Cardiff Three' case), where convictions were set aside on the basis that confessions had been obtained by means of oppression, following evidence that interrogating officers had continued to shout at one of the appellants the words they wanted him to say over 300 times, despite his denials of guilt. The court commented upon the importance of officers complying with the letter and spirit of the Codes of Practice.

Prior to the 1984 Act a confession would only be admitted if it were voluntary. This meant that it should not have been induced 'by fear of prejudice or hope of advantage exercised or held out by a person in authority'. This seems to be the general purport of s76(2)(b) although it is of wider application than the previous rule. It remains for the defendant to raise the question of the confession's having been made in consequence of something said or done, and for the saying or doing to render unreliable the confession obtained in consequence. Presumably the repetition of 'in consequence' is not merely pleonastic or intended for emphasis but requires that the confession is made as a consequence as well as the unreliability being consequential.

A confession which has been excluded may not affect the admissibility in evidence of facts discovered as a result of the confession – although the facts should not be related to the confession itself – or of showing that the accused speaks, writes or expresses himself in a particular way.

At common law, following the decision in *R* v *Sang* [1980] AC 402, the judge's discretion to exclude evidence which had been improperly obtained was to be exercised on the basis that evidence should be admitted provided that its effect was not more prejudicial than probative. Pre-PACE authorities reveal a relaxed approach. Thus in *R* v *Leatham* (1861) 8 Cox CC 489, Crompton J expressed the view that 'It matters not how you get it; if you steal it even, it would be admissible in evidence.' Similarly in *Kuruma, Son of Kania* v *R* [1955] 1 All ER 236, Lord Goddard CJ expressed the view that if evidence was admissible the court would not be overly concerned with how it had been obtained. Lord Widgery CJ said much the same thing in *Jeffrey* v *Black* [1978] 1 All ER 555, where an unlawful search of the defendant's premises was undertaken and cannabis discovered there after he had been arrested for stealing a sandwich.

'I have not the least doubt that an irregularity in obtaining evidence does not render the evidence inadmissible. Whether or not the evidence is admissible depends on whether or not it is relevant to the issues in respect of which it is called.'

In Australia, Barwick CJ succinctly put the problem in *R* v *Ireland* (1970) 126 CLR 321:

'On the one hand there is the public need to bring to conviction those who commit criminal offences. On the other hand there is the public interest in the protection of the individual from unlawful and unfair treatment. Convictions obtained with the aid of unlawful and unfair treatment may be obtained at too high a price.'

In *R* v *Maqsud Ali, R* v *Ashiq Hussain* [1965] 2 All ER 464, murder suspects went voluntarily with police officers to a room where they were left alone. In their conversation there incriminating remarks were made and tape-recorded by a hidden microphone. In the Court of Appeal it was said: 'The criminal does not act according to the Queensbury rules. The method of the informer and of the eavesdropper is commonly used in the detection of crime'; see further *R* v *Khan* (1994) The Times 1 June.

In the Courts-Martial Appeal Court Lord Macdermott CJ said in *R* v *Murphy* [1965] NI 138, after the accused had been convicted when he had made disclosures of information useful to an enemy to police officers posing as subversives:

'Detection by deception is a form of police procedure to be directed and used sparingly and with circumspection: but as a method it is as old as the constable in plain clothes and, regrettable as the fact may be, the day has not yet come when it would be safe to say that law and order could always be enforced and the public safety protected without occasional resort to it.'

Section 78 of the 1984 Act now provides a statutory basis for the trial judge's discretion. It states:

'(1) In any proceedings the court may refuse to allow evidence on which the prosecution proposes to rely to be given if it appears to the court that, having regard to all the circumstances in which the evidence was obtained, the admission of the evidence would have such an adverse effect on the fairness of the proceedings that the court ought not to admit it.
(2) Nothing in this section shall prejudice any rule of law requiring a court to exclude evidence.'

This section curiously refers to the 'fairness of the proceedings', although it also speaks of the circumstances in which the evidence was obtained. It must be assumed that it is referring to the general fairness of the obtaining of the evidence, rather than the fairness of the proceedings as such.

In *R* v *Mason* [1988] 1 WLR 139 the Court of Appeal held that 'evidence' for the purposes of s78 included a confession notwithstanding that confessions were expressly dealt with by s76. Thus a confession that was admissible through not falling foul of s76(2) could nevertheless still be excluded on the grounds of its unfairness. Mason, who had been arrested in connection with an arson offence, was told by the police that they had glass fragments of the petrol-filled bottle used to perpetrate the offence on which they had Mason's fingerprints. In reality this was simply a trick, and the police thought it would be fair, even if deceitful, in that Mason would not have confessed if he knew that he had nothing to do with the bottle. Watkins LJ was highly critical of the tactics practised by the police, and in quashing the conviction, was clearly at pains not to be seen to be encouraging the use of such tactics.

Difficulties still exist where evidence has been obtained through the use of officers working 'under cover'. *R* v *Smurthwaite* [1994] Crim LR 53, suggests that if an officer is in the role of an *agent provocateur*, the courts are likely to exclude evidence thus obtained, but not where it is clearly D who initiates the criminal activity (eg soliciting a plain clothes policeman to carry out a contract killing.) Even so, some cases are very close to the line (for example plain clothes officers making test purchases; *DPP* v *Marshall* [1988] 3 All ER 683; and *R* v *Christou* [1992] 3 WLR 228, officers running a 'shop' to catch handlers selling off stolen goods; evidence admissible in both cases).

The courts have indicated that if the activities of the undercover officer can be said to amount to interrogation (as opposed to entrapment) the evidence obtained may be ruled inadmissible because the safeguards laid down in PACE and the Codes of Practice will not have been complied with. Hence, Mr Justice Ognall threw out the case against Colin Stagg for the murder of Rachel Nickell because his 'confession' had been induced by repeated and persistent questioning by a WPC posing as Stagg's girlfriend; see (1994) The Times September 15

17

Recent Cases

17.1 The functions of the House of Commons – parliamentary privilege

17.2 The Crown

17.3 Arrest, search, seizure and interrogation

17.1 The functions of the House of Commons – parliamentary privilege

Prebble v Television New Zealand Ltd [1994] 3 WLR 970 Privy Council
(Lords Keith, Goff, Browne-Wilkinson, Mustill and Nolan)

Defence in libel case – whether impugning proceedings in Parliament

Facts
Television New Zealand broadcast a programme in which allegations were made of impropriety on the part of the Labour government. The plaintiff, the minister for state-owned enterprises, alleged that the programme had defamed him by implying, inter alia, that he had misled the House of Representatives concerning the government's policy on the sale of state-owned industries. The defence contended that either the programme had not conveyed any defamatory meaning, or to the extent that it had, its contents were true. At first instance those elements of the defence that sought to rely on statements made in proceedings in Parliament in order to refute the plaintiff's claim were struck out, on the basis that reliance on them infringed Article 9 of the Bill of Rights 1689. The decision was upheld by the Court of Appeal, but in addition a majority of the court held that the plaintiff's action should be stayed unless and until privilege in respect of the statements relied upon was waived by the House of Representatives. The Privileges Committee of the House of Representatives had concluded that it did not have the power to waive the privilege. The plaintiff appealed to the Privy Council against the stay of his action and the defendants sought to appeal against the upholding of the first instance decision to strike out parts of the defence submission.

Held
The plaintiff's appeal was allowed and the action allowed to proceed. The defendants' appeal was dismissed.

Extract from the judgment:

'It is common ground that Article 9 is in force in New Zealand by virtue of section 242 of the Legislature Act 1908 and the Imperial Laws Application Act 1988.

If Article 9 is looked at alone, the question is whether it would infringe the Article to suggest that the statements made in the House were improper or the legislation procured in pursuance of the alleged conspiracy, as constituting impeachment or questioning of the freedom of speech of Parliament.

In addition to Article 9 itself, there is a long line of authority which supports a wider principle, of which Article 9 is merely one manifestation, viz that the courts and Parliament are both astute to recognise their respective constitutional roles. So far as the courts are concerned they will not allow any challenge to be made to what is said or done within the walls of Parliament in performance of its legislative functions and protection of its established privileges: *Burdett* v *Abbot* (1811) 14 East 1; *Stockdale* v *Hansard* (1839) 9 Ad & El 1; *Bradlaugh* v *Gossett* (1884) 12 QBD 271; *Pickin* v *British Railways Board* [1974] AC 765; *Pepper* v *Hart* [1993] AC 593. As Blackstone said in his *Commentaries on the Laws of England*, 17th ed. (1830), vol 1 p163:

> "... the whole of the law and custom of Parliament has its original from this one maxim, 'that whatever matter arises concerning either House of Parliament, ought to be examined, discussed, and adjudged in that House to which it relates, and not elsewhere.' "

According to conventional wisdom, the combined operation of Article 9 and that wider principle would undoubtedly prohibit any suggestion in the present action (whether by way of direct evidence, cross-examination or submission) that statements were made in the House which were lies or motivated by a desire to mislead. It would also prohibit any suggestion that proceedings in the House were initiated or carried through into legislation in pursuance of the alleged conspiracy. However, it is the defendant's case that the principle has a more limited scope. The defendant submits, first, that the principle only operates to prevent the questioning of statements made in the House in proceedings which seek to assert legal consequences against the maker of the statement for making that statement. Alternatively, the defendant submits that parliamentary privilege does not apply where it is the member of Parliament himself who brings proceedings for libel and parliamentary privilege would operate so as to prevent a defendant who wishes to justify the libel from challenging the veracity or bona fides of the plaintiff in making statements in the House.

The first of those submissions is based on the decision in the New South Wales Supreme Court *R* v *Murphy* (1986) 64 ALR 498. In that case a judge was being prosecuted for an alleged offence. The principal Crown witness had previously given evidence to a select committee of the Senate relating to matters in issue in the trial. The question arose whether, in the course of the criminal trial, the witness's earlier evidence to the select committee could be put to him in cross-examination with a view to showing a previous inconsistent statement. Hunt J held that Article 9 did not prohibit such cross-examination, even if the suggestion was made that the evidence given to the select committee was a lie. He further held that the statements of the select committee could be used to draw inferences, could be analysed and be made the basis of submissions. Almost immediately Commonwealth legislation, the Parliamentary Privileges Act 1987, made it clear that *R* v *Murphy* did not represent the law of the Commonwealth. Section 16(3) of that Act provides "for the avoidance of doubt" in relation to proceedings of the Parliament of the Commonwealth as follows:

"In proceedings in any court or tribunal, it is not lawful for evidence to be tendered or received, questions asked or statements, submissions or comments made, concerning proceedings in Parliament, by way of, or for the purpose of – (a) questioning or relying on the truth, motive, intention or good faith of anything forming part of those proceedings in Parliament; (b) otherwise questioning or establishing the credibility, motive, intention or good faith of any person: or (c) drawing, or inviting the drawing of, inferences or conclusions wholly or partly from anything forming part of those proceedings in Parliament."

That Act, therefore, declares what had previously been regarded as the effect of Article 9 of the Bill of Rights 1689 and section 16(3) of the Act of 1987 contains what, in the opinion of their Lordships, is the true principle to be applied.

It is, of course, no part of their Lordships' function to decide whether, as a matter of Australian law, the decision of Hunt J was correct. But Article 9 applies in the United Kingdom and throughout the Commonwealth. In their Lordships' view the law as stated by Hunt J was not correct so far as the rest of the Commonwealth is concerned. First, his views were in conflict with the long line of dicta that the courts will not allow any challenge to what is said or done in Parliament. Second, as Hunt J recognised, his decision was inconsistent with the decision of Browne J in *Church of Scientology of California* v *Johnson-Smith* [1972] 1 QB 522 (subsequently approved by the House of Lords in *Pepper* v *Hart* [1993] AC 593) and *Comalco Ltd* v *Australian Broadcasting Corporation* (1983) 50 ACTR 1, in both of which cases it was held that it would be a breach of privilege to allow what is said in Parliament to be the subject matter of investigation or submission.

Finally, Hunt J, based himself on a narrow construction of Article 9, derived from the historical context in which it was originally enacted. He correctly identified the mischief sought to be remedied in 1689 as being, inter alia, the assertion by the King's Courts of a right to hold a Member of Parliament criminally or legally liable for what he had done or said in Parliament. From this he deduced the principle that Article 9 only applies to cases in which a court is being asked to expose the maker of the statement to legal liability for what he has said in Parliament. This view discounts the basic concept underlying Article 9, viz. the need to ensure so far as possible that a member of the legislature and witnesses before committees of the House can speak freely without fear that what they say will later be held against them in the courts. The important public interest protected by such privilege is to ensure that the member or witness *at the time he speaks* is not inhibited from stating fully and freely what he has to say. If there were any exceptions which permitted his statements to be questioned subsequently, at the time when he speaks in Parliament he would not know whether or not there would subsequently be a challenge to what he is saying. Therefore he would not have the confidence the privilege is designed to protect.

Moreover to allow it to be suggested in cross-examination or submission that a member or witness was lying to the House could lead to exactly that conflict between the courts and Parliament which the wider principle of non-intervention is designed to avoid. Misleading the House is a contempt of the House punishable by the House: if a court were also to be permitted to decide whether or not a member or witness had misled the House there would be a serious risk of conflicting decisions on the issue.

The defendant's second submission (that the rules excluding parliamentary material do not apply when the action is brought by a member of Parliament) is based on the decision of the Supreme Court of South Australia in *Wright and Advertiser Newspapers Ltd* v *Lewis* (1990) 53 SASR 416. In that case the plaintiff was a member of the South Australia House of Assembly. The plaintiff made an allegation in the House that the first defendant, Wright, had obtained an advantage as a result of his close association with a former government. Wright wrote a letter to the second defendant, a newspaper, which published it. The letter accused the plaintiff of abusing his parliamentary privilege and of cheap political opportunism. The plaintiff sued alleging that the letter was libellous. The defendants pleaded justification, qualified privilege and fair comment. The case was one therefore in which the plaintiff's integrity in making statements in the House was determinative of the action: the letter was plainly defamatory and unless the defendants could challenge the truthfulness of what the plaintiff had said in Parliament, they had no defence. King CJ with justification described the result of allowing the action to proceed without such evidence being admissible as follows, at pp421–422:

> "It must be observed at the outset that if the view argued for by counsel for the Attorney-General and the plaintiff is correct, the result is remarkable. A Member of Parliament could sue for defamation in respect of criticism of his statements or conduct in the Parliament. The defendant would be precluded, however, from alleging and proving that what was said by way of criticism was true. This would amount to a gross distortion of the law of defamation in its application to such a situation. Defamation in law is by definition an *untrue* imputation against the reputation of another: ... If the defendant were precluded from proving the truth of what is alleged, the Member of Parliament would be enabled to recover damages, if no other defence applied, for an imputation which was perfectly true. Moreover the defence of fair comment would often be unavailable, as in the present case, because it would not be permissible to prove the factual foundation for the expression of opinion. The defence of qualified privilege might be seriously inhibited because the defendant would be prevented from answering an allegation of express malice by proving the facts as known to him. If this is the true legal position, it is difficult to envisage how a court could apply the law of defamation in a rational way to an action by a Member of Parliament in respect of an imputation relating to his statements or conduct in the House, or could try such an action fairly or adjudicate upon it justly. If on the other hand such an action is not justiciable, other difficulties and injustices arise ... A Member of Parliament would be deprived of the ordinary right of a citizen to obtain damages for defamation in such circumstances notwithstanding, the privilege being that of the Parliament not of the member, that he might be quite willing to have all the ordinary defences put forward and adjudicated upon by the court."

The South Australian Supreme Court solved the dilemma pointed out by King CJ by holding that the privilege does not extend to prevent challenges to he truth or bona fides of statements made in Parliament where the maker of the statements himself initiates the proceedings. The court considered, at p426, that such a limitation on normal parliamentary privilege would not inhibit the member from exercising his freedom of speech "because he would be aware that his actions and motives could not be examined in court unless he instituted the proceedings which rendered such examination necessary."

Although their Lordships are sympathetic with the concern felt by the South Australian Supreme Court, they cannot accept that the fact that the maker of the statement is the initiator of the court proceedings can affect the question whether Article 9 is infringed. The privilege protected by Article 9 is the privilege of Parliament itself. The actions of any individual member of Parliament, even if he has an individual privilege of his own, cannot determine whether or not the privilege of Parliament is to apply. The wider principle encapsulated in Blackstone's words quoted above prevents the courts from adjudicating on issues arising in or concerning the House, viz whether or not a member has misled the House or acted from improper motives. The decision of an individual member cannot override that collective privilege of the House to be the sole judge of such matters.

In reaching its conclusion, the South Australian Supreme Court did not advert to the Parliamentary Privileges Act 1987, presumably because that is a Commonwealth statute which does not regulate the privileges of the South Australian State legislature. They relied on two earlier authorities. In the first, *Adam* v *Ward* [1917] AC 309, the plaintiff was a Member of Parliament who had alleged in the House of Commons that X, an army officer, had been guilty of improper conduct. The Army Council thereafter conducted an inquiry in which they exonerated X. The Army Council sent their findings (which included unfavourable comments on the plaintiff) to the press, which published them. The plaintiff then sued the Army Council for libel. Qualified privilege was pleaded. The House of Lords upheld the claim to privilege and the speeches contained stringent criticisms of the plaintiff's conduct. At no stage was the question of parliamentary privilege raised. The only legal issue in relation to which parliamentary privilege could have arisen was whether the publication by the Army Council of its findings to the whole world was so wide as to go beyond the qualified privilege to which those findings were entitled. For this purpose it was held that the fact that the words had been uttered by the plaintiff in the House fully justified the publication by the Army Council through the press. Therefore there was no issue in that case which questioned the truth or propriety of what had been said in Parliament: the only material point was the fact that the allegation against X had been made in Parliament. Therefore the decision provides on basis for an argument that statements in the House can be questioned where the plaintiff is the Member of Parliament ...

... Their Lordships are acutely conscious (as were the courts below) that to preclude reliance on things said and done in the House in defence of libel proceedings brought by a member of the House could have a serious impact on a most important aspect of freedom of speech, viz the right of the public to comment on and criticise the actions of those elected to power in a democratic society: see *Derbyshire County Council* v *Times Newspapers Ltd* [1993] AC 534. If the media and others are unable to establish the truth of fair criticisms of the conduct of their elected members in the very performance of their legislative duties in the House, the results could indeed be chilling to the proper monitoring of members' behaviour. But the present case and *Wright's* case, 53 SASR 416, illustrate how public policy, or human rights, issues can conflict. There are three such issues in play in these cases: first, the need to ensure that the legislature can exercise its powers freely on behalf of its electors, with access to all relevant information; second, the need to protect freedom of speech generally; third, the interests of justice in ensuring that all relevant evidence is available to the courts. Their Lordships are of the view that the law has been long settled that, of these three public interests, the first must prevail. But the other two public interests cannot be ignored and their Lordships will revert to them in considering the question of a stay of proceedings.

For these reasons (which are in substance those of the courts below) their Lordships are of the view that parties to litigation, by whomsoever commenced, cannot bring into question anything said or done in the House by suggesting (whether by direct evidence, cross-examination, inference or submission) that the actions or words were inspired by improper motives or were untrue or misleading. Such matters lie entirely within the jurisdiction of the House, subject to any statutory exception such as exists in New Zealand in relation to perjury under s108 of the Crimes Act 1961. However, their Lordships wish to make it clear that this principle does not exclude all references in court proceedings to what has taken place in the House. In the past, Parliament used to assert a right, separate from the privilege of freedom of speech enshrined in Article 9, to restrain publication of its proceedings. Formerly the procedure was to petition the House for leave to produce Hansard in court. Since 1980 this right has no longer been generally asserted by the

United Kingdom Parliament and their Lordships understood from the Attorney-General that in practice the House of Representatives in New Zealand no longer asserts the right. A number of the authorities on the scope of Article 9 betray some confusion between the right to prove the occurrence of parliamentary events and the embargo on questioning their propriety. In particular, it is questionable whether *Rost* v *Edwards* [1990] 2 QB 460 was rightly decided.

Since there can no longer be any objection to the production of Hansard, the Attorney-General accepted (in their Lordships' view rightly) that there could be no objection to the use of Hansard to prove what was done and said in Parliament as a matter of history. Similarly, he accepted that the fact that a statute had been passed is admissible in court proceedings. Thus, in the present action, there cannot be any objection to it being proved what the plaintiff or the Prime Minister said in the House (particulars 8.2.10 and 8.2.14) or that the State-Owned Enterprises Act 1986 was passed (particulars 8.4.1). It will be for the trial judge to ensure that the proof of these historical facts is not used to suggest that the words were improperly spoken or the statute passed to achieve an improper purpose.

It is clear that, on the pleadings as they presently stand, the defendant intends to rely on these matters not purely as a matter of history but as part of the alleged conspiracy or its implementation. Therefore, in their Lordships' view, Smellie J was right to strike them out. But their Lordships wish to make it clear that if the defendant wishes at the trial to allege the occurrence of events or the saying of certain words in Parliament without any accompanying allegation of impropriety or any other questioning there is no objection to that course.'

17.2 The Crown

Act of State

Littrell v *United States of America (No 2)* [1994] 4 All ER 203 Court of Appeal (Nourse, Rose and Hofmann LJJ)

Sovereign immunity – whether medical treatment by military personnel governed by acta jure gestionis

Facts

The plaintiff, whilst serving as a member of the United States forces in 1987, received medical treatment at a United States military air base in England, the treatment being provided by American military personnel. As a result of the treatment the plaintiff sought damages in negligence from both the United States government and the Ministry of Defence. Following interlocutory proceedings the court ruled that the Ministry of Defence should not be a party to the action, and the case against the United States continued on the basis that the matter was governed by customary international law. The United States contended that, under customary international law, it was immune from suit as the matter fell within acta jure imperii (exercise of sovereign authority) and not acta jure gestionis (private or commercial law matter).

Held

The matter was governed by the common law, which incorporated customary international law, as it stood at the time the claim arose. As the action arose out of the treatment of a member of its own armed forces, at its own military base, conducted by its own military staff, there was no possibility of the action falling within the scope of acta jure gestionis. Therefore the United States was immune from suit.

Comment

The decision confirms the view, expressed in cases such as *The Parlement Belge* (1879) 4 PD 129, that treaty provisions (such as article VIII para 5 of the Agreement regarding the Status of Forces of Parties to the North Atlantic Treaty 1951) do not form part of domestic law unless expressly incorporated by Act of Parliament.

17.3 Arrest, search, seizure and interrogation

R v *Chief Constable of South Wales, ex parte Merrick* [1994] 1 WLR 663
Queen's Bench Division (Ralph Gibson LJ and Smith J)

Right of a prisoner to consult privately with a solicitor

Facts

The applicant, a remand prisoner, was being held in the cells at Cardiff magistrates' court following an unsuccessful bail application. His request to consult privately with his solicitor after the hearing was refused. The police at the court had adopted a policy of not permitting interviews between prisoners and solicitors after 10.00 am, unless there were good reasons for the interview not having taken place earlier, and it was possible to grant access given the other demands on resources. The applicant had requested an interview in the middle of the afternoon. The applicant, by way of judicial review, sought a declaration that the policy being followed at Cardiff magistrates' court was unlawful in that it resulted in a denial of his right to consult with a solicitor under s58(1) of the Police and Criminal Evidence Act 1984.

Held

The application would be granted in part. Section 58(1) of the Police and Criminal Evidence Act 1984 did not extend to a prisoner held in custody at a court following a refusal of bail, but at common law he did have a rig ht to consult with a legal adviser as soon as was reasonably practicable.

Extract from the judgments, per Ralph Gibson LJ:

'It was not necessary, in my judgment, for Parliament to apply s58(1) to a person on remand and held in custody in the cells of a court in order to secure to that person the right to consult a solicitor. At common law a man in custody is entitled to consult a solicitor at an early stage of the investigation. The only qualification was that he could not delay the investigation by asking to see a solicitor if the effect would be to cause "unreasonable delay or hindrance ... to the process of investigation or the administration of justice": see *R* v *Lemsatef* [1977] 1 WLR 812 where the decision was based upon principle C of the Judges' Rules. The right of a person in custody at a court to consult a solicitor can, in my judgment, be no less than that of a person in detention in the course of investigation of a suspected offence under the rules of common law which preceded the Act of 1984 and which were not abrogated by that Act. That right in my judgment is on request to be permitted to consult a solicitor as soon as is reasonably practicable. It follows that if s58(1) applies to a person in custody in the cells at CMC his right, when he asks, is to be permitted to see a solicitor as soon as is practicable; and, if s58(1) does not apply, his right when he asks is to be permitted to see a solicitor as soon as is reasonably practicable. There may be cases in which such a difference would be decisive. This, for reasons which will appear, was not such a case.

(vi) The right to consult a solicitor is not, so far as concerns a person in custody, a free standing right of uniform extent irrespective of the circumstances. So far as concerns questioning of a person by the police and treatment of him after arrest, and while he is in custody before charge, the primary purpose is to ensure that the questioning is fair and that his legal rights may be preserved and protected, in particular that he should understand and, if he wishes, have resort to his right to be silent: see *R* v *Walsh* (1989) 91 Cr App R 161, 163. To that end, it is necessary that the right should be secured to such a person at that stage to consult a solicitor privately at any time while the inquiry proceeds and "as soon as is practicable;" and, subject to the exceptions listed in paragraph 6.6 of PACE Code of Practice C, a person who wants legal advice may not be interviewed or continue to be interviewed until he has received it. After a person has been charged, and is in custody at a court on remand, the primary purpose of the right to consult a solicitor is to ensure that the trial, and all ancillary proceedings, such as applications for bail, are conducted fairly and effectively. To that end, it is necessary that the right should be secured to such a person at such time or times as will enable the proceedings to be fairly and effectively conducted by him or on his behalf. A significant difference between a person in detention or custody but before charge, whose conduct is under investigation by the police, on the one hand, and a person in custody after charge on remand in the cells of a magistrates' court, on the other hand, is that the court stands between the person in custody and the prosecutor, and the court, provided that complaint is made by or on behalf of the accused, is well able to ensure that any preceding failure to provide sufficient access for an accused to a solicitor is not permitted to prejudice the conduct of the proceedings on the behalf of the accused. The court can direct, or indicate its opinion – I have discussed the distinction above – that the accused is to be allowed sufficient access to his legal advisers before the hearing of the case, or of any ancillary proceeding, will proceed.

(vii) The right under s58(1) is not absolute in the sense that there is a breach of duty by any person to which s58 applies if the requirement by a person in custody is not at once met by being enabled to consult a solicitor: the request must be met "as soon as practicable", apart from the permitted exception which is not here relevant. "Practicable" in its dictionary meaning is defined in the *Shorter Oxford English Dictionary* as "capable of being carried out in action; feasible" and in *Webster's Dictionary* as "possible to be accomplished with known means or known resources". In *Dedman* v *British Building & Engineering Appliances Ltd* [1974] 1 WLR 171, the Court of Appeal considered the meaning of the word as used in the Industrial Tribunals (Industrial Relations, etc.) Regulations 1972 (SI 1972 No 38) with reference to the time for presenting a complaint. Scarman LJ said, at p179:

"Upon the point of construction of 'the escape clause' I agree with Lord Denning MR. The word 'practicable' is an ordinary English word of great flexibility: it takes its meaning from its context. But, whenever used, it is a call for the exercise of common sense, a warning that sound judgment will be impossible without compromise. Sometimes the context contemplates a situation rarely to be achieved, though much to be desired: the word then indicates one must be satisfied with less than perfection: see, for example, its use in s5 of the Matrimonial Property Act 1970. Sometimes, as is submitted in the present case, what the context requires may have been possible, but may not for some reason have been 'practicable'. Whatever its context, the quality of the word is that there are circumstances in which we must be content with less than 100 per cent: and it calls for judgment to determine how much less."

(viii) It follows, in my judgment, whether s58(1) applies or not, that which is to be regarded as complying with the duty to permit consultation with a solicitor "as soon as practicable" or, if s58(1) does not apply, "as soon as is reasonably practicable", requires consideration of the circumstances of the accused, and of the police in charge of the cells. Those circumstances include the other duties of the police and the immediate demands upon them when the request is made. It is to be noted that the word "practicable" is not in s58 qualified by the word "reasonably" as it was, for example, in s68(2) of the Act of 1984 as first enacted. If the police undertake the task of controlling persons in custody at a court, it is, in my judgment, their duty to comply fully with the obligations imposed by the law upon any person performing such a task and it is irrelevant that the officers of the particular constabulary are assigned to the task "voluntarily" and without – if it be the case – any legal duty previously imposed upon the constabulary. The law does not, however, impose a duty upon the constabulary, or upon particular officers within it, to meet a request for access to a solicitor made by a person in custody at a court forthwith or at a time when it is not "practicable" having regard to the other immediate duties of the officers and the number of them available, provided that the resources made available are reasonably sufficient to ensure that such a request is, so far as is reasonably foreseeable, capable of being met so as to satisfy the primary purposes for which such access is required.

(ix) Accordingly, in my judgment, there is in cases such as this no significant difference, so far as concerns securing to persons in custody the substantial benefits of the right to consult a solicitor, between that specifically enacted by s58(1) and that secured to such a person by the common law. I conclude that, upon the construction of the provisions of s58, in its statutory context, and having regard to the substance and effect of the common law of which Parliament was aware, s58 did not apply to the applicant in the circumstances in which he was on 12 May 1993.'

As regards the implementation of the policy, his Lordship observed:

'The one particular defect in the policy which, in my judgment, was unlawful was that it authorised or permitted the gaolers to refuse access to a solicitor on the sole ground that the request was made after 10 am without reference to the question whether it was reasonably practicable to allow access at once or within a period of time ...

... If the policy had been that, after 10 am, access would be arranged as soon as was reasonably practicable, having regard to the demands upon the police at any time, there would, in the absence of other circumstances not raised in this case, be no objection to the policy as such because it would not necessarily give rise to the likelihood of the denial of the right of a person in custody to access to legal advice. It is to be emphasised that the primary consideration is the right of the person in custody and the duty to give effect to it. The fact that the policy is not shown to have been erroneous when announced will not necessarily justify every decision made under it.'

Index

HLT Publications

HLT books are specially planned and written to help you in every stage of your studies. Each of the wide range of textbooks is brought up-to-date annually, and the companion volumes of our Law Series are all designed to work together.

You can buy HLT books from your local bookshop, or in case of difficulty, order direct using this form,

The Law Series covers the following modules:

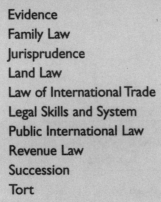

Administrative Law
Commercial Law
Company Law
Conflict of Laws
Constitutional Law
Contract Law
Criminal Law
Criminology
English Legal System
Equity and Trusts
European Union Law

Evidence
Family Law
Jurisprudence
Land Law
Law of International Trade
Legal Skills and System
Public International Law
Revenue Law
Succession
Tort

The HLT Law Series:
A comprehensive range of books for your law course, and the legal aspects of business and commercial studies.

Each module is covered by a comprehensive six-part set of books
● Textbook
● Casebook
● Revision Workbook
● Suggested Solutions, for:
● 1985-90
● 1991-94
● 1995

Module	Books required	Cost
To complete your order, please fill in the form overleaf	Postage	
	TOTAL	

Prices (including postage and packing in the UK):
Textbooks £19.00; Casebooks £19.00; Revision Workbooks £10.00; Suggested Solutions (1985-90) £9.00, Suggested Solutions (1991-94) £6.00, Suggested Solutions (1995) £3.00.

For Europe, add 15% postage and packing (£20 maximum). For the rest of the world, add 40% for airmail (£35 maximum).

ORDERING

By telephone to 01892 724371, with your credit card to hand

By fax to 01892 724206 (giving your credit card details).

By post to:

HLT Publications,
The Gatehouse, Ruck Lane, Horsmonden, Tonbridge, Kent TN12 8EA

When ordering by post, please enclose full payment by cheque or banker's draft, or complete the credit card details below.

We aim to dispatch your books within 3 working days of receiving your order.

Name

Address

Postcode

Telephone

Total value of order, including postage: **£**

I enclose a cheque/banker's draft for the above sum, or

charge my   ☐ Access/Mastercard   ☐ Visa   ☐ American Express

Card number

☐☐☐☐   ☐☐☐☐   ☐☐☐☐   ☐☐☐☐

Expiry date

☐☐☐☐

Signature

Date

Publications from **The Old Bailey Press**

Cracknell's Statutes

A full understanding of statute law is vital for any student, and this series presents the original wording of legislation, together with any amendments and substitutions and the sources of these changes.

Cracknell's Companions

Recognised as invaluable study aids since their introduction in 1961, this series summarises all the most important court decisions and acts, and features a glossary of Latin words, as well as full indexing.

Please telephone our Order Hotline on 01892 724371, or write to our order department, for full details of these series.